CAPTAIN LENOIR'S *Diary*

The subject of this painting is thought to be Thomas Isaac Lenoir, portrayed as a young man at about the time he moved to his father's property along the East Fork of the Pigeon River in Haywood County, N.C., in 1846. Artist unknown. *Collection of Fort Defiance Museum, Lenoir, N.C.; used by permission.*

Captain Lenoir's Diary

Tom Lenoir and His Civil War Company from Western North Carolina

Carroll C. Jones
Foreword by Terrell Garren

Captain Lenoir's Diary: Tom Lenoir and
His Civil War Company from Western North Carolina
copyright © 2010 by Carroll C. Jones

All rights reserved. No portion of this work may be reproduced without the express written permission of the author or publisher. Images not in the public domain or owned by the author are used by permission.

PUBLISHED BY WINOCA PRESS
An imprint of Bookadelphia • Lubbock, Texas USA • www.Bookadelphia.com

Available direct from the publisher, from your local bookstore, or from the author at ccrymes.jones@gmail.com

Printed in the United States of America • First edition, November 2010 / second printing, 2016

LIBRARY OF CONGRESS CATALOGING-IN-PUBLICATION DATA
Jones, Carroll, 1950—
 Captain Lenoir's diary : Tom Lenoir and his Civil War company from Western North Carolina / Carroll C. Jones ; foreword by Terrell Garren.
  p. cm.
  Includes bibliographical references and index.
  ISBN 978-1-935619-00-0 (cloth) — ISBN 978-1-935619-02-4 (trade pbk.)
 1. Lenoir, Thomas Isaac, 1827-1882—Diary. 2. Confederate States of America. Army. North Carolina Infantry Regiment, 25th. Company F. 3. North Carolina—History—Civil War, 1861–1865—Regimental histories. 4. United States—History—Civil War, 1861-1865—Regimental histories. 5. United States—History—Civil War, 1861-1865—Personal narratives, Confederate. 6. North Carolina—History—Civil War, 1861–1865—Personal narratives. 7. United States—History—Civil War, 1861–1865—Campaigns. 8. Soldiers—North Carolina—Haywood County—Biography. 9. Haywood County (N.C.)—Biography. 10. Lenoir family. I. Title.
  E573.525th.J67 2010
  973.7—dc22
                                                                2010024580

Cover and interior designed by Barbara Brannon
On the cover: portrait presumed to be Thomas Isaac Lenoir, artist unknown; collection of Fort Defiance Museum, Lenoir, N.C.; used by permission. Pages from Thomas Lenoir's Civil War diary, collection of Hugh K. Terrell and the late Emily Michal Terrell; used by permission.

"The Den" by Hugh K. Terrell. *Used by permission.*

In Memory of
Emily Michal Terrell

Contents

List of Illustrations and Maps ix
Lenoir Family Tree xv
Foreword xvii
Preface xxi
Introduction 1

PART I THOMAS LENOIR'S EAST FORK LEGACY

Thomas Lenoir, Haywood County Pioneer 9
Thomas Isaac Lenoir: A Son's Coming of Age 21
Dutiful Endeavors on the East Fork 31
A Volunteer Company from Forks of Pigeon 59
Captain Lenoir's Diary 75
    November 1861 77
    December 1861 119
    January 1862 151
    February 1862 171
    March 1862 183
    April 1862 195
    May 1862 207
In War's Aftermath on the East Fork 227

PART II HISTORY AND ROSTER OF THE HAYWOOD HIGHLANDERS

The Haywood Highlanders' Civil War Journey: The Last Three Years 245
A Closer Look at the Haywood Highlanders' Civil War Service 255
    Carolina Coastal Duty.. 255
    Seven Days' Battles 261
    Maryland Campaign 271
    Fredericksburg... 281
    North Carolina / Virginia Coastal Defense 289
    Richmond / Petersburg Defense: The Last-Ditch Effort 309
Lifting the Shroud of Time 341
The Last Highlanders Standing 363
Afterword... 369

Appendix A: Haywood Highlanders—Roster and Service Records......... 375
Appendix B: Haywood Highlanders—Casualties of War 393
Appendix C: Haywood Highlanders—Every Move They Made 395
Appendix D: Selected Excerpts from the Lenoir Letters................. 407
Notes 439
Bibliography... 463
Index 469

Illustrations and Maps

Thomas Isaac Lenoir, about 1846 . . . . Frontispiece
"The Den" by Hugh K. Terrell v
Thomas Lenoir's Civil War diary, front and back covers xx
Thomas Lenoir's Civil War diary, interior pages xxii
Forks of Pigeon, Haywood County, North Carolina 6
Sunlight breaking over the mountains 8
Survey authorization granted by the Buncombe County surveyor
   to Thomas Lenoir in August 1806 10
Col. Thomas Lenoir, about 1807 11
Gen. William Lenoir 13
East Fork region of Haywood County, North Carolina, about 1833 17
Picking wild flowers 20
Fort Defiance plantation home, Caldwell County, North Carolina 22
Thomas Isaac Lenoir at about age 23, circa 1840 24
Chesapeake and Ohio Canal aqueduct 26
Clearing the field 30
Tom Lenoir's Western North Carolina 33
Thomas Isaac Lenoir, about 1846 34
Tom Lenoir's cavalry officer's commission, 1847 42
"The Den," Tom Lenoir's East Fork home 44
Tom Lenoir's specifications for the "Pigeon River
   Turnpike Road," 1860 48–49

"Going off to join the fray"... 58
Fort Sumter Barrage, Apr. 12, 1861... 61
Gov. Zebulon Baird Vance, 1862... 62
Col. Joseph Cathey... 65
Tom Lenoir's commission as captain in the 25th Regiment N.C. Troops,
    June 29, 1861... 66
Col. Thomas L. Clingman... 69
Gen. James G. Martin's Special Order No. 335 to
    Col. Thomas L. Clingman, Sept. 12, 1861... 71
"A Very Raw Recruit"... 74
"A Formidable Line" by Walton Taber... 76
Battle of Port Royal Sound... 92
Fort Beauregard, Port Royal Sound, South Carolina... 92
A Confederate encampment, by Conrad Chapman... 93
Vicinity of Grahamville, S.C., and the Charleston & Savannah R.R., 1861... 117
"Rebs" by Alfred Rudolf Waud... 118
Gen. Robert E. Lee... 122
Gen. Robert E. Lee, mounted on Traveler... 122
Ordnance list for the Haywood Highlanders, Dec. 21, 1861... 123
Holy Trinity Episcopal Church, Grahamville, S.C.... 148
Captain Lenoir's diary entry for Dec. 28, 1861... 149
Confederate entrenchments... 149
"Rebs Foraging" by Alfred Rudolf Waud... 150
Captain Tom Lenoir's discharge document for Alfred Burnett... 163
Vicinity of Grahamville, S.C., and Camp Lee during the Civil War... 168
"Rebs Eating Corn-on-the-Cob"... 170
Captain Lenoir's inventory of the effects of a Haywood Highlander
    who perished from disease... 180
Letter, Tom Lenoir to Lizzie Garrett Lenoir, Feb. 18, 1862... 181

"Making Corn Meal during a Rest" by William L. Sheppard 182
Captain Lenoir's pay statement for period ending Apr. 30, 1862 185
"Confederate Sharpshooters" by Allen C. Redwood. 194
"Rebs Roasting Corn" by Alfred Rudolf Waud. 206
Bill submitted by Joseph Cathey to Captain Tom Lenoir for
   outfitting the Haywood Highlanders, July 1861 216–17
Final entry in Captain Lenoir's diary, May 19, 1862 225
"Early Ploughing" 226
Rufus Theodore Lenoir, about 1875 228
Walter Waightstill Lenoir, about 1843 228
List of tenants from Tom Lenoir's memorandum book, 1866 236–37
Gravestone of Tom and Lizzie Lenoir, Bethel, N.C. 242
Journey of the Haywood Highlanders through the Civil War 244
Capt. James Madison Cathey. 246
Col. Henry M. Rutledge. 248
Brig. Gen. Robert Ransom. 249
"Rebels on the March" 254
Muster roll of Company F, 25th N.C. Troops, April 1862 258–59
"Rushing into the Mouth of Death on Malvern Hill"
   by Thure de Thulstrup 260
The Peninsula Campaign, June 25–July 1, 1862 269
"Crossing the Potomac into Enemy Territory". 270
Harpers Ferry, Virginia, during the Civil War 273
Dunker Church, Sharpsburg, Virginia 276
Battle of Antietam Run, Sept. 17, 1862. 279
Before Marye's Heights; illustration by Allen C. Redwood 280
Marye house at Fredericksburg battlefield 284
Sunken road under Marye's Heights at Battle of Fredericksburg. 286
Battle of Fredericksburg, Dec. 13, 1862 287

"C.S.S. *Albemarle* Under Construction in a Corn Field" by M. H. Hoke 288
Gen. Matt W. Ransom 291
Maj. Gen. Daniel Harvey Hill 291
Gen. Robert F. Hoke 291
CSS *Albemarle* 303
Map of Eastern North Carolina, 1863 307
"A Dangerous Occupation" 308
Gen. Bushrod Johnson 312
Gen. P. G. T. Beauregard 312
"Planting the Mine" by Alfred Rudolf Waud 317
"Crater Explosion" by Alfred Rudolf Waud 318
Capt. James Allen Blalock 321
Bombproof shelters at Petersburg, Virginia 324
Red trenches of Petersburg, Virginia 327
Attack upon Fort Stedman 329
Interior of Fort Stedman 333
Siege and battles of Petersburg 339
"As Brave a Man As Ever Met the Enemy" by Walton Taber 340
Lt. Joseph T. Cathey 346
Lt. William Harrison Hartgrove 346
Lt. Garland Sevier Ferguson 346
The Singleton brothers, William A.S. Columbus,
    John C., and James Anderson 353
Garland S. Ferguson 361
William Hartgrove, or "Captain Hack" 361
"Rebel" by Alfred Rudolph Waud 362
"Going up" or "going over" to the enemy 364
Rebel prisoners at the Battle of Five Forks, April 1, 1865 367
"Hobbled Rebel" by Edwin Forbes 368

Letters

Thomas Lenoir to General William Lenoir, September 16, 1806 408

Tom Lenoir to Thomas Lenoir, August 10, 1843 409

A.C. Hartgrove to Thomas Lenoir, January 3, 1846 410

Thomas Lenoir to Tom Lenoir, March 28, 1846 411

Tom Lenoir to Thomas Lenoir, February 13, about 1847 412

Tom Lenoir to Rufus T. Lenoir, October 16, 1852 413

Tom Lenoir's Christmas Letter, December 25, 1852 414

Tom Lenoir to Rufus T. Lenoir, January 14, 1854 415

Tom Lenoir to Rufus T. Lenoir, August 5, 1854 418

Tom Lenoir to Rufus T. Lenoir, December 15, 1855 419

Tom Lenoir to Thomas Lenoir, October 19, 1860 420

Tom Lenoir to Rufus T. Lenoir, December 14, 1860 421

Laura Lenoir to Tom Lenoir, May 23, 1861 422

Tom Lenoir to Rufus T. Lenoir, June 10, 1861 423

Tom Lenoir to Rufus T. Lenoir, June 18, 1861 424

Tom Lenoir to Walter Lenoir, July 2, 1861 425

Tom Lenoir to Walter Lenoir, September 15, 1861 426

Tom Lenoir to Rufus T. Lenoir, August 14, 1865 427

Tom Lenoir to Rufus T. Lenoir, March 27, 1866 428

Tom Lenoir to Walter Lenoir, June 10, 1874 430

J. M. Gwyn to Walter Lenoir, July 30, 1876 431

Walter Lenoir to Tom Lenoir, February 11, 1879 432

Mr. R. V. Welch to Capt. T. I. Lenoir, June 20, 1879 433

Tom Lenoir to W. B. Gwyn, December 12, 1879 434

Mamie (Mary) Lenoir to Aunt Sade, January 12, 1880 435

Walter Lenoir to Tom Lenoir, November 27, 1880 436

Walter Lenoir to Rufus T. Lenoir, December 19, 1881 437

Rufus T. Lenoir to Walter Lenoir, January 8, 1882 438

Lenoir Family Tree

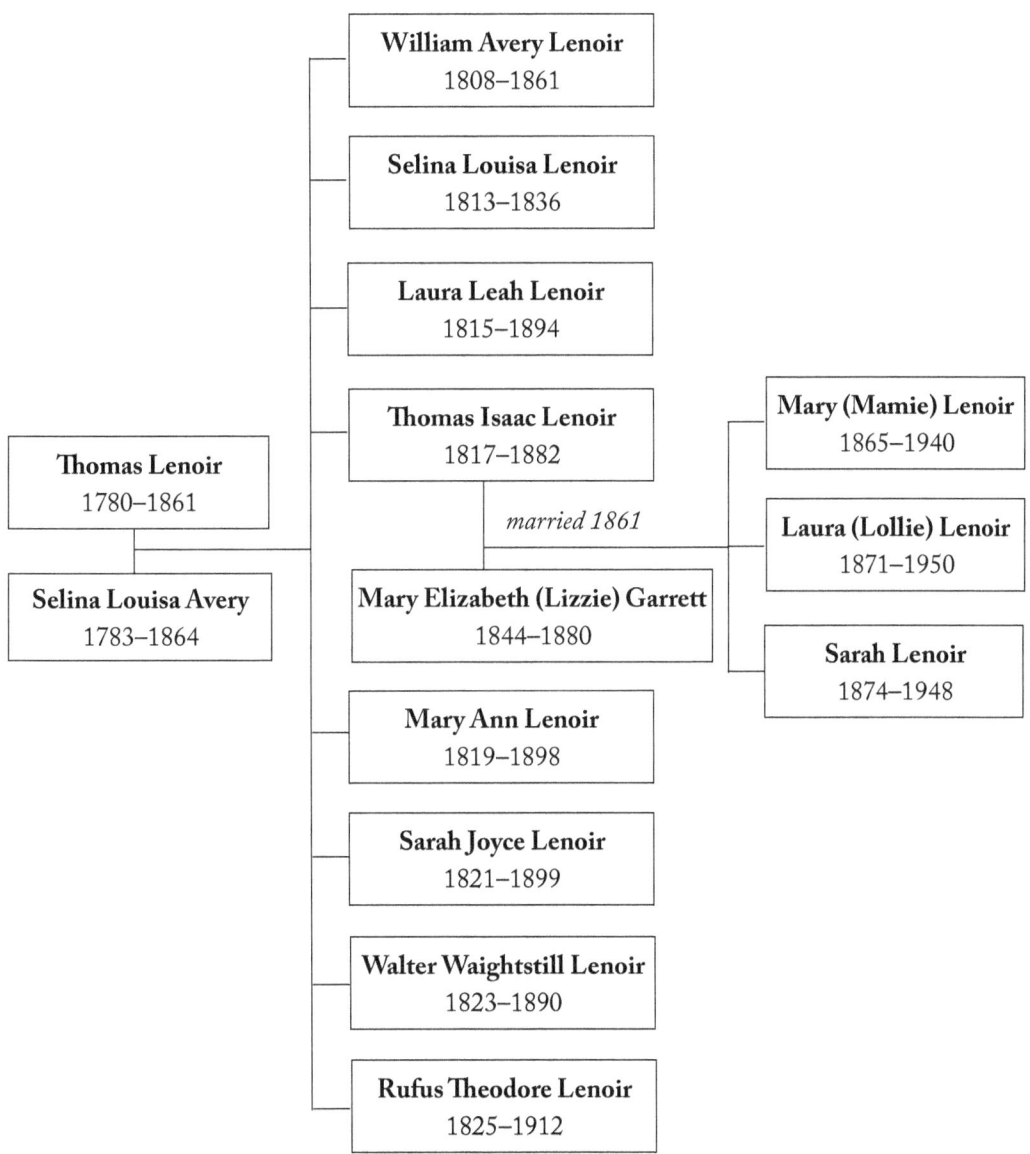

Foreword

WHEN WHITE SETTLERS FIRST WALKED the ridges of the continental divide in the highlands of Western North Carolina they discovered some of the most pristine water sources found anywhere on earth. One of those special places was the headwaters of the Pigeon River in what is now Haywood County, North Carolina. It was here on the East Fork of the Pigeon River where the ancestors of Thomas Isaac Lenoir acquired thousands of acres of land shortly after the turn of the nineteenth century.

Carroll C. Jones provides the reader with a solid understanding of this early period and how it contributed to the region's involvement in the American Civil War. Lenoir was not only a successful farmer and businessman but also, like most landed Southerners of the era, an economic beneficiary of the "peculiar institution" of slavery. And, as Jones shows, he was a natural leader of men.

So it was in 1861 that Lenoir found himself struggling with the rising tide of war. As a man of property, he certainly had an economic interest in the South's fortunes. But as a civic and community leader he probably felt the burden of responsibility and duty. At age forty-three, no one expected him to fight. In the early period of the war there was no conscription law; yet Lenoir did what men have done throughout the ages: he donned a uniform and marched off to war.

He organized the Haywood Highlanders and served a year as captain of what became Company F of the 25th North Carolina Infantry.

In this perceptive portrait of Captain Lenoir, Jones draws upon his considerable knowledge as the author of the award-winning history *The 25th North Carolina Troops in the Civil War: History and Roster of a Mountain-Bred Regiment*, a masterpiece of diligent primary-source research. From this foundation Jones digs even deeper, presenting a detailed account of the Haywood Highlanders in the current work.

We follow the Haywood County men to Camp Patton in Asheville, North Carolina, where they begin training as Confederate soldiers. Jones exploits Lenoir's diary of the first year of the war to give us more background on this little known period of the regiment's experience on the coasts of North and South Carolina.

Recording the company's defense of the coastal region, Jones follows the Haywood County volunteers to the raging war in Virginia. It is here that the regiment joins the famed Army of Northern Virginia and their legendary leader, Confederate Gen. Robert E. Lee. Jones then guides us through a three-year stint that includes some of the greatest battles in all American history. The Haywood Highlanders were there at the Seven Days' Battles and Malvern Hill. They were there on Marye's Heights at Fredericksburg and the bloody fields at Antietam. Good fortune did come their way when the regiment was ordered back to North Carolina in 1863: having marched long and fought hard since the war's inception, they were spared the Battle of Gettysburg.

These weary but brave men returned to Virginia, where they fought through the bloody battles of 1864 until war's end. They were in the trenches at Petersburg, the last Confederate offensive at Fort Stedman, and the closing battles at Five Forks and Sayler's Creek. When the last roll was taken at Appomattox Court House none of the names from Company F, 25th Regiment, Ransom's Brigade of the Army of Northern Virginia appeared on it. But Haywood Highlanders were surely there, scattered along the roads with many dead, wounded, or captured.

Jones completes this marvelous work by giving us an easy-to-follow and carefully compiled roster and service records for the Haywood Highlanders. A detailed analysis of casualty information, excerpts from Lenoir's letters, and numerous maps and illustrations serve the casual reader, amateur historian, and professional scholar alike. Jones's dedicated work provides a comprehensive view of a special group of men caught up in a common destiny of their time.

Carroll C. Jones has preserved detail and focus that might have been lost forever without him. It is a part of our history and heritage that should never be forgotten.

Terrell Garren

Thomas Lenoir's Civil War diary: front (left) and back covers. *Courtesy of Hugh K. Terrell.*

Preface

Soon after publishing a history of the 25th Regiment North Carolina Troops, I came upon a related primary-source document that was rich beyond my wildest dreams. A newfound friend, Charles Cathey, made me aware of the existence of a personal diary kept by Captain Thomas Isaac Lenoir during the Civil War. Lenoir—son of Thomas Lenoir, who pioneered Haywood County and was a respected politician and leader in the county, and grandson of General William Lenoir, a famed Revolutionary War hero and state politician—was the first commander of the Haywood Highlanders. This Civil War company of volunteers from the Forks of Pigeon region of Haywood County became attached at the outset of the war to the 25th Regiment North Carolina Troops. Cathey furthermore informed me that he in fact possessed a copy of Lenoir's journal that had been meticulously scanned from the original held in the collection of Emily Michal Terrell of Canton, North Carolina. The little-known document had been lovingly cared for over the years and passed down through the Lenoir-Michal family to Mrs. Terrell, a great granddaughter of Captain Lenoir. She most generously gave me permission to obtain a copy from Cathey for further personal reading and study.

Captain Lenoir's treasured diary—only 5¾ inches in height and 4 inches in width—is handsomely bound in a dark-green, embossed leather cover. On the lightly-ruled white leaves of the journal the captain first inscribed his thoughts in pencil beginning on November 1, 1861. Later on in the war he switched entirely to pen and ink to make his recordings, which conclude with an entry dated May 19, 1862. The leather front cover, still in surprisingly good condition after all these years, wraps over the page

Friday Camp Lee
Nov. 15 near Grahamville S.C.
" Walked most of the way from
R.R. Station — Arrived here
with Co. Cathey & a few others
between 9 and 10 O'clk. A.M.
" Balance of the day was
spent in cleaning off ground,
spreading tents, digging wells
& sinks &c. &c —

Saturday
Nov. 16 Men have been working
on our Street & the wells.
drilled one hour in fore noon
Dress parade this evening, &
orders against wrestling were
read — Paymaster coming
next Tuesday — Rolls to make
out before Monday morning!!!

Sunday Camp —
Nov. 17 Sunday inspection this
morning, & dress parade
this evening — I have have
at work all day upon the
pay rolls & not done yet —
Refused an invitation to
dine with Capt. Scriven (I
believe is the name —

Have had sore tongue &
chap'd lips, & bad cold
& been in bad condition for
writing, but have done a good
deal of it today —
We had a little ice & a big
frost this morning, & it is
quite cold again tonight

edges and fastens with a simple tab attachment to the back cover, fully enclosing and protecting the contents of the little book.

Charles Cathey's readily legible copy of the diary presented an excellent document for reading and study. Over the course of several months in late 2008 and early 2009 I worked intently to decipher, transcribe, study, and annotate the Lenoir diary. Primarily, I sought a more intimate understanding of the Haywood volunteer company's activities during the first year of the war. Also, in order to show my appreciation, I wanted to present to Mrs. Terrell, and to Charles Cathey, an accurate transcript along with the annotations I could offer as a serious amateur historian.

The notion to use this diary study as the centerpiece of a book covering Thomas Isaac Lenoir's life and the history of the Haywood Highlanders was by no means intuitive or spontaneous. It was an idea that developed over time as I gradually perceived the extraordinary historical wealth of the journal's contents and the value of the annotations that I had produced to frame the captain's writings. Additionally, I understood that the diary study described very well the locations and the activities of the Haywood Highlanders during the initial year of the war. But due to Captain Lenoir's comparatively short service with the company—he resigned from the Confederate army after serving only one year—the story ends rather abruptly.

It was manifest to me that readers left uninformed of the continuing service and sacrifice of the Haywood Highlanders through the Civil War stood to benefit from a more comprehensive account. Having previously written a history of the company's regiment, I decided that it would be a relatively straightforward undertaking to sharpen my focus and develop a brief historical chronicle of the company's actions for the final three years of the conflict. With that in mind and with the continued encouragement and support of Mrs. Terrell, I launched into the development of this project, choosing to bookend the diary study with a running sketch of Captain Thomas Isaac Lenoir's

Opposite: Excerpts from Thomas Isaaac Lenoir's Civil War diary: front endpapers (top) and entry for Nov. 15–17, 1862. *Courtesy of Hugh K. Terrell.*

life and experiences on the East Fork of Pigeon River in Haywood County, and to conclude with a history and roster of the Haywood Highlanders.

The biographical information for Lenoir and his family was obtained from several established sources: the Lenoir Family Papers in the Southern Historical Collection of the University of North Carolina's Wilson Library; the Thomas Lenoir Papers contained at the Duke University Library; the several Lenoir family letters and documents held in the collection of Hugh K. Terrell and the late Emily Michal Terrell, as well as interviews with Mrs. Terrell; the private collection of Lenoir family letters and documents owned, curated, and held by Ike Forester of Lenoir, North Carolina; essays on the Lenoir family history written by Emily Michal Terrell and her husband, Hugh K. Terrell, published in book 3 of Evelyn Coltman's *Legends, Tales, & History of Cold Mountain*; two books by Thomas Felix Hickerson, *Happy Valley* and *Echoes of Happy Valley*; and William L. Barney's little book, *The Making of a Confederate: Walter Lenoir's Civil War*.

No pretension is made or implied that this work represents a comprehensive biography of the life of Thomas Isaac Lenoir. However, an intensive perusal of the numerous extant letters that he and his father penned, as well as letters written to these men, has offered some insight into many important events and travails in the life of Captain Lenoir. The information gleaned from all of the above sources was compiled, interpreted, and stitched together to fashion a glimpse of Thomas Isaac Lenoir and to capture the essence of the boy, the young man, the farmer, the slaveholder, the Civil War commander, and the family man.

In this volume the transcription of Captain Lenoir's diary is presented in a typographical format reproducing the features of Lenoir's handwritten pages as faithfully as possible. Alongside each day's entry I have provided historical context and annotations of the text, borrowing judiciously from my earlier work, *The 25th North Carolina Troops in the Civil War: History and Roster of a Mountain-Bred Regiment*. Additionally, new details and findings regarding the duty performed by the 25th

N.C. Troops at Grahamville, South Carolina, offer vivid descriptions of the coastal encampment and tantalizing clues into the soldiers' lives.

While the greatest portion of the work in preparing this book involved close reading of old letters and records and careful preparation of documentary transcriptions, high-tech research methodologies were used as well. Internet services provided ready access to valuable resources such as *The War of the Rebellion: A Compilation of the Official Records of the Union and Confederate Armies* (*Official Records*) and Walter Clark's *Histories of the Several Regiments and Battalions from North Carolina, in the Great War 1861–1865*. Moreover, through the service provided by Footnote.com the compiled records of the Confederate army held in the National Archives were accessed, and minute service details for the individual soldiers and the company were obtained.

Finally, the roster and service records for the Haywood Highlanders included at the end of the book are taken directly from the seventh volume of *North Carolina Troops, 1861–1865: A Roster*, published by the North Carolina Division (now Office) of Archives and History in 1979. The data from that work have been paraphrased and reformatted with permission. For more detailed information about each soldier, you may obtain a copy of the entire book at http://nc-historical-publications.stores.yahoo.net/125.html.

Emily Michal Terrell, the proud guardian of Captain Tom Lenoir's Civil War diary and keeper of Lenoir family lore in the East Fork region of Haywood County, passed away as this book's manuscript reached its final stages. Before her death she was able to review the early drafts of the story and offer keen insight into the Thomas Isaac Lenoir family. I can say with absolute conviction and certainty that Mrs. Terrell approved of the treatment given to the diary and the many Lenoir family letters and documents that were incorporated into this narrative. Just as importantly, she also agreed with my assessment of Tom Lenoir's sense of duty, which drove both his original move to Haywood County in 1846 and his later decision to accept the command of the Civil

War volunteer company from his neighbors. Moreover, Mrs. Terrell fully comprehended the difficulties that Tom Lenoir encountered in the post-bellum Reconstruction era, and she felt empathy for his struggles to eke out a living for himself and his family by farming his land along the East Fork of the Pigeon River. Therefore, for her eager and valuable contributions, including the generous loan of Captain Lenoir's diary, it is my honor and pleasure to dedicate this book to the memory of Emily Michal Terrell.

Others contributed as well to help fill the gaps and complete the story of Captain Tom Lenoir and his band of Civil War volunteers. Upon his wife's passing, Hugh K. Terrell opened for my purpose his beautiful home with its bounty of Lenoir artifacts and resources and provided a continuation of Lenoir family support. I will be forever grateful for this kindness as well as the opportunity to renew an old friendship too long lapsed by distance and time.

Another Lenoir descendant with whom I became acquainted and subsequently indebted to is Ike Forester (Ike's great great grandfather was Tom Lenoir's younger brother, Rufus.) Becky Phillips, executive director of the Fort Defiance Museum in Lenoir, North Carolina, made me aware that Ike was the proud guardian of another important cache of Lenoir family documents. I soon discovered that he indeed possessed an abundance of Lenoir letters and records, and we quickly developed a fruitful friendship. Ike was generous to the extreme in sharing his precious resources with me. Moreover, we opened a line of e-mail communication in which viewpoints on the Lenoir personages were exchanged, genealogical lines discussed, and, most important, Ike's Lenoir knowledge base tapped. Additionally, Ike reviewed the entire manuscript of this book and made numerous useful comments and corrections. For his generosity and constructive assistance I offer my deepest appreciation.

Matthew Turi and his staff at the University of North Carolina's Wilson Library were extremely professional and helpful in serving up boxes and boxes of Lenoir family documents contained in the Southern Historical Collection. The many long days spent sifting through this extraordinarily valuable historical information were not only fascinating but perhaps the most rewarding of my career. Also, I am appreciative of the efforts of researcher Diane Richard, who scoured the collection of Lenoir memorabilia at Duke University and the North Carolina State Archives to turn up several nuggets of correspondence between the Thomas Lenoirs, father and son.

And to my many friends in Western North Carolina who have in some way donated time and assistance to further my efforts I am profoundly beholden. That applies especially to Charles Cathey for his historical insight into the Forks of Pigeon region of Haywood County and his contribution of the copy of Captain Lenoir's diary that was the inspiration for this work; to Edie Burnette for her endeavors as my local agent and confidante and for the wonderful map she produced of Forks of Pigeon, which is included within these pages; and to Terrell Garren, noted and highly regarded Civil War historian, for vetting my manuscript and offering not only his insightful thoughts but the book's foreword.

Last, there are no words that I can invoke to sufficiently express my feelings of gratitude to Maria. For her steadfastness, everlasting support, and devotion I can only say "Thanks." She will understand the rest.

CAPTAIN LENOIR'S *Diary*

Introduction

The fall of Charleston's Fort Sumter in April 1861 prompted President Abraham Lincoln to call for military forces to suppress the Southern insurrection, one he felt was "too powerful to be suppressed by the ordinary course of judicial proceedings."[1] His precipitous action not only pushed the state of North Carolina to secede from the United States in May 1861, but it also effectively incited many of the citizens of Haywood County, in far western North Carolina, to turn against their country. Soon after the Old North State declared its allegiance to the Confederate States of America, farmers and farmers' sons began flocking out of the highlands surrounding the upper reaches of Haywood County's Pigeon River to defend their mountain homeland from what they deemed vile invaders.

Thomas Isaac Lenoir, a landholder, slaveowner, and farmer from the Pigeon River's East Fork region, and Col. Joseph Cathey, a respected farmer, merchant, and politician in the Forks of Pigeon community, assembled a band of zealous volunteers who had poured out of the hills to fight the Yankees. Lenoir, at the age of forty-three, was unanimously elected captain of the fledgling military unit his mountaineers styled the "Haywood Highlanders." On July 18, 1861, after the requisite number of men had enlisted to form a company, Captain Lenoir marched the Haywood Highlanders off to Asheville, North Carolina to join the fray. At the training camps in Asheville the Haywood volunteers began learning the rudiments of soldiering and were quickly assimilated into the 25th Regiment North Carolina Troops as Company F. For the ensuing months the captain recorded in his personal diary the various activities and movements of his company as well as many other events and observations that he deemed noteworthy. The commander's recordings not only lay bare the plight and lifestyle of the average Civil War soldier, but reveal the initial modest military contributions made by the Haywood Highlanders during the first year of the war.

The opening chapters of Part I of this book establish Thomas Isaac Lenoir's presence in Haywood County on a large farm beside the East Fork of Pigeon River and explore his career as a bachelor farmer and slaveholder before the Civil War. Lenoir's life changed abruptly with his election as captain of the Haywood Highlanders, and the full content of his wartime diary unveils the extraordinary circumstances and the innermost feelings and perspectives of a participant in the war. The concluding chapter of this section follows Captain Lenoir home from the war after his abrupt resignation from the rebel army, and resumes the story of a struggling agrarian career on the East Fork of Pigeon River.

Part II recounts the Haywood Highlanders' travails in the Civil War from the point in April 1862 when Captain Lenoir resigned, through the balance of the War for Southern Independence. A brief summary highlights the important events and contributions made by Company F during the last three years of the war and sets the stage for a closer examination of the real service rendered by the company. Frequently, histories of Civil War regiments and companies are so murky that present-day readers have little notion of the actual work that the military units performed. First-hand accounts told and even recorded by the soldiers themselves many years after the war were occasionally remembered inaccurately. Too often exaggerated embellishments were added to romanticize the Civil War experience. Consequently, the veracity of these historical tales and testimony eroded with repetition and time through subsequent generations. One of the primary objectives of this work, then, is to lift the shroud of obscurity that has hidden the genuine deeds and service performed by the Haywood Highlanders and to offer the reader a clearer lens through which to view the authentic accounts of the mountain boys during the Civil War.

It is manifest that the Haywood Highlanders' record, though meritorious, did not shine more brilliantly than those of most other Confederate Civil War companies. For nearly a full year after the first passionate Haywood men enlisted they fired no shots at the enemy. However, over the subsequent six months the Highlanders participated with Gen. Robert E. Lee's Army of Northern Virginia in one significant engagement and three major battles. Following that period of hard service the company once again fell into a lengthy spell (approximately sixteen months) of monotonous coastal defense duty in eastern North Carolina and southeastern Virginia. Then, suddenly, as the fourth year of the war began to unfold, they were ordered to the trenches protecting Richmond and Petersburg, Virginia—the very same saps they had worked alongside slaves earlier in the war to construct. Earthworks, "gopher holes," and bombproof shelters were home to the Haywood Highlanders for the last year of the war, and from these entrenchments they fought, suffered, and died.

The journey of the Haywood Highlanders through the Civil War closely paralleled those of the 25th Regiment North Carolina Troops and Ransom's Brigade. Company F, as the Highlanders were designated, remained attached to the 25th Regiment for the entirety of the war. Likewise, the regiment remained an integral unit in Ransom's Brigade from April 1862 until the surrender of Lee's army at Appomattox Court House in April 1865. A history of the 25th Regiment North Carolina Troops by the author (*The 25th North Carolina Troops in the Civil War: History and Roster of a Mountain-Bred Regiment*) illuminates the path of the regiment as it coursed from theater to theater through the horrible conflict. While a detailed recounting of the general events and movements of the Haywood Highlanders would be in a large degree redundant, in this work I have examined several distinct phases of the company's service which include extended periods of routine duty interrupted by periods of fierce fighting and terrible hardships. The periods of Carolina coastal duty, Seven Days' Battles, Maryland campaign, Fredericksburg, North Carolina / Virginia coastal defense, and Richmond / Petersburg defense receive additional scrutiny.

From the training camps at Asheville, North Carolina, through these various periods of service, the names of some 131 men filled the company's rosters. However, over the course of the war a number of factors and influences worked insidiously to diminish the fighting strength that the Haywood Highlanders could muster. Many brave men perished from the ravages of disease; other lives were snuffed out by the enemy's well-aimed and lethal projectiles. The wounded and disabled were numerous, as were those who were captured and trotted off to prisoner-of-war camps. Also, some mountaineers chose to resign, if eligible, or transfer to other units. And, of course, the war severely tested the mettle of all the mountain men who went to war. As a result, more than a few of the Highlanders abandoned their brethren in the field and went over to the enemy, or skulked back to the hills to hide out for the balance of the sectional conflict. For each of the various phases of the war the casualties and losses suffered by the company have been compiled and presented here. This information is intended to give readers an appreciation for the sacrifices made by the mountain men and the multitude of factors that gradually wore away the fighting capacity of the company.

Notably, when the last dark months of 1865 finally arrived, only twenty-seven Haywood Highlanders were left in the Petersburg trenches to battle the Yankees. The names of these stubborn and stalwart men who persevered through it all—perils of war, deprivations, and separation from loved ones— should never be forgotten. To the degree possible, considering the quality and accuracy of the extant Civil War service records, I have endeavored to identify these last few remaining Haywood Highlanders who were left to fight from the hideous trenches of Petersburg. And only about half of those standing survivors were original company enlistees. Their names especially—the men who served for almost four years while denying the enemy's efforts to kill them and resisting the deadly camp diseases and temptations to desert—are illuminated for all to know and revere.

Whether readers' interests are directed to the intriguing biographical accounts of Captain Lenoir, his diary's contents, or the history of the company he commanded, I hope this book will provide a deeper understanding of the sacrifices made by all who participated and lived through the American Civil War. And I hope, as well, that readers will come to share this writer's appreciation for the captain and a band of mountain-bred rebels from Forks of Pigeon known as the Haywood Highlanders.

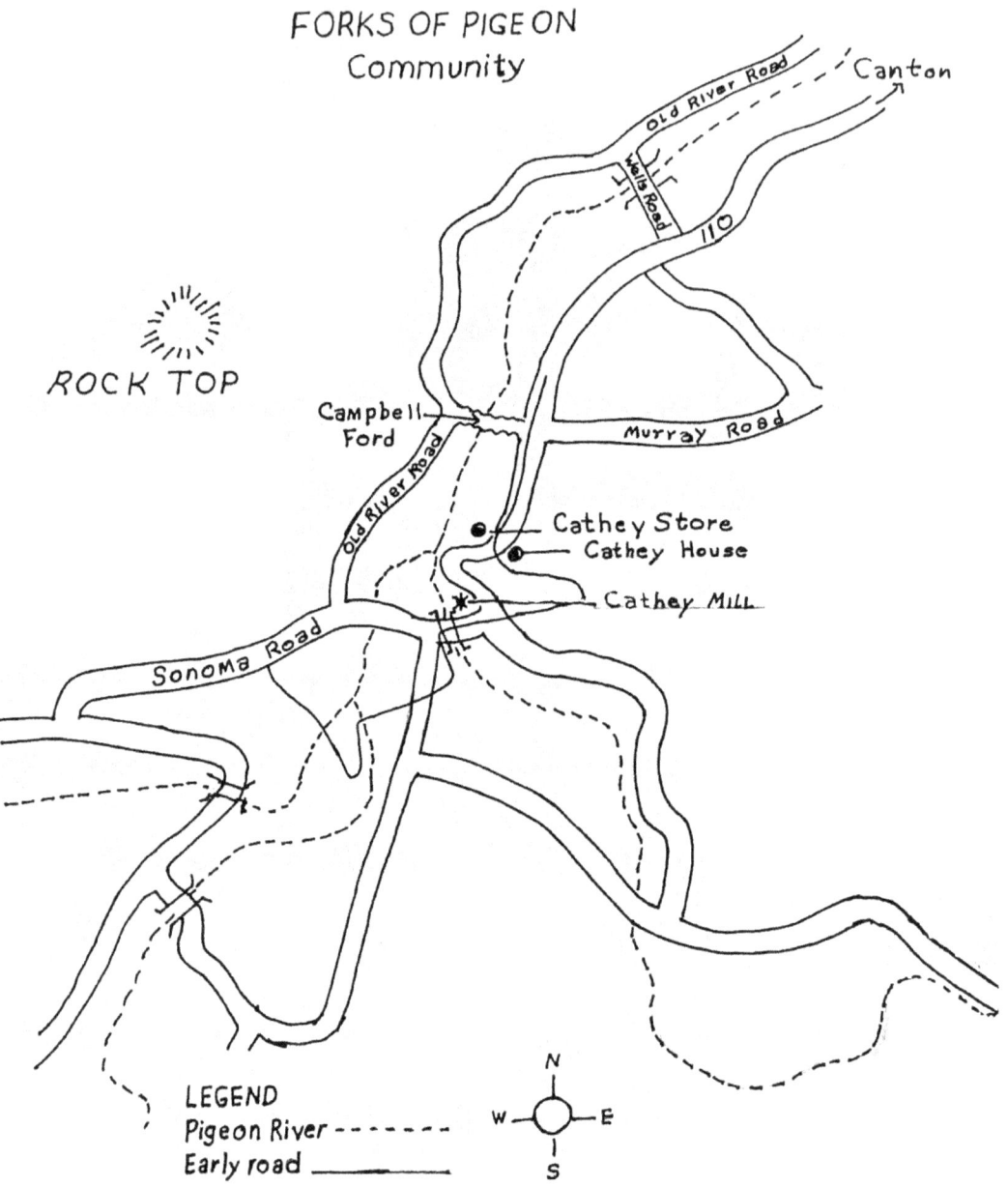

Forks of Pigeon, Haywood County, North Carolina. *Map by Edie Hutchins Burnette; used by permission.*

Part I
Thomas Lenoir's East Fork Legacy

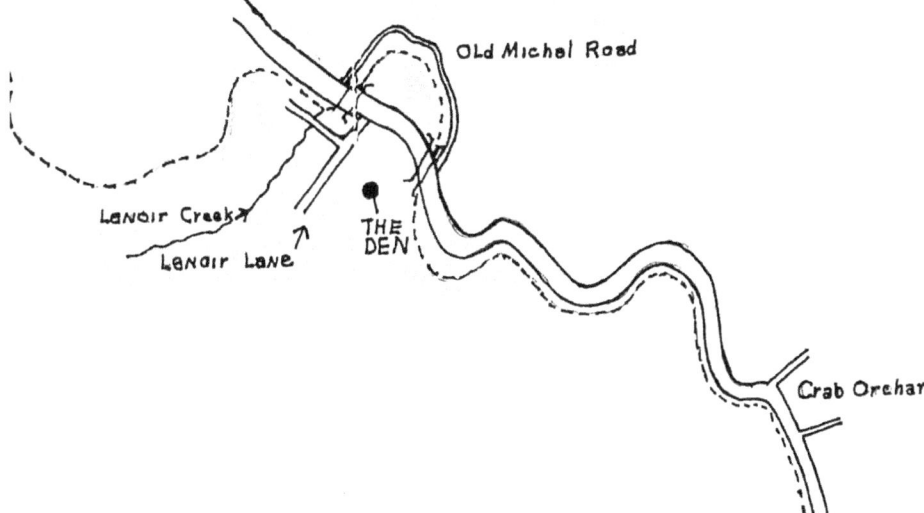

Sunlight breaking over the mountains. *Harper's New Monthly Magazine*, vol. 61, June–Nov. 1880.

Thomas Lenoir, Haywood County Pioneer

In the years immediately preceding the American Civil War the highland regions of Western North Carolina were not devoid of working farms dependent on slave labor for economic success and survival. One of the several instances of such a socioeconomic enterprise existed along the East Fork of the Pigeon River, deep within the remote mountain recesses of Haywood County. In that rural and rugged outpost of antebellum society Thomas Isaac Lenoir lorded over holdings comprising almost 5,000 acres of land and at least eighteen slaves. The mountain farmer had styled his East Fork quarters with the seemingly appropriate name "Bachelor's Den," reflecting his own unmarried status since reluctantly moving from Wilkes County to his father's Haywood land in 1846. At that time the property had been held by the elder Thomas Lenoir for almost forty years, yet managed by local agents and overseers for more than half that period.

In 1806, or maybe a year before, Thomas Isaac Lenoir's mother had been offered a large tract of land along the East Fork as a wedding bequest from her father, Waightstill Avery. At the time Avery, a lawyer and the first attorney general of North Carolina, was the largest slaveholder in Burke County and one of the earliest land speculators purchasing vast tracts of the former Cherokee territories in Western North Carolina. In September 1806 the elder Thomas Lenoir wrote in a letter to his father, Gen. William Lenoir, "Louisa has a wish to go to Buncombe and to gratify her curiosity. I have consented to go with her." Haywood County had not yet been partitioned from Buncombe, and Thomas Lenoir's wife, Selina Louisa Avery Lenoir, was apparently

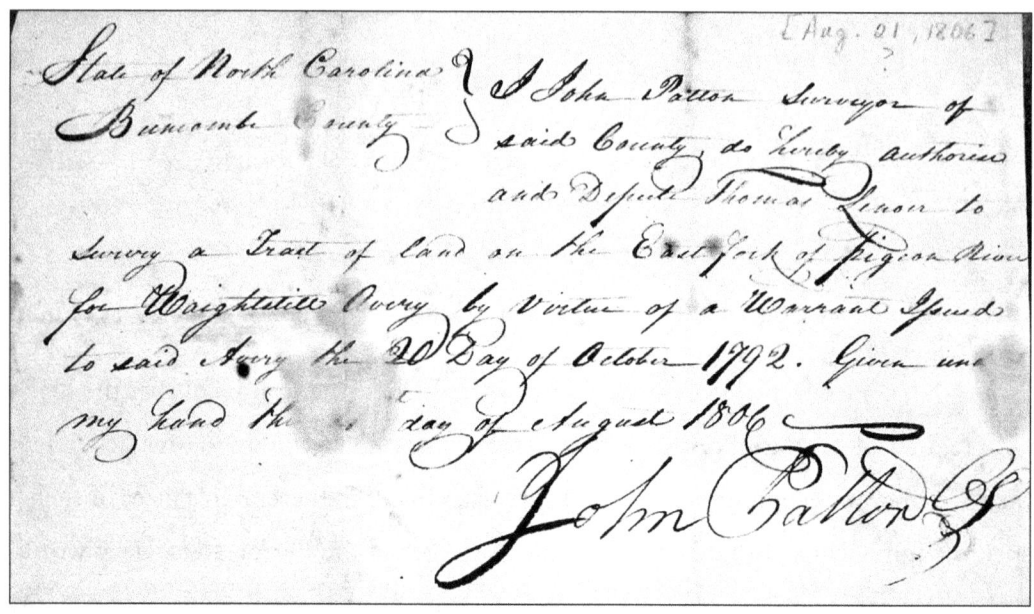

An authorization granted by the Buncombe County surveyor in August 1806 allowed Thomas Lenoir to survey Waightstill Avery's tract of land on the East Fork of Pigeon River. *Southern Historical Collection, Wilson Library, University of North Carolina at Chapel Hill; used by permission.*

eager to make a trip to the western frontier to see the much talked-about mountain property she had acquired. Having agreed to the trip, Thomas wrote further to General Lenoir:

> It does not afford me much pleasure to reflect on the unprofitable manner in which I have spent so much time in the prime of life and to think of my present situation, that I am without a home, without any flattering prospects of getting one that will be agreeable, and without any appariant [sic] means of rendering society that service, or my Friends that satisfaction. I could wish, causes me much uneasiness . . . . . I have heretofore felt no disposition to settle myself on the land which Col. Avery talks of giving to Louisa on Pigeon River, but in my present circumstances, I should be very willing, provided Col. Avery would make her a right to it, and it was clear of the incumberance [sic] of law suits etc.[2]

Col. Thomas Lenoir, father of Thomas Isaac Lenoir, as a young man, probably just before he relocated with his bride to the mountains of Haywood County along the East Fork of Pigeon River in 1807. Pen and ink sketch, approx, 6" x 8". Artist unknown. *Collection of Fort Defiance Museum, Lenoir, N.C.; used by permission.*

Reading his letter more than two hundred years after it was scratched with quill and ink reveals how despondent and uneasy about his future the young Thomas Lenoir was. The options before him seem to have been limited.

After receiving authorization from the surveyor of Buncombe County to survey Waightstill Avery's property grants, Thomas escorted Louisa into the western mountains in September 1806 to see the land of promise and hope.[3] Surprisingly perhaps, the Lenoirs found Avery's holdings along the East Fork valley dotted with the crude log shelters of farmers and likely squatters. A memorandum written by Thomas Lenoir during this trip lists these first settlers in the area as tenants. Recorded as they lived starting at the upper settlement and moving down the river were John Robbins, John Morrison (noted as a Scotsman and a woman hater), William Earp, Tobias Harp, Byrum Jones, Ben and Thomas Vines, Josiah Daniel, Jeremiah Daniel, Rowland and I.

Smith, Charles and Elijah Henson, John Lemmonds, William Stegiel, William Spivey, and Robert Jones. These men and their families inhabited various plots of ground that had been cleared and styled with names such as the Big Bottom, Black Walnut Cove, Crab Orchard, Black Walnut Bottom, Glade, Morgan's Bottom, Poplar Bottom, and the Island. They were true pioneers in every respect and were, in fact, the first white immigrants to chop down the virgin forests and cultivate the rocky soil along the East Fork.[4]

Apparently undeterred by the remote and rugged terrain they encountered, the young Lenoir couple elected to settle upon the "Pigeon River" land tract. In 1807, during the first cold months of the year, Thomas and Louisa loaded up their belongings and, with livestock and slaves in tow, made the arduous trek from Fort Defiance, the Lenoir family plantation located in Wilkes County, across the Blue Ridge into the hinterland of the Pigeon River's upper tributary waters.[5] On the brow of a hillside overlooking the East Fork of Pigeon River, brawling bold and clear through a verdant highland valley, they constructed a cabin of poplar logs for shelter and began raising livestock, growing grain crops, and leasing land to meet expenses. The East Fork venture seems to have gotten off to a promising start, for soon after making the move to Haywood, Thomas wrote to his brother informing him of progress:

> I have got a promising <u>little</u> crop of corn, wheat and Oats and my little stock of Cattle horses and hogs appears to thrive very well in this good range which helps to make Louisa and myself better satisfied with our new home than we expected to be, when you was at the poplar cabbin [*sic*]. I fear you disliked the place so much when you was there that you will never come to see us any more; but I think if you was there now you would have a much better opinion of the country.[6]

The Lenoirs were not alone in their extreme efforts to claim and possess the lands and forests west of the Blue Ridge. During the decades following the Revolutionary War, European pioneers of every ilk—Scots-Irish, English, and Germanic—began finding

Gen. William Lenoir, father of Thomas Lenoir and grandfather of Thomas Isaac Lenoir, was a famed Revolutionary War hero, statesman, surveyor, and plantation owner in Western North Carolina. His plantation home, called Fort Defiance, was located in Wilkes County (which later became Caldwell County) and was home to Thomas I. Lenoir for the greater part of his youthful years. Artist unknown. *Collection of Ike Forester, Lenoir, N.C.; used by permission.*

their way through the mountain passes and establishing homesteads throughout the wild river valleys. Soon after Thomas and Louisa settled on their mountain property the far western lands of the state were detached from Buncombe to form a new county. Settlers rapidly populating the former Cherokee Indian territory had lodged an appeal with the state's General Assembly declaring the distance to the courthouse in Asheville too great and inconvenient. Moreover, they pleaded that the roads were frequently impassable, especially during the winter season.[7] Thus in 1808 the state legislators established the new county of Haywood, its name borrowed from the sitting treasurer of North Carolina, John Haywood.

North Carolina's newest geographical subdivision included all of the land along the Pigeon River and its tributaries and encompassed the region extending from the Pigeon watershed to North Carolina's border with Tennessee. In 1810 the assistant marshal making the Haywood census described the county as comprehending "the western part of the State of North Carolina west of Rutherford and Buncombe Counties." The census taker went on to emphasize in his report to the state's marshal that the "settlements on Fines Creek & the East fork of pigeon also lye [sic] very remote from the Body of the County." Although the county was large in area, the enumerator reported there were only 384 families living within its borders and included 2,780 "Inhabitants of every description."[8] Among those scarce Haywood County pioneer inhabitants residing on the East Fork of Pigeon River, far "remote from the body of the county," were Thomas and Louisa Lenoir.

Thomas did not limit himself to simply constructing a homestead for Louisa and himself. If he wished to become a prominent and successful farmer and landholder there were many essential farming tasks to be performed. He and his slaves worked feverishly to erect quarters for the bonded Africans, to clear fields, to make grain crops, to split rails by the thousands and lay up fencing to contain the stock, to plant fruit trees, and to fashion bee gums, among untold other jobs.

As if all this was not enough to occupy his time, Lenoir quickly established himself as a respected political leader in the new county. His name is prominent in the earliest annals of the county and even appears in the General Assembly's bill establishing Haywood; he was designated one of three commissioners whose stated responsibility was to erect public buildings for the county.[9] Additionally, he acted as a grand juror in the first session of the Superior Court held in Asheville after the county's formation; and during the formative years of Haywood County's existence he represented the county in the state's General Assembly.[10]

There can be no doubt of Thomas Lenoir's affinity for politics and his willingness to serve for the public good. He proudly wrote to his father in 1809 of being appointed by the Haywood Court as "Overseer of the Path up the East Fork." Furthermore, he informed General Lenoir, "Big Tom Love & Little Tom Lenoir are the only Candidates at present in the Commons [North Carolina House of Commons]."[11] Tom Love of Waynesville, a wealthy landowner and slaveholder, was a dominant political figure in Haywood during the county's early years. The younger Thomas Lenoir's comparison of himself and Love likely referenced the significant contrast in political stature more than physical size. Nevertheless, the humorous styling of his comment points to a wit and humility which was surely not lost on his neighbors and local citizens. Such traits would go far in increasing his popularity and his own political standing in the county as well as the state. Haywood County constituents elected Thomas Lenoir to the lower house of the state legislature five out of the first six years of the county's existence.

At the outbreak of war in 1812 with Great Britain the mountaineers residing in Haywood became apprehensive of their Cherokee neighbors. It was rumored that the Indians, allied with the British government, had been supplied with new muskets and ammunition and were in a warlike posture. Thomas Lenoir wrote to his father that many citizens were considering "forting," or building safe houses to afford protection from Indian attacks:

> Some exagerated [sic], or rather false accounts, of the proceedings and threats of our Cherokee neighbors have several times, so much alarmed some few of the citizens of this County, that they have been on the point of Forting, and some of my neighbors I believe are at this time too much scared to sleep good of nights etc. [T]his is a circumstance that makes me rather unwilling to leave home long, least, a few Scare Crow Stories about the Indians, should cause some of my neighbors & my Negroes, to run off in my absence and neglect my crop etc. It has been reported that the Cherokees have by some means, been furnished with a considerable number of new British muskets and a quantity of Ammunition, and that they and the Creek's have not long since Stolen about 100 horses out of the frontiers of Georgia. The report about muskets is generally believed to be groundless, and that of the horses, to be much exaggerated.[12]

The Indian attacks against Haywood's citizens did not come off as feared. However, the State of North Carolina enlisted militia troops to defend against the British foe, and Haywood County was not exempted. Thomas Lenoir was appointed a major in the state militia and summoned to Wadesborough in 1815 along with his Haywood militia company "for the defense of the Southern Frontier." The troops remained there for a short time but did not engage the enemy or leave the state's borders before being mustered out of service.[13]

The years in the rural and remote outpost of society which Haywood County represented at that time were not easy for Thomas and Louisa. Court weeks in Haywood and Buncombe, regular militia musters at Waynesville, and occasional stints at Raleigh serving in the General Assembly allowed Thomas some opportunities to interact with citizens beyond the neighborhood and mingle with a somewhat more cultured side of society. He was commissioned colonel of the Haywood regiment of militia in 1818 and would have been required to participate in the frequent gatherings and activities of the military unit.[14] At shooting matches in Asheville during court sessions Thomas found a venue to satisfy competitive urges and demonstrate his professed prowess wielding a flintlock musket. In a letter to his brother William he boasted, "Me and my gun are much dreaded where we are known by these Buncombe marksmen."[15]

However, no such diversions or avails were extended to Louisa, who was confined to her log house, caring for the young offspring she and Thomas were producing with some regularity. By the close of the year 1821 six children (and one other, who died as an infant) had been born on the East Fork to the Lenoirs.[16] The small children, along with the constant and perplexing issues of managing a working farm that included approximately thirty-five slaves, were not enough to keep Louisa's mind wholly distracted from the dreariness and loneliness of her domestic situation.

It might be supposed that Thomas and Louisa, the progeny of wealthy families and owners of great tracts of mountain land and many slaves, were well situated and highly successful. The value of their real property and chattel was much higher than the standard of the mountaineers living in Western North Carolina at the time. However, the labors of their slaves were not extended toward raising profitable cash crops such as cotton, rice, and sugar cane as was the case with the wealthy planters in the lower South and southern coastal regions. Instead, crops of corn and wheat they raised were

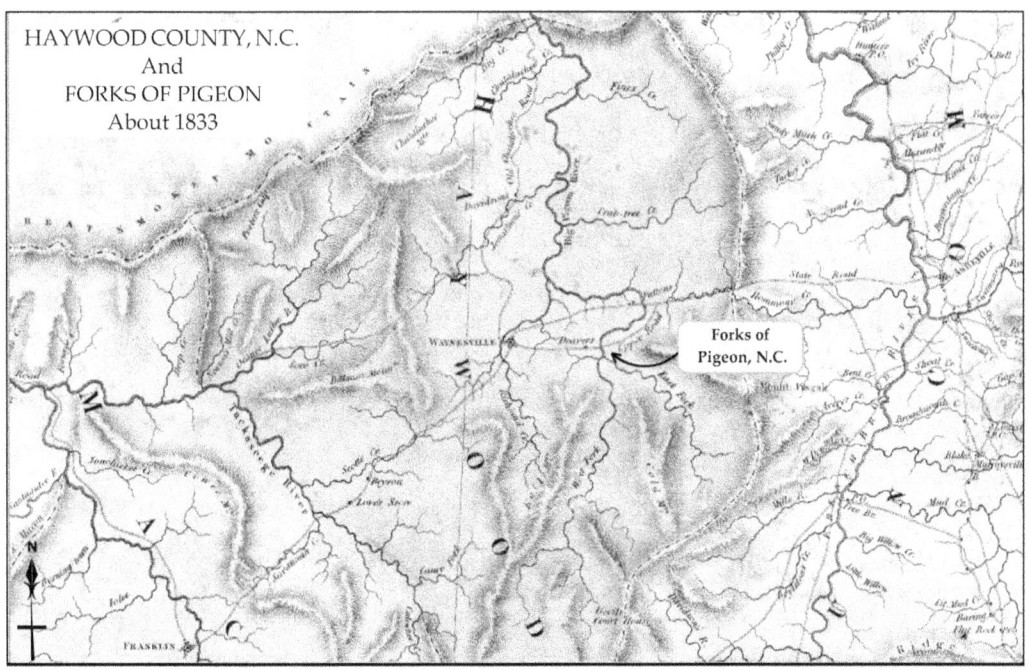

In 1833 the first crude county roads connected the East Fork region and Forks of Pigeon with Waynesville to the west and Asheville to the east. *Library of Congress, Maps Division.*

sufficient only to sustain themselves, the slave families, and the livestock. Leasing parcels of their land and raising and selling stock—cattle, mules, horses, sheep, and hogs—offered the best chances of earning a profit. Yet due to the scarcity of cash in the region the animals, as well as any surplus grain products, were usually bartered for other goods or services. And the payments for leased land by tenants usually amounted to obligations of some share of the crops raised or for other services rendered in favor of the Lenoirs.

In 1816 Thomas lamented in a letter to his brother, "My expenses for two years past have so far exceeded my incomes that I am nearly moneyless."[17] Five years later he summarized his financial situation in a letter to his father, recapping the cash on hand, money owed to him and the dim prospects for collecting it, debt obligations, and pending lawsuits inherited from his father-in-law. The net value of all these debits and credits was so dismal that Thomas was inclined to affirm to General Lenoir: "By the above statement, you will perceive that I am poor . . . . . and I entertain but little hope of ever acquiring great wealth."[18] So it is abundantly clear that the East Fork Lenoir family, although rich in heritage, land, and personal property (including their large slaveholdings), was just able to eke out a living in Haywood's mountains and subsist along with the other hardy pioneers of lesser means and station.[19]

Neither were Louisa and Thomas pleased with the prospects of raising a family in a place where there were no schools and the children were growing up as wild as Indians. Thomas wrote of living in a "dark hollow" and confided in a letter to his brother, "When I write or think of my children something whispers in my ear, this is not a suitable place to raise them in."[20] It is manifest that the Lenoirs were not content in Haywood and not satisfied with their primitive circumstances. And it had become abundantly clear to them that wealth and riches could not be easily accumulated by farming with slave labor on their vast East Fork landholdings. Fortunately, however, in 1821 Thomas was presented with a way to escape the dark, lonely Pigeon mountains. General Lenoir extended to him a proposition to return to Wilkes County and assume much of the responsibility of running the business and affairs at the family's plantation home, Fort Defiance. This opportunity seems to have much pleased and even flattered Thomas:

> As regards my moving to Wilkes, my mind has not materially changed since I saw you and have uniformly intended to go, provided you continued to think it would suit your conveniences & be satisfactory to you, Moma [sic], and friends generally. The fact is ever since we first talked on that subject, the idea of leaving the Pigeon mountains, and returning to my native country and friends, has been a pleasing one; and I believe Louisa has been more pleased with that expectation than myself; but when meditating on this subject, I can truly say, that I've never felt any rush to go, provided I could think, in so doing, I should transgress on your convenience, or occasion you any dissatisfaction of mind, or thereby give any of my near friends any just cause to think hard of either yourself or me. and have always felt like a small

hint from you that my going would probably have those effects, would be sufficient to make me cheerfully and willingly abandon the idea (although a pleasing one) of going altogether.[21]

Thomas and Louisa Lenoir finally did become convinced that their removal back to the Fort would not transgress on the general's "convenience," and they chose to take up his generous offer. In 1822 they packed up their children and belongings in a "little" wagon borrowed from General Lenoir and took flight to Wilkes, vacating the Haywood mountains, yet leaving most of their slaves behind to attend to the farm and livestock.

Picking wild flowers. *Harper's New Monthly Magazine*, vol. 61, June–Nov., 1880.

Thomas Isaac Lenoir: A Son's Coming of Age

Five-year-old Thomas Isaac (Tom) Lenoir likely had mixed emotions at leaving the beautiful mountain habitat of his birth. The close, familiar confines of the log cabin's interior would have offered security and comfort to him, having spent much of his short life at the hearth's side warming in front of the fire. He would have grown attached to the family's slaves, cared for farm animals that he called by name, climbed the steep mountainsides, and swum and fished in the cold waters of the East Fork River. However, he surely would have been delighted with the relocation to his grandparents' fine plantation home and likely made the adjustment to his new environment easily and quickly. The youth would have instantly made new friends in the surrounding countryside and among the slaves quartered at Fort Defiance.

Also, there were schools in that neck of the woods that he would have attended soon after relocating to Wilkes. Even before reaching the age of twelve Tom was packed off to a boarding school in Burke County to further his education. And apparently he was a scholar of extraordinary ability. The instructor at the school reported to the elder Thomas Lenoir that the young pupil was among the first in the class in reading, writing, and arithmetic. The teacher added, "He has been remarkably studious for a boy of his age; and attentive to his business, both in, and out of school. Sometimes I think he studies rather too closely for a boy of his weakly appearance, But this I think is erring on the safest side."[22]

The early boarding-school experience, along with his attendance in 1837 at the Bingham School in Hillsborough, were only preparatory steps to help Tom gain

Gen. William Lenoir's plantation home, Fort Defiance, was originally constructed in 1792. Enlarged in 1822 to accommodate Thomas Lenoir's growing family, the house was continuously occupied by Lenoir descendants until 1961 and has now been fully restored. *Courtesy of Fort Defiance Museum.*

admittance in 1838 to the state's university at Chapel Hill.[23] Gen. William Lenoir, Tom's grandfather, had been a founding member of the school's board of trustees and for a brief period its first president. It is doubtful that this status won any special privileges for the grandson, but it surely held him in good stead with the president of the university and former governor, David Swain, with whom Tom was able to develop a warm personal relationship. While attending the university Tom found that rooming in the village was much more suitable for study than taking a room in the dormitories, where the company was annoying and the noise intolerable.[24] He boarded with William Green, chaplain of the school and a professor of rhetoric and logic. It was a pleasant living situation; Tom later wrote to his brother, Walter, that Mr. Green's house seemed "more like home to me than any place in the world, except the Old Fort."[25] However, Tom's tenure at Chapel Hill was a brief one. In May of 1839, after only one year of college study, he elected to leave academia, supporting his decision with the following explanation to his father:

> "If I were five or six years younger & had plenty of money I would like very much to spend a year or two more at Chapel Hill, but under present circumstances I have no idea of doing so, but calculate on improving my self in future by studying alone—When I leave Chapel Hill I expect to feel very much like a fish out of water, in consequence of having no settled business to engage in, but hope that you will give me some advice upon that subject—[26]

Tom landed a job quickly with the backing and help of President Swain. He was appointed as an assistant marshal to take the Wilkes County census in 1840 and returned to Fort Defiance to reside and work. In addition to riding through the outlying Wilkes communities and enumerating the county's population, Tom assisted his father and brother with the management of business matters at the plantation. Moreover, Tom's grandfather, Gen. William Lenoir, had died in 1839, leaving an enormous estate to divide among beneficiaries and creditors. As the executor of the large estate, Thomas Lenoir depended on Tom to collect debts, settle accounts, and even perform occasional surveying work to delineate land tracts and untangle property legal suits.

However, by 1842 Tom must have grown restless at Fort Defiance and felt a yearning to strike out on his own and establish himself in some profitable occupation. He was twenty-five years old and still harbored no resolute ideas for an appropriate career that might suit him and earn some money. In the spring he accompanied his brother William to Alabama, where the older Lenoir was attempting to recover money owed him from various business ventures. Not long after Tom's return from the South

Thomas Isaac Lenoir at about age twenty-three, circa 1840. *From Thomas Felix Hickerson,* Happy Valley: History and Genealogy *(1940).*

to Caldwell County (formed from parts of Wilkes and Burke Counties in 1841) he received a job offer from a Mr. J. Dunlap, who was a merchant and store owner in the village of Asheville.[27] Dunlap evidently desired to have Tom clerk in his store, and the young Lenoir immediately responded to the employment opportunity with a letter mailed in August of 1842:

> Being out of employment I have concluded to accept your offer, & will endeavor to be in Asheville by the 25th of this month. I hope that I shall be able to discharge to your satisfaction, the duties which may be incumbent upon, & incidental to me, while in your employment, & acting as your Clerk. as I am unexperienced in that capacity, I cannot promise to do better than my <u>best</u>. hope that you will find me desirous of promoting your interest & attentive to your business.[28]

Although he was inexperienced as a clerk, Tom's endeavors in that capacity met with approbation from his new boss and earned an enduring friendship with the man. Nevertheless, by mid-1843 the brief clerical stint at Asheville seems to have come to an end. It was in that time frame when Tom and his younger brother, Walter, started out on foot from Fort Defiance on a tour of the northern states.

The young Lenoir men from the hills of Western North Carolina undertook the journey to gain an impression of the land of Yankee thrift. They trudged on foot through the Shenandoah Valley, visiting the Natural Bridge and caverns as they passed by. Their route took them through Strasburg, Winchester, and Harpers Ferry; and from there the footworn boys walked along the towpath of the Chesapeake & Ohio Canal all the way to the Federal City, Washington. As Tom described in a letter to his father, "[We] walked by the side of the Canal 61 miles to Washington City—This canal appeared to us, to be a stupendous work—The aqueducts across the Monocacy & Catoctous [Catoctin] are splendid—The Monocacy is near 200 y^{ds} wide where the aqueduct crosses." Tom could not have known as he marveled at the aqueduct spanning the mouth of the Monocacy River that the Confederate Civil War company he would later command would participate in an attempt to destroy the structure.

Both young men wore out their shoes and clothes on the way to Washington, and it seems they drew much attention as they "footed" it through the villages of the Virginia countryside. Tom wrote to his father: "We generally trudge through the vilages [sic] with our coats & vests both off and sometimes attract considerable attention – & are very much amused at questions which are often asked us—Many persons think we are mechanics—some ask us if we are not tailors, ship carpenters [etc.]." After sightseeing for a few days in Washington, Tom and Walter rode in train cars and boats as they continued their northward tour and visited the cities of Philadelphia, New York, and Boston. On the return trip home they altered their course so as to pass through Cincinnati, Ohio, Lexington, Kentucky, and finally eastern Tennessee, where their uncle William Ballard Lenoir's residence and vast business enterprises were

Tom and Walter Lenoir marveled at the Chesapeake and Ohio Canal and the aqueducts such as this one, where the canal carries vessels across the Monocacy River. *Library of Congress, Prints and Photographs Division.*

located.[29] It was surely an impressionable experience for the brothers as they were able to comprehend a country of vast industrial resources that was mostly devoid of slavery and populated with citizens of abolitionist persuasions. In later years, as the United States was being torn apart by the political implications of the "peculiar institution" of slavery, both Tom and Walter likely reflected back upon what they had witnessed on this trip. These memories were placed in the balance as they carefully weighed their loyalties to the United States and those to the Confederate States.

For the next couple of years Tom apparently worked on and off for James Gwyn II, his brother-in-law, in a mercantile business at Wilkesboro, North Carolina. Likely, he clerked for Gwyn & Hickerson and in 1845 even made a second trek to New York City to purchase goods and supplies for the store. From New York he hurriedly scratched out a letter to his father, giving news of his arrival there and informing the senior Lenoir that he had "scarcely commenced buying goods yet, find them rather higher than I anticipated—have no idea when I will get through." Always conscious of his father's feelings toward him, Tom offered an apology for his brevity: "Please excuse my letter—I am writing in a crowded bar room, & in a hurry."[30]

Tom's father had retained his Haywood County landholdings and served as an absentee landlord over the East Fork farm and mountain lands. In the immediate years following the Lenoir family's return to Fort Defiance Joseph Cathey acted as Thomas Lenoir's agent, handling problems and issues as they arose and until such times as Lenoir could make periodic visits and take care of things personally. Overseers to manage the farm and slave affairs were employed by Colonel Lenoir over the many years that he remained detached from Haywood. In about the year 1840 Augustus Columbus (A. C.) Hartgrove, a seemingly responsible young man who was twenty-eight years old at the time, was employed by Tom's father to manage the Haywood County East Fork business.[31] He oversaw the work of the slaves who still resided at the farm's quarters and tended to their many needs and issues. Additionally, Hartgrove saw to the plowing and planting and harvesting of crops; raising and caring for stock; killing and butchering of swine; selling and bartering of grain products and livestock and hams; handling tenant affairs; and various other responsibilities. A steady stream of correspondence between employer and employee demonstrates the nature of the business affairs on the East Fork concern and the close relationship that developed between Thomas Lenoir and Hartgrove.

In March of 1844 Hartgrove reported to his employer about the passion for prospecting that had hit Haywood: "The gold fever is started again in haywood. I am told they are a going to start about 200 hands in the west end of the county and there has been a company of men in the pink beds a testing and mining land."[32] In the fall of the next year Hartgrove wrote of a problem with one of the tenants: "I had sold eight head of cattle but when I came to gather them we could not find but 7 head of them & them that we did find was wild & part of them not verry [sic] fat. I have no doubt that Reece has neglected his business as stock keeper this summer. I do believe he would do his duty better if he did not get so well paid for it." Besides this bit of advice Hartgrove wrote to his boss that all were getting along "tolerable well" and that although he had not yet gathered any corn he would commence the next week and would finish "digin" potatoes the next day.[33] Three months later, in January 1846, the East Fork overseer wrote a letter to Thomas Lenoir that gave a tally of the number and weight of hogs killed. Also revealed was the fact that Hartgrove had "not finished gathering corn yet. I have both big cribs full & over 300 bu to gather yet." But that was not all the mountaineer farmer communicated to Thomas Lenoir.

An important message had been conveyed to his boss at Fort Defiance in a previous correspondence, and Hartgrove simply desired to follow up and remind Lenoir of what he had written. "I mentioned to you in my last letter that I did not expect to continue with you any longer than my time was out but I have arranged my business so that I could stay until next fall if you want me." He went on to request that Lenoir send him word whether the extended services would be needed and explained, "The reason I want [to] know is that I have contracted for a piece of land & have a chance of renting it next summer & I cannot rent it until I know whether I stay any longer with you or not.."[34]

Upon learning that his overseer had resigned, Thomas Lenoir would have found his Haywood worries dramatically multiplied, presenting a dilemma not easily resolved. At the age of sixty-five he knew there were only a few more trips to Haywood left in him. With each passing year these journeys over poor mountain roads had become significantly more difficult for the aging man. Selling the vast tracts of mountain land was apparently never a serious possibility or consideration. The senior Lenoir eventually concluded that what was needed was someone—some young, intelligent, responsible, enterprising, and strong individual—to move to the East Fork land and take control of the farming business and the management of the slaves and tenants' affairs; someone who could run the plantation better than A. C. Hartgrove had done and better than he and Louisa were able to do decades earlier. That was what was needed. But who could he find to carry out such a demanding duty? As it turned out Thomas Lenoir had to look no further than his immediate family.

Clearing the field. *Harper's New Monthly Magazine*, vol. 61, June–Nov., 1880.

Dutiful Endeavors on the East Fork

ON MARCH 6, 1846, the elder Thomas Lenoir arrived in Asheville late in the evening after a long day's ride from Burke County. He wearily wrote to Louisa from his Buncombe lodging that he found "the road <u>much worse</u> than I ever saw it before at any season of the Year, and being much vexed and jerked by the scaring and jumping of my <u>foolish</u> horse, causing me to be very sore and much fatigued." The correspondence reveals that Colonel Lenoir was on his way to Haywood to attend to matters at his East Fork farm and expected to meet Tom there. Tom, in fact, did not leave Fort Defiance for the East Fork until March 16, arriving after dark on March 20 with a dog named "Frank" tagging along.[35] His father was surely happy to welcome him into the dimly lit cabin safe and sound. Their reunion that evening would be a fateful one.

As it happened, the colonel had made up his mind to ask Tom to move to Haywood and take charge of the family farming venture there. It is not known how the elder Lenoir posited the opportunity to his son. However, the substance and tone of the request can be inferred from a letter written three weeks later. Writing from Asheville, en route back to Caldwell County, Colonel Lenoir apparently felt inclined to take one last occasion to advise his son:

> I pray, that You may be endowed with sufficient strength of body and mind, to encounter the many <u>perplexing</u> difficulties, that await you, in such a manner, as to acquire the respect of all your acquaintances, and to afford you the great consolation, of a consciousness, of having endeavored to do your duty: Do not confine yourself too close to the Qr. [Quarter] but go to

Preaching, and other places, where you can enlarge your acquaintance and hear and know something of the opinions and transactions of the people in the neighborhood and other places, always leaving the necessary orders about locking Doors etc. etc. when You leave the Qr.[36]

Clearly it can be discerned from Thomas Lenoir's phrasing "having endeavored to do your duty" that Tom was motivated to remove to the lonely Haywood country out of a sense of obligation to father and family. As a dutiful son and full of respect and admiration for his esteemed father, Tom could not possibly have refused and disappointed him. And just as Col. Thomas Lenoir had been without flattering prospects or home in 1806 when he reluctantly decided to relocate into the dark mountains with Louisa, Tom himself was still casting about trying to find a suitable niche in society—until his father found one for him. Besides wishing Tom well in his new responsibility Thomas advised his son that A. C. Hartgrove, the former overseer, would be "one of your best counselors as who to trust and as to what measures would be most advisable to take" to secure payment of doubtful debts. And in a manner that left no qualms, the young Lenoir was instructed to write every two weeks and "oftner [sic] in case of unexpected occurrences."[37]

Such was the start of Thomas Isaac Lenoir's farming career on the banks of the East Fork of Pigeon River. For the ensuing fifteen years he lived alone in his father's old log house which he first styled Bachelor's Retreat and later, Bachelor's Den. With his father's slave families offering companionship as well as the labor for the farming concern, Tom fell in beside these men and women and bent himself to the hard, exasperating work of raising crops, horses, mules, cattle, sheep, and hogs for subsistence and profit. It would be a long learning process as he struggled to cope with the whims of the weather and the significant effects these natural forces produced on his grain and fruit crops. He studied and discovered how to treat diseases and injuries affecting his livestock as well as the slaves. Constantly, he intervened to resolve petty issues as well as more serious consequential difficulties within the slave population. And he

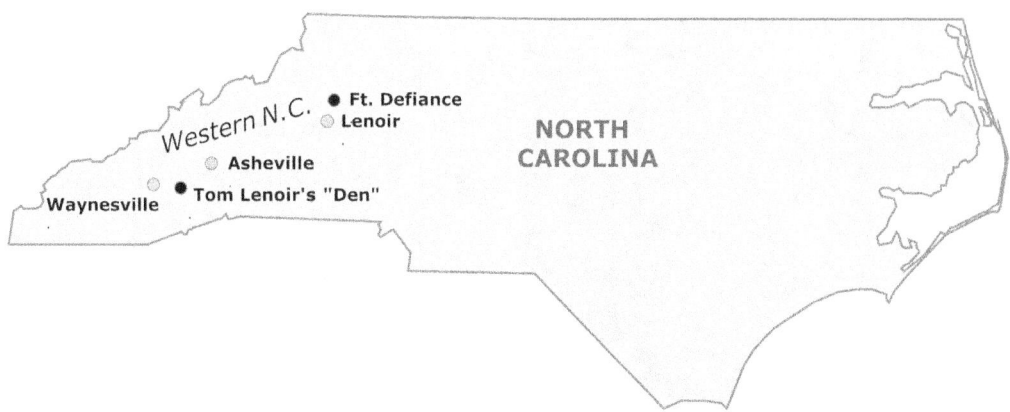

Tom Lenoir's Western North Carolina. *Map by Carroll C. Jones.*

administered justice related to their squabbles and behavior—on rare occasions even having to resort to severe disciplinary measures. He enjoyed both cozy relationships with tenants who were good stewards of his land and provided profitable yields, and endured troublesome partnerships with ornery or lazy renters who failed to produce payments for their land or take proper care of the stock entrusted to them. With the guidance and support of local natives such as Joseph Cathey and A. C. Hartgrove, Tom persevered through this apprenticeship and gradually developed into a respected farmer and citizen.

Numerous surviving letters to "My Dear Father" and to "Dear Tom" attest to the close communications between father and son. This correspondence is filled with mundane recordings about livestock, weather, crops, tenants, land, trading, debts and financial concerns, local politics, slave affairs, and the news of family and happenings at either Fort Defiance or Bachelor's Den. Moreover, their letters are laced with beautiful prose, rich stories, witticisms, folksy jokes, and descriptions of events and people that allow present-day readers to step back in time and tread in the Lenoirs' footsteps. Many of the elder Lenoir's letters to his son indicate a deep remorse for Tom's having to live in such a rural and lonely setting. Just three months after he left Tom to fend for himself

The subject of this painting is thought to be Thomas Isaac Lenoir, portrayed as a young man at about the time he moved to his father's property along the East Fork of the Pigeon River in Haywood County, N.C., in 1846. Artist unknown. *Collection of Fort Defiance Museum, Lenoir, N.C.; used by permission.*

in Haywood Thomas Lenoir confessed to his son: "I often think of you, and wish that you were more agreeably situated as regards society and the prospects of doing much good."[38]

An 1852 letter from Tom's mother, Louisa, includes the following lament: "It would do no good to tell you about all the heart aches I have had about the way you have had to live in this troublesome world."[39] Sister Sarah wrote in April 1846: "I feel very sorry, when I think how lonely you must feel sometimes, when you are in the house by yourself. I send you some seed, you must plant them for my sake, they will remind you of me."[40] It is manifest that the entire Lenoir family—parents, brothers, and sisters—kept Tom foremost in their thoughts and were very anxious about his solitary situation in "them big mountains." In response to Sarah's letter, Tom dashed off a reply in which he offered a remedy for his desolate existence: "You appear to feel much sympathy for my lonely situation—I therefore hope that you will write frequently, as that will be the best means of alleviating it—unless some of you will come to see me."[41]

Thomas Lenoir's inclinations to express empathy for his son's lonely circumstances did not suppress an urge to proffer instructions and advice in almost every letter. Regarding one of the troublesome tenants, Colonel Lenoir instructed Tom:

> You appear to not have complete confidence in the sayings and doings of the [one of the tenant families]; I never liked them, and consider them as having descended from a bad stock, on the side of their Mother; and I have long somewhat feared that [name withheld] was a Lazy, hiddeous [*sic*] and malicious man, that would not be too good to inflict a private injury to a man by killing or worring [*sic*] his stock, or by other means, and I have often thought he should not be continued in my employ any longer; but partially from the fear of offending him and his connections on the West Fork, (who could easily cause me much trouble) and partly out of pity for his family, he has been permitted yet to remain.[42]

Thomas Lenoir wrote further that he wanted his son to get rid of this hateful tenant if practicable before the next winter. On the other hand the father often demonstrated a more lenient side toward his tenants, as when he tendered this wise counsel to his son in a separate letter: "I hope You will not only make corn enough for yourself, but some to spare to your Tenants, some of whom, have been so long accustomed to being supplied at the Quarter [Lenoir's farm], will probably conclude to move off to where some body will make corn for them."[43] At this time there were at least ten tenant farms spread across Tom's property, lying mostly above him on the East Fork of Pigeon River. Heeding his father's counsel he tread easily with the tenants and did not demand payment of their debts in cash money, but took their labor services and shares of crops, wool, and stock instead.

However, it was not an easy matter to overcome the prejudices built up over the years among some of the long-time tenant families. Josiah Anderson likely expressed the sentiments of a few others when he grumbled, "[I]t's a serious & candid fact that Tom Lenoir has imposed on the people of the E. Fork by preventing their getting lands on which they could make a support." Once when Tom refused to rent to Anderson a portion of his father's Crab Orchard property, the old man was reputed to have said that Tom "was serving him just like the boy did his master's monkey. Who, when told to chop its tail off, began at the tip & cut off a short piece at a time, saying that he was afraid it would kill it to cut it all off at once."

At the schoolhouse located on Anderson's tenant farm neighbors would gather to hear the circuit-riding Methodist preacher. In this aspect of community life, Tom put aside any hard feelings between himself and the disgruntled tenant and established a Sunday school library in the schoolhouse, stocking it with children's religious books and magazines ordered from New York. Moreover, he selflessly devoted himself to instructing the younger generation with lessons of moral guidance, most assuredly selected from the literature of the library he had provided.[44] Regarding this devotion of personal time and resources he wrote to his father in 1853:

> I have appointed next Sunday to open my Sunday S. Library up there, & take care of a class in the S. School. The latter is a task that I undertake from a sense of duty though very reluctantly—feeling that I have heretofore been too negligent about a matter of so much importance to the rising generation—at the same time regretting much that I am so poorly qualified to instruct any one.[45]

And Tom was no stranger to the religious camp meetings that punctuated the late summers in the Pigeon Valley and elsewhere in Haywood County during the antebellum years. He frequently made references to them in his correspondence, and regarding one two-week period in September 1854 which seemed to be particularly active with religious fervor he wrote:

> There was a Presbyterian C. [Camp] Meeting at Bethel last week near old E. [Eli] Deaver's—and a Methodist Campmeeting on Hominy (seven miles from Asheville) the week before—and a Baptist Association on Crabtree at the same time. I was at Bethel three days but came home each night. Several persons joined the Presbyterians but there did not appear to be as much excitement and noise as is common at Methodist Meetings.[46]

As if he had not been filled with enough excitement and spiritual zeal by the Presbyterians, Tom went on to record that he had intentions to go down to Shook's (near present-day Clyde) and participate in the Methodist camp meeting that was then under way. And it seems that the excitement generated by these revivals was at times much too intense for some repenters to bear. Concerning one unfortunate soul Tom reported to his father that "Polly Trull, daughter of Ab Trull, lately died in Henderson & I am told that some persons think that her death was probably caused by her great excitement at a campmeeting a short time before."[47]

The African men, women, and children who were bonded into slave service on the East Fork farm provided the manual labor to support Tom's enterprise. They cooked, laundered, wove, sewed, plowed, planted, harvested, picked fruit, gathered, smithed, carpentered, chopped wood, carried water, split rails, built fencing, tended stock, slaughtered swine, rendered lard, and performed every other task imaginable and required on the farm. Although the actual number of slaves on the Lenoir plantation varied somewhat (they were transferred occasionally to and from Fort Defiance in Caldwell County), by the year 1860 Tom had two enslaved families totaling eighteen individuals who lived in four slave houses on his farm.[48] Being unmarried and without a passel of children with whom he could share the labor burdens of farming, Tom would have found the slaves' services indispensable. And in the Southern economy of the era, as personal property they were his most valuable assets, other than the land, and could be readily exchanged for cash, real estate, or other items of high value. Yet they required much in the way of sustenance and demanded inordinate amounts of Tom's time and attention to supervise and properly care for. And, as he often reminded his correspondents, the bonded men and women were a never-ending source of trouble for him.

For example, a slave by the name of Riley was anxious to get a wife among the slaves attached to the Osborn farm, located in the community. Tom wrote to his father that Riley, however, was not "atall" willing to belong to Osborn. Riley suggested that if

Tom would sell him to Colonel Blaylock he knew of two men who would secure the payment; but Tom did not believe him. Tom told Riley that in order to accommodate another of his slaves, named Larkin, he would swap Riley for the girl Larkin desired. The account becomes so convoluted it is almost beyond understanding today. Tom advised his father that "He [Riley] is often complaining, but is the briskest hand on the plantation, & behaves as well as any of them—If you allow him to have a wife away from home, the pricedent [precedent] will play the mischief with the balance." Tom summarized the situation tersely: "[T]hese things cause me a good deal of vexation."[49]

In another letter dispatched to Fort Defiance Tom allowed the frustration caused by his bondsmen to be transferred through his pen to paper. He wrote, "The others are as well as common, but some of them cause me a great deal of vexation, & I can't help wishing sometimes that the whole race were back in Africa."[50] On rare occasions Tom's irritation would evolve into something of a more serious and consequential nature. There were at least a couple of instances when the extraordinary actions of the East Fork slaves surpassed even Tom's lofty levels of patience and tolerance; and the master resorted to the stern disciplinary measures of the lash. Once, after he took a whip to one of his slaves for insolent and disrespectful behavior, Tom was apparently compelled to confess to someone of the drastic punishment that he had inflicted. Opening a letter he had previously closed and sealed, he added a postscript to his brother Rufus in which he confided the sordid details of the punitive business:

> I called up Erwin this morning, & told him that it was necessary to give him a sound thrashing, that I had been deferring it that I might be cool etc. that I was then ready to attend to him, but would first give him a chance to run away, & that if he wished to run he must do so while I went to the house to get something to tie him up with. [B]ut if he ran I would plan ways to catch him without putting myself to much trouble. I went to the house but he wouldn't run, but followed me over to the new stables, quietly took off his shirt, & I tied him fast to the horse rack, & I commenced pretty sharply upon him, but he begged & promised fair [?], & I stopped sooner

than I expected, talked to him a while, & untied him. He said he was glad it was over, & that he felt better <u>satisfied</u> than he had done since that Tuesday morning. that he had not felt right since then, that he knew he was going to get it etc. I think fully as well of him as before & if he had a different sort of a wife would rather have him than any of them. I feel as if I had got over one trouble. All Well.[51]

Yet there was another time when Tom was not as confident of such passive behavior on the slave's part, nor of his own physical ability to manhandle and mete out punishment to a stout slave boy named Isaac. Although Isaac was a "good ditcher" and "pretty good hewer" and carpenter, Tom thought this youngest son to be spoiled and wanted rid of him "for the good of the others." So he resolved to sell Isaac and hired two men to come up to the farm, apprehend the young man, and cart him off to the Asheville jail. Posing as Tom's guests, the men called at the Den one night and slept over. The next morning, as the unsuspecting Isaac was eating his breakfast in the kitchen, Tom stepped in with the two hired hands and identified Isaac as "the boy that must be whipped." Isaac immediately jumped up from the table and made for the door, but the strong men were prepared for his escape attempt, and they grabbed the frightened boy and wrestled him to the floor. A long scuffle ensued until Isaac was finally overpowered into submission, tied up, and stripped of his clothes. During the "muss" the henchmen disarmed the slave of a long, keen two-edged knife and two rocks concealed in his pockets. Then, using a long strip of sole leather tacked to a hickory stick, they deliberately proceeded "to give him [Isaac] a very genteel paddling which set him to begging very humbly in a very short time." Tom had to pay the two men twenty dollars for their services and incurred additional expenses for lodging Isaac in the jailhouse at Asheville. In a matter of days the slave boy was sold for $1,100 to Mr. J. W. Patton of Asheville. Patton intended to resell him in Alabama, where strong field hands were always in high demand and the slave trade more lucrative.[52]

It seems from the epistolary record that Tom's slaves were forever sick or "grunting," as he so often expressed it. He applied himself to reading up on medical matters in books and utilizing this knowledge in the treatment of his ailing slaves and livestock. However, early on as a newcomer on the East Fork, Tom was not so well versed or comfortable acting as a doctor to his servants. When a slave woman by the name of Patsy came down with an illness, he thought hers was a "gone case." In a posting to his father, Tom recounted Patsy's circumstances, describing the urgency of the situation, the methods of treatment employed, and Tom's growing and abiding respect for his neighbor Joseph Cathey:

> On Wednesday night she [Patsy] was much worse & complained of great pain in her side, tongue looking very badly, & her pulse at the rate of 190 to 200 pr. min.—gave her more calomel & applied another large blister.
>
> On Thursday evening I thought it was a "gone case", & so did Col. Cathey, (who was kind enough to come & stay with me two nights, & on whose advice I would sooner depend than on the advice of any of the Haywood doctors –) for she seemed to be rapidly sinking, & could not move hand or foot & seemed to have no pulse atall –
>
> We had her arms and legs bathed in warm water in which we put a good deal of mustard, & gave her a teaspoon full of French brandy about once pr. hour—until her pulse became better.[53]

Patsy came around and recovered in a few days and became stouter than ever, as she observed to Tom. On a later occasion of illness, however, she sent out for a granny to come to her bedside. Tom was drafting a letter to Rufus at the time and commented with a dose of feigned bother: "[B]ehold two [Grannys] came here and have been in my room a good part of this morning entertaining me with interesting discourses connected with changes of the weather, moon, etc., etc." Their methods were a mystery to him: "[O]ne of them was in here a few minutes ago for a teaspoonful of gunpowder, I think it is about time for me to decamp—where I have read of some horrible explosions lately—but after all it may turn out to be just a flash." Later, as he was concluding his correspondence to his brother, Tom added a postscript explaining the granny's concoction: "That old woman has come in again, and says that she put the powder in some tea for Patsy—Did you <u>ever</u>! Well I have heard of Gunpowder tea, but never before of tea made of the real genuine <u>Brimstone</u> gunpowder." Tom appears to have been genuinely surprised and incredulous over the gunpowder-tea affair and ended the matter by stating to Rufus, "I have no idea of trying the <u>Gunpowder tea</u> as a diet, believing it rather explosive, yet I think it may furnish to old bachelors, food for some very <u>wholesome</u> <u>reflections</u>."[54]

On October 17, 1846, in response to the United States' declaration of war with Mexico over the seceded territory of Texas, a militia troop of cavalry was organized in Waynesville, North Carolina. Approximately forty Haywood citizens volunteered their services as dragoons and elected Thomas I. Lenoir as the captain of the unit. The election to such a respected capacity was surely a reflection of how fully Tom had been assimilated and accepted into Haywood County society, only seven months after he had removed to the East Fork. He was officially commissioned in 1847 by the governor of North Carolina as captain of cavalry in Haywood County attached to the 19th Brigade of the North Carolina Militia. Though the unit was never called into active service, over the course of the war and afterwards the dragoons mustered and drilled regularly. On one occasion, for instance, Tom recorded that he "had to muster on Alice Gray on last Saturday, as Zack was lame. she acquitted herself pretty well. The company is improving slowly. Our next muster will be on the 4th July."[55] On yet another occasion of a parade in Waynesville in which the dragoons were to strut their horses down the village's main dirt roadway, Captain Lenoir, thinking his own horse sufficiently unimpressive for the procession, borrowed and rode one of Joseph Cathey's mounts.[56]

Tom occasionally escaped his solitary confinement at Bachelor's Den by making trips outside of the state to sell and buy livestock. Moreover, he ventured northeastward across the mountains at least once per year, usually during the winter, to visit with family and friends at Fort Defiance. But a letter posted in 1848 reveals yet another

The State of North Carolina,

To *Thomas I. Lenoir*

Greeting:

WE, reposing special trust and confidence in your patriotism, valor, and military skill, do hereby commission you a *Captain of Cavalry in Haywood County attached to the 19th Brigade of North Carolina Militia* you having been thereunto elected by the ~~Officers of the~~ *volunteer Troop* ~~Regiment~~; and (after taking such oath or oaths as are necessary for your qualification,) you are hereby vested with the authority and command belonging to the said office, that you may promptly and diligently perform the duties thereof, as prescribed by law and military discipline: In the discharge of which, all officers and soldiers under your command, are required to yield to you their ready obedience.

IN WITNESS WHEREOF, HIS EXCELLENCY, WILLIAM A. GRAHAM, our Governor, Captain General, and Commander in Chief, hath signed with his hand these presents, and caused our GREAT SEAL to be affixed thereto. Done at our City of RALEIGH, on the *3rd* day of *June* in the year of our Lord one thousand eight hundred and forty-*seven* and in the 71*st* year of our Independence.

BY THE GOVERNOR:

Private Secretary.

Tom Lenoir's commission as Captain of Cavalry in Haywood County in 1847 was signed by North Carolina governor William A. Graham. *Lenoir Family Papers, Southern Historical Collection, Wilson Library, University of North Carolina at Chapel Hill; used by permission.*

reason that allowed him to break out of the East Fork surroundings. A New York City postmark and the contents of the letter indicate that Tom had made another procurement venture to the northern city. Just as he had done in 1845, he went in the capacity of a buyer for Gwyn & Hickerson, brother-in-law James Gwyn's Wilkesboro, North Carolina, mercantile business. Judging from the apparent discretion that Tom was given as well as the amount of money he either paid out or was allowed to make commitments for, he had obviously gained an enormous level of respect and trust from Gwyn. While in the city he reported to his brother-in-law, "Dry goods, hats, etc. were so cheap, that I could not help buying. At least they seemed cheap to me, and I hope that you will not regret the amt. of the purchases." Tom spent approximately $4,300 acquiring dry goods for Gywn & Hickerson and placed an order for milling machinery for which he deposited $5,190. The dry goods were being shipped by steamer, and Tom himself had not made up his mind at the time whether to return by the "bay route [by boat down the Chesapeake Bay]."[57]

In 1850 a fortuitous opportunity came Tom's way that would have enabled him to change his situation and vacate the Haywood mountains for brighter prospects elsewhere. His uncle William Ballard Lenoir, Thomas Lenoir's older brother, was a very prosperous farmer and businessman in Tennessee, and he extended an invitation for his nephew Tom to move west and go to work in his cotton-manufacturing mills that produced yarn and batting. Thomas Lenoir, to his credit, expeditiously relayed his brother's message to Tom:

> I have not liked Tommy's situation and prospects in Haywood, and have been thinking lately that he might live more to his notion here, than where he is; I don't know what he is making for himself, nor do I know what we can afford to give him, but if you can part with him and he is willing to change situations, I think we will do such a part for him that he will have no reason to regret it.

"The Den," shown here in an undated photograph, fell into disrepair after Thomas Isaac Lenoir's death in 1882. Fashioned from hewn logs, the little cabin abode is where Tom lived a confirmed bachelor's life for years on his East Fork farm before marrying Mary Elizabeth (Lizzie) Garrett in 1861. Family lore suggests that the lean-to addition to the back of the house, clad with sawn boards, was a kitchen that the young Lizzie insisted upon having. Note that the chimney has either been demolished or has fallen into ruin and out of view on the far side of the house. *Collection of Hugh K. Terrell and the late Emily Michal Terrell; used by permission.*

The uncle further elaborated that the job would entail much travel, and Tom would be employed making contracts and thread collections (collecting debts).

It is a certainty that Thomas Lenoir was extremely appreciative of how his son had managed the Haywood farming operation over the past four years, effectively relieving him of a greater part of the burdens and responsibilities there. Although knowing very well the consequences of his brother's proposal, Colonel Lenoir passed the communication along to his son, word for word, and added his own heartfelt sentiments in hopes that they might facilitate Tom's decision, one way or another. The colonel wrote:

> I will write to Brother William today (being the first mail since the rect [receipt] of his letter) and say to him, that as regards your change of situation, occupation or residence, and the propriety and policy thereof, I shall submit intirely [sic] to your own discretion; which I am willing to do, as you have arrived to an age that you ought to be capable of judging for yourself, and believing as I do, that in deciding on a matter of so much importance, you will duely [sic] consider, the whys and wherefores a change should be made, and the prospects of being financially benefited thereby: One of my most ardent wishes, is for your prosperity and happiness, both of which may be materially effected by some conclusion you may shortly come to; and should you be permitted to live to an old age, and denied the pleasure of looking back on a long life, spent in as profitable a manner to yourself and the world, as it might have been, I fondly cherish the consoling hope, that You will have the great consolation of knowing, that you have generally, if not always, endeavored to do what your judgment dictates as the best.[58]

Tom eventually declined his uncle's invitation and stayed on in Haywood for reasons that are not completely clear. Perhaps a filial reverence and love for his father tipped the balance away from Tennessee. And, after all, he had a duty to perform and was not about to fail in fulfilling his father's expectations and needs. Or maybe that was not the deciding factor at all. It is highly possible that a growing fondness for "them big mountains" and the career he was slowly forging on the East Fork was enough to sway him in favor of remaining in Haywood County.

By 1850 Tom had his roots firmly planted and growing into his father's land on the East Fork. Over the ensuing years he became a fixture in the community and a respected farmer. He routinely attended the Haywood Court sessions in Waynesville, where he met with acquaintances and leaders of the county. During one court-week session in March 1855, with the temperatures lodged firmly below twenty degrees Fahrenheit, Tom attended court every day but one, riding back to the East Fork Den each night.[59] These were important meeting opportunities that offered Tom the chance to sell his livestock, make stud-servicing arrangements for his bulls or stallions, peddle his bacon hams, pay his debts, and dun his debtors. Once he wrote to brother Rufus asking him to tell their father "that I was in Waynesville dunning his Debtors all day yesterday, but did not collect one red cent & do not expect to collect any soon."[60] Another time after he had been to Waynesville during court week he observed to his brother: "I was in Waynesville yesterday but did not see one case of intoxication, but I am sorry to know that the only reason was that they couldn't get the critter. The place had been drunk dry. The cause of temperance seems to make but slow progress in the County."[61] Evidenced in this last excerpt is Tom's disdain of intemperate behavior in regards to alcoholic drink, whether distilled or fermented.

The log structures on Tom's East Fork farm had been built many years before by his mother and father, having been maintained over the years by the slaves under the supervision of either Colonel Cathey or overseers such as A. C. Hartgrove. It seems that Tom continued to live in the old cabin that he variously styled Bachelor's Retreat or Bachelor's Den. However, by 1854 he found the corn cribs and stables so far in disrepair that they were apt to tumble down at almost any time and determined to build new ones. For that enterprise he employed Etheldred Blalock, the same carpenter who had built Col. Joseph Cathey's grist mill just a few years before, to frame the structures. The slaves and other workmen supervised by Blalock felled the timber, hewed the logs, and split the chestnut shingles that Tom complained in a letter to his father ought to have been seasoned more. A building site was chosen "between the spring and the creek" and the same plan of the recently constructed cribs at Fort Defiance was utilized. He estimated that it would take "four or five hands a week or more to level the spot, prize & roll out the rocks, & make a convenient road for the wagon to get to them [cribs]." The sills of the cribs measured twenty-two feet long by seven feet wide, Tom reported. "In order to keep the rats out," he wrote, "I wish to raise them about two feet from the ground on locust blocks, but am afraid it will not be quite so substantial as I would like—but hope they will not tumble down."

Not being one easily contented or tolerant of shiftlessness in others, Tom offered a scathing assessment of the pace of the crib construction work:

> I expected them to have been completed long ago, but find that no one can calculate with any certainty as to when things can be done in this Country—for there seems to be little punctuality in this Community—especially as to working promises—and when men say positively that they will come to work on a certain days they fail (I think) at least half the times, & seem to think that the slightest inconvenience to themselves, or the gratification of any little whim of their own, is a sufficient excuse, for disappointing a neighbor, or injuring him to any amount.

Implicit in this indictment of his builder and the other workmen that Tom had contracted to construct the cribs is the fact that the vital structures were not likely to be completed and ready to receive the corn crop, made and still in the field, before the hardest winter weather set in. Worrisome as the project might have been for Tom, the cribs were finally completed. And as testament to the design and the skill of the builders, one of those log corn cribs has survived the years and still stands today on the spot chosen by Tom "between the spring and the creek."[62]

More of Tom's energies were devoted to stock-raising than any other farming activities or initiatives. Livestock represented his highest source of investment and also offered the greatest potential for income. He must have been turned by a natural inclination for working with farm animals and have developed a good eye for stock as well, because it was a profession in which he became quite engrossed in and proficient at. Tom's father had made a remark to him early on: "I am truly sorry You are so unfortunate with stock, in which You appear to take more interest than any of my other sons; but hope you will not despair of having better luck in future."[63] Although he surely

Above and opposite: In 1860 Tom Lenoir recorded the specifications of the "Pigeon River Turnpike Road." Tom was obviously the overseer of the construction project, which ran all the way to the Henderson County Line. Interestingly, his father had been appointed "Overseer of the Path up the East Fork" in 1809, fifty years earlier. *Lenoir Family Papers, Southern Historical Collection, Wilson Library, University of North Carolina at Chapel Hill; used by permission.*

had many occasions through the years to despair over stock misfortunes, he persisted and encountered some luck along the way, just as his father had wished. As proof of his stock-raising prowess, judges at the 1853 and 1854 Haywood County Agriculture Fair and Cattle Shows awarded to Tom the premium prizes for best livestock entries. In 1854, for example, he gathered first honors for best colt under one year old, best horse three years old, best ram lamb, and best ewe lamb. These awards won for the East Fork farmer both acclaim and cash rewards ranging from two to three dollars. Tom confided to brother Rufus that he would have won still more accolades "but for a rule of our Society which prohibits any Member's drawing so many premiums."[64]

Tom generally kept more than a hundred head of cattle through the winters, which he contracted with tenants to help him look after. Although in the spring many of his neighbors without large landholdings would drive their herds to the Shining Rock balds to range, it appears that Tom did not have to resort to that practice. His vast properties along the East Fork of Pigeon offered sufficient pasturing grasses for not only the cattle but the large flocks of sheep that he and his tenants raised and the horses and mules that he worked.

The hogs were released into the wild forests in the springtime and allowed to feed and grub all summer long on nature's bounty of green plants, roots, and mast. Come the first cold weather of autumn the slaves and dogs would be sent out to round up every swine that had escaped the ravages of the wolves and black bears inhabiting the woods. Those hogs that could be found were coerced back to the farm's pens, where they were fattened up on corn and then slaughtered, often dozens at a time. Sides of pork, salted down and hung in an enclosed smokehouse to cure, would sustain Tom and his slaves through the winter. More important, these valuable bacon hams became an economic currency that was bartered for profit—when paying buyers could be found—or for credit, or other needs on the farm. One of numerous messages on the subject of farm trade that Tom sent to his father and brothers reveals that Colonel Cathey's wagon emptied the smokehouse of sixty-four middling hams weighing a total of 2,202 pounds. At seven cents per pound Tom earned $150 for the single transaction, a good portion of which was most certainly credited to his account at Cathey's store.[65]

The bottom fields along the creeks and river were routinely planted with corn, rye, wheat, oats, and clover. Wheat was sown after the clover crop was made, and Tom felt so strongly about the benefits of the clover rotation that he once opined to his father, "I am becoming more & more confirmed in the opinion that clover should be the great crop of this country."[66] Corn, of course, was indispensable not only to Tom but to the entire rural community. When not eaten directly "on the cob" it was routinely shelled by the slaves and taken to the mill to be ground into meal. Tom recorded that when corn was plentiful and the cribs were full, the slaves would shell and measure up "fifteen bushels of corn, which is the amt. that we send weekly to mill, for cows, calves, horses, negroes, dogs, & chickens.[67] By 1857 a threshing machine had been introduced in the Pigeon Valley by two of its most prominent farmers, Col. Joseph Cathey and Ephraim Osborn. They had formed a partnership and invested in the mechanized contraption which was usually powered by horses walking on a treadmill. Farmers and all the laborers they could muster carried the shocked wheat from the fields and fed it into the machinery which separated the seed, or grain, from the chaff. Tom was one of many who tried out the newfangled thresher that first year and was rewarded with 175 bushels of clean, golden wheat grain.[68]

Remnants of the original fruit orchard that Tom's mother and father had planted a half century earlier were still alive and producing during Tom's tenancy at Bachelor's Den. However, in 1854 he bent himself to replanting many of the apple trees, which had long suffered the ravages of the severe mountain winters. In March he recorded, "I have spent about a week lately in planting out appletrees, & have set out more than 100—More than 50 are in the old orchard, & the bal. [balance] over the creek on the hill side opposite Garden and cabbage patch." He was indeed proud of his efforts and allowed that he had learned much about the nursery business—so much so that he entertained thoughts of writing a chapter or so to Rufus on the subject.[69] However, this enthusiasm for planting fruit trees did not carry over to Tom's beekeeping business. He observed that many of his tenants and neighbors were extremely productive beekeepers. Old Josiah Anderson, for example, had about forty gums in 1857 per Tom's reckoning, and the Plotts had more than one hundred. Tom, on the other hand, had only eight. He confessed to his father that the bee gums "have probably been very rich, but have done me but little good, owing to neglect, which is attributable to procrastination, laziness, and disinclination to be stung."[70]

Life on the East Fork encompassed more than work, drudgery, and bee stings. At times it offered a bit of excitement and pleasurable diversion. Tom reported to his father in the winter of 1847 about a great frolic the boys had with a bear while he was away trying to tame some wild shoats. The exhilaration of the affair can still be sensed in the words that Tom penned on a cold February day:

> Some of the boys were setting up coal wood, & one of them standing in the shop [blacksmith], when a large bear came pacing along on the track of the hogs with his head down, & passed between them and the orchard fence with[out] appearing to notice them, & went on to the cabbage patch where he seemed disposed to climb the fence & take hold of my berkshire [hog], but some of them called the dogs, & he turned back & jumped into the orchard where [it] met the dogs, (for they all (four) happened to be at the house), & they turned him toward the cribs & he jumped into the yard, & the dogs fought him around the cribs & all over the garden, & across the creek—When he would attempt to climb the fences or trees they would pull him back until they worried him almost down—One of the boys shot

him 3 times, & another beat him with a hand spike, but he was still able to travel a little, & sized [seized] Bruce [one of the dogs] by the head and was biting him cruelly, when one of them fell upon [him] with an axe & put an end to him—He was almost too poor to pork, but was as long a bear as I ever saw, & a real old hog thief no doubt.[71]

A pleasurable distraction for Tom and a few of his neighbors occurred during a February cold snap in 1850 when the temperatures bottomed out around zero and the waters of the Pigeon River and its East and West Forks froze solid. It was on that occasion that Tom was asked to entertain a bunch of highlanders at Osborne's Mill. In a posting to his brother Rufus, which also bore the news of a "big hog" that was killed weighing in at 586 pounds, Tom proudly recounted an ice-skating exhibition that he put on for the locals:

> Osborn's Old Dutch Miller said that the poys [boys] wanted me to go down & scoot some for them & I went down on Saturday morning, & scooted until about 12 oclock—The ice was strong but rough—There were twenty or thirty persons there to see the show—& only one of them had ever seen a pair of skates before—They were much pleased—& no doubt thought me a great skater."

Tom's muscles were so sore afterward that he "felt a good deal like a foundered horse for 2 days afterward" but was soon able to "stand up to the rack" again."[72]

Even in the most extreme weather conditions the mountaineers found activities to amuse and entertain themselves. It is plausible to believe that the elderly Dutch miller who worked at Osborne's Mill may have been the only person to have seen a pair of ice skates before this event. And where Tom may have come by his skates and learned how to scoot is anyone's guess. Possibly he purchased the pair on one of the excursions to the northern states that he made in the years prior to 1850.

Interestingly, Tom exhibited his affability, and loneliness, by opening up his log abode to wealthy tourists visiting the Western North Carolina mountains. Planters and businessmen and their families, escaping the stifling heat, humidity, and diseases attendant to the lowcountry climate of the Carolinas, habitually retreated to the mountains to summer. Many availed themselves to the soothing and healing waters at Deaver's Sulphur Springs Hotel in Buncombe County (located near Hominy Creek in today's West Asheville). Hotel patrons who sought thrill and sport ventured into Haywood's wild mountains on hunting and fishing expeditions, even finding their way to the remote East Fork region and to Tom's farm. They surely must have been bewildered to find there a man of education, letters, and culture living alone amongst the slaves and farm animals. Tom came to host these parties from the "Springs" and acted as a guide by leading them into the heavily wooded mountains to find game and to the swift waters of the East Fork of Pigeon River to fish for wild trout. Even notable southern gentlemen such as the youngest son of John Calhoun, the famed statesman from South Carolina and early champion of slavery, states' rights, and secession, "came up" to visit Tom; and he generally delighted in their companionship and the opportunity to lead them into his own private wilderness.[73]

In the fall of 1848 Tom mentioned in one of his letters that "[t]he hunting party from Sulphur Springs were out last week, & staid with me on Monday, Tuesday & Wednesday nights. There were as many as nine beside myself sometimes. Of course some of them slept on the floor & three in a bed at that. They killed only one deer, & caught but few fish."[74] One year later he scribbled an afterthought in a letter to his sister, Sarah: "Should those <u>Big Bugs</u> come to see me from the Springs, I will have a long yarn to tell you some of these days, but I wish they may put it off for a while at least, as Old Jenny is now on the grunting list."[75] A subsequent letter to his brother indicates that the "Big Bugs," as Tom styled the wealthy visitors from the Sulphur Springs Hotel, did finally make it out to Bachelor's Retreat: "The Hunting Party came out on Thursday. Some of them went home on Tuesday, & some staid until yesterday. They killed but one deer & caught very few trout. I expect they were sadly disappointed."[76] Tom's slave cook, "Old Jenny," was apparently off the sick list by then and able to dish out cornmeal hoecakes, fresh milk, and other tasty fares sufficient to satisfy the appetites of the mostly unsuccessful sportsmen.

Throughout the 1850s Tom made several trips to Tennessee, Kentucky, and Virginia to inspect the livestock industry in those states. The primary objective of his visits was to sell some of his horses and mules, examine different breeds of cattle, inspect Thoroughbred horse stock, and learn about any innovative stock practices that might be transferable to the mountains of Western North Carolina. In 1853 he corresponded to brother Rufus that he had sold ten steers to a Tennessee man who planned to drive them to Kentucky. Tom submitted that "the cattle will probably be kept there one year—then driven to Missouri & converted into oxen for the great Western emigration."[77] A quest for purebred cattle and a market for his own stock led him to Columbia, South Carolina, in 1857 to a state fair. It was his first trip to that region and even afforded an opportunity to visit the plantation of Wade Hampton, one of the wealthiest planters in the South, who would later become a famed Confederate cavalry leader and politician during the Reconstruction era.

Tom was the first Haywood County farmer to raise blooded stock and was said to keep the finest purebred cattle in the county.[78] It seems apparent that as early as 1853 he was already breeding Devonshire cattle. In one of his routine letter reports to his father he wrote, "The little Devonshire bull is so great a rascal about breaking fences that we have to keep him chained all the time."[79] Even today this very same line of Devon cattle can be seen grazing the verdant pastures bordering the East Fork of Pigeon River on land still owned by Tom Lenoir's descendants. One can only wonder if the blood of the little "rascal" bull might still flow in that fine herd.

For all of the years that Tom lived on his father's land he never intimated in his letters a desire to possess any of the vast East Fork property, totaling 4,620 acres by Tom's estimate. However, in a letter to the elderly Lenoir in October 1860, Tom broached the subject and let his wishes in that regard be known: "I do not think that I have any talent for speculating in lands, but more of a disposition to hold on to them,

& be particular & <u>stingy</u> about timber." With that said Tom finally expressed to his father his long pent-up desires:

> I know nothing atall about what disposition you intend to make of your lands here, as you never gave me the least intimation about it & I believe I never mentioned the subject to you except once when I only remarked that if I ever got able, & if you thought it would be proper, I would like to own all of your lands lying below the Black Walnut bottom tract, & if I am to remain in Haywood, I still think that I would like to own that much, & that it would be important in me to [not] attempt to own more land than that as I do not consider myself smart enough to run much in debt for land, & then make the money by farming soon to pay for it—This would be contrary to my experience so far, & to what I have observed in others."[80]

Tom goes on to suggest to his father how the property could be divided into an upper tract and a lower tract of similar acreages. He thinks that it is probable that the soil on the upper half is a good deal better than that on the lower section. Nevertheless, Tom preferred to have the lower half for several reasons: it contained more level land and cleared land (although some was worn out); he would have less worry about titles; and he felt more at home at the "Old Den," which was located on the proposed lower tract. Thomas Lenoir must have placed considerable stock in the words and wishes expressed by his son. Within just three months, in January 1861, the patriarch was dead; however, he had left provisions for Tom to inherit the lower tract of the East Fork property. The youngest brother, Rufus, ended up with the family's plantation property at Fort Defiance in Caldwell, and brother Walter inherited the upper tract of land along Haywood County's East Fork River, which included the Crab Orchard field.[81]

William, the oldest brother, took his own life in May of 1861. For years he had been haunted by melancholic maladies and poor luck or judgment in his business ventures. Apparently overwhelmed by a growing burden of financial debt, the alarming drums of war, and his father's death, William abruptly ended his life with a single rifle shot to the head. A final desperate note that he had scribed earlier in a memorandum book offers this portent query, "[O]h how can I live & be deranged[?]" With no ready way out of his troubles he simply concluded, "God bless us all and Save me."[82]

In 1860, upon the eve of civil war in the United States and still living a confirmed bachelor's life at the Den, Tom could look backward on his fortieth birthday. The records and the letters reveal no romantic interests, or hints thereof, in Tom's life since his removal to Haywood. The Lenoir family members, friends, and neighbors had made their attempts at matchmaking, but to no avail. It seems that Tom's stock, his slaves, and a never-ending pressure to make a profit from his father's resources provided ample worry and occupied almost the entirety of his time. Yet in about 1860 a bug apparently began nibbling away at Tom, and as the months wore on this bug gnawed and bit and set its teeth deeper and firmer until, lo and behold, the infernal love bug had hold of him—this being contrary, of course, to what Tom ever expected or even professed. Years before he had emphatically stated in a letter to Rufus that he "never intended to be bitten by one of them critters [women] upon top of this green earth."[83] Well, whether intended or not, he was indeed bitten by a female critter named Lizzie Garrett from Haywood County.

Mary Elizabeth Garrett was born on February 4, 1844, to William Green Berry Garrett and his wife, Martha Jane Rogers Garrett. Although twenty-seven years older than the girl, Tom was overcome with an infatuation for her too strong to be denied. Lizzie's father and Tom were friends and of a like age. William Garrett was a prosperous landowner and slaveholder from the Jonathan Creek Valley area of west Haywood, and his and Tom's business interests would certainly have drawn them together, especially during court sessions. Undoubtedly, Tom had been acquainted with Lizzie for several years. In 1859 correspondence between Tom and the Norwoods (Joseph and sister Laura) in Lenoir confirm that Tom made arrangements for Lizzie to board with them while attending Davenport Female College, which was located in the town.[84]

More than a year later, in December of 1860, Tom wrote to Rufus saying that he had promised Lizzie Garrett's father that he would go to Lenoir and bring Lizzie home from school. However, a grumbling Tom scribbled to his brother that he did not know where he was to get a good safe buggy horse: "My buggy is just standing here rusting & rotting, and I have nothing to work it—I don't believe that anything has been hitched to it in twelve months."[85]

By the spring of 1861 the defiant acts of secession by several southern states had created an elevated level of anxiety and excitement across the region. The unilateral action taken by the Confederate forces in bombarding and forcing the surrender of the United States government's Fort Sumter, in Charleston, South Carolina, sparked the tinder and subsequent inferno that roared into the southern border states—North Carolina among them. Long buggy rides with young Lizzie Garrett and the stimulation of the rebellious times must have galvanized Tom and Lizzie to hurriedly act upon the strange emotions that had unexpectedly engulfed them. In June 1861 Tom unleashed a bombshell for his brother Rufus's consumption: "When this & the exciting state of the times is taken into consideration together with the fact that I am going to be married on next Thursday morning!!!!!"[86] His bachelor days were soon to end, and coincident with the breakup of one union—the United States—Tom and seventeen-year-old Lizzie Garrett were determined to form their own matrimonial union.

"Going off to join the fray." From Rod Gragg, *The Illustrated Confederate Reader* (1989).

A Volunteer Company from Forks of Pigeon

Tom Lenoir was not bent to politics as was his father. While the Southern fire-eater politicians ranted and raved on the virtues of secession he anxiously watched and listened and waited for sane moderators to find a remedy to the nation's discord over the ills of slavery. Tom, along with most of the citizens of Haywood County did not condone the reckless behaviors demonstrated by rebellious states voting to secede from the United States.

In November 1860, while lamenting in a letter to brother Rufus how far behind his farming affairs were, Tom rationalized the situation by explaining: "Perhaps these small matters prevent my thinking & grieving as much about the foolery of our Southern neighbors, and the danger of our government, as I otherwise would do."[87] One month later he expressed in yet another letter to Rufus his thoughts on the country's political situation: "I do not yet think we have had sufficient cause to secede but this aggressive policy of the Black Republicans will sometime, if they do not now, drive us from a Union once so dear but now so little respected."[88]

Joseph Cathey was of a like mind, it seems. He wrote to a newspaper editor in Waynesville at the time that he identified himself with the South and that "North Carolina would not have her convention in session until after Lincoln would be in office, and would have indicated his policy."[89] Other respected leaders and politicians in Western North Carolina espoused similar feelings. David W. Siler of Macon County offered an opinion endorsed by a majority of the mountaineers: "My policy is to hold to the Union, until every remedy has been [tried] and if that fails it will be time enough then to get out."[90] Zebulon B. Vance, the popular Buncombe Congressman and Unionist, urged his native constituents to err on the side of restraint: "We have everything to gain and nothing on earth to lose by delay, but by too hasty action we may take a fatal step we can never retrace—may lose a heritage we can never recover."[91]

The "watch and waiters" like Tom Lenoir, Joseph Cathey, Zebulon Vance, and a majority of the Western North Carolina highlanders waited until the rebel cannon fire on Fort Sumter had subsided and President Lincoln had issued his fateful proclamation of April 15, 1861. The president's reaction to the rebellious aggression at Charleston's harbor was to call for 75,000 militiamen to be enlisted into national service to put down an insurrection "too powerful to be suppressed by the ordinary course of judicial proceedings." This course unleashed such a furor across the South that the "watch and waiters" eagerly joined with the secessionists and began clamoring for military action to protect their homeland against the Yankee invaders. North Carolina's governor, John W. Ellis, immediately replied to Lincoln's call for troops by stating, "I can be no party to this wicked violation of the laws of the country and to this war upon the liberties of a free people. You can get no troops from North Carolina."[92] A bitter Unionist in the state penned the following observation: "[T]he Union sentiment [in North Carolina] was largely in the ascendant and gaining strength until Lincoln prostrated us. He could have adopted no other policy so effectual to destroy the Union."[93] On May 15, 1861, one month after Lincoln's proclamation, delegates of the North Carolina secession convention met and voted to break from the Union. In just days a relieved Confederate President Jefferson Davis officially welcomed the state into the confederation of seceded states, and North Carolina began raising military troops to defend against the Northern foe.

Throughout the Civil War the western section of North Carolina and eastern Tennessee was host to a significant population of citizens who remained loyal to the United States government. Nonetheless, as the news of the fall of Fort Sumter, Lincoln's proclamation, and the results of North Carolina's secession vote filtered into the rural Forks of Pigeon community where Joseph Cathey's general store, postal office, and mill were located, mountaineers flooded out of their homesteads and congregated

On Apr. 12, 1861, Confederate batteries at Charleston, South Carolina, opened fire on the United States government's Fort Sumter, and thirty-three hours later the fort's garrison was forced to surrender. President Lincoln's bellicose proclamation calling for troops to put down the rebellious Southern insurrection pushed states such as North Carolina, which had been reluctant to secede, to the side of the Confederacy. Harper's Weekly, *Apr. 27. 1861.*

at Cathey's mercantile enterprises. There they anxiously caught up with the latest reports concerning the rebellion and entered into passionate discussions about forming a militia company of their own. Nervous and excited young men wishing to enhance their levels of fervor and courage looked to friends and neighbors for encouragement and stimulation. Older farmers surely worked at times to incite their younger neighbors, while possibly discouraging any warmongering thoughts among their own sons. Gradually, over a period of a month or so, a nucleus of the male inhabitants of the countryside surrounding Forks of Pigeon committed themselves to become part of a local military company. Joseph Cathey's sons, James Madison and Joseph Turner,

Zebulon Baird Vance, shown here on the occasion of his inauguration in 1862, was the wartime governor of North Carolina. The Asheville native had been a leader of the Unionist movement in the state's western mountains prior to the Civil War. However, upon North Carolina's secession he zealously took up the Confederate banner, first as the colonel of the 26th North Carolina Troops and subsequently as governor. *Courtesy North Carolina Department of Archives and History.*

were at the center of this organizational effort. Not only did they work to cajole and convince friends, neighbors, and acquaintances to join with them, but they lobbied for the selection of one of the area's farmers to become their captain. That man—the person they wanted to lead them to war—was the respected farmer from the East Fork region, Tom Lenoir.

On the morning of June 10, 1861, after his slaves had saddled a horse for him, Tom mounted up and rode down the East Fork of Pigeon River to Cathey's Store. He planned to find some quiet spot there where he could compose a letter and then post it to his brother Rufus. However, upon arrival at Cathey's he found it full of people who "were talking, whistling, etc." Moreover, the postmaster had already arrived to make up the mail and would not allow Tom much time to write. Therefore, he sat amongst his neighbors and hurriedly scratched out a note to Rufus informing him of his impending marriage to Lizzie Garrett. Although this was by far the most important news that Tom communicated, he nevertheless fed Rufus some other tidbits which reveal much about the rebellious events quickly transpiring in Haywood County. Samuel Bryson had told

Tom that another Haywood volunteer company was already formed in Waynesville and would be leaving for Raleigh in the coming week. Also, Tom went on, "My friends seem determined to get up a company for me, & I think it probable that it will be filled up after a while, but not before 1st July." Though there still were not the requisite number of men (approximately one hundred) to establish a company, Tom predicted that it should fill by sometime in July.

The letter to Rufus contains not only information about Tom's involvement in the volunteer company, it also divulges his personal thoughts about accepting the command if offered to him. He wrote:

> If I were not peculiarly situated I would not think it my duty to go just now, but this section of the County is determined to make a comp[any] & not unite with the other Company & from what I hear there is no probability of their selecting any body else to command them & no man could think of declining under such circumstances.

It is clear that Tom sensed that it was his duty, if selected, to command the company of mountaineers, and he could not think of letting his friends and neighbors down. He was a man who saw his responsibility clearly. Just as he was "peculiarly situated" when his father asked him to take over management of the Haywood affairs, he again found himself in a peculiar situation where he could not refuse his duty. Though, as he explained to Rufus, he did not believe he was the right man for the job, he recognized "that it will be my duty to pitch in when ever they ask me." Tom went on to offer that his health was only "tolerable," expressing doubts as to the effect that camp life might have upon him.[94]

Perhaps Tom had been instilled with these doubts from a letter he received just the week before from his older sister, Laura Norwood. Incredulous that Tom was seriously considering joining the company, she chastised him for the lack of consideration for their mother, who had been so severely tried of late (Louisa had already suffered the loss of her husband and a son in 1861). Additionally, she did not believe that Tom's constitution would hold up under a long campaign. But her primary argument against his joining the army was that he could do much more from home to help the cause: "I am decidedly of the opinion that you can serve your country better by staying at home and making bread and meat for our soldiers to eat than by going to be a soldier yourself at this stage of the game." Laura's admonitions, while also serving her own interests, made very astute and valid points that were later proved accurate. As it turned out the South would not be able to produce sufficient food to sustain its armies. And Tom was forty-three years old and had always been rather sickly. His later army experience would demonstrate that his health was not up to the task of commanding troops in the field during wartime. Laura also pointed out to her brother, "[T]here seems to be no lack of troops in the field at this time and there are many more who are willing to go and who cannot serve their country so well in any other capacity."[95] Her heartfelt and well-intended sentiments and advice fell on deaf ears, as events transpired.

Tom's wedding to Lizzie Garrett came off as he predicted on June 13, 1861. He jokingly reported to Rufus that "a nice Young Lady came home with him, & was seen riding behind next day on his big bay horse over the river to the strawberry patch, & that he took her down to preaching last Sunday in a buggy, & was rather late … & every body was grinning at him & he grinned back at them." Tom also teased that it was said that he and the little flax-headed gal behaved rather well away from home but it might be "right hard to find out how they carry on in The Den." He explained that he had been trying to study military tactics but had not been able to make much progress in that or any other kind of tactics.

He also reported to Rufus on the progress being made in filling the volunteer company from Forks of Pigeon. At the time there were only about fifty volunteers willing to sign up, and Tom did not believe the company would be made up before the crops were harvested in the fall.[96] Little did he realize how hurried things were soon to become.

Joseph Cathey was a respected farmer and merchant from Forks of Pigeon in Haywood County. Along with his sons, Joseph Turner and James Madison Cathey, "Colonel" Cathey helped to raise volunteers to form the Haywood Highlanders. *Collection of Charles Cathey; used by permission.*

Only two weeks later, on July 2, 1861, the volunteer company from Forks of Pigeon met to drill and elect officers. On the Saturday before, June 29, the total number of volunteers had grown to seventy-one, and Tom seems to have expected that number to increase further by the day's end. As expected, Thomas I. Lenoir was elected captain of the company by a unanimous vote. Other officers (commissioned at a later date) and non-commissioned officers were also elected that day: Etheldred H. Blalock, 1st Lieutenant; James A. Burnett, 2nd Lieutenant; James Madison Cathey, 3rd Lieutenant; Joseph Turner Cathey, 1st Sergeant; Sergeants—William Cathey, Garland Sevier Ferguson, William Henderson; Color Corporal—Humphrey P. Holland; Corporals—Thaddeus C. S. Hyatt, John G. Burnett, Isaac W. Roberson; Musician—William N. Allman.[97]

On this same day Tom wrote to his brother Walter about the company and inquired whether Walter himself was still interested in joining. Apparently the topic had been discussed previously; Tom mentioned that he had not yet entered Walter's name on the roll but had told the others that his brother spoke of coming. "After seeing

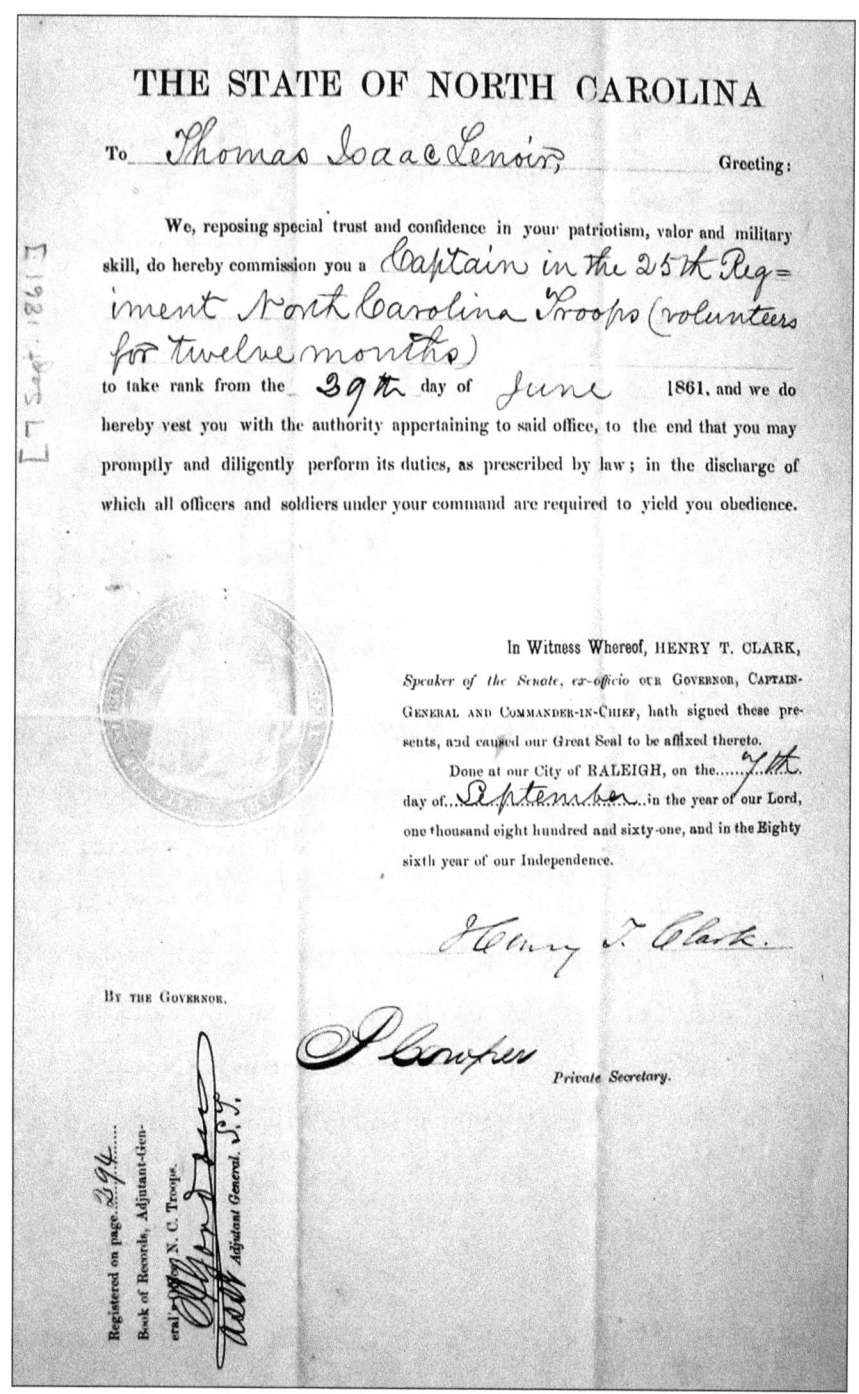

The State of North Carolina commissioned Tom Lenoir as "Captain in the 25th Regiment North Carolina Troops (volunteers for twelve months)." *Lenoir Family Papers, Southern Historical Collection, Wilson Library, University of North Carolina at Chapel Hill; used by permission.*

a company from Cherokee (Captain Francis) pass last Saturday," Tom continued in his letter, "I am better pleased with the looks of my men." Tom also informed Walter that Joseph Cathey planned to leave July 4 for Asheville, where he would catch the stage to Morganton and entrain there for Raleigh. He was to act on behalf of Tom and the company and offer the services of the Haywood Highlanders to the state, obtain officer commissions, and receive requisite instructions and orders.[98]

Tom took the opportunity to bring his brother current on matters of a more personal nature as well. "It looks like making a mashup of my business here," he wrote, "but it wont [sic] do to look back now." Tom obviously harbored worries about what would happen to his farm, his slaves, his stock, and his Haywood affairs while he was off to war. His likely plan, as he informed Walter, was to employ A. C. Hartgrove as an overseer to give some attention to his business. This friend and native farmer, who had worked so faithfully as an overseer for Thomas Lenoir decades earlier and who had helped Tom get his feet on the ground when he first came to Haywood, was the man to whom Tom again turned to for help. Hartgrove was eventually hired with the charge of going out to the East Fork one day per week and looking in on the boys and their work.[99]

Additionally, Tom told Walter that Lizzie and two of her sisters were probably going to board with Joseph and Laura Norwood in Lenoir while they attended the girls' college. Last, Walter had suggested on some prior occasion that Tom take the slave Uriah (Henry Uriah Lenoir) with him wherever the army duty took him. Uriah could read and write and was very highly regarded by the Lenoir siblings. Tom responded, however, that he would not be willing to do so unless Walter himself went along with the company, his reluctance suggesting that the twenty-six year old slave belonged to Walter at the time. Nevertheless, Tom did ultimately accept Walter's suggestion. Uriah accompanied Tom during his Confederate army service and, in addition to the chores he performed, was of tremendous assistance to the commander during periods of hardship and sickness.[100]

The Haywood Highlanders marched out of Haywood County on July 18, 1861, destined for Asheville, North Carolina. Asheville was then, as it is today, the largest town in Western North Carolina, and the main center of trade and a hub for the primitive road network leading into and out of the western highlands. Haywood's mountain boys arrived in Asheville the next day and immediately encamped at Camp Patton, where other companies were assembling.[101] Judge Garland Ferguson of Waynesville later wrote of his earliest wartime experience at Asheville: "As each successive company took its position in camp the guard line was extended and the civilian began to do duty and learn the step and maneuvers of the soldier."[102]

On July 20 the company known as the Haywood Highlanders was mustered into the service of the state of North Carolina and by the middle of August had been organized with nine other mountain companies to form a regiment—the 15th Volunteers North Carolina:

Company	Location	Captain
Company A	Henderson County	Captain Balis M. Edney
Company B	Jackson County	Captain Thaddeus D. Bryson
Company C	Haywood County	Captain Samuel C. Bryson
Company D	Cherokee County	Captain John W. Francis
Company E	Transylvania County	Captain Francis W. Johnstone
Company F	Haywood County	Captain Thomas Isaac Lenoir
Company G	Georgia and Clay / Macon / Cherokee counties	Captain William S. Grady
Company H	Buncombe / Henderson counties	Captain Frederick R. Blake
Company I	Buncombe County	Captain George W. Howell
Company K	Buncombe County	Captain Charles M. Roberts

Captain Lenoir's company was designated Company F at the time of the regiment's formation. The name "Haywood Highlanders" would remain only in the minds and sentiments of that first contingent of men who had trudged out of Haywood to defend the homeland. But to the state and later the Confederate army the Highlanders would be forever known as Company F of the 25th North Carolina Troops.

Asheville lawyer and politician Thomas L. Clingman espoused the rhetoric of the Southern fire-eaters before the Civil War and lobbied fervently for secession in the Western North Carolina mountains. He was the first colonel of the 25th Regiment North Carolina Troops and served in that capacity until being promoted to brigadier general in April 1862. *Library of Congress, Prints and Photographs Division.*

As was the protocol at the time, the various company captains and commissioned officers were responsible for electing their regimental commanders. Consequently, Captain Lenoir and the other company officers huddled and chose the Honorable Thomas L. Clingman to become the colonel of the 15th Volunteers. Clingman was a longtime resident of Asheville and before the war had been a prominent politician and statesman, having served in both houses of the United States Congress. Moreover, he was one of the most ardent secessionists in the mountains, spewing the rhetoric of the Southern fire-eater politicians and inciting the mountaineers to join with the other states in a new Southern confederacy. St. Clair Dearing, a former regular officer in the U.S. Army, was elected lieutenant colonel, and Henry Middleton Rutledge was elected major. Rutledge, born to wealth and privilege in the plantation society of South Carolina's lowcountry, was a seasonal resident of Flat Rock, North Carolina.

The Haywood Highlanders and the other companies of the regiment drilled continuously to learn the step and maneuvers of the soldier at Asheville's Camp Patton. On or about August 30, as Captain Lenoir's diary reveals, the regiment moved to Camp Clingman on the eastern outskirts of Asheville. During the period of encampment there Tom wrote to brother Walter on September 15 informing him of his situation and general affairs. He said that "all were tolerably well" and that the size of the company was not increasing much; it proved to be one of the smallest in the regiment. Tom was not pleased with a few of his men and hurriedly scratched: "[W]e have 3 or 4 in it [company] now that ought not to have been received, & I wish they were out again—Recruits will be more closely examined in future." He went on to discuss his daily regimen. The captains and other company officers were volunteers, not professionals, and most had no prior soldiering experience, with the exception of duty with local militia units. The educational process these raw officers underwent during the first months of the war to learn their proper duties was extremely intense. Tom describes his own experience:

> "I find it requires very close application in myself to make any progress – & my time is more fully occupied than it ever was at school or college—We have to recite two hours pr. day to Col. Dearing, be drilled by him one hour, & drill our companies two hours – & then attend battalion drill one hour, making six hours work besides studying lessons, etc., etc."[103]

Captain Lenoir also informed Walter that the regiment had not received arms yet and had no clear plan: "It is said that we will meet Col. Clingman as we go to Raleigh. We know nothing as to where we will be sent from Raleigh." Orders had in fact been sent to Col. Clingman the day before Tom penned this letter, and the company would promptly find themselves on the march.

One other item of interest that Tom passed along to Walter indicates that there had been some discord within the regiment while the colonel was away.

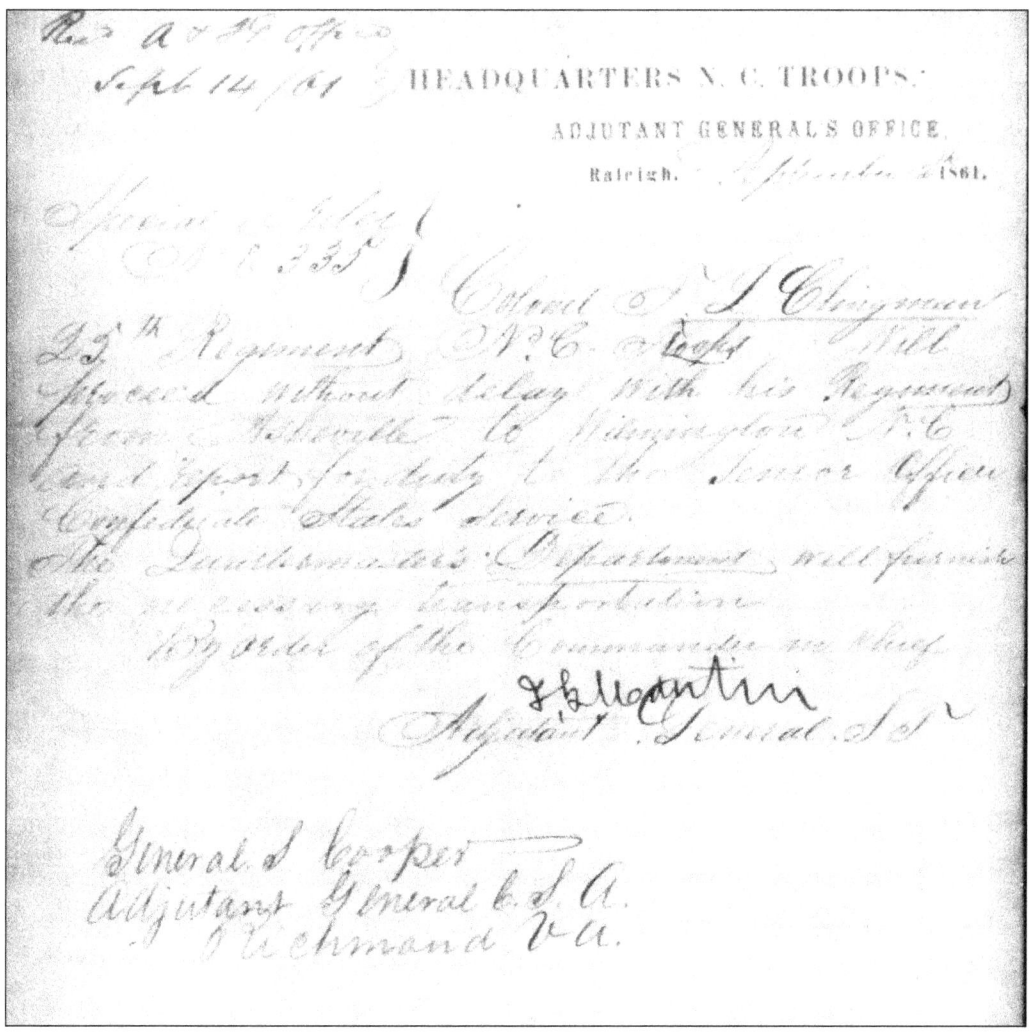

Special Order No. 335 from Gen. James G. Martin, adjutant general of State Troops, dated Sept. 12, 1861, directs Col. Thomas L. Clingman to proceed with his 25th Regiment N.C. Troops from Asheville to Wilmington, N.C., "without delay" (www.footnote.com, accessed 2009).

We had some little trouble in the camp Friday night—but I think the worst of it is past—Some members of some Companies were trying to get up a rebellion alledging [sic] as the reason that the discipline was such as they would not submit to—None of my company were engaged in it—The ring leaders were arrested & are now in jail in Asheville—three of them.[104]

The independent mountaineers were already having problems submitting to army rules. The problem would become increasingly acute as the war progressed and the regiment fell under the command of Brig. Gen. Robert Ransom, a professional soldier and notorious disciplinarian.

Colonel Clingman, who was not with his regiment in Asheville at the time, received orders on Sept. 14 from Gen. James G. Martin, adjutant general in charge of all the North Carolina state troops, to proceed "without delay with the 25th Regiment N.C. State Troops" to Wilmington, North Carolina, and report to the senior officer Confederate States Service.[105] The 15th Volunteers N.C. had already been redesignated as the 25th Regiment N.C. State Troops. However, the regiment would not be officially transferred from the service of North Carolina to the service of the Confederate States Provisional Army until Sept. 29, 1861, following its arrival in Wilmington.

Colonel Clingman's orders were to move "without delay." At last, four days later, on Wednesday, Sept. 18, Captain Lenoir's Company F struck camp and marched with the other companies of the regiment out of Asheville. Local citizens and family members had flocked into the town to see the Highlanders off.[106] The throngs of applauding, kerchief-waving supporters would have surely offered loud cheers of encouragement and even wept tears of pity and sorrow as the men paraded away. The soldiers followed the road leading eastward up the valley of the Swannanoa River and trod its path as it wound its way up the Blue Ridge Mountains. Escaping the mountains through the Swannanoa Gap, the men tramped down the winding roadway as it descended the eastern slope of the range and coursed by the Old Fort post office, through Pleasant Gardens, and toward the nearest railhead, at Morganton. There most of the Haywood Highlanders would have gazed in wonderment and marveled at the very first steam locomotive train they had ever laid eyes on.

The regiment entrained at Icard Station in Morganton and rode the rails of the Western and North Carolina Railroad to Raleigh, North Carolina, where they arrived on Sept. 25. At the state's capital city the 25th Regiment disembarked and pitched camp for a couple of days while waiting to draw their uniforms. On Sept. 27 General

Martin issued another special order to Colonel Clingman while his regiment was camped at Raleigh. Obviously not pleased with the pace of movement of the mountain troops, the general's order read in part: "Colonel T. L. Clingman, 25th Regiment N.C. Troops will proceed today with his Regiment to Wilmington N.C. and report for duty to General Anderson, C.S. Army or officer in command of the Confederate Troops."[107] Thus prodded and proudly donning the new gray uniforms furnished by the state of North Carolina, the regiment's troops embarked for Wilmington at ten o'clock at night on Sept. 27, the same day the order was issued.[108]

A soldier from Jackson County who was attached to Company B described the new uniforms in a letter that he wrote to a friend back home:

> "We all have Drawd our uniforms and tha ar as fine as hart [there] Can [be.] tha ar a gray sack Coats with a Row of the finist Brass Buttons up the Brast [breast]. the Pants is prety much the same onley tha is a Black Stripe up the ledgs. tha ar nice and Caps all so."[109]

Surely, all of the troops were as pleased with their uniforms and basked in their new military attire as they lurched and bumped down the tracks to Wilmington behind a hissing, wood-burning locomotive belching steam, smoke, and fire into the Carolina darkness.

The Haywood Highlanders, along with the balance of the regiment, arrived in Wilmington on Sept. 28, 1861, and encamped at Camp Davis on Mitchell's Sound. Two days later they were issued arms (Mississippi rifles by one account) and equipment and began training and learning how to make deadly use of their new weaponry.[110] For the next seven and a half months the Haywood Highlanders and the 25th Regiment N.C. Troops would perform coastal defense duty for the Confederate army in North and South Carolina—the beginning of an arduous involvement in the conflict that would continue longer, and take them to more remote battlefields, than they could ever have imagined.

"A Very Raw Recruit." *From Robert Underwood Johnson and Clarence Clough Buel, eds.*, Battles and Leaders of the Civil War *(1989), vol. 1.*

Captain Lenoir's Diary

AMONG THE MANY SOLDIERS WHO RECORDED their daily experiences and thoughts during the Civil War was Capt. Thomas Isaac Lenoir. His notes begin on Nov. 1, 1861, when the Haywood Highlanders were encamped at Wilmington and end in May 1862 after his resignation from the army. The leather-bound pocket journal which he carried home from the war has survived for one hundred and fifty years, lovingly and carefully passed from one family generation to the next. Today, the once matter-of-fact recordings in the diary open a window into a time when the convulsions of war washed across the United States.

Captain Lenoir wrote about his company's activities, sickness among the troops, and his own daily occupations, including the burdensome administrative paperwork, or "troublesome institutions," as he called the business. Curiously absent from the journal's contents are any statements revealing the captain's own political sentiments with which to gauge the depth of his persuasion and commitment to the cause. However, the pages abound with personal observations of the natural and biological world surrounding him as well as non-professional medical opinions, which often differed from those of the doctors. Backaches and headaches plagued Captain Lenoir throughout his military career, and he routinely recorded his sufferings and miseries caused by these afflictions. Most strikingly for the modern-day reader, the devotion and love that he felt for his young wife, his "dear Lizzie," jumps out of the pages. The captain pines for her at night from the Confederate encampments and often bemoans the fact that he has received no letter that day.

Captain Lenoir was a well-educated man of his time, and both his journalism skills and his writing style were exceedingly fine. The contents of his diary are not difficult for modern readers to follow. Annotations and commentary have been added primarily to assist readers in keeping Lenoir's journal entries in context with the ongoing war and related events along the middle and South Atlantic coastline. Explanations are provided only where supplemental information seems helpful.

"A Formidable Line" by Walton Taber. *From* The American Heritage Century Collection of Civil War Art *(1974)*.

November 1861

> *1861*
> *Nov. 1*
> *The 25th Regiment is still here at Camp Davis near Wilmington, N. C.*
>
> *The Haywood Highlanders (now Company F.) left the Forks of Pigeon for Asheville on the 18th of July 1861_ Arrived at Asheville on the 19th & were mustered into service at Camp Patton near Asheville on Saturday morning the 20th of July 1861 & moved to Camp Clingman near Asheville (I believe) on the 30th day of August*

Four months after his enlistment in the Haywood Highlanders, Tom Lenoir was inexplicably motivated to begin keeping a journal of his wartime experiences. His initial diary entry, dated Nov. 1, 1861, runs several pages as he records the noteworthy events and activities leading up to that date.

Tom records from memory or other sources that the Haywood Highlanders marched out of Forks of Pigeon on July 18, 1861, and arrived at Asheville, North Carolina, the next day. Their route undoubtedly coursed through the village of Pigeon River (present-day Canton) and from there followed the Western Turnpike to Asheville. Upon their arrival in Asheville, the largest town in Western North Carolina, the Haywood Highlanders encamped at Camp Patton with other mountain companies beginning to spill into the town. "As each successive company took its position in camp the guard line was extended and the civilian began to do duty and learn the step and maneuvers of the soldier," wrote Garland Ferguson.[111]

Tom's journal states that the Haywood Highlanders were mustered into the service of North Carolina on July 20, 1861, one day after their arrival in Asheville. By the middle of August the company along with nine others had been assembled into a regiment styled the 15th Volunteers, North Carolina. This was a short-lived designation, as the regiment was soon to become the 25th Regiment North Carolina Troops. On or about Aug. 30, as Tom recollected, the company packed up and moved from Camp Patton to Camp Clingman, another Confederate training camp located on the outskirts of Asheville.[112]

1861
Nov. 1 [continued]
Camp Davis

*The 25th Regiment left Asheville on the 18th Sept. & arrived in Raleigh on 25th Sept_ (at 10 ock A.M.) Left Raleigh at Wilmington for Wilmington on 27th at 10 Oclock P.M_ Arrived in Wilmington on 28th about 11 Oclk A.M., And on same evening 28th arrived at Camp Davis_ & arms were distributed to the Company on the 30th Since that time Yankee vessels have been frequently seen & have from the encampments_*

As the sun rose over the Blue Ridge on Sept. 18, 1861, the Haywood Highlanders and the other nine companies of the 25th Regiment N.C. Troops broke camp at Camp Clingman and marched off to war. Reaching the nearest railhead at Morganton on or about Sept. 20, many of the men looked on in wonderment as they laid eyes for the first time on a real steaming and hissing locomotive train.

Days later, after the excited men finally embarked at Morganton, Tom recorded that the regiment arrived in the state's capital city of Raleigh on Sept. 25. Uniforms and supplies furnished by the state were distributed to the troops and in a couple of days they once again entrained, bound for the eastern coastal region of North Carolina. Per Tom's diary the regiment arrived at Wilmington on Sept. 28; they encamped at Camp Davis, located on Mitchell's Sound. There the troops were issued arms, Mississippi rifles by one account,[113] and began to drill and train and learn how to effectively use their new weapons.

One of the troops wrote that the regiment was camped not more than two hundred yards from the beach, and steamboats and steamships could be seen from the camp, "running all the time." He continued: "[I]it is a grand seen [*sic*] to see all the steamers Running up and down to and fro ... the fleet [Union navy] is seen every day and we are looking for an attack in very short time."[114]

Although not mentioned by Tom in his journal, the 15th Regiment Volunteers was transferred from the service of North Carolina to the service of the Confederate States Provisional Army on Sept. 29, 1861. The unit, made up almost exclusively of mountain companies from Western North Carolina (Company G, or the Highland Guards, consisted of approximately 133 men from north Georgia), was given the permanent designation of 25th Regiment North Carolina Troops. From then until war's end the unit was a viable fighting force within the Confederate army, and the Haywood Highlanders company remained appended to the 25th Regiment N.C. Troops for the duration.

Apparently not all of Tom's time was taken up by his military duties. He recorded in his journal that he sailed to the beach on two different occasions and, not unlike today's beachgoing tourists, enjoyed splashing around in the surf and picking up seashells. His companions on the second sailing excursion were regimental officers and company captains like himself.

Col. St. Clair Dearing was actually the lieutenant colonel of the regiment. Maj. Henry Middleton Rutledge, who was born to a wealthy planter family from the South Carolina lowcounty and a seasonal resident of Flat Rock in Henderson County, was only twenty-two years old at the time. He was later elected to command the 25th Regiment, and the "boy colonel" would lead his band of mountain rebels through some of the fiercest battles of the Civil War.

1861
Nov. 1 [continued]
Camp Davis

I have sailed down
*to the beach twice_*
Once with Col. Clingman
& we enjoyed a fine sea
bath_ & I picked up shells
and was delighted [?] *with a view*
of the Atlantic & the
white breakers etc. we
saw two ships at a distance
   The second excursion
was with Co^l*. Dearing,*
Maj^r*. Rutledge, several of*
the captains, & M^r*. Bradley*
*& his wife, & two Daughters_*
We went in a nice boat
& had a pleasant sail.
returned to M^r*. Bradley's*
& took tea,

1861
Nov. 1 [continued]
Camp Davis

This has been a dreary dark day, & I have been working hard at Muster Rolls – Troublesome institutions! We have heard of a large Yankee fleet sailing South, & we suppose it is intended to attack some point on the coast of N. C. probably with the view of marching to Wilmington, & last night I heard about 20 reports discharges of cannon in a Southerly direction & we suppose they were down about Confederate Point_ They were fired between 2 & 3 Oclk at night

The diary accounts show that throughout Tom's service to the Confederacy he was burdened by the tedious responsibility of maintaining the company's muster and payroll records. Apparently those "troublesome institutions" fell heavy upon the captain's shoulders and not to an adjutant or clerical person. It is manifest that he worried constantly to insure that every penny owed to his men was received or accounted for.

Tom recorded that a large Yankee fleet had been spotted sailing south, and he supposed that it was a naval expedition aimed at the extremely critical Southern port city of Wilmington, North Carolina. Located on the Cape Fear River and defended by coastal fortresses such as Fisher, Caswell, and others, the deep-water port provided a haven for speedy steam-powered blockade runners slipping through the Union's naval cordon. The vital military supplies, foodstuffs, and domestic goods delivered by the sleek vessels were immediately shipped by rail to Southern military depots, and commercial centers dependent on them to sustain the South's war effort.

As would become apparent, the Yankee armada was indeed steaming on a southerly heading, but it would bypass Wilmington, where Captain Lenoir and the Haywood Highlanders were stationed, for a more vulnerable Confederate target on the South Atlantic coastline.

This day's journal entry contains Tom's first observation of the Civil War soldier's incessant plight with the elements. Tents provided by the Confederate government were used when available for shelter from the sun, rain, sleet, and snow. However, as can be discerned from Tom's experience, the tents often leaked badly and were uncomfortable. Of course during later campaigns requiring long marches, daily troop movements, and strategic maneuvers the Haywood Highlanders camped out in the open air, sometimes without blankets, where "during the . . . nights the beds were roomy but cool."[115]

The Outer Banks fort Tom mentions is Fort Hatteras, which was surrendered to Union Gen. Benjamin Butler's amphibious landing force approximately one month before. Hatteras was one of North Carolina's busiest ports, almost equaling the level of Wilmington's commercial maritime trade, and was targeted early on by Union war planners as they looked for strategic leverage points for their blockading efforts. Butler's Federal naval squadron bombarded forts Clark and Hatteras, and a landing force of Yankee soldiers forced the final capitulation of these facilities on Aug. 28, 1861.[116]

Tom reports more accurate intelligence information on the Union fleet's position than the day before. The flotilla had actually been seen steaming north of Savannah, Georgia, near Port Royal Sound in South Carolina waters surrounding Hilton Head Island. As a result, Confederate planning was hurried and rumors spread that the 25th N.C. Troops might be ordered to Charleston, South Carolina, to defend against the expected Yankee intrusion.

1861
Nov. 2
Camp Davis

We had a tremendous rain last night, and a considerable storm, the water in the Sound unusually high_ Tents leaked badly_ & were very uncomfortable but we hope that some of the Yankee vessels are wrecked, & that the fort at Hatteras is washed away

It is reported that a part of the fleet has been seen near Port Royal S. C , & that there is a probability of our being ordered to Charleston immediately_ This has been a cool winday day

> *1861*
> *Nov. 3*
> *This has been quite a cool day_ We had preaching in the encampments today by a Methodist Minister (name unknown) We have been ordered to be in Wilmington tomorrow at noon with two days provisions, to be reviewed by Genl. Anderson I disapprove of it, because it will probably make a good many men sick as they will be com = = pelled to wade some & some have had measles & others will probably be taking it tomorrow_ & then if we should be ordered to Charleston tomorrow, it would be much better to know it before leaving the camp_ But I am bound to obey, & if my back should be well enough, I expect to toddle with the balance_*

Each side in the sectional conflict thought their rationale for going to war superior to the other's and believed that God's assistance and intervention in their behalf was relatively assured. However, to reinforce the likelihood of His alliance the soldiers were increasingly motivated to attend Sunday services and preachings where their sins could be forgiven, the virtues of their struggle extolled, and God's understanding sought.

In the Confederate Civil War camps a religious fervor increasingly infected the rebel soldiers who sought to shirk the seductive influences of sin and receive spiritual and philosophical reinforcement. Their hopes and belief in the cause were stretched thin as great enemy forces were arrayed against them and as they gradually realized their extreme disadvantages in war-making resources. The Haywood Highlanders were no different than their rebel brethren in these religious respects, and, as Tom records, Sunday services and preachings were the norm in their encampments whenever conditions allowed and preachers were available.

Besides the church service on this particular Sunday, Tom received orders from his regimental field and staff to move his company to Wilmington with two days' worth of provisions. There Brig. Gen. Joseph R. Anderson, a Virginian and West Point graduate, who on Sept. 3 had been ordered by President Davis to North Carolina to assume command of the coastal defenses at Wilmington, was to review the troops and likely to assess their combat readiness.[117]

Of note also in this day's journal entry are Tom's comments that he disapproves of the orders and fears that the march to Wilmington might make his men sick. He was constantly concerned about the men's health and was becoming more aware of the lethal menace of infectious and camp diseases. There had already been cases of measles, and he foresaw that there would inevitably be more.

It is evident from Tom's chronicles that he suffered back problems throughout his service in the Confederate army. On this day he records that because of a bad back he could not lead his company to Wilmington for the review by General Anderson. Instead Colonel Clingman left his ailing captain in charge of the encampment, and Tom busied himself addressing myriad issues and infractions of a minor nature.

Picket guards were sent out to find a reported traitor, but they came back empty-handed. The night pickets returned to camp at daylight with news of an enemy steamer spotted within a few miles of their line. Also, Tom had to deal with two servants who were caught bringing spirituous liquors into camp. For that violation of trust and regulations the two slaves were ordered confined in the guard tent.

And it seems apparent from Tom's account of the day's activities that George Eleanor Christopher and his brother Henry, both of whom belonged to the Haywood Highlanders, had been fighting the previous night. Eleanor was placed under guard over night, but Tom had him released in the morning so that he could participate with the company at the Wilmington inspection. Immediately upon Eleanor's return to camp he was ordered back to the guard tent.

1861
<u>Nov. 4 – Monday</u>
Camp Davis

*My back was not well enough to allow me to go to Wilmington today & so I was left in charge of the encampment_*
  *Sent out picket guard & six men in search of a supposed Traitor_ They didn't catch him_*
  *The pickets which returned this morning reported that a large steamer remained within a few miles of them last night, & then steamed Northward this morning early_*
  Welch's Andy & John Jackson (a fine mulatto) of T. D. Bryson's company were both detected in attempting to bring spirituous liquors into Camp today & I sent them to the Guard tent, & the whiskey is still in my possession_ 9 Oclock I have just ordered Eleanor Christopher back to the guard tent, he was sent there last night for fighting his brother H. & released this morning to go to Wilmington to be reviewed

1861
Nov. 5 – Tuesday

*About 2 Oclock P.M. today received Orders to start to Charleston_ In less than two hours the Regiment were on the march for Wilmington Left T.C.S. Hyatt to take care of the two sick viz' Blaylock & Bugg_ Just when we were Hasting from Camp Davis a M^r. J.A. Sanders came to me & said that he had heard that I was unwell with pain in the back & very kindly offered me his little pacing horse to ride to Wilmington_ Some of the companies reached Wilmington before sundown & several after dark Co^l. Clingman got off for Charleston about 9 Oclock P.M. with two companies only viz' Capt. Jonstone's & Cap. Blake's_ Co^l. Dearing started about 11 Oclock with 3 companies namely Capt. Francis, Capt. Blake and Capt. Grady_*

The Haywood Highlanders remained stationed at Wilmington, presumably at Camp Davis, for approximately thirty-seven days. On the afternoon of Nov. 5 Tom received orders for his company to start to Charleston, South Carolina. In less than two hours the Highlanders had broken camp and were on the march to the Wilmington railroad station. However, two men in his company who had fallen sick, Sgt. James Blalock and Pvt. Henry Tilman Bugg, were left behind in the care of Cpl. Thaddeus Hyatt.

On that excited day an angel was apparently looking out for Tom. Still suffering from chronic back pain, he would have been hard pressed to make the march of some few miles on foot. However, as the companies were hasting from camp a kindly gentleman by the name of J. A. Sanders offered Tom the use of a little pacing horse, thus enabling the captain to accompany his troops.

The van of the regiment reached Wilmington as dark was setting in. At around 9:00 Colonel Clingman embarked for Charleston with two companies—Capt. Francis Johnstone's Company E and Capt. Samuel Bryson's Company C. Lieutenant Colonel Dearing and three more companies got off around 11:00. These were Capt. John Francis's Company D, Capt. Frederick Blake's Company H, and Capt. William Grady's Company G.

Tom entered this day's events in his journal while on board the train running rapidly for Charleston. He, Major Rutledge, and the remaining five companies were stranded at the Wilmington rail depot all night as they waited for the next train. The major received a dispatch from Colonel Clingman asking that a telegraph be sent ahead to Charleston requesting breakfast for the colonel and the two companies he was escorting. However, Tom and Major Rutledge found the telegraph office closed until the next morning.

It was a long, restless night for Tom. He slept but little on the floor of a depot room along with approximately three hundred men. Rising early, he and Major Rutledge sent the telegraph to Charleston and began making preparations for the train march.

1861
Nov. 6 – Wednesday

On the Road to Charleston running rapidly It is a bad place to write I slept but little last night until midnight was expecting orders to move_ About one received a dispatch from Co^l. Clingman requesting ~~tela~~ *Co^l. D or Maj^r. Rutledge to telegraph to Charleston for breakfast for 2 companies Went to the T. office with M^r. Sawyer_ It was closed & we were told that it would not be opened again until 8 Oclk this morning_*

*Went back to Depot & slept a little in a room with 3 companies say near 300 men_*

Went early this morning with Maj. R. to T. office & he left a dispatch for Charleston _

1861
<u>*Nov. 6*</u> *[continued]*

*I then called at M^r. P. K. Dickinson's (I believe the P in his name is Pratt) and heard M^rs. D. read a chapter in Bible, & her mother M^rs. London offer up a most eloquent & affecting prayer_ ~~Took~~ Was much struck with M^rs. London and think that she must be an excellent old Lady_ We left Wilmington at 2 Oclock P.M. Maj^r. R. and five ^5 companies Capt. Roberts, Capt. Thad. (Howel's and Edney's) Bryson^ & Haywood Highlanders & here we go! jolting along crowded in uncomfortable cars to fight the Yanks_*

After briefly assisting Major Rutledge at the telegraph office Tom found time to call on an acquaintance living in Wilmington, Pratt K. Dickinson. During the visit it appears that his host's wife and mother-in-law ministered to his spiritual side by reading a chapter from the Bible and offering an "eloquent & affecting prayer."

Finally, at 2:00 in the afternoon the five companies boarded the uncomfortable rail cars and embarked along the Wilmington & Manchester Railroad for Charleston to "fight the Yanks." In addition to Tom's Company F the last straggling companies were Capt. Balis Edney's Company A, Capt. Thaddeus Bryson's Company B, Capt. George Howell's Company I, and Capt. Charles Roberts's Company K.

Tom and the trainload of troops were delayed for several hours at the "little town" of Florence, South Carolina, which lies approximately one hundred miles west of Wilmington. Although the reason for the hold-up is not revealed, it was likely due to the troops having to switch railroads and trains, as the line running to Charleston from Florence was the Northeastern Railroad. After being detained for the entire night the five companies finally got off at daybreak and reached Charleston between the hours of 10:00 and 11:00 that same morning, a trip of just over one hundred miles. Tom notes that the route had taken them across one large river whose name escaped him (the Santee River) and through a great deal of cypress swamp.

Still suffering from a severe headache as well as continued back pain, Tom found quarters for his company in Charleston's American Hotel. All of the regiment's troops were accommodated there with the exception of Capt. Johnstone's Company E. To make room for so many men the furniture was removed from the dirty hotel rooms and the men undoubtedly slept on the floors.

The company commanders rated better lodging, it seems. At the Charleston Hotel on the corner of Pinckney and Meeting Streets Tom found a room where he was able to take a bath and catch a couple of hours of sleep. He awoke at around 9:00 that evening and for the first time since sunrise had something to eat.

1861
Nov. 7 – Thursday

Were detained several hours at a little town called Florence Left Florence about day--break, & reached Charleston between 10 & 11 A.M. Crossed one large river the [blank] *passed a great deal of cypress swamp on high trestle_*

 Charleston, S.C
*Came down between Cooper & Ashley Rivers_ The Cooper on our left or East of us, & the Ashley on our right_*

 *Had severe head ache, & my back still paining me_*

 The Regiment (excepting Cap. Johnstone's Company) were quartered at the American Hotel_ All the furniture was removed & the rooms were very dirty_ I went to the Charleston Hotel_ Took a bath, went to bed & slept two hours & a half got up at 9 Oclock, got a little supper (the first thing that I had eaten since sunrise)

1861
Nov. 7 [continued]
Charleston
*Went back to the American Hotel after 10 Oclock_ found the men hungry_ Supper was served to them after 10 Oclock_ & now it is nearly midnight, & I must yet write a few lines (not withstanding headache) to my own Dear little wife_ We are ordered to rise at 5 Oclock, take the cars at 7 Oclock_ & we will probably reach the vicinity of Port Royal in time to be in the fight in afternoon of tomorrow_ We hear that a portion of the Yankees fleet have passed Port Royal_ We hear tonight also that Hatteras has been retaken but have no particulars_*

After taking his supper at the Charleston Hotel Tom went back over to the American Hotel to check on his men. He found them hungry, but that condition was soon remedied as supper was served to them after 10:00 p.m. Finally, with his men's appetites satisfied and other needs looked after, Tom made his way back to his room by midnight. Although weary from the lack of sleep and by the interruption of the normal daytime/nighttime routine and suffering the constant pain of a headache, Tom could not close his eyes for some much-needed rest until adding a few lines in a letter to his "own Dear little wife."

It was only with the revelation that orders had been received to embark the cars at 7:00 in the morning for Port Royal, South Carolina, that Tom put down his pen. His last thoughts as he settled down for a few hours of troubled sleep were likely for his boys and the expected fight with the Yankees on the morrow's afternoon.

Tom awoke at 4:30 in the morning thankful that the headache was clear but still bothered by back pain. He soon found that Pvt. John Trull of the Haywood Highlanders was sick and obtained through the regiment's surgeon, Dr. Solomon S. Satchwell, a ticket of admittance for the ailing man to enter the Confederate States Hospital. Before he left Trull with the other stricken men from the regiment Tom obtained the pledge of a Mr. Lane from North Carolina ensuring that the private would be taken to the hospital.

Again writing on a jolting train as it clamored along the steel rails toward Port Royal, Tom scratched out that his men were unable to get sufficient provisions that morning. He paid $3.55 from his own pocket to buy bread for them. To this accounting he noted an outlay of $3.90 at Camp Davis to procure meal for the boys so that they could have some bread, plus additional expenditures at Asheville of $2.50 to buy a pair of shoes for one man, and $1.00 for a blank book. But in Tom's way of thinking during those tense hours before a highly anticipated and likely clash with the enemy "these were just small matters, until a man's purse fails him."

1861
<u>Nov. 8 – Friday</u>

*Slept but little last night_ Got up at half after 4oclock_ clear of the head ache, but my back no better_ got from D^r. Satchwell a ticket of admittance into the Confederate States Hospital for J. Trull & left him with Capt. Howel's sick men_ A gentleman by the name of Lane from N.C. promised to see ~~that~~ him carried to the hospital On the Savannah R.R. hurrying on to Port Royal_*
*The men could not get much provisions this morning & I paid out for bread for them just before starting ~~$3.55~~ =   3.55 and while at Camp Davis for meal for them   3.90 and at Asheville for a pair of shoes for one   2.50 and towards a blank book - 1.00 & also some other little articles cost forgotten but these are small matters until a mans purse fails him_*

1861
<u>Nov. 8</u> [continued]

The Troops marched from the American Hotel about 8 oclock crossed Ashley river on a long bridge,_ March to R.R. station & waited until about 10 oclock & the Regiment started on a long train of open cars, & here we go at eleven oclock_ The sun scorching hot, & burning my ears owing to having on a cap which I bought in Charleston_ After 3 oclok P.M arrived at our stopping place an old field in Beaufort Dist and near Coosawhatchie P. Office & there found a Reg^t. from Spartanburg Dis^t. Co^l. Edwards and L^t. Co^l. _ & Maj^r. T.Y. Farrow

The troops of the 25th Regiment had vacated Charleston's American Hotel around 8:00 in the morning and marched across a long bridge spanning the Ashley River to the railroad station. After boarding a train of open cars the troops started south at about 10:00 over the recently opened Charleston & Savannah Railroad line that hugged the Atlantic coast all the way to Savannah, Georgia.

Tom notes that the sun was scorching hot that fall day, and as a result his ears were sunburned from exposure. He attributes that little bit of misfortune to a new Confederate cap purchased in Charleston, one that obviously offered little protection for his ears.

Around 3:00 in the afternoon, after traveling approximately sixty-five miles, the train screeched to a halt near an "old field" in the Beaufort District of South Carolina. The location was near the Coosawhatchie station and post office and very close to Port Royal Sound, where Tom had heard the Yankee fleet was threatening and where he had expected to fight soon.

Coosawhatchie was the final destination for the Haywood Highlanders, and they along with the rest of the regiment quickly piled off the cars. Interestingly, Tom bothered to record that another Confederate regiment was encamped nearby (the 13th Regiment South Carolina, commanded by Col. Oliver Edwards), and he attempted to log the names of its commanding officers. This regiment that had just recently been organized in Columbia, South Carolina, would later be attached to the Army of Northern Virginia and see heavy service at such notable places as Chancellorsville, Gettysburg, and Petersburg.[118]

The Haywood Highlanders set up camp in the old field near Coosawhatchie and next to the railroad tracks. Since their baggage did not arrive with them they spent the cool night under the stars without tents for shelter. Tom says that when the baggage finally did reach them on this day, they relocated their camp slightly to the south in the direction of Savannah and on the eastern side of the railroad tracks. The boys were told that the Yankee vessels could approach within thirteen miles of where they were. Again they were situated in an old farm field, this time on land that Tom thought unsuitable for camping because it was too low and damp and not apt to drain heavy rainfalls.

News quickly reached them that the Yankee fleet had entered Port Royal and had taken the Confederate batteries that guarded its approaches. The news was old, as it turned out. Two days before, on Nov. 7, a Union armada of no fewer than eighty ships under flag officer Samuel du Pont sailed into the waters of Port Royal Sound and within just a few hours bombarded the two protective sand forts, Walker and Beauregard, into submission. Because of its location midway between Charleston and Savannah, Port Royal was a place of high strategic value that could be used as a base of operations and as a coaling station to supply the North's growing blockading fleet patrolling the entrances to the important Southern coastal cities. Immediately the Union began landing forces and soon gained complete control of Hilton Head Island and the surrounding waters of Port Royal Sound. It would be proven that Union domination of this region not only was important for maintenance of the blockade, but it provided a stage for the first steps toward reconstruction. There was a distribution of land to the freed slaves (much of it later negated); early attempts were made toward educating the freedmen; and many of the former slaves were recruited into the Union army.[119]

1861
Nov. 9 – Saturday
Coosawhatchie

*Slept last night without tents_ The baggage came up today, & in the afternoon we moved about ¼ mile South towards Savannah, & encamped on the East side of the R.R. in an old field, & a part of the tents stand on low damp ground which I believe will be covered with water when it rains & we are told that the Yankee vessels can approach within 13 miles of us _ We learned yesterday that the Yankee fleet had entered Port Royal, & had taken both our batteries_*

The news is confirmed today but we have conflicting accounts

Opposite, above: This painting of the Battle of Port Royal Sound depicts the Union warships sailing in a circle as they fire in turn on the Confederate forts Beauregard on the left and Walker on the right. *From Robert Tomes,* The War with the South: A History of the Great American Rebellion *(1862).*

Opposite, below: Confederate Fort Beauregard was situated to the north of South Carolina's Port Royal entrance. On Nov. 7, 1861, a powerful Union armada easily outgunned and overwhelmed the sand fort's defenses and captured the rebel facility along with all of its ordnance. *Library of Congress, Prints and Photographs Division.*

Above: A typical Confederate encampment, by Conrad Chapman. At Grahamville's Camp Lee—much like the arrangement shown here—the Haywood Highlanders lived amid the pine trees and Spanish moss. With plenty to eat, a comfortable climate, and an enemy indisposed to attack the rebel defenses, the mountain boys led a relatively easy army life. *Library of Congress, Prints and Photographs Division.*

Nov. 9 [continued]

from the fight_ Some say that our troops behaved disgracefully, & others say that they fought bravely until all their guns but one was dismounted by the enemy's superior guns_ etc. etc. We also hear that Beaufort is deserted, but that the Yanks are afraid to land supposing that the retreat was connected with some trap to catch them_ It has been very hot today, and I fear many of us will be sick if we remain here long_ When the baggage was unloaded we found each Company's portion of scattered from one end of the train to the other & a good many small articles were lost

Reports reaching Tom and the Haywood Highlanders were mixed regarding the resoluteness of the Confederate defensive actions during the battle for Port Royal. Although by some accounts the troops "behaved disgracefully," they were simply overwhelmed by the firepower of the powerful Yankee warships. More than sixty men were killed or wounded by the bombardment and, as a result of the rebels' hasty retreat, more than forty pieces of ordnance, mostly heavy caliber, and a large number of arms and personal baggage were left behind.[120] One Confederate officer later reported that the incessant artillery fire from the naval vessels "rent [the Confederate flag] into so many shreds that no piece could be found."[121]

Had the Haywood Highlanders arrived a couple of days sooner they almost certainly would have been participants in the fight that Tom had imagined. As it turned out, however, the Union forces did not press the thing and were satisfied, for the time being, with their advantage and foothold on Hilton Head Island. Tom, on the other hand, was left to fret over the coastal heat, his men's health, and the company's baggage which was "scattered from one end of the train to the other."

It was not an easy night for Captain Lenoir. Although he slept under a tent, he complained that the old corn rows had not been leveled and he had to lie across one with his hips elevated higher than his head and feet.

The Haywood Highlanders rose early for the usual Sunday morning inspection. As the men stood at attention in files, the officers examined their muskets one by one to insure that they were clean and in proper order. On this morning a few cartridges and caps were found spoiled.

It was an excessively hot day for autumn, and Tom noted that a good many of his men were complaining. At supper he dined with Capt. St. Clair of the Confederate Navy, whom he likely had just met, and was introduced to a caffeinated tea made from the crushed leaves of the yaupon plant. It seems that the tea was not too unpleasant, and after eating a few of the yaupon red berries he thought the concoction had a laxative effect on him. The naval commander expressed the surprising fact that the people of Richmond believed there were nearly 27,000 rebels arrayed against the Yanks at Port Royal. Tom may or may not have been aware at the time that, in actuality, there were probably fewer than 7,000 troops in and around the area, all of these being under the immediate command of Brig. Gen. R. S. Ripley.[122]

On Nov. 6 Confederate States President Jefferson Davis had dispatched Gen. Robert E. Lee to Coosawhatchie to assume overall command of the Department of South Carolina, Georgia, and East Florida. Davis was concerned for the safety of key coastal cities such as Charleston, Savannah, Georgetown and Jacksonville; the railroads linking them; and the important plantation country surrounding them. Effectively this was the exposed underbelly of the Deep South, and Davis entrusted its care to Lee, a man he held in highest esteem. Unfortunately, the very day that General Lee arrived to take over his new command the Union armada struck.

1861
Nov. 10 – Sunday
Coosawhatchie

*We had as usual Sunday inspection this morning, & found some cartridges & caps spoiled_ I slept badly last night The high old corn ridges were not leveled in our tent, & I lay across one with my hip on it & higher than either my head or my feet_*

*Today has been excessively hot & a good many men are complaining_*

*Capt. St. Clair of the Navy took supper with me tonight, & says that the people in Richmond believed that there were twenty seven thousand men [(]27,000) here ready to repel the Yanks_*

Tried the [blank] *tea for the first time_ I think it about as good as Black tea_ & I also eat several spoonsfull of the little red berries_ They at first seem quite bitter but afterwards appear rather pleasant to the taste & I believe that they acted as an aperient on me_*

1861
Nov. 10 [continued]

Capt. St. Clair thinks that the Yankees have one of best navies in the world_ & praises their vessels, their guns, & the manner in which their men are drilled, & thinks that we can whip them when out of the range of those guns on land but that they can land almost any where

Nov. 11 - Monday
Coosawhatchie – Camp Beauregard

Was detailed Officer of the Day for today, but owing to my back–ache L^t. Blalock had to act_ We got no news of importance this morning Our Co^l. is still speaking of moving to an other encampment & I hope we will get a better _ Settled with J.M. Cathey & J.T. Cathey & E. Smith & my accounts are squared with them all up to this morning _ Returned Wesley Henson 50 cts & I now owe nobody in the Regiment any thing that I remember, except good wishes

During the course of their meal Captain St. Clair, Tom's dinner companion, heaped high praise on the Union navy. He especially lauded their vessels, their guns, and the manner in which their sailors were trained and drilled. Although in his estimation they could land wherever they chose, the Confederate army could whip them once beyond the range of their dominant guns.

Tom's back pains persisted on this day and he could not perform the officer-of-the-day duties that fell upon him. He assigned the responsibility to 1st Lt. Etheldred Blalock of his Haywood Highlanders (making it apparent that the "Blalock" who was left sick back at Wilmington along with Private Bugg was Sgt. James Blalock). Etheldred Blalock, about forty-four years old at the time, was an able man who had been a millwright and carpenter in the Forks of Pigeon community before the war.

It appears from the journal entry that Colonel Clingman believed the regiment would soon be moved to another location. The notion would appeal to Tom since he still thought very little of the company's present encampment site, now styled as Camp Beauregard in his diary. And it is clear from his record that Tom was not entirely bedridden with his back as he went about settling personal debts with various men from the company. So pleased was he to close out the accounts that he concludes his day's notes by writing he owed nobody in the regiment anything "except good wishes."

The Haywood Highlanders were posted on guard duty from 9:00 the previous evening until 8:00 this morning. Tom also wrote that he neglected to record on the previous day that Mr. Lawrence Massilon Keitt had given a speech to the regiment before the evening dress parade. Keitt was a South Carolina politician known for his fire-eater sentiment. He served in the Confederate congress and later as a colonel in the Confederate army. Tragically he, along with many other brave soldiers, was mortally wounded at the Battle of Cold Harbor.

The famous orator complimented the Old North State for the bold step it took on the 20th of May, 1775, and also on the 20th of May, 1861. The earlier date coincides with the signing of the Mecklenburg Declaration of Independence by a bunch of citizens from North Carolina's Mecklenburg County, supposedly the first declaration of independence from England made in the thirteen colonies.[123] The later date references North Carolina's delayed action to secede from the United States. Keitt went on in his attempt to incite the rebellious instincts of the mountain boys and raise their spirits to say that the state's later deliverance from Yankee subjugation was a greater achievement than the escape from British rule. These words would certainly have raised loud hurrahs from the ranks and a cheer in Tom's heart.

This day was another hot one in the South Carolina lowcountry, and the Haywood Highlanders were surely thankful that there was no drilling. Captain Moore's artillery unit of approximately 110 men and six brass cannon was located close by, and Tom took an opportunity that evening to walk over to visit and check out the heavy ordnance.

1861
Nov. 12 – Tuesday
Camp Beauregard

*The Haywood Highlanders were on guard duty from 9 Oclock yesterday until 8 this morning_*
I omitted to mention that on yesterday evening just before dress parade we had a speech from the Hon. M^r. Keit of S.C who complimented the Old North State for the course she took both on the 20th of May 1775 & also on 20th May 1861 – & said that the deliverance from Yankee thraldom was a much greater achievement than the deliverance from British thralldom

This has been a very hot day & a few companies of troops have passed on the cars towards Savannah
No drilling today _
Went over this evening to where Cap. Moore's battery of six brass cannon from Wilmington are stationed _

1861
Nov. 13 – Wednesday
Camp Beauregard

The 8th Reg^{t}. N.C.V. arrived last night or early this morning Co^{l}. Ratcliff, L^{t}.Co^{l}. Mears Maj^{r}. Tate They have stationed at Camp Wyatt near Wilmington N.C. Co^{l}. Cathey arrived this evening bringing us butter, lard, bacon, apples and a great many things for the Company something for almost every man_ He brought 64^{lb} bacon & 20^{lb} lard from the Den, and [blank] ^{lb} *butter, & 1 barrel of apples_ A. Crawford came with Co^{l}. Cathey & rejoined his company today*

Sometime during the early morning hours another regiment of North Carolina volunteers from Wilmington arrived on the train and bivouacked at Camp Beauregard. Although Tom refers to the unit as the 8th North Carolina Volunteers under the command of Col. James D. Radcliffe, on the very next day the regiment would be officially designated as the 18th Regiment North Carolina Infantry State Troops.

It may have been a surprise to Tom and the rest of the Haywood Highlanders when Col. Joseph Cathey of Forks of Pigeon rolled into camp. He was accompanied on the long journey by Pvt. Amos Crawford, who had been sick when the company left Asheville and had been left behind on furlough for thirty days. Although it is possible that Colonel Cathey, a highly respected merchant and county leader, came by rail, having embarked at the closest railheads of either Morganton, Greenville, or Spartanburg, it is presumed that he made the long trip by wagon based on the quantity of goods that he delivered to the Haywood men. Tom wrote that Cathey brought something for almost every man including bacon and lard from Tom's East Fork farm, Bachelor's Den.

Colonel Clingman received orders to move the 25th Regiment to Grahamville, South Carolina, situated approximately nine miles to the southwest of Coosawhatchie and just east of the Charleston & Savannah Railroad. There he was instructed to "occupy a point on the Honeywood road in advance of Grahamville" with the intent to guard the town and cover the roads leading from Tenny's and Boyd's landings on the Broad River. Further, he was advised to "establish depots and obtain supplies of subsistence at Grahamville, as far as possible."[124] This would prove not to be a difficult proposition as the plantation country surrounding the new encampment produced rice, cotton, Indian corn, and sweet potatoes in abundance.[125]

Clingman's orders were a consequence of Gen. Robert E. Lee's hurried appraisal of the situation around Port Royal Sound and the ineffectiveness of the Confederate defense against the Union battleships and gunboats. In addition to reinforcing the existing defensive works around the Charleston and Savannah harbors, Lee decided to withdraw the Confederate forces from scattered posts along the coast and assemble them at the most probable points of Federal advance, just beyond the range of the menacing gunboats.[126] Grahamville's location along the strategic coastal railroad opposite the Union lodgment at Port Royal Sound was chosen as a point of concentration, and the 25th Regiment N.C. was moved into position to defend it.

After having their dinner (lunch) the Haywood Highlanders packed up and marched to their new post at Grahamville.

1861
Nov. 14 – Thursday
R. R. station near
to Grahamville, S.C.

After dinner today took down the tents & piled all the baggage on the side of the R. Road _ about 3 oclk put it in the cars. & all the sick and complaining with it

The Companies marched for the new encampment near Grahamville, & said to be about 3 miles from this Station_ We waited for the mail train to pass_ then started a little before 4 oclock arrived here & unloaded the last of the baggage just before sundown_ found no wagons started some men off

1861
Nov. 14 – [continued]

with blankets to the encampment tried to get wagons to send tents to our men _ but all were engaged _ Spread our tent _ & several others near the baggage, & had supper prepared _ At 8 Oclock the boys quarreled some about the wagons, but we agreed to wait until the next load _ At about ½ past 8 Oclock got a wagon & started most of the tents & about nine oclock sent another wagon with part of the mess chests

Although it was not a long march from Camp Beauregard to Grahamville (about nine miles), it was one that tested Tom's administrative capacities and patience. After loading their baggage and "all the sick and complaining" on the train cars the boys started on foot for Grahamville around 4:00 in the afternoon. Upon arriving there they found their baggage and unloaded it just as the sun was setting. Unfortunately, no wagons could be secured to haul their stuff to the new encampment, so Tom started some of the men off on foot to the new campsite with blankets. He and the others stayed behind at the railroad tracks and waited until a means to transport their belongings and accoutrements became available. The few wagons were likely being used by other companies of the regiment, and Tom notes that the boys argued over the situation. Spreading a tent near the tracks, they took their supper, and as wagons became available Tom sent most of the tents first and then the mess chests along to their new post.

Tom, Col. Joseph Cathey, and all those Haywood Highlanders who slept overnight near the railroad started early for their new encampment. As this site was close by, they reached it between 9:00 and 10:00 in the morning. Most assuredly, they sought out the rest of the men and began assessing the plot of ground allocated for the company by the regimental commanders. The balance of the day was spent "cleaning off the ground, spreading tents, digging wells and sinks, etc." Tom's heading for the day's journal entry, "Camp Lee," indicates that Colonel Clingman wasted little time in naming the regiment's new post.

Apparently Camp Lee was laid out in such a manner that the quarters for each company were lined up in two rows with the intervening space designated as a street. The morning hours were taken up with the Haywood Highlanders working on Company F street and digging wells in the vicinity. In the evening there was a dress parade at which Colonel Clingman or someone on his staff read aloud a stern prohibition against wrestling in the camp.

A sense of dreaded anticipation can be discerned in Tom's closing note for the day. The Confederate paymaster would arrive on the coming Tuesday, which meant that the company payroll had to be completed the day before, probably in duplicate or triplicate—and, of course, by hand.

1861
Nov. 15 – Friday
Camp Lee

near Grahamville, S.C.
Walked most of the way from R.R. Station _ Arrived here with Co^l. Cathey & a few others between 9 and 10 Oclk. A.M
Balance of the day was spent in cleaning off ground, spreading tents, digging wells & sinks etc. etc. __

Nov. 16 – Saturday
Camp Lee

Men have been working on our street & the wells. drilled one hour in forenoon Dress parade this evening, & orders against wrestling were read __ Paymaster coming next Tuesday_ rolls to make out before Monday morning!!!

1861
Nov. 17 – Sunday
Camp Lee

Sunday inspection this morning, & dress parade this evening_ I have been hard at work all day upon the pay rolls, & not done yet _ Refused an invitation to dine with Capt. [Trezevant] I believe that's the name __

Have had sore tongue & chapped lips, & bad cold & been in bad condition for writing, but have done a good deal of it today __ We had a little ice & a big frost this morning, & it is quite cold again tonight

As usual this Sunday held for the Haywood Highlanders an inspection in the morning and an evening dress parade. Between those events Tom worked interminably on the pay rolls, which he did not complete. He complained of a sore tongue and chapped lips along with a cold to boot. And to top things off the weather was turning cold as they awoke that morning to ice and a heavy frost—not very conducive for writing, of which Tom did a lot that day. It seems that the day's events kept Tom so busy that he even turned down a dinner invitation from Captain Trezevant, whose company of cavalry occupied a position in advance of the 25th Regiment in observation of the Broad River and Boyd's and Tenny's landings.[127]

Although Tom had thought the muster and pay rolls would be finished by morning, he worked on them for most of the day. He again declined a dinner invitation, this one having been extended by his commanding officer, Lieutenant Colonel Dearing. Tom writes that he is not well; it is likely that the pressure and effort of completing the pay roll had worn him down.

The morning hours brought the sound of cannon fire to the attentive ears of the Haywood Highlanders at Camp Lee. Many supposed the action was down about Bluffton, some fifteen to twenty miles south of Grahamville. However, the only Confederate force located in that region at the time was a cavalry unit commanded by Lt. Col. Colcock, with orders to observe only.[128] The artillery noise was likely emanating from the Yankee gunboats patrolling the rivers and inlets of Port Royal Sound.

The Confederate paymaster did not arrive as expected on this day. All of Tom's earnest work to get the pay rolls—those "troublesome institutions"—ready on time was for naught.

1861
Nov. 18 – Monday
Camp Lee

Worked at the muster & pay rolls most of the day
 Was invited by Co^l. Dearing to dine with him him but did not go_ felt unwell & had too much to do _
 Nothing of much interest has occurred here today _

Nov. 19 – Tuesday
Camp Lee

Heard about fifty cannon this morning after breakfast, supposed at the time by some to be at Bluffton, & by others to be at other places _
 *There was but little done in camp today_ expecting the Pay master all day_*
 About 8 Oclock

1861
Nov. 19 [continued]
Camp Lee

Tonight we received orders to be ready to march at half past nine tonight_ allowing us about 1 ½ hours_ Only five Companies were ordered to be ready B.C.D.E. & F_ We had quite a splutter in making preparations, & then after getting ready & waiting a long time were told that the order was countermanded_ Went to bed about 11 Oclk. I had equipped myself with sword & pistol overcoat & blanket, haversack with bread, a few apples_ 1pr. sock, 1pr. gloves a little sugar & coffee ground, 1 tin cup & the Ambrotype of my Dear Wife __ As much as an invalid could well march with

At 8:00 in the evening the Haywood Highlanders received orders to prepare for a march in less than two hours' time. Only half of the regiment's companies were so ordered: in addition to Company F, companies B, C, D, and E. After what Tom described as "quite a splutter" the boys finally readied themselves and were raring to go by half past nine. And then they waited—until finally there came down another order countermanding the original one. It surely must have been a disappointment to many of the mountain boys, who had yet to fire a shot at the enemy.

As can be gleaned from Tom's notes, he had prepared himself well for the anticipated march and action that night. Included in the heavy load he planned to tote were his weapons (sword and pistol) and other accouterments—clothing, coffee, and the most treasured possession of all, an ambrotype of his "Dear Wife" Lizzie.

Tom slept well for a change, with the Catheys keeping him company inside his tent. Col. Joseph Cathey, his civilian friend from Forks of Pigeon who had helped recruit many of the Haywood soldiers, was at fifty-eight years of age still supple and strong enough to sleep on the ground. Next to Colonel Joe lay one of his sons, 1st Sgt. Joseph T. Cathey, and on a cot slept the other son, Lt. James Madison Cathey. Both of these young Cathey boys would eventually give their lives in service to the Confederacy.

1861
<u>*Nov. 20 – Wednesday*</u>
Camp Lee

*Slept pretty well last night with Co^l. Cathey & J.T. Cathey on the floor & Lieut. J. M. Cathey slept on his cot_*
  Drill master Edward Smith left us on the 18th_ I was sorry to part with him_ I think he ~~is a young man~~ has many good traits of charater ~~besides being~~ & also a very good stock of common sense, is a pretty good judge (for his age) of human nature, & can appreciate a favor_ He asked me to write to him _ His address is
    E. Smith – Averasboro
      Harnette Co. N.C.

1861
Nov. 21 – Thursday
Camp Lee

*No drill today_ The Pay Master ____ Mitchell is here & paid A. & C. Companies this evening_ No war news Camp quite quiet_*

Nov. 22 – Friday
Camp Lee

Three companies B.D.& F. were drill in Battalion drill today_ Several Companies including Co. F. were paid today (excepting the commissioned officers) – The amount paid over to me for the noncommissioned officers and privates, was $4149.89=$4149.89 & I have distributed it all except to H.T. Bugg at Wilmington & six others who are at Grahamville hospitals

The Confederate paymaster, undoubtedly burdened with new Confederate currency, arrived at Camp Lee and proceeded to issue the soldiers pay for their loyal service. He and any assistants who might have accompanied him surely scrutinized carefully the rolls and ciphers of the individual company commanders before releasing the funds. Only two companies, A and C, received their compensation on this day.

A battalion composed of the Haywood Highlanders and two other companies practiced military maneuvers and drilled as a body during the day. Tom's hard work on the pay rolls was rewarded as he received more than $4,000 from the paymaster to distribute to the men of Company F. High time, he must have thought. This was the first pay the men had received since joining up for the fight in the summer.

The record shows that Henry Tilman Bugg was still sick back at Wilmington; six other men had also fallen ill and were being cared for in the Grahamville hospitals. An epidemic of contagions and camp diseases would in due time ravage the regiment during their service at Grahamville's Camp Lee.

Tom had just heard news of a fight at Pensacola, Florida, with a great deal of conjecture concerning how effective Gen. Braxton Bragg's cannon fire might have been. The report of the bombardment was accurate, as it turned out. On the morning of Nov. 22 Union-controlled Fort Pickens, along with two Federal warships, opened fire on the Confederate mainland defense works at Pensacola commanded by Bragg. The battle lasted eight hours and was resumed on the next day. Loss of life was small on both sides, and the primary damage was the destruction of the villages of Warrington and Woolsey adjoining the Confederate naval yard at Pensacola.[129]

The paymaster, who was still at Camp Lee, doled out the pay for the commissioned officers of Tom's Company F, a day after the noncommissioned soldiers were paid. Tom wrote that he received "just" $1,532.65 for the commissioned officers, suggesting that he had anticipated even more funds. As a captain commanding an infantry company Tom earned $130.00 per month, and he signed a payment voucher for a total of $524.33. It appears that he was paid for four months and one day of service to the Confederate States.[130]

1861
Nov. 23 – Saturday
Camp Lee

*Heard today of a fight at Pensacola_ The rumor is that the firing commenced yesterday & had continued (up to last dates) four hours without loss on our side, & Bragg was firing slowly but with what effect we know not_*

*I hope he has something better than grape to give the Yanks_*

The Paymaster handed me today for the commissioned officers of Company F just $ 1532.65
For the Capt. $ 524.33
" 1st Lieu^t. = 363.00
" 2nd D^o. = 322.66
" 2nd D^o. = 322.66
           $1532.65=1532.65
*and it was distributed among them immediately_*

1861
Nov. 23 [continued]

*This pays said Commissioned Officers up to 31st Oct. 1861_ They in making out their accounts calculated from the date of their Commissions June 29th 1861 James A. Burnett lifted, tonight, a note which I held on him for $15.00 I charged him no interest_ The note was given at Camp Clingman near Asheville for a small pistol_ I received a letter tonight from my Dear Wife dated 18th Nov. & mailed 21st (day before yesterday) at Lenoir_ It came so quickly that I think there was probably some mistake in the Post mark It is now nearly bed time but I must answer that letter_*

The additional day's pay that Tom received is clearly for the single day in June that he served after receiving his commission on June 29, 1861. The same holds true for the other commissioned officers of the company, 1st Lt. Etheldred H. Blalock, 2nd Lt. James A. Burnett, and 3rd Lt. James M. Cathey.

The much-needed currency the men received began rapidly exchanging hands to settle debts for money owed to one another. For instance, Tom writes that James A. Burnett paid him for a pistol that he sold to the lieutenant at Camp Clingman in Asheville. It was a common thing for soldiers and civilians alike during this period to lend and borrow money from one another. The transactions were usually formalized with a note or scrap of paper documenting the particulars of the deal and signed by the debtor. Tom's diary, filled with accountings of such matters, demonstrates not only the manner in which the debts were tracked but the care and attention devoted to this personal business.

It was a good day. Tom at last received payment for his service with the Confederate army, was reimbursed for at least one note he was holding, and, joyously, received a letter from his dear Lizzie. The letter was postmarked in Lenoir, North Carolina, where Lizzie was boarding with Tom's sister and brother-in-law, Laura and Joseph Norwood, while attending the town's female college.

The cool, crisp, autumn mornings continued in the Carolina coastal country, and as the Haywood Highlanders threw off their blankets and arose out of their tents they found a white frost covering the grounds of the encampment. It was Tom's turn to serve as officer of the day, and he immediately posted the guard pickets at 8:00 that morning.

After staying with the Haywood Highlanders for eleven days Col. Joseph Cathey bid his sons and the mountain boys good-bye and started in his wagon for Savannah. It is presumed that Cathey aimed to stock his wagon with goods to carry back with him to Forks of Pigeon. These would be sold or bartered at his store, which was the commercial and trading hub of the community.

However, before he left the camp Lt. Ephraim Young of Company E gave Cathey $160.00 to be credited against a note Tom held on Young. The note was in the hands of Augustus C. Hartgrove, the overseer of Tom's farming business in Haywood County, and Cathey was to deliver the money to Hartgrove. Tom also turned over to Colonel Cathey $10.00 of Pvt. James M. Henderson's army pay to be handed over to Henderson's wife back home. The private was very ill at the time, and Tom was holding his money for him.

1861
Nov. 24 – Sunday
Camp Lee

*Another white frost this morning_ Guard mounted at 8 Ock. A.M. & I am Officer of the Day_*

*Col. Cathey left us between 12 & 1 oclock today, & Lieut. E. H. Blalock started with him for Savannah_ B. will return on Tuesday next_*

E. Young paid over to Col. C. $160.00 to be credited on a note due me which was left with A.C. Hartgrove

*I sent ten dollars $10.00 of Jas. M. Henderson's money by Col. C. to be paid over to Henderson's wife (He is very low with Typhoid fever.) & I will keep the bal for him_*

1861
Nov. 25 – Monday
Camp Lee, S.C.

After much trouble today succeeded in drawing pay for our Company Commissary N. J. Ferguson served from 20th July to 15th August & recd. =$ 6.25 B. F. Edmonston from 15th Augt. to Oct. 3rd & recd. =$ 12.00 R. C. Osborne from Oct 15th to Oct. 31st & recd. = $ 4.00
$22.25
From the 3rd to 15th Oct. the First Sergeant served, but was not allowed any pay for it_ Heard this evening that the Yanks had been shelling Tybee Island about 20 miles below Savannah although the fortifications had been evacuated for several weeks I suppose they were afraid of <u>*Masked Batteries*</u>

The Confederate Civil War soldiers were forever hungry, especially during the waning stages of the war. During the siege of Petersburg, Virginia, there would be periods when the daily ration for the men was usually no more than one pint of corn meal and an ounce or two of bacon. After the war one rebel who endured severe privations at Petersburg quipped: "I was hungry . . . so hungry that I thanked God that I had a backbone for my stomach to lean up against."[131] Even in the early years, however, the regimental and company commissaries had the thankless job of foraging and providing food to the troops. As can be seen in Tom's diary entry, he had a hard time drawing pay for his commissaries, who apparently earned an extra twenty-five cents per day for their additional responsibilities. From the time of the company's formation in July 1861 through October three men acted as commissaries for Company F: privates Nathan Ferguson, Benjamin Edmonston, and Roland Osborne.

On Nov. 24 the Yankees crossed the Savannah Bar with eight vessels and made a lodgment on Tybee Island, which General Lee's Confederate forces had evacuated.[132] Lee had little concern about the enemy taking the islands in front of Savannah and thought the Yankees would find little advantage in holding them once done with their pillaging. Having seen to the obstruction of the Savannah River, he pushed to complete the strengthening of Fort Pulaski, which protected the city.[133]

Tom received further news this day that Union forces were quickly occupying Tybee Island, just as they had Hilton Head Island less than three weeks before. His intelligence regarding the artillery battle at Pensacola on the 22nd demonstrated the Confederate slant painted by General Bragg's dispatches. Residential villages surrounding Confederate Fort McRae had been destroyed by the Union bombardment, and the cannon duel had actually shown that the coastal batteries were ineffective against the Union's Fort Pickens.[134]

After the company's morning drill Tom visited his sick men in the hospitals around Grahamville, and all seemed to be improving. He took the opportunity, while in the village, to find a whetstone and had his sword sharpened. Afterwards, when he got back to camp he wrote a letter to A. C. Hartgrove in Haywood County. He wanted to notify his overseer about the money Col. Cathey was carrying to him and advised Hartgrove regarding his livestock matters and some fencing around a grave.

1861
Nov. 26 – Tuesday
Camp Lee, S.C.

Heard this morning that 500 Yanks had landed on Tybee Island_ & that the firing at Pensacola had ~~ceas~~ ceased without much damage being done to the Confederates The loss on the other side unknown

Nov.27 – Wednesday
Camp Lee

*Company drill one hour in forenoon_ in afternoon went to Grahamville & visited three hospitals & ground my Sword_ Our sick men seem to be improving_*
*Wrote to A.C. Hartgrove about my stock , & about some money sent by Co^l. Cathey_ & about the paling for [?] grave_*

1861
Nov. 28 – Thursday
Camp Lee S.C

*Battalion drill in forenoon beyond Grahamville_ Gathered some Yopon or (Cassina) to make tea_ Eat about half tea cup full of the red berries & they opperated twice as a mild cathartic_ I think they had the same effect on me once at Camp Davis & will try to get some one else to make the same experiment perhaps it may result in the discovery of a valuable medicine_ No news of much interest from Savannah or elsewhere today except the prospect of a little flareup between England & Lincoln's Government on account of the seizure of Mason & Slidell, but in an English vessel_ but don't believe that we can hope for much from England_*

In the forenoon Tom's company joined the others of the regiment for battalion drill on the outskirts of Grahamville. After official duties were suspended for the day he gathered more yaupon leaves for brewing the tea substitute that he was quickly developing a keen taste for. The concoction was described as having "in a less degree, the same exhilarating or sustaining effect as coffee, is very wholesome, & might with propriety be adopted as a permanent substitute for it."[135] Tom was, for some reason, inclined to eat some of the red berries from the yaupon plant, and he comments once again about the purgative effect they had on him. He even entertains whimsies of having discovered a valuable medicine, little realizing that the native Americans had brewed yaupon potions for medicinal and ritual purposes centuries earlier.

Tom held little prospect that England would intervene on the Confederate side as a result of the *Trent* affair involving James Mason and John Slidell. On Nov. 8 the two Confederate diplomats aboard the British ship *Trent* were impressed by the Union navy and hauled back to the United States as contraband of war. Infuriated by the unlawful detention of their ship and the seizure of the Southern officials, the British government began spewing rhetoric that threatened war with "Lincoln's Government." However, President Lincoln and his cabinet had no desire to start a second war and narrowly averted it by releasing the Southern envoys in December 1861.[136]

One of the men from Company A, Pvt. Walter Salisbury, died during the night at the age of about seventeen years. Tom gives the cause as typhoid fever, although the Confederate records state the youth died from an "unreported cause." It was not an isolated case as the houses, or "hospitals," in Grahamville were quickly filling up with soldiers suffering from occurrences of measles, mumps, diarrhea, pneumonia, and a variety of other illnesses.

Ever-present dysenteries, fevers, and upper respiratory infections were so prevalent during the war that the average infantry soldier was twice as likely to die from a camp disease as he was from a battlefield injury. Another reason—one especially true for the mountain boys in the 25th Regiment N.C. Troops—was that the rural life styles of many of the Civil War soldiers had protected them from such childhood diseases as measles, mumps, chicken pox, and scarlet fever. When they came to live together in camps with large groups of men, thousands died of these diseases in the early stages of the war. And in fact almost one-third of all Civil War casualties were caused by sickness.

Tom continued to worry about Pvt. James Henderson of the Haywood Highlanders, who was still in one of the Grahamville hospitals. "It is a sad thing," he writes, "to be sick so far from home and in a crowded room with other sick men."

1861
Nov. 29 – Friday
Camp Lee

*One of Company A. a M^r. Salisbury died of typhoid fever last night_ When he died he was lying in the same bed with James M. Henderson, & had been for a week_*

*Henderson is quite low with the same disease_ Has had no operation on his bowels, since last Saturday or Sunday I hunted up D^r. Satchwell this evening to inform him of this fact; but he said that he was already aware of it, & intended that it should be so, & also said that in some extreme cases of that disease he had allowed this state to continue for two weeks, & especially when the bowels had been previously, much affected_ Henderson seemed to have a good deal of fever this evening, & I feel quite anxious about him, but do not know of any thing that I can do to relieve him or to make him more comfortable now that that he has a bed to himself_ It is a sad thing to be sick so far from home & in a crowded room with other sick men_*

1861
<u>*Nov. 29*</u> [continued]
Camp Lee

Six houses in Grahamville are now occupied by our sick & they are all crowded_ A large majority of the cases are measles_ several are typhoid fever_ One of mumps_ The Ladies about Grahamville have been very kind to our sick, & deserve our gratitude for ~~*supplying*~~ *their assiduity in supplying them with wholesome food_ Nothing of much interest has occurred in Camp today The Auction of knives, pistols watches, extra clothing etc. is going on in some of the streets tonight, as has been usual for several nights past_ The Boys seem to be enjoying themselves finely not with standing about 190 were reported sick this morning*

Tom's brother, Walter Waightstill Lenoir, who would later attach himself to Company F at Camp Lee, offered a good description of Grahamville in a diary of his own that he kept. "The village of Grahamville, about a mile from our camp, is a town of singular appearance, the houses being sparsely scattered through the primeval forest of pine for more than a mile, yet with so little interruption to the original growth that you seem still to be in the midst of the forest when you are in the midst of the town."[137]

Six of the houses enveloped by Grahamville's pine forest were now crowded with men stricken with cases of measles, typhoid fever, and mumps. The women of the village fed these fallen soldiers, lavishing much care and attention on them.

Back at camp the healthy and semi-healthy rebels spent their off hours in the streets, it seems, trading knives, pistols, watches, clothing, and other desirous items. Though these men were "enjoying themselves finely," Tom notes that a staggering number of 190 others were reported sick.

The Haywood Highlanders fell into alignment for a monthly inspection as the sun climbed up from the eastern horizon. Hours later as the solar orb waned in the western sky the company formed with the regiment for dress parade. This final formal ceremony was one where the troops were assessed, reports of roll calls received, and important orders read.[138]

It is interesting that Tom's diary is almost devoid of personal political thoughts, opinions, and sentiments other than an occasional cynical remark about the Yanks. He fails to reveal anywhere in the journal the motivating factors that led him to leave his "Den" and young bride and march off to war at a relatively advanced age. Instead, he fills the pages with notes and comments on subjects such as botany, medicine, wildlife, nature, personal excursions, and business matters. On this particular date he records a lesson learned from a local wagoner on the uses and virtues of Spanish moss, the prolific beardlike plant that grows and hangs from trees in the Southeastern coastal regions. He learned that the plant could be fed green to livestock, was good food for milk cows but "only tolerably good" for horses, and had to be cured and dried properly before stuffing into mattresses.[139]

Tom also reveals a few scant details about the site that Camp Lee occupied. He records the depth of the water table, describes the quality of the soil and water, and notes the characteristics of local flora.

1861
Nov. 30 – Saturday

Camp Lee
*Monthly inspection this morning, & dress parade this evening, but no drill_*
*Had one well filled and another dug in the afternoon We strike water here at the depth of six to 8 feet_*
*I was told by a negroe wagoner today that the long moss (which hangs in such abundance on the trees here) is good food for milk cows & mules, but only tolerably good for horses_ It is necessary to scald it before using it for beds, in order to kill it & stop the growth_ It is considered unwholesome to sleep on while green or in a growing state Sometimes large quantities are put in pools of water to kill it & then dried for matteresses It is fed to stock green_ It is to be seen on some pines but seems to be more generally on other trees_*
*We are in the midst of a beautiful pine grove_ The ground level & sandy and the water tolerable_*

1861
Nov. 30 [continued]
Camp Lee

*Along the brances, the
Bay tree is found in great
numbers, but small & scarcely
large enough to deserve the name
of tree_ It is an evergreen*

Opposite: This 1861 vintage map clearly shows the village of Grahamville, S.C. and its strategic location adjacent to the Charleston & Savannah Railroad and near the Broad River. *Library of Congress, Maps Division.*

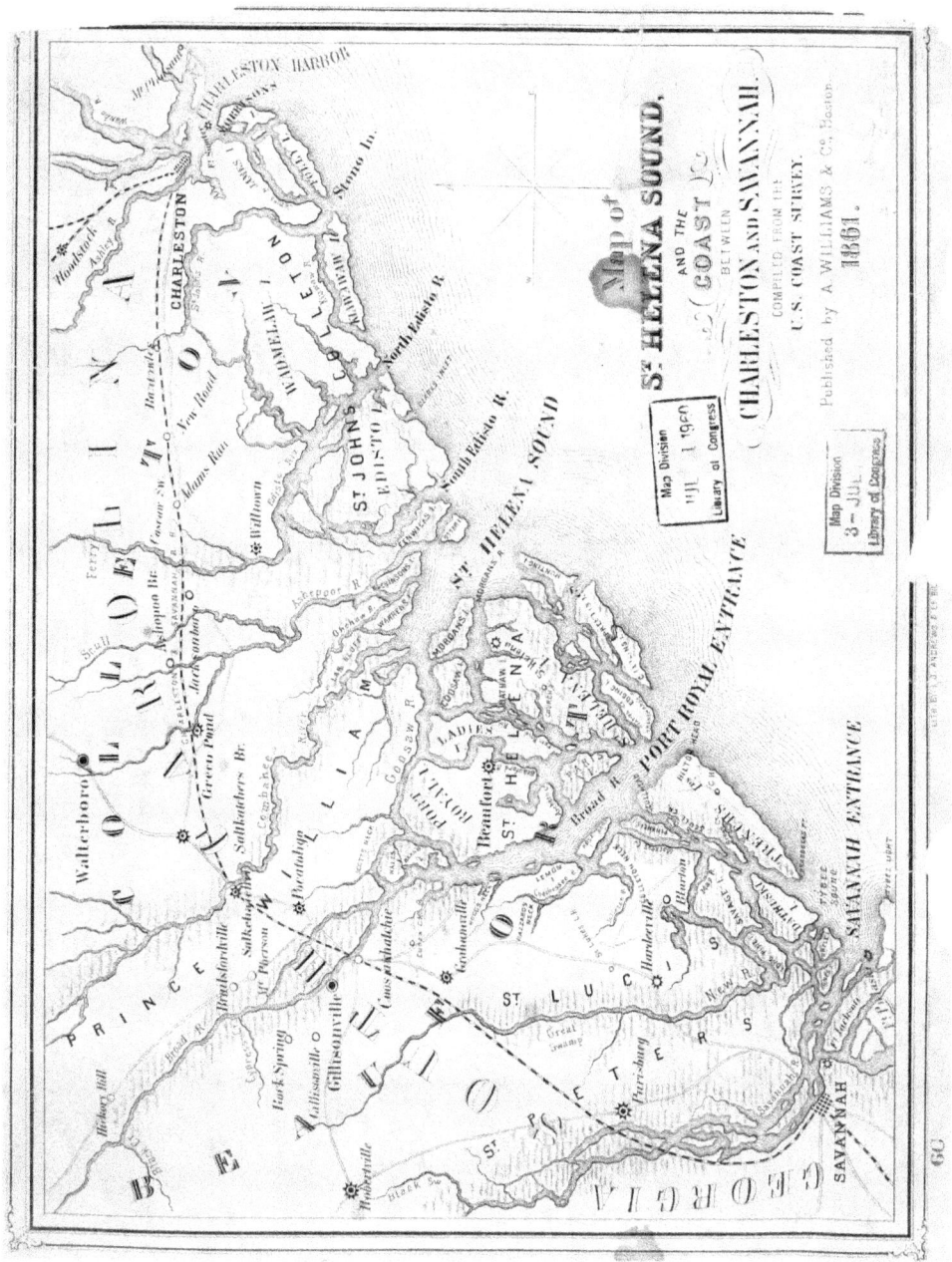

"Rebs," sketch by Alfred Rudolf Waud. *Library of Congress, Prints and Photographs Division.*

December 1861

Captain Lenoir's headache returned on the first of December, along with symptoms of illness that were so rampant in camp. However, he felt well enough to attend church services and enjoyed a message from 2 Samuel delivered by the Rev. Arthur Wigfall, rector of nearby Holy Trinity Episcopal Church in Grahamville.[140]

Under the escort of Company A and most of the other officers of the regiment the body of Pvt. Walter Salisbury was taken to the Grahamville railroad depot. From there the corpse was shipped back to his home and family in Henderson County, North Carolina, for a proper burial.

1861
<u>Dec. 1 – Sunday</u>
Camp Lee

I have had headache all day & otherwise felt unwell, & a little feverish_
The Rev. M^r. Wigfall preached in camp today_ His text was the 45th verse of the 17th Chap_ of Second Samuel_ I thought his discourse a very good one_
Company A. and most of the officers went to excort the remains of Salisbury to the R.R. Depot_
Calvin Edney was sent to Henderson Co. N.C. with the body_ We heard some heavy firing in the forenoon a little West of South_

<u>Dec. 2 – Monday</u>
Camp Lee S.C.

Nothing of importance to chronicle today_ made out Monthly report today
Recitations by the Officers to the Lieut. Co^l. commenced again today_ Several new cases of measles_ 228 reported sick today_

1861
Dec. 3 – Tuesday
Camp Lee S.C.

*Officer of the Day Had Ja^s. Coker of Comp. G. & H. H. Rice Comp. B. both arrested for gambling_ Three men from different Companies were sent to the guard tent for fighting No letter from my Dear Wife for a week_*

Dec. 4 – Wednesday
Camp Lee S.C.

*Was relieved by new Officer of the Day at 8 Oclock A.M. Company has all been on guard duty that were able Went to Battallion drill at 9 ½ Oclock A.M. After dinner went to hospitals in Grahamville James Henderson still very low with typhoid fever_ Nine there sick from Company F. five of them are measle cases_ John G. Burnett among them, & quite sick_ About 240 sick in Regiment The tattoo has been sounded No letter from Lizzie_ Must write her tonight yet_*

As officer of the day Tom had to deal with some men from the regiment's other companies who got out of line and committed petty infractions. 1st Sgt. James Coker of Company G and Pvt. Henry Rice of Company B were both arrested for gambling. And three other men from different companies, who were not named, were sent to the guard tent, as well, for fighting.

Gladly relieved of the officer-of-the-day duties at 8:00 in the morning, Captain Lenoir got dressed, strapped on his sword, and attended Battalion drill with the rest of the Haywood Highlanders—those who were not sick. The men who had all been on guard duty through the night manned the picket lines. At those advanced posts they maintained a lonely and usually boring vigil, watching for the enemy and any threatening movements or incursions against Camp Lee, Grahamville, and the railroad.

After taking his dinner Tom hiked over to Grahamville to visit the sick in the hospitals and look in on Pvt. James Henderson, who was still "very low" with typhoid fever. And Henderson was not the only Haywood Highlander laid up there. There were eight others, five of whom were apparently infected with measles, including Cpl. John G. Burnett. However, these nine cases were but a small portion of the 240 soldiers from the 25th Regiment who were counted sick. That number equated to an average contribution to the infirmaries of about twenty-four patients per company. Nonetheless, the worst was yet to come.

Forever worried about James Henderson's condition, Tom went back to Grahamville in the morning hours to try and secure a quiet room for the private. Rev. Arthur Wigfall of the village's Episcopal church assisted Tom in this endeavor, and to no avail. Although unsaid in the journal, there were either no rooms available in Grahamville or the inhabitants of the little town were not willing or were afraid to omit a man with typhoid fever into their homes.

As the captain returned to camp from the hospitals, where the toll of the sick stood at 250, ten more than the previous day, he spotted Gen. Robert E. Lee in the distance just riding off. The general had established headquarters at Coosawhatchie following his arrival on Nov. 7 and had immediately begun making inspections of the Confederate defensive works along the South Atlantic coast. He traveled from Charleston to Savannah and points in between and found the existing defenses woefully inadequate to resist Union amphibious campaigns. After giving strict orders and laying out the work to be executed, General Lee quickly established a routine of personally inspecting the rebel lines within riding distance of Coosawhatchie.

He set a grueling pace starting out early in the morning on his horse, Traveler, and returning late at night. On one day he rode a distance of 115 miles.[141] It is a certainty that General Lee rode down to the works in front of Grahamville, where the mountain boys were toiling, on more than this one occasion. However, they may not have bothered to take much notice. After all, at that point in the war, before Lee and the Army of Northern Virginia began forging magnificent battlefield successes in Virginia, the general's star had not yet risen.

1861
Dec. 5 – Thursday

Camp Lee S.C.
*Went to Grahamville this morning to try to procure a quiet room for Ja^s. Henderson to be moved to_ Called on Mr. L[?] & various other persons, & was accompanied & assisted in my enquiries by the Rev^d. M^r. Wigfall, but failed to get a room_*

Between 11 and 12 Oclock heard some heavy firing 15 or 20 guns a little East of South returned to Camp a little after 12 & & saw Genl. Lee at a distance just riding off

*About 250 reported sick in the Regiment_*

*No letter from Lizzie yet_*

Right: Gen. Robert E. Lee was sent to South Carolina in November 1861 to take command of the Confederacy's South Atlantic coastal defenses. *Library of Congress, Prints and Photographs Division.*

Lee's headquarters at Coosawhatchie was within riding distance of Camp Lee, where the Haywood Highlanders were garrisoned. Occasionally the mountain boys were able to catch glimpses of the general as he rode on horseback to inspect their work on the defenses—much as he is depicted in this contemporary postcard view, below.

An ordnance list for Company F of the 25th Regiment N.C. Troops dated Dec. 21, 1861, reveals that the Highlanders were in possession of eighty-eight muskets, one rifled musket, and eighty-nine bayonet scabbards, among other accoutrements of war. *Lenoir Family Papers, Southern Historical Collection, Wilson Library, University of North Carolina at Chapel Hill; used by permission.*

1861
Dec. 6 – Friday
Camp Lee

Had Battallion drill today Heard heavy firing occasionally through the day_ sometimes in the direction (as I suppose) of the mouth of the Savannah River & sometimes towards Port Royal Two hundred & fifty seven reported sick today in the Reg^t. Henderson thought to be better Letter from W.W. Lenoir today dated 3^d & stating that all were well & that he would come soon_ Paid for well bucket for the Company   87 ½

The ten companies of the 25th Regiment N.C. participated in a battalion drill even though approximately one-fourth of the men were absent sick and many others probably not well. The rumbling sound of cannon fire could be heard, as on most days, far off in the distance toward Port Royal to the east and the mouth of the Savannah River to the south.

Tom received a letter from his younger brother, Walter, stating that everyone in the family was well and that he would soon join Tom and the Haywood Highlanders at Camp Lee. Walter was living in Caldwell County at the time and had been busy since the summer trying to settle the estate and affairs of their brother, William, who had died by his own hand in May of 1861. Only a couple years prior to that Walter had endured the death of his infant daughter in 1858 and watched helplessly as his wife, Nealy, succumbed to tuberculosis one year later.[142]

It was not a very noteworthy day, by Tom's own admission in his record. He settled all personal financial accounts with James Madison Cathey and his brother Joseph Turner Cathey. Distant thuds of cannon fire could be heard far beyond the southeastern horizon.

A Haywood County man who belonged to Company C died of disease on this day: Pvt. James Winchester, age twenty-five. Although Tom stated that he died from typhoid pneumonia, Confederate records list the cause of death as measles. Winchester's company ordered a coffin from Savannah and began making plans to send the body back to Haywood.

The number of sick men continued on a relentless trend upward. Thirty-four more were committed to the hospitals over the preceding day, bringing the total sick count for the regiment to 291.

1861
Dec. 7 – Saturday
Camp Lee, S.C.

*Settled with James, & Turner Cathey all our accounts to date_*

Nothing of special interest to record tonight except the death of J. Winchester

*Heard a few cannon but don't know what the Yanks were shooting at_*

James Winchester of Capt. Bryson's Company C. from Haywood died today. The Doctor says of Typhoid Pneumonia_ He had scarcely recovered from Measles

His Company intend sending his body back to Haywood, & have sent to Savannah for a coffin

291 reported sick today

1861
Dec. 8 – Sunday
Camp Lee, S.C.

Augustus Carrel of Capt. Grady's Company G. died tonight, about, seven Oclock_ I saw him but a short before he died in one of the hospitals in Graha He was a native of G^a. the son of a widow_ was attacked with something like pneumonia, but his death was supposed to have been caused by an over dose of morphine_ 299 reported sick today_ Went up to the hospitals after dark_ Henderson seems to be a little better

Dec. 9 – Monday
Camp Lee, S.C.

Capt. Thad. C. Bryson's Company C. left Camp before 8 Oclock this morning to escort the body of James Winchester to the R.R. Depot. 316 reported sick today

Augustus Carroll of Company G died during the night. Tom knew the twenty-one-year-old man and had looked in on him at the hospital just a short time before he expired. The records indicate that Carroll simply died from "disease," yet Tom states that he was suffering from pneumonia-like symptoms and even suspected that the real cause of death was a morphine overdose.

Augustus Carroll was a Georgia boy, as were approximately seventy percent of the men who formed Company G. Over the course of the war some 133 men from Georgia filled the ranks of Captain William S. Grady's Company G and fought with the 25th Regiment N.C. Troops. Captain Grady himself was later promoted to major of the 25th Regiment.

At nightfall Tom walked up to Grahamville and made the hospital rounds, where he found Pvt. James Henderson doing a little better.

In the early morning hours Capt. Samuel C. Bryson (not Capt. Thaddeus C. Bryson, as Tom erroneously reports) and the men of Company C escorted the body of James Winchester to the Grahamville depot. Upon reaching the railroad the soldiers would likely have bowed together for a short prayer and then watched in silence as the remains were loaded onto a car to be shipped to Haywood County.

Tom reports a shocking 316 men sick in the hospitals or laid up in their tents, twenty-five more than the day before.

Suffering from another headache during the night and concerned for his sick men, Tom slept but little. He arose from his bed several times to check on privates Alfred Burnett and Green Berry Abbott. These men were apparently coming down with measles, as was Uriah, who was Tom's personal servant in the war (although the personal property of his brother Walter). Uriah had been employed at Tom's East Fork farm in Haywood immediately prior to the war.

The number of sick men on the regimental rolls reached 324 this day. Since the remaining diary entries do not reveal a higher count it is believed that during this period of one or two weeks the epidemic that beset the regiment reached its peak. Although one-third of the rebel soldiers at Camp Lee were sick, this figure is consistent with the proportion of overall casualties due to sickness throughout the war. But at that early period of the conflict the threat of the contagions and camp diseases such as diarrhea must have been truly alarming to commanders and men alike.

It is apparent that Tom received a short furlough, whereupon he decided to accompany Lieutenant Colonel Dearing on a diversion to Savannah, ostensibly to buy a new uniform. The important Southern coastal town was approximately twenty-five miles from Camp Lee, and interestingly the two commanders opted to make the trip in a buggy instead of riding the rail cars.

At Savannah they first stopped off at the Marshall House to check in and later paid a visit to the home of Lieutenant Colonel Dearing's brother-in-law, a Mr. Harding. There Tom was introduced to the colonel's mother, whom he thought "a fine looking old lady," and presumably to Dearing's sister and other family members. Either at the Hardings' or elsewhere Tom played his first game of billiards. After first watching the others play he tried his hand at the game and "played worse than [he] expected to do." The disappointment at his lack of skill in the game etched in these few diary words can still be discerned today.

1861
Dec. 10 – Tuesday
Savannah G^a

Had head ache last evg. was up several times to see Alfred Burnett and Berry Abbot & Uriah
*The two first have measles & I suppose the other is taking it_ 324 reported sick in the Reg^t. today_*
Left the Camp about half past two P. M. in a buggy with Co^l. D. for Savannah, to buy for my self a Confederate coat and pants_ Reached the City just before dark Stopped at the Marshall House_ After supper went to M^r. Harding's He is Cashier of Bank & Co^l. Dearings Brother in law Saw the Co$^{l's}$. Mother at M^r. H^s. She is a fine looking old Lady about 70 years old
Play my first game at Billiards with Co^l. Dearing I played worse than I expected to do, after seeing others play

1861
Dec. 11 – Wednesday
Marshall House [?]
Savannah Georgia

Had quite late breakfast went to a Silver Smiths & left 4 watches to be repaired Went to D.B. Camp (tailor) had my measure taken for coat & pants & paid him in advance = 70.00 (45.00 for the coat & 25.00 for pants) & in addition to that I will have to pay for the lace to go on the sleeves_!!!! At one time thought that I had lost my money & was in somewhat of a stew for a few minutes but soon found it_ After buying books, portfolios, envelops & various other articles for The 'Haywood Highlanders' Started with Co^l*. Dearing in a buggy to see the Town & Surroundings We drove around Town a while started down the shell road – (so called because it is made for twelve miles of Oyster shells_) it is one of the very nicest roads that I ever saw_ We drove down it a few miles, & then turned to the left to see a cemetery called Buenaventura* ~~Bonoventure~~ *(I believe is the spelling)*

It appears that Tom took a room at the Marshall House and resided there for the duration of his stay in Savannah. This four-story brick establishment with its signature iron veranda, the first hotel in Savannah, was built in 1851 by businesswoman Mary Marshall.[143] The accommodations must have suited Tom, for he apparently slept later than accustomed and had a late breakfast.

While Tom was taking in the sights of the historic city the first order of business was to find a silversmith's shop, which he soon came upon. He left four watches with the craftsman there to be repaired. Undoubtedly, not all of these timepieces were Tom's, and as a favor to some of the boys he must have brought theirs to get fixed as well. Next he found a tailor's shop and had his measure taken for a new coat and pair of pants. Paying out seventy dollars in advance (more than half his monthly salary), he seems to have been surprised at the cost, and even yet had to pay for the lace, or braid, to go on his uniform sleeves.

Tom continued his shopping spree around Savannah and purchased books, portfolios, envelopes, and other articles for the Haywood Highlanders. At one point he thought that he had lost all of his money but after a few stressful minutes of being in "somewhat of a stew" he located it again.

Eventually, these necessary procurement tasks were wrapped up, at which time Tom accompanied Lieutenant Colonel Dearing in a buggy as they toured the city and its surroundings. Taking a road paved in oyster shell fragments that Tom referred to as "one of the very nicest roads" that he had ever seen, the two rebel commanders had a leisurely and enjoyable drive to the renowned Bonaventure Cemetery.

The two Confederate officers proceeded down the fine oyster shell road in a southeasterly direction from Savannah, then turned into the grounds of the Bonaventure Cemetery. The beauty and serenity of the place immediately captivated Tom, and he very ably and vividly recorded his impressions. Tom's descriptions evidence his botanical interests and his fascination with the natural world around him.

Botanist and naturalist John Muir, who would visit Bonaventure Cemetery shortly after the war, was similarly impressed. Muir wrote: "Bonaventure to me is one of the most impressive assemblages of animal and plant creatures I ever met." He went on to catalogue the same avenue of live oaks that Tom describes in his dairy entry: "The most conspicuous glory of Bonaventure is its noble avenue of live-oaks. They are the most magnificent planted trees I have ever seen, about fifty feet high and perhaps three or four feet in diameter, with broad spreading leafy heads. The main branches reach out horizontally until they come together over the driveway, embowering it throughout its entire length, while each branch is adorned like a garden with ferns, flowers, grasses, and dwarf palmettos."[144]

1861
Dec. 11 [continued]

*but generally called Bonnyventure_ But I think the pronunciation by no means appropriate and decidedly a misnomer, as a view of it impresses the beholder (Co^l. D. says it is Buenaventura) with feelings very different from those of mirth and gayety_*

It is three or four miles in a South.Easterly direction (I believe) from Savannah & on a branch of the Savannah river (I believe)

It is in a large grove of Live Oaks which were planted in beautiful straigh rows by one of the first Governors of G^a. (Genl. Oglethorpe)

Some of the trees are perhaps two feet in diameter, & branching so as to form beautiful archways in every direction, & almost every branch has the long moss hanging down from it in profusion, & imparting to the whole scene a peculiarly grave solemnity which induces feelings of Sadness, & requires but little aid from Fancy to enable ~~one to imagine~~ *the visitor to imagine that they have been purposely clad in their Sombre drapery which hangs in such mournful silence over the Dead_*

1861
<u>*Dec. 11*</u> *[continued]*

*Among them was one Magnif-
-icent Magnolia, & two very
large Palmetta trees_ The
tops of the Palmettas seemed quite
flourishing, but the whole trunk,
look like rotten wood_
Within one little iron enclosure
around a monument, I saw beautiful
roses in bloom, & the prettiest
white flower (a Japonica) that
I ever saw (all in Dec^r.!!!
I was sorry that I had so
little time to admire the roses
etc._ It was nearly dark when
we returned to the City_
Upon the whole it was a very
pleasant ride & I am much obliged
to Co^l. Dearing for it_
As we went down, we saw
several Yankee vessels in the
distance, & could see the smoke
'curling' up from those in motion
I made a little trial at a
game of billiards_ & thought
it a beautiful game, but it
would require too much time in
practicing to play well, therefore
I discard it as worthless_*

As Tom and his companion, Lieutenant Colonel Dearing, toured Savannah's Bonaventure cemetery, the large magnolia and two large palmetto trees attracted their attention. The palmettos especially drew Tom's keen eye. And within a private space surrounded by iron paling he marveled at the beautiful flowers that were in bloom. The *Camellia japonica,* an import from the Far East, had by the mid–nineteenth century become one of the South's favorite blossoms. Its showy flowers bloomed during the winter months.

It was nearly dark before the two men rolled back into the city with Tom lamenting the fact that he had so little time to admire the roses. Based on the journal entry Tom was manifestly delighted with the excursion, and he was much obliged to Dearing for taking him on the pleasant ride. As a matter of fact, it seems evident that Tom had struck a cordial friendship with the colonel, sharing not only this trip with him but entertaining several previous dinner invitations.

The colonel, a professional solder who had resigned his commission in the U.S. Army upon Georgia's secession from the Union, would resign from the Confederate army in the spring of 1862. Old records and various sources cloak Dearing's resignation with references to dissipation and drunkenness. However, these accusations that accompanied him from his prior U.S. Army service had been absolutely refuted.[145] Nowhere in Tom's diary are there disparaging notes about his commander nor hints or other evidence of a drinking problem. (Surely Tom's temperance leanings would have precluded friendly relations if the rumors about Dearing had been true.)

That night Tom gave billiards another trial but decided to abandon it. Too much time, he decided, would be wasted in becoming proficient at the game.

Tom embarked on the rail cars early in the morning to return to Grahamville station, apparently leaving Lieutenant Colonel Dearing behind for an extended stay with his family. Flying along down the tracks, he strained to get a good look at the rebel troops posted in camps at the northwestern outskirts of Savannah, but the barricade fences were too high and he could only glimpse the tops of the tents.

The swamp bordering the Savannah River crossing impressed Tom as the dreariest-looking place he had ever seen. Along the way he observed thick cane stands and forests full of trees draped with "gloomy" Spanish moss. Cypress groves abounded, and Tom marveled at the sensation that overcame him upon staring out of the train.

1861
<u>Dec. 12 – Thursday</u>
Camp Lee, S.C.

Left Savannah this morning at about seven Oclock
  *Could only get a peep at the Brigade which is encamped on the race Course_ The paling is so high that, from the cars, I could only see the tops of their tents except at one point as we flew along in the cars_*
    *Nothing else attracted my attention much until we entered the apparently interminable swamp on the Savannah River It appeared to me to be the most intensely dreary looking place that I had ever seen_ The cane stands very thick generally among the timber & the timber is laden with gloomy moss_ However, among the tall Cypress trees there was but little if any cane_ & we passed through some extensive groves of them, where they stood very thick & were very tall & straight & as we flew swiftly by they appeared to me moving rapidly around in large circles_ an appearance which I had never before observed to be given to the trees by passing them rapidly either in R.R. cars or on horse back_*

1861
Dec. 12 [continued]

*We soon passed Hardeeville where a Reg^t. or two are stationed_ & then to Grahamville Station & to the encampment about 10 oclock, & found ~~the Sick~~ some of the sick better, & some about as I left them_ a few new cases of measles_ Negroe boy, Uriah among them_ In the evening the Charleston train brought news of a great fire in Charleston but I hope the account is exaggerated_*

Dec. 13 – Friday

*The news of the great fire at Charleston is confirmed, & I now fear that for once the news was not exaggerated_ Maj^r. Rutledge lost some property by the fire_*

The train soon passed Hardeeville on its way to Grahamville station, approximately fifteen miles beyond. Arriving at about 10:00 in the morning, Tom likely checked on the sick in the Grahamville hospitals before making his way down to Camp Lee. He found some of the sick better and some little changed. There were a few new cases of measles including Uriah, his servant—actually a young man of about twenty-six years.

News of a great fire in Charleston reached Camp Lee. On the night of Nov. 11 and during the next day this disastrous fire, the largest ever to affect the city, swept the business district east of King Street and near the Cooper River. Aided by a stiff breeze, it destroyed a sizeable segment of the city.[146]

Days later one contemporary publication printed: "[T]he conflagration assumed a formidable character, nearly equaling the most extensive conflagration on the American continent."[147] Heaped upon the effects of the blockade and with the threat of Yankee invasions imminent from Port Royal and Savannah, this catastrophe in the spiritual center of the South came as a significant blow to the South.[148]

The family of Maj. Henry Middleton Rutledge owned a house on Tradd Street in Charleston, and it was lost in the inferno.[149] The young officer himself had inherited from his grandmother the magnificent rice-growing Hampton Plantation located north of Charleston near the banks of the South Santee River.

Thirty-five of the Haywood Highlanders were counted sick on this day, and still among them was Tom's servant, Uriah. The rest of the company's men were occupied with picks and shovels fortifying their position as per General Lee's orders. About fifty of the mountain boys were detailed to work on new breastworks east of camp and down the road in the direction of Beaufort. These defenses were certainly devised to protect against stealthy enemy movements and assaults originating from the Broad River with its numerous potential landing points such as Boyd's and Tenny's landings.

Tom's naturalist instincts were piqued by a large black fox squirrel that he saw, probably among the tall pine trees surrounding the camp. He notes that it was entirely black with the exception of a small white spot on its nose.

Pvt. Perry Franklin's condition had worsened, Tom noted, and he went on to state that the private would not be able to head home soon. The illness is not identified here nor elsewhere in the diary, but the Confederate records show that Franklin was discharged from the army on Jan. 20, 1862, by reason of disability. Later in the war he would join the 62nd Regiment N.C. Troops for a brief period before being discharged again for sickness.

1861
<u>*Dec. 14 – Saturday*</u>
Camp Lee

Thirty five sick in Co. F. besides negroe Uriah
*Nothing of much interest to record today_*
About fifty men were detailed today & put to [work] *throwing up breatworks about* [?] *miles down the road towards Beaufort_*
*Saw a large fox squirrel today entirely black excepting a small white spot on his nose They are said to be numerous about here, & get fat on on the pine seed_*
Bought two chamber pots today for the use of the sick in Company "F" = 1.00
Perry Franklin is worse & I fear he can't start home soon

1861
Dec. 15 – Sunday
Camp Lee

*Went to Church at 11 Oclock & heard the Rev. M^r. Wigfall I then went to all the Hospitals & found all my men improving that were in Grahamville_ Had a conversation tonight with Co^l. Clingman upon the subject of clothing for N.C. volunteers_ He says that N. Carolina agreed with the Confederate States that She (N.C.) would furnish the clothing for all the troops which She furnishes to The C. States, & C. States agrees to pay N.C. $50.00 per year for each one, & C. S. Government has now sent $25.00 here for each soldier's clothing for first six months_ or thus Co^l. Clingman says that the Quarter Master of this Regt. has now in his hands Twenty six Thousand dollars =$ 26000.00 which was sent to pay N.Carolina for clothing this Reg^t. six months That the State agreed to clothe it one year for $50.00 for each man & that we are now to look entirely to the State alone for clothing & the State now demands that we relinquish all claim on this money before She furnishes us any more clothing_*

Tom attended church service at 11:00 and heard a sermon delivered by the Rev. Arthur Wigfall. By this time he had become well acquainted with the preacher and likely walked over to the Holy Trinity Episcopal Church in Grahamville to attend the morning service (see illustration, p. 148). Afterward he visited his men in the hospitals and found all of them improving somewhat.

That night Tom met with Colonel Clingman, who informed him of an arrangement arrived at between the State of North Carolina and the Confederate States government for clothing the troops. He learned from the colonel that the state had agreed to supply the necessary clothing for all those troops raised and organized in North Carolina. Actually, in late September 1861 the State Legislature directed Adjutant General James G. Martin to provide winter clothing for the state's troops when it became clear that the Confederate army could not meet the demands. General Martin immediately appointed Maj. John Devereaux as chief quartermaster, and Devereaux wasted little time procuring every yard of cloth available to be converted by factories and the women of the state into military garments.[150]

Colonel Clingman informed Tom that the Confederate States agreed to reimburse the state of North Carolina $50.00 per year for every soldier clothed. And in fact the quartermaster of the regiment had received from the Confederate States a payment of $26,000 to cover the cost of clothing for the first six months. The state rightfully lodged a claim for this money, since it had provided uniforms for the regiment, and demanded that Colonel Clingman relinquish the funds.

The staggering sum of $26,000 was delivered to the regiment's assistant quartermaster, Capt. William H. Bryson, by the Confederate States government as a clothing payment for all of the troops. It covered only the first six months and was, therefore, a reimbursement of $25 (one-half of the annual agreed-to amount of $50) for every man in the regiment. It can easily be derived that the payment covered the clothing costs for a total of 1,040 (or thereabouts) soldiers in the 25th Regiment N.C. Troops. All of these men had been provided "some clothing," as Tom put it, by the State of North Carolina. And with the term "some" lay the difficulty.

Apparently Tom, Colonel Clingman, and the other commanders did not believe that all of the men had been equally clothed. A necessary settlement would have to follow once the articles furnished to each man were determined and the price for each piece established. More "troublesome institutions," Tom surely thought, as he and the other commanders of the regiment weighed and sorted through their options to deal with the clothing payments. Colonel Clingman ultimately recommended that the money be relinquished to the state and, as can be seen from Tom's journal entry, a sophisticated accounting system would have to be devised to track the clothing requisitions and reimbursements for each soldier in the regiment. Acting upon the colonel's proposal Tom, and likely all of the company commanders, signed a relinquishment to the state of all monies paid to the companies of the 25th Regiment for clothing.

1861
<u>*Dec. 15*</u> *[continued]*

She has already furnished us some clothing, & consequently there is a settlement pending with Her, but we do not know the price of any of the articles & consequently ~~have but idea~~ *cannot tell how much is yet due to the men in clothing_*

*He recommends that we relinquish the money, make requisitions for such articles only as we need, & then if we do not draw the $50.00 in clothing the state will pay over the balance to the men_*

<u>*Dec. 16 – Monday*</u>
Camp Lee

Signed a relinquishment to the State of all money due from C. States to any Company for clothing, & handed it to Q.M. W^m. Bryson, but made out no requisition, only told him we needed some shoes

1861
Dec. 17 – Tuesday
Camp Lee

*Nothing of much interest to record for today except the death of Jno. Marshall one of the Regimental Color Guard_ He is from Henderson or McDowel County, & is to be sent home for burial_ He belongs to Company A. or the Edney Grays_*

Dec. 18 – Wednesday
Camp Lee

Two Companies B.&C. were sent off this afternoon without tents to some breastworks down toward Port Royal Co^l. Dearing returned from Savannah today bringing me a sword for which I paid $ 35.00 and a belt costing 4.00

Tom wrote of another death in the regiment. Pvt. John H. Marshall from the Edney Grays, or Company A, died from an undisclosed cause, though it is suspected that he succumbed to one of the ubiquitous diseases attacking the young men in camp. The twenty-five-year-old soldier, who was dark-complexioned and unusually tall for the era, standing a full six foot four inches in height, had been chosen by his company brethren to serve in the honorary color guard of the regiment. The color guards bravely carried the flag of the regiment into battle so that the men could form and rally around it and the generals could easily spot the regiment's location on the field. The audacious flag bearers, in addition to the colonels, offered the most conspicuous targets among the throngs of soldiers in the confusion of battle, and consequently suffered an extremely high mortality rate during the Civil War.

Companies B and C were ordered off to man some Confederate breastworks down toward Port Royal Sound. And Lieutenant Colonel Dearing returned from his week-long trip to Savannah, bringing with him a sword that Tom had apparently ordered during his brief stay in the city. The sword and accompanying belt cost $39, which equated to almost one-third of his monthly salary as captain.

Tom was not pleased with the sword that Lieutenant Colonel Dearing had secured for him. He said that it "didn't spring back quite straight when bent" and to one with an eye for perfection and excellence, this flaw or peculiarity was unacceptable. However, Maj. Henry Rutledge found the sword quite satisfactory and bought it from Tom; and it is highly probable that this young major, later elevated to colonel of the regiment, waved Tom's bent sword over his head as he led the men of the 25th Regiment N.C. into the many battles ahead.

Major Rutledge bought the weapon on credit and promised to pay Tom when he next drew his salary. It is enlightening that Tom noted in the diary that Capt. Frederick Blake and others were witness to the transaction. These informal business deals among the men apparently either required a note or verification by eyewitnesses of the oral contract, no matter the station of the individual.

1861
Dec. 18 [continued]

*I did not precisely like the sword & sold it to Major Rutledge at $ 35.00 to be paid when he next draws his wages as Maj^r. _ Capt. Blake & others were present_ I told the Major that my only objection to the sword was that it didn't spring back quite straight when bent_ but he said it was straight enough for him_*

1861
Dec. 19 – Thursday
Camp Lee, S.C.

*We hear today that on yesterday Capt. Moore of Wilmington N.C. with only two of his guns fired upon a Yankee gunboat and killed 25 or 30 without loosing a man_ hope it is so_ We also hear that some of the enemy's gun boats have been running up the Edisto & Stone Rivers The Yankees seem to grow saucy, - but they stick closely to their vessels_ The papers seem to be rejoicing over the prospect of a rupture between England & the Yanks but I have not much hopes of it. About 250 reported sick now, but a great many others are not fit for service_*

Dec. 20 – Friday
Camp Lee S.C.

Nothing of interest for today several companies including Company "F" have been working on the fortifications_ Perry Franklin seems worse

Reports filtered into Camp Lee that Captain Alex D. Moore's battery of the 1st North Carolina Artillery had been put into action the previous day against a Yankee gunboat.[151] Moore's cannon fire, it was claimed, killed twenty-five or thirty Yankees without Moore himself losing a man. The veracity of this news cannot be readily substantiated from existing records. However, as Tom noted, the Yankees were growing bold and adventurous, and their gunboats were increasingly making runs up the numerous rivers leading inland from Port Royal and St. Helena sounds and the large rivers on either end of Edisto Island.

Just two days earlier, on Dec. 17, four enemy vessels crossed the bar and began steaming up the North Edisto River. A small Confederate force of almost three hundred men was forced to evacuate Rockville, midway between Edisto and Kiawah Islands, for fear of being isolated and cut off from their rear.[152]

On the same day and nearer to where the Haywood Highlanders were stationed a Union force crossed the Coosaw River to Chisolm's Island, just north of Beaufort, and captured a whole party of Confederate pickets from the 14th Regiment South Carolina Volunteers.[153] No Union casualties were reported, thus it is unlikely that this skirmish was the one that provoked the fire from Captain Moore's battery.

Still in the news was the ongoing threat that the United States and Britain might go to war over the *Trent* affair, but Tom's instincts led him to believe that it would not come to that. The number of sick men from the ranks stood at 250, a significant number but down somewhat from the peak reached ten days prior.

The Haywood Highlanders spent the day working on General Lee's fortifications.

Just yesterday an ailing Pvt. Perry Franklin appeared to be doing worse in Tom's opinion; however, on this day he seemed to be faring a little better, as did the other sick men. A young sergeant in the Haywood Highlanders, eighteen-year-old Garland S. Ferguson, was stricken with what Tom thought to be a "plainly marked" case of measles. The boy's eyes and the eruptions all over his body were symptomatic of the contagious viral disease. Although Ferguson had suffered through a severe case of measles a few years earlier, Tom's intuition and the many occurrences of the disease that he had witnessed over the past months led him to diagnose this as an unusual second attack.

Lieutenant Colonel Dearing apparently was able to secure for Tom a more suitable sword than the first, and Tom promptly paid him for it.

Tom had previously received word from his brother Walter that he was coming to Grahamville and would muster in with the Haywood Highlanders. From the conclusion of the captain's daily entry it is manifest that not only was he anxiously anticipating Walter's arrival, but he was bitterly disappointed in not receiving a letter from his wife, Lizzie.

1861
Dec. 21 – Saturday
Camp Lee

*Perry Franklin is thought to be a little better today & also most of the others sick_*
*Garland S. Ferguson seems to have measles_ his eyes & the eruption all over him seem to show it be a plainly marked case, & yet he had it severely 4 or 5 years ago_ This is evidently a second attack, but a light one_*
*I am to be Officer of the Day tomorrow and must go to bed_*
Paid Co^l. Dearing for sword which I ordered from Savannah & which came today $ 35.00 in Capt. Francis' Tent
*No letter from Lizzie_*
I suppose W.W. Lenoir will come tomorrow

1861
Dec. 22 – Sunday
Camp Lee

*Officer of the Day today Several of the companies were out of wood today Cut & hauled some, I carried some, & carried some on their shoulder Walter W. Lenoir did not arrive_ Borrowed a horse & sent J. W. Norwood to the Depot to meet him_*

Dec. 23 – Monday
Camp Lee

*Another death today Samuel Tucker one of Capt. Johnston's men_ He died in Grahamville, (I believe) from a relaps after having measles_*

As officer of the day Tom helped the men from various companies in the regiment gather wood for the camp fires. Though a captain and slaveowner and a man plagued with a chronic back ailment, he was not above shouldering and carrying the wood himself.

Tom borrowed a horse and sent Pvt. John Wall Norwood of Company C to Grahamville Station to meet his brother Walter. Norwood was the son of James H. Norwood of Waynesville, North Carolina, who had been a distant relative and friend of Tom's before losing his life in 1852 on the western frontier while working as an Indian agent. The young Norwood would have been able to recognize Walter, and for that likely reason drew the assignment to retrieve him. The eighteen-year-old Norwood, whose sister later married Garland Ferguson of the Haywood Highlanders, would sadly lose his life at the Battle of Fredericksburg in December 1862.[154]

Alas, Tom's brother did not arrive on any of the trains passing through Grahamville on this day and, as it came to pass, did not reach Camp Lee until after the new year was rung in.

Another man from the regiment's Company E died in Grahamville this day. Nineteen-year-old Pvt. Samuel Tucker from the newly formed North Carolina county of Transylvania died from "disease," as reported in the Confederate records. Tom's note, however, reveals even more information and indicates a belief that the young soldier died from a relapse of measles.

Two other men died the previous night, in addition to Private Tucker: privates Andrew J. Wilson of Company B and Wiley Duncan of Company K. All three men were presumed to have expired from pneumonia after having the measles.

Captain Lenoir and the Haywood Highlanders participated in a battalion drill somewhere west of Grahamville from Camp Lee. As Tom returned through Grahamville he looked in on his men in the hospitals there and found "poor" Amos Reece very low. The doctors thought it unlikely that the young man would live to see "the morning again on the earth."

Tom records that Pvt. Perry Franklin and Cpl. John Burnett had recovered somewhat, and is surprised that Pvt. James Henderson had come down with the measles.

1861
Dec. 24 – Tuesday
Camp Lee

Two men (beside Tucker)
died last night but I didn't
hear of it until this morning
Three in less than 24 hours !!
all from something like
pneumonia after having measles
The other two were
A.J. Wilson of T.D. Bryson's Co.
& _____ Duncan of Capt. Robert's Co.
Went to Batallion drill
& as we returned through
Grahamville stopped to see
the sick_ Poor Amos Reece
is very low & the Doctors think
that he will hardly see
the morning again on The Earth.
Perry Franklin & John Burnett
*both seem a little better_*
   Was surprised to find
James Henderson with Measles
But he still seems to be improving

1861
Dec. 25 – Wednesday
Camp Lee

*Amos Reece died last night about one Oclock We will try to send him home_ No tin to be had in Savannah_*

Dec. 26 – Thursday
Camp Lee, S.C.

Had coffin made for Reece & coal burnt to pack around it, & a large box to contain The coal & coffin_ The work was superintended by Lieu^t. E. H. Blalock & [?] (I was sent by Co^l. Clingman to superintend the construction of some fortifications about 1¼ miles N.E. of the encampment) Lieu^t. Blalock informs me that A. Reece was laid in his coffin with a new blanket wrapped around him, with his uniform pants & coat on, & then a few ^{lbs} of cotton put in to fill up the coffin_ The bottom of the large box was then covered with charcoal beaten fine & packed

The doctor's worries proved accurate. Pvt. Amos M. Reece, a Haywood Highlander, died of pneumonia around 1:00 on Christmas morning. Only twenty years old, he hailed from the East Fork of Pigeon area, where Tom maintained his farming enterprise. Interestingly, when Tom first settled in the East Fork region more than a decade earlier, his father had warned him about David Reece, Amos' father, who was a tenant farmer on the Lenoir lands. He wrote that the elder Reece was "malicious and lazy" and not above killing and maiming a man's stock out of spite.[155] Now Tom was only concerned with giving the remains of young Reece due care and respect and getting them back to the family as soon as possible; but there was no tin to be found in Savannah with which to seal the body.

Tom was sent by Colonel Clingman to direct the pick-and-shovel work on fortifications being constructed a little more than a mile northeast of Camp Lee, which was nearly opposite Boyd's Landing. He left Lt. Etheldred Blalock in charge of constructing a coffin and large box for Private Reece's remains. Not only had Blalock been a carpenter and mechanic back at Forks of Pigeon previous to the war, he had even constructed a water-powered mill for Col. Joseph Cathey. The great pains, labor, and respect that Blalock and the Haywood Highlanders gave to the job of preparing Reece's remains for shipment to Haywood is abundantly clear. The body was clothed in his uniform, shrouded with a new blanket, and then carefully placed in a coffin which in turn was placed into the large box. The bottom of the box was covered in charcoal that had been pulverized to absorb odor and moisture.

Again on this day Captain Lenoir was sent by Colonel Clingman back to the fortifications to direct the ongoing construction work. While he was occupied in this endeavor the Haywood Highlanders and Company B escorted the bodies of Reece, Wilson, and Duncan to Grahamville and sent them back to the mountains to their families. Jesse McMinn of Henderson County was entrusted to accompany the bodies and see that they reached their proper destinations. It is not known whether this man was Pvt. James N. McMinn of Company A or simply a civilian from Henderson who was visiting the troops at the time. In any case McMinn was instructed to take the body of Reece to Asheville, and if no one was there to receive it then carry it on to Haywood.

To defray expenses along the way Sgt. Joseph Turner Cathey handed over to McMinn $64. This sum of money was made up from part of a death fund the boys had contributed to as well as the $12.75 that Reece had in his pocketbook when he died. Clear instructions were given to McMinn to pay over any remaining funds to Col. Cathey at Forks of Pigeon, who would ensure that the money was returned to the boys at Camp Lee.

1861
Dec. 27 – Friday
Camp Lee

*I was sent back to superintend the work on the fortifications_ Company F. & Company B. went out to the R.R. Depot to carry the bodies of A. Reece, A.J. Wilson & ___ Duncan The other corpse Saml. Tucker was sent yesterday_*

*The three that were started today were put under the care of Jesse McMinn of Henderson Co. who promised to take the body of Reece to Asheville & if necessary to Haywood_ Sixty four dollars (64.00) were handed to him by J. T. Cathey to defray expenses, which $ 64.00 was a part a fund of $101.75 one hundred & one dollars & 75cts raised by adding to the $ 12.75 which was found in his pocket book_*

The sum of Eighty nine dollars which was subscribed & paid in by the Company with the understanding that the surplus after defraying all the expenses of his burial should belong to the subscribers in proportion to the amount paid in by ~~him~~ each _ I paid into that fund -- $ 5.00 & also the $ 12.75 left by A. Reece_ Others subscribed but have not paid up_ The amount will reach (=$ 105.75)

1861
<u>*Dec. 27*</u> [continued]

*So there is now left of said fund in the hands of J.T.Cathey $37.75 & M^c.Minn promised to pay over to Co^l. C. whatever may be left in his hands to be returned to the Company_*

<u>*Dec. 28 – Saturday*</u>
Camp Lee

Spent a part of this day at the breastworks, staking off & directing_ Most of the embankments are quite light & only intended to protect our men against small arms_ The bank of sand is four feet & 9 inches high about two feet wide at top & on a base of seven & a half feet, kept perpendicular on the inside by a wall of logs or poles, & sloped on the side next the enemy, to the edge of the ditch which is seven feet & a half wide, and only deep enough to afford sand for the wall____

Tom continued to apply his attention and energies to the defense works east of camp. His responsibility was to stake off the construction and then superintend the work to make certain that it was structurally stable and could offer adequate protection for the men against enemy small arms and cannon fire. Tom' detailed journal entry fully describes the geometry and measures that were adhered to in building the fortifications. These specifications can be seen in the diagram on page 149.

Captain Lenoir's directions for constructing the embankments ran counter to Colonel Clingman's careful explanations for carrying out the work. Although the colonel had pursued a scientific career in addition to politics prior to the war, Tom found that his mathematical dimensions for constructing the embankments would not work. The base of Clingman's berm was not sufficiently wide relative to the height for the sand to lie in a stable repose. In order to gain a secure embankment Tom had to widen Clingman's suggested base width by fifty percent.

And it is apparent that the regiment's troops had not been toiling alone at the defense works. Tom's diary entry indicates that Negro slaves (almost certainly impressed from the surrounding plantations) had been employed to labor alongside the rebel soldiers. The English-based creole spoken by the slaves so amused Tom, and seemingly differed so much from the colloquial speech of his own slaves at the East Fork farm, that he recorded some of their expressions, such as "wid we" and "bring we." In fact the rich patois was Gullah, which incorporated words and structures borrowed from the West African languages and heritage of the men and women bonded into servitude in the Carolina lowcountry.

Moreover, Tom got another lesson from the slaves on preparing and using the Spanish moss that grew and hung in such profusion from the lowland trees. The black moss, as they called it, was cured by scalding it and burying it for a few weeks. After preparation in this manner, it had many uses in those days, including being woven into black saddle blankets. Tom had seen such blankets in his Haywood mountains, where they were referred to as rugs.

1861
Dec. 28 [continued]

These proportions make the sloped side about as steep as the sand will lie (all sand) but Co^l. Clingman directed me to have it built 4 feet 9 in & two feet on top upon a base of 5 feet, but I found that those proportions would not do, & had it constructed on a base of 7 feet 6 in___

I was much amused at some of the expressions of the negroes — such as wid we, bring we etc.

Made another discovery concerning the long moss_ Some of the black saddle blankets which I have seen among the mountains (called rugs) are made of it

*The negroes called it black moss but it is the common long moss prepared by scalding or burying if for a few weeks, & I suppose the bark is destroyed, & the inner & tough part left_ Bunches of it may be found hanging about in the woods quite black, but not quite so tough as that which is properly prepared_*

1861
Dec. 29 – Sunday
Camp Lee, S.C.

*Was not very well this morning_ Attended to Sunday inspection_ (Made out duplicate inventories of the effects left by Amos Reece & handed them over to the Adj^t. one is to be kept by him & the other to be sent to Adj^t. Genl. Looked over his love letters & tore off the names of the Girls_ & put them with his little pocket book comb etc. to be sent to his Father Wrote to Mason Morfit at Weldon inclosing him a transportation ticket for Tilman Bugg & requested him to answer soon, & send him along_ I directed to Mason Morfit Acting Transp. Ag^t. C.S.A_*

Dec. 30 – Monday
Camp Lee, S.C.

Rec^d. a letter tonight from M^r. Garrett asking me to send a name for his boy, & I have just answered it suggesting Roscoe_ I also asked him to sell 4 mules for me at any price which might think proper

Although feeling unwell Tom attended Sunday dress inspection and then sat down to tediously record in duplicate an inventory of the effects of Amos Reece. These papers were handed over to the regiment's adjutant, 2nd Lt. Wesley Freeman, who would keep one and pass the other up to the adjutant general's staff.

Young Reece was not married, but he apparently corresponded with more than one girl back home at Forks of Pigeon. After reviewing the love letters Tom thought it wise to remove identifying information before sending them along to Reece's father with other personal items.

Pvt. Henry Tilman Bugg had been convalescing at Wilmington ever since being left there on Nov. 5, when the regiment was rushed to South Carolina, or so Tom thought. The captain wanted him back in the ranks as soon as possible and wrote to the Confederate acting transportation agent at Weldon, North Carolina, asking him to send Bugg to join his company at the front.

Tom received a letter from his father-in-law in Haywood County requesting that he suggest a name for the man's newborn son, Lizzie's younger sibling. William Greene Berry Garrett was not only Lizzie's father but also a longtime friend of Tom's. Before the war Garrett had been a strong Union man; he had voted against secession at both 1861 elections held to determine North Carolina's position on the matter.[156] The name "Roscoe" struck Tom as a good one for a boy and he responded with that idea to Garrett, along with a request to handle the sale of four of his mules. Apparently Garrett was not as partial to the name "Roscoe" as was Tom, however, since none of his later offspring were so named.

In an old field beyond Grahamville Colonel Clingman inspected the troops of the 25th Regiment N.C.. Tom thought the inspection came off tolerably well and commented that there were a good many ladies there observing—a common custom during the war. He also noted that all of the sick men in the encampment and hospitals were inspected.

If Tom paused on this last day of the year to look backward, there would have been many historical occurrences and life-changing events to reflect upon. He had witnessed the breakup of his country and secession of his native state in the spring, married Lizzie Garrett in June, and marched off to the Civil War in July. The entire latter half of the year was consumed for him in learning the rudiments of making war and leading his band of mountaineer warriors. As of the year's end Tom and his Haywood Highlanders had not engaged the enemy in hostile action but were surely desperate to do so. Thus far the only enemy they had battled was sickness, and it had taken a mighty toll from the company and the regiment. As Tom so eloquently put it: "The old year is gone, and has carried many brave hearts with it."

1861
Dec. 31 – Tuesday
Camp Lee

The usual Monthly inspection by the Co^l. today in an old field beyond Grahamville
  It went off tolerably well a good many Ladies were there
   The sick were inspected some in the encampment & some in the Hospitals
    *The old year is gone, & has carried many brave hearts with it_*

Grahamville's Holy Trinity Episcopal Church opened its doors for worship to the men of the 25th Regiment North Carolina Troops while they were garrisoned at Camp Lee. The building, which still stands today, was completed in 1859 and escaped destruction in 1864 when Union forces torched the rest of the village. *From the Colcock-Hutson Collection, University of South Carolina Law Library, http://law.sc.edu/colcock-hutson/the_places/grahamville.shtml*

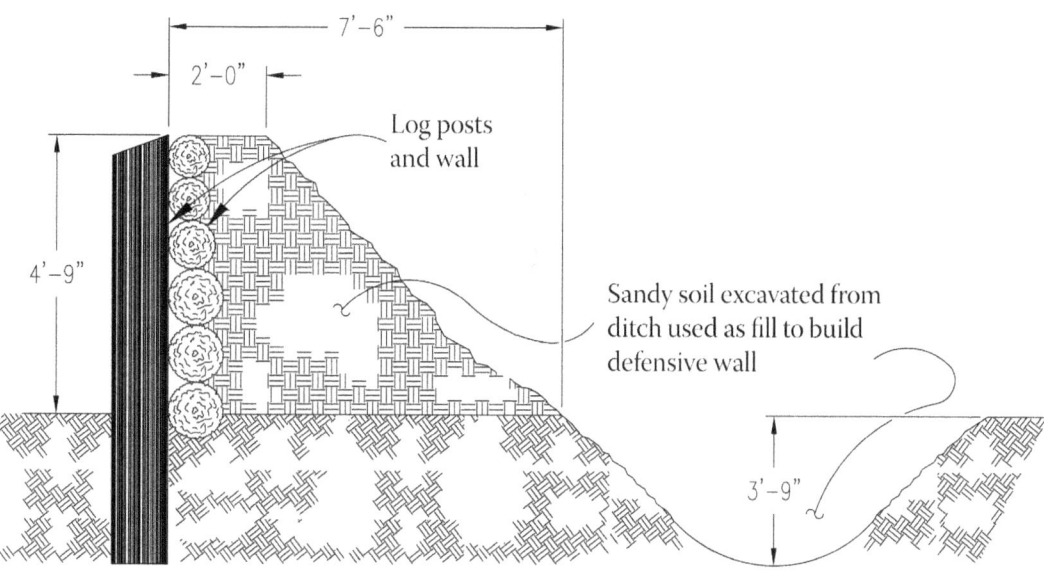

In his diary, Capt. Thomas I. Lenoir described with meticulous detail how the rebel troops at Grahamville's Camp Lee constructed earthworks from which to defend against Union incursions and attacks against the Charleston & Savannah Railroad. Evidence of the defensive fortifications can still be seen today at the site of the Battle of Honey Hill. *Diagram by Alan Neubauer.*

"Rebs Foraging," sketch by Alfred Rudolf Waud. *Library of Congress, Prints and Photographs Division.*

January 1862

The Haywood Highlanders rang in the new year by being posted on guard duty watching for enemy forays from the Broad River. Captain Lenoir had appointed Lt. Etheldred Blalock to carry out the officer-of-the-day duties for the 25th North Carolina Troops while he filled out muster rolls.

Tom was apparently rousted from the drudgery of his paperwork with an invitation to dine with his colonels. He readily accepted this invitation, although he would later come to regret it. Included among the afternoon dining party were Reverend Wigfall, colonels Clingman and Dearing, and probably Major Rutledge. In spite of Tom's strong objections to having a glass of wine that afternoon, it is apparent that Colonel Clingman was insistent that his captain take a glass. And Tom gave in to this undue pressure so as not to be thought "singular" by the others.

That night when he came down with another one of his severe headaches he attributed it to the small amount of wine that he had imbibed. In Tom's opinion the colonel was entirely out of line in insisting on overriding a guest's wishes in the matter.

1862
<u>Jan. 1 – Wednesday</u>
Camp Lee, S.C.

*Company F was on guard duty_ Lieut. Blalock acted as Officer of the Day & I worked at muster rolls_*
At 3 Oclock took dinner with our Cols & the Revd. Mr. Wigfall_ And in order to prevent being though[t] singular I allowed myself to be persuaded to take half of a very small glass of wine, & I now have headache which I attribute to that _
I never thought it true hospitality to <u>insist</u> on a Guest to eat or drink any thing contrary to his wishes He should be allowed to judge & choose for himself after being informed of the nature & composition of the ~~drink~~ (drink or food)
But Col. C. seems firmly convinced that stimulants would be beneficial to me, but I am convinced to the contrary

1862
Jan. 2 – Thursday
Camp Lee, S.C.

*Have finished those troublesome muster & pay rolls They are both together this time_ One is to be sent to Richmond, two to be furnished to the Paymaster, & one to be kept with the Company papers_ The pay roll is to be cut off of the one sent to Adj^t. Genl. at Richmond_ I suffered much with a severe head ache last night & have been unwell all day today, & have now come to the conclusion that I am taking a second attack of measles More than a dozen men in Company F & a great many in the Regiment have had what appears to be a second attack of measles_ The pneumonitory symptons and the eruption following them appears to be precisely similar except that they are much milder & very few of the men have been <u>laid up</u> by it, Yet some of them were quite unwell for several days & one told me that he thought his second attack worse than the first_ None who have had measles recently have this disease which is strong evidence to my mind that it is measles_ Not withstanding the Doctors say that ~~there~~ no man ever had measles twice_*

The captain worked on and completed the company muster and pay rolls. He still complained about how annoying these tasks were, but at least this time he was able to reconcile the two. And he complains of another severe headache during the previous night. Feeling unwell throughout the day to boot, Tom finally diagnosed that he must have come down with a repeat case of measles. Moreover, he determined that many more in Company F, and the rest of the regiment, were suffering from a second attack of measles as well. These conclusions were reached notwithstanding the fact that the doctors tending to the regiment's sick men assured him it was not possible to contract the disease twice. However, the evidence led Tom to believe otherwise.

The engagement between "our folk and the Yanks" referenced in this day's diary entry occurred the day before, on Jan. 1, when a Union force of approximately three thousand men, protected by their gunboats, crossed the Coosaw River north of Beaufort and landed near Port Royal Ferry, 12 to 15 miles from Colonel Clingman's defenses. The 14th South Carolina Volunteers under the command of Col. James Jones were manning the fortifications at the ferry and offered stubborn resistance under the duress of a severe shelling from three Federal gunboats on the river. The Confederate troops eventually evacuated the earthworks at Port Royal Ferry, leaving behind a twelve-pounder iron cannon. They hurriedly established a new defense line further inland toward Garden's Corner. The records of this skirmish list the casualty estimates at two Union soldiers killed and twelve wounded, compared to eight Confederates killed and twenty-four wounded.[157]

Tom's anxious anticipation of the arrival of his brother from Caldwell County ended on this evening. Walter arrived on the train eager to join the Haywood Highlanders as an independent, armed, and equipped soldier serving at his own expense. This willingness to "fight for nothing," as Tom put it, was certainly not a common undertaking, but men of wealth and means were apt to serve in this manner to demonstrate their devotion and support for the Southern cause.

1862
Jan. 2 [continued]

The same Doctors say that there is no such disease as milk sickness, & that such cases as are so called, are generally typhoid fever cases_ & yet the Mountain people say that a great many typhoid fever cases, are really cases of milk sickness

We hear tonight of an engagement between our folk & the Yanks some 12 or 15 miles from us but which we lost about 15 men but have not heard particulars

Moore's battery from Wilmington & Co^l. Jones' Reg^t. S.C. and a Ten. Reg^t. under Co^l. Jones were said to have been in the action

Jan. 3 – Friday
Camp Lee

Walter W. Lenoir arrived here this evening directly from Caldwell_ He comes to join my Company as an independent armed & equipped at his own expense_ expects to feed himself & fight for nothing__

1862
Jan. 4 – Saturday
Camp Lee, S.C.

*Nothing of importance to record for today_ Co^l. Clingman gave W. W. Lenoir permission in writing to pass the guard lines until further ordered_*

Jan. 5 – Sunday
Camp Lee

*W.W. & myself dined with our two Co^{ls}. today They both appeared to be in a fine humor & we were very agreeably enter-
=tained both by their conversation & <u>turkey</u> _*

Jan. 6 – Monday
Camp Lee

*Nothing of importance for today_*

From the scant reports in Tom's diary the next several days were evidently devoid of significant military activities. It surely was a period when the two Lenoir brothers renewed brotherly bonds, exchanged news of a personal nature, and simply caught up with the events in each other's lives. And Tom would have spent a good deal of this time assimilating Walter into army ways and introducing him to the men of the company, other company commanders, and the field and staff of the regiment. Walter was about to make the sudden and sobering transition from a civilian gentleman's standard of living to the Spartan, rustic existence of a private soldier in the Confederate army.

There are no records that can be found, however, which indicate that Walter officially mustered into service with the Haywood Highlanders. He simply walked through the guard lines of Camp Lee, with Colonel Clingman's explicit permission in writing, and commenced to live and work as a Confederate soldier serving with Tom's Haywood Highlanders. Walter wrote in own diary, "I attached myself as an independent to the company of which my brother .... is capt." He went on to explain what this independence meant: "I furnish my own army outfit and rations, and expect to do duty as a private."[158]

But before beginning his new lifestyle and service in the Confederate army Walter was invited, along with Tom, to dine with Colonel Clingman and Lieutenant Colonel Dearing. From Tom's journal entry it is obvious that the two colonels were in a "fine humor" and thoroughly entertained the Lenoir brothers with not only their lively and intelligent conversation but with an offering of turkey as well.

Sounds of cannon fire from the east and southeast wafted back to Camp Lee throughout the day and into the evening. No evidence can be found in the records of this action, but the Confederate cavalry pickets apparently brought back some spent shells as proof to show the boys.

On this same day, Jan. 8, General Lee, who was in Savannah inspecting the work on the defenses, wrote to the adjutant and inspector general in Richmond and reported on the state of affairs along the coastline between Charleston and Savannah. Lee summarized his thoughts on the enemy's next probable course of action: "I have thought his purpose would be to seize upon the Charleston and Savannah Railroad near the head of the Broad River, sever the line of communication between those two cities with one of his columns of land troops, and with his other two and his fleet by water envelop alternately each of those cities."[159] This statement clearly demonstrates that General Lee remained convinced of the likelihood of a Federal attack against the critical railroad in the low-lying country in front of Grahamville or Coosawhatchie. And, of course, prepared and still poised near the head of the Broad River for that anticipated Yankee thrust were the 25th N.C. Troops.

Tom was overjoyed to receive three boxes packed full of clothes and food and many things he "had been wishing for." Two of the boxes had been sent from Fort Defiance by his mother and his wife, Lizzie, to whom he whimsically refers as "Mrs. M. E. [Mary Elizabeth] Lenoir."

1862
Jan. 7 – Tuesday
Camp Lee, S.C.

Nothing of importance

Jan. 8 – Wednesday
Camp Lee

Heard some cannons early in the morning & frequently all through the day about East of us_ Home Cavalry pickets have come in tonight & brought some shells which they say were fired at them today near Palmetto Island

  Since dark tonight we have heard a good deal of cannonading about S.East.

  *Rec^d. three boxes today from Two from Fort Defiance & one from Tucker's Barn_*
They contained many things which I had been wishing for & among them a p^r. of nice gray pants made by M^{rs}. M. E. Lenoir, of homemade jeans, & also a coat pattern of the same sent by my Dear Mother__
Two p^r. drawers & two shirts all of homemade linsey <u>very nice</u>

1862
Jan. 8 [continued]

The little box from Tuckers Barn contained dried peaches dried apples, & some nice little apples called Hall's Seeding (one of J.C.N's favorites) cakes pickles, blackberry wine etc.

Jan. 9 – Thursday
Camp Lee, S.C.

Nothing of interest for today except the ball given by the officers of the 25th to the Ladies of Grahamville as a kind of expression of thanks for their kindness to our sick men_ I am sick myself tonight & could not go, but paid ten dollars (10.00) towards paying the expenses of it_ W.W. Lenoir went_ A band of musicians from Savannah are in attendance & a cook from Savannah was also sent for & I suppose he came_ W.W. went dressed entirely in homemade goods

It is noted that one of the three boxes Tom received from Caldwell County was from Tucker's Barn. Tucker's was the original name of the community which became Caldwell's seat of government when the county was formed in 1841. The new county seat was given the name of "Lenoir" in honor of Tom's grandfather, Gen. William Lenoir.[160] As can be seen, however, Tom was still accustomed to referring to the settlement as Tucker's Barn. The crate was packed with fruit and included apples of a variety named Hall's Seeding that were a favorite of Tom's brother-in-law, Joseph Caldwell Norwood. Interestingly, Tom's benefactors thought he might be in need of some blackberry wine, which might seem a little odd after the regrettable wine affair with his colonels on New Year's Day. Yet, Tom was not averse to taking a drink every now and then; he just believed it should be done in moderation.

The officers of the 25th N.C. Troops organized and gave a ball for the ladies of Grahamville. It was their way of expressing thanks to the local women for the assistance and kindness they had bestowed to the regiment's sick men. Tom contributed ten dollars toward the expenses of the gala but did not go due to his not feeling well. However, Walter was able to attend the event and Tom noted—proudly it seems—that his brother was clothed from head to toe entirely in homespun "goods."

Dr. Solomon Satchwell's diagnosis for the illness which had attacked many men in the regiment, including Tom, was "Bastard" measles. The captain's earlier amateur observations and opinion turned out to be reasonably accurate. Bastard measles, or rubella, was a contagion which presented similar symptoms as measles but was much less serious, running its course in approximately seven days.[161] Perhaps tongue in cheek, Tom considered the ailment to be not as bad as "legitimate" measles.

The ladies' ball on the prior evening had apparently gone off well, but Tom notes with chagrin that some of the "small" officers drank a little too much, or "got rather tight," as he put it. It is presumed that he was referring to the company officers below his own captain's rank and perhaps one or more minor regimental staff members.

William Welch from Haywood County had made the long trek from Waynesville to South Carolina's coast to pay a visit to his kith and his son, 1st Lt. William Pink Welch of Company C. The elder Welch had played an important role in making Haywood and served terms as a state senator and many years as clerk of court. He was also a merchant in Waynesville as well as a successful farmer, and Tom thought him sufficiently distinguished to attach the term "Esquire" after his name.[162] The son, Lieutenant Welch, eventually distinguished himself in the defense of the Southern cause. He served honorably and with excellence in the 25th Regiment N.C. Troops and later with the Second Regiment Engineer Troops, C.S.A.[163] Upon the conclusion of the war in 1871 William Pink Welch married Sarah Lucinda Cathey of Forks of Pigeon, the daughter of Col. Joseph Cathey.[164]

1862
Jan. 10 – Friday
Camp Lee, S.C.

*Still unwell with (what D^r. Satchwell calls) bastard measles_ Rather a sorry disease, but not so bad as the legitimate measles_*

*I am told that some of our small Officers got rather tight last night_*

Jan. 11 – Saturday
Camp Lee

*Wm Welch Esq. from Haywood Co. N.C. arrived this evening_*

*W.W. Lenoir went hunting with Maj^r. Rutledge_ Killed one Snipe & 1 Lark_*

1862
Jan. 12 – Sunday
Camp Lee, S.C.

M^r. Patterson a Baptist preached in the encampment today He is from Buncombe N.C. After dinner went to Grahamville to see our sick_ They all seem better_ Genl. Pemberton was here at Dress parade this evening_ I did not get a good look at him He is a small man_ with very dark beard, I did not see him with his hat off_ I wrote to Lizzie tonight & it is now near 11 Oclock & I must to bed__

A Baptist preacher from Buncombe County, Mr. Patterson, provided the spiritual uplift that the soldiers attending his Sunday service in Camp Lee sought. After that was over and Tom had taken his dinner he visited the sick in Grahamville's hospitals. Likely just recovering from the effects of rubella himself, Tom as always remained concerned for his men and extremely vigilant of their welfare.

At the evening dress parade the commander of the Fourth Military District of South Carolina reviewed Colonel Clingman's 25th North Carolina Troops. Although Tom did not get a good look at Brig. Gen. John C. Pemberton (who would be promoted to major general in a couple of days and later to lieutenant general), he wrote that the man was small and wore a very dark beard. General Pemberton was a northerner by birth and a southerner by choice and would later gain a great deal of notoriety while commanding and surrendering the besieged Confederate forces at Vicksburg, Mississippi, in 1863.[165]

Most of Tom's concerns over the ensuing couple of days appear to have been for the distribution of winter overcoats to his men. Eighty-eight Haywood Highlanders (all but two of the enlisted men) decided to take the overcoats supplied to them by the State of North Carolina. Implicit with their decision to take the coats was that the temperature along the Southern coast was sufficiently cold that they were needed; and the mountaineers did not have adequate outerwear to stay warm.

A committee (of unknown makeup) established that the average value for the overcoats was $12, which would be counted against each man's annual allotment of $50 for clothes. It is obvious that the coats were not of equal quality, and the men of Company F contrived a means to balance the benefits. When they next drew their pay, including a clothes allowance, those fortunate soldiers who had received the finest overcoats would pay the difference to the ones who had received the lower-quality ones. The manner in which the prices of each coat were determined and the difference calculated, accounted for, and paid is left unsaid; these troublesome issues surely compounded the administrative burdens of the officers of the Haywood Highlanders.

The diary entries detailing the specifics of the overcoat business demonstrate that there were only ninety enlisted men in Company F. Adding Tom and his three lieutenants and excluding Walter Lenoir, the total number of mountaineers counted on the company's muster roll during those early days of 1862 totaled just ninety-four.

1862
Jan. 13 – Monday
Camp Lee, S.C.

Alfred Burnett this day paid me 70 cents which I told him would settle in full an old Book Account which he owes me of 76 cts
　　*Eighty eight of the comp^y. this day decided to take the overcoats & I this evening received two boxes containing the 88 over coats_*

Jan. 14 – Tuesday
Camp Lee

Nothing of importance excepting the distribution of over coats_ 88 were distributed among Company F_ each enlisted man except John Jones & H.T. Bugg got one. The average price put upon them by a Committee was twelve dollars_ And the understanding among them was that the price should be equalized when they next drew their pay, by those who got the finest coats paying the difference to them who got the lower priced.

1862
Jan. 15 – Wednesday
Camp Lee, S.C.

*Rained a little today James Nichols settled a little debt of 3.00 by a note on Henry J. Sorrels for $ 2.50 and fifty cents in cash_*

Drew stationary today for the first time drew 5 [quires] paper, 12 pens 12 envelops, ½ oz. wafers 2 sticks sealing wax_ a little twine (not a ball) 1 small bottle (or vial) ink 1 stamp, 1 wafer box, 1 pencil 1 paper folder__ and gave duplicate requisitions & receipts

Jan. 16 – Thursday
Camp Lee

I don't remember any thing of interest today

Tom's diary accounts for this day and the next are indicative of the inactive service the Haywood Highlanders had fallen into at Camp Lee in midwinter and the continuing lack of military aggressions by the Yankees in the Port Royal area. The only items deemed worthy of jotting down in his diary were the settlement of a debt held over Pvt. James Nichols of Company C and the acquisition of writing supplies, for which he gave duplicate requisitions and receipts.

Brother Walter Lenoir's diary offers a glimpse of the men's daily routine and easy soldier's life: "The soldiers of this regiment are having a very easy time. They have had no fighting to do, are in a healthy & pleasant location & have abundant time to amuse themselves, running, leaping, playing ball, exercising on a pole, throwing heavy weights, & such other athletic sports as they choose to get up. They have even erected a large log house for dancing, and have another, fifty feet by thirty, for the same purpose nearly finished. In one part of the camp is a log house erected for singing, where the sound of sacred music is daily heard. The music like the dancing, is rude and & uncultivated. But both serve to give some variety to the monotonous life of the soldier in camp. The use of ardent spirits is restrained as much as possible by the exertions by the Col. and others of the officers. Card playing is much too common, but I suppose not more than usual in camps."[166]

Colonel Clingman demonstrated his confidence in Tom's capability and judgment by appointing him president of the regiment's court martial, or military court. Also appointed as judges to serve with him were 1st Lt. William Herbert from Company D and 2nd Lt. John Robinson from Company E.

Tom and his fellow officer-jurors convicted two men for passing the guard lines and leaving camp without permission. They also found a third soldier guilty of being absent for about three days. All three were sentenced to be confined under guard and subject to a specified number of days of hard labor. None of the three offenders were attached to the Haywood Highlanders. Electing to do all the writing and recording of the court's findings himself, Tom found the clerical work to be "quite burthensome."

1862
Jan. 17 – Friday
Camp Lee

Acted as President of Reg^t.
Court Martial consisting
of 1st L^t. W^m. H. Herbert &
2nd L^t. John C. Robinson &
myself _____

Jan. 18 – Saturday
Camp Lee

On Court Martial,
again today_ Have had
all the writing to do myself
and find it quite burthensome

Jan. 19 – Sunday
Camp Lee, S.C.

The Court Martial has
been disolved_ Three
prisoners have been tried
*and convicted of offences_*
David Moss of co. "G" of
crossing the guard lines &
being absent without permission
And Ezekiel Kuykendall
of the same offence &
they were sentenced to
to be confined in charge
of the Guard for ten days at hard
*labor_*

1862
Jan. 19 [continued]

*I forget the name of the other prisoner, He was con= =victed of being absent about three days, & sentenced to 15 days hard labor in charge of the guard_ I have had to work hard the greatest part of this day & until ten oclock at night in trying to get discharges, certificates etc. ready for Alfred Burnett & Perry B. Franklin who wish to start tomorrow for their homes in company with Joshua Inman and Eli Deaver & Ths. Franklin Who will carry the remains of ____ Spivey a Corporal of Company "C" He died last night_*

For the greatest part of the day Captain Lenoir worked on the discharge papers for privates Alfred Burnett and Perry B. Franklin, both of whom were being released from the Confederate army due to physical disability. These men wanted badly to get off the next day on their long trip back to the mountains. They were to be accompanied by Pvt. Joshua Inman of Company F; Eli Deaver from Forks of Pigeon, who was the father of Pvt. Rufus L. Deaver of Company C; and Thomas Franklin, the father of Private Franklin.[167] Almost certainly the elder Franklin had heard of his son's pending discharge and had come to Grahamville to provide support and assist in taking his son home.

This small band was also to accompany the remains of Cpl. William M. Spivey of Company C, who had died during the night, back to Haywood. Although the Confederate records state the young twenty-year-old soldier died of an "unreported cause," most assuredly he succumbed to disease.

> Alfred Burnett of Capt. Tho. I. Lenoir's Company "H" of the twenty fifth Regiment of N.C. Volunteers of Confederate States Army was enlisted by Tho. I. Lenoir of 25th Regiment N.C. Vol. in Buncombe County in the State of North Carolina on the 14th day of Augt. 1861 to serve twelve Months. He was born in Buncombe County in the State of North Carolina, is twenty six years of age, five feet & Eight inches high, fair complexion, blue eyes, dark hair, & by ~~profession~~ occupation a farmer when enlisted a farmer.
>
> During the last two Months said soldier has been entirely unfit for duty ~~at least~~ _____ days.
>
> I believe that the disability of said soldier has been caused by an attack of typhoid fever followed by measles, the hay a stupid cough &his nervous system appears to be so much deranged, that I think ~~he~~ ~~kept in~~ (if retained) he will continue to be nothing but an Encumbrance to the service —
>
> Camp Lee near Grahamville S.C.
> Jany 18th 1862
>
> Tho. I. Lenoir
> Capt. 25th Regt. N.C.
> Comdg. Cor "H"

One of the "burthensome institutions" that Captain Tom Lenoir complained about in his diary was the inordinate amount of paperwork the army required him to fill out. In this draft copy of a discharge document for Alfred Burnett, he wrote that the soldier's nervous system had been wrecked by disease. If retained, Captain Lenoir reported, Burnett would continue to be "nothing but an Encumbrance to the service." *Lenoir Family Papers, Southern Historical Collection, Wilson Library, University of North Carolina at Chapel Hill; used by permission.*

1862
Jan. 20 – Monday
Camp Lee

Discharges were signed by Co!. Clingman this morning for Alfred Burnett, & Perry B. Franklin dated today and Alfred Burnett sold his claim to James A. Burnett for $ 29.20 & they both started for Haywood this morning I loaned the money to L^t*. Burnett & took his note & returned four muskets & accoutrements to Ordnance Officer*

Jan. 21 – Tuesday
Camp Lee, S.C.

*Another man of Company "C" died last night his name _____ Stevenson_ I went on duty as Officer of the Day this morning The rain is now (8 oclock) at night falling rapidly_*

Tom's hard work on the previous day preparing discharge papers for privates Burnett and Franklin was rewarded with Colonel Clingman's signature and approval. The discharges that Tom labored to write indicate that Franklin was being released "in consequence of physical disability existing before his enlistment." Burnett, on the other hand, was disabled by what Tom thinks was "an attack of typhoid fever followed by measles." He further recorded on the discharge: "He has a severe cough & his nervous system appears to be much deranged, that I think (if retained) he will continue to be nothing but an Encumbrance to the service."[168]

The two men, along with the other Haywood escorts, left for home as planned with the body of Corporal Spivey. Tom was left with their four muskets and accoutrements to hand over to the company ordnance officer.

Another man from Company C died during the early morning hours of an unreported cause. Eighteen-year-old James H. Stevenson, a private, lost his battle for life at Grahamville before ever having the opportunity to confront the Yankee invaders. He, like Corporal Spivey the previous day and so many others, was surely felled by a contagion.

Although the Jan. 9 gala for the ladies of Grahamville must have gone off quite well, the funds raised by the officers were apparently insufficient to defray the expenses of the party. Lt. John Phinizy of Company G came around soliciting more money to make up the shortfall in the "party matters," and Tom grudgingly contributed another five dollars. He was obviously irritated for having to pay a total of fifteen dollars toward a "frolic" he did not attend nor had expected to.

Tom noted that it was quite a stormy night and expressed a hope that the Yankees at Hatteras were feeling its brunt as well. Undoubtedly, news of Union Gen. Ambrose E. Burnside's expedition against North Carolina had reached Camp Lee. Tom would have learned that a fleet of Yankee vessels of every description sailed into the Cape Hatteras waters on Jan. 13 and had begun a determined struggle against the weather, tides, and outer sand bar at Hatteras Inlet to reach the protected water of Pamlico Sound. What he would not have known was that the expedition's first objective was the capture and occupation of Roanoke Island, and from that lodgment they aimed to initiate operations against New Bern and the coastal railroad infrastructure. Burnside's orders had come down from Gen. George B. McClellan and were devised to work in cooperation with an overall Union strategy to overwhelm the Confederate resistance and defenses and capture Richmond, Virginia, the capital of the Confederacy.

For almost two weeks upon their arrival off Hatteras Inlet the Union fleet was lashed by one storm after another. On Jan. 23, as they waited for the weather to turn and enter Pamlico Sound, one of the men aboard a Union vessel wrote: "[T]he wind blew a perfect hurricane, and caused many vessels to drag anchor and some to break their cables, and so drift down with the tide."[169] It would seem that the Yankees were indeed getting the "full benefit" of the weather, as Tom had wished.

1862
Jan. 22 – Wednesday
Camp Lee

Paid Lt. Phinesy today, $5.00 to help the Committee of arrangements to settle up their Party matters_ I had paid Capt. Walker $10.00 before the party came off_ which makes = $15.00 paid toward a frolic which I did not attend or expect to attend

*Paid today $2.00 to L^t. Freeman to be sent to M^r. Cowper (Private Lee to Genl. Clarke) for commission Settled accounts yesterday with James Cathey & J.T. Cathey & Uriah_*

Jan. 23 – Thursday
Camp Lee

*This is quite a stormy night & we hope that the Yankee fleet at Hatteras are getting the full benefit of it_*

1862
Jan. 24 – Friday
Camp Lee

Made a bedstead for W. W. Lenoir & myself today and will sleep in our new cabin tonight

Jan. 25 – Saturday
Camp Lee, S.C.

This has been a very bright pleasant day sunned bed clothes etc. & made shelves, gun racks etc. etc. for our new cabin

Jan. 26 – Sunday
Camp Lee

*Went to Hospital in forenoon_ W^m. B. Rhodes is quite sick, & talks very wildly_ James Henderson & John Burnett seem to be improving, but slowly_ Had preaching this afternoon here inside the lines & near the Guard Tent by a Young Baptist preacher who read his sermon holding it up all the time_*

Over the past few days it is obvious that Tom and Walter had been busily engaged in constructing more permanent and suitable winter living quarters than the army tents offered. On this day and the next the brothers added the finishing touches to their own log cabin by fashioning a bedstead to sleep in and shelves and gun racks along the walls for organizing and storing their things. Only a few days earlier Walter had written to their brother Rufus about the captain's supervision of the construction details and their chances of moving into the structure: "If we remain here we will soon have a cabin, but Tom is having it built so nicely that I fear we will be moved before it is furnished so that we can get into it."[170]

This certainly was not the only log shelter constructed at Camp Lee. Walter left records of his own that described how the men sang and danced in two log buildings they had raised, "where the sound of sacred music is daily heard." It is fairly obvious that the various company "streets" lining Camp Lee would have included several other such semipermanent structures for living quarters.[171]

Although the epidemic diseases that pervaded Camp Lee throughout November and December of 1861 had subsided to some degree, men were still falling sick and even dying of the scourges. Tom reports that Pvt. William B. Rhodes of his company was very sick and talking wildly. Two other unwell men, privates James Henderson and John Burnett, were slowly improving. The unfortunate Henderson had long been suffering from the effects of typhoid fever, ever since Nov. 24 of the previous year, when his name first appeared in Tom's journal.

This day did not pass without a Sunday religious service in camp. Tom notes that a young Baptist preacher delivered his sermon inside the guard lines. However, the youthful minister's experience level and oratory skills must have been considerably lacking because, as Tom points out, the preacher held the sermon in front of him and read the whole thing.

Tom observed that he had been neglectful of his diary, having failed to record an entry for the past three days. However, he had been very busy, it seems, working with Walter to survey and mark out a connecting road from Camp Lee to the main road linking Grahamville and Coosawhatchie. The new road ran only about a mile or so before intersecting the main road. Such a basic road project would not have taxed the professional skills of the Lenoir brothers, both of whom had been surveyors in their youthful days and had laid out and helped construct more involved turnpike ventures across mountainous terrains. They had learned the surveying profession from their father, Thomas, who had been a land surveyor as was his father before him, Gen. William Lenoir. The only apparent complication that Tom encountered was running with his compass and maintaining a due north heading while suffering the effects of yet another of those "sick" headaches that so afflicted him during his Civil War service.

1862
<u>Jan. 30 – Thursday</u>
Camp Lee, S.C.

*My journal has been neglected I was out today to finish marking out a road from the Camp Lee to the road leading from Grahamville to Coosawhatchie_*
  W. W. Lenoir & myself at the request of Co^l. Clingman ran with a pocket compass & partially marked lately a line running due North from the encampment. It reaches the Coosawhatchie road at about a mile & ¼ I think perhaps only a mile_ & about a half mile west of a breast work which has been lately thrown up across said Coosaw^e. road I suffered a great deal in the afternoon from sick head ache which I suppose was brought on by quitting the use of coffee for 24 hours

1862
Jan. 31 – Friday
Camp Lee

William B. Rhoads died last night a little after midnight, & a Private in Capt. Francis' Compy. died about two hours afterwards_ Both were at The Hospital in Grahamville I have acted as Off. Day today_ We had the usual Monthly inspection

Sadly, another one of Tom's Haywood Highlanders died during the night. Pvt. William B. Rhodes, who had been talking "wildly" a few days before, died from a bout with typhoid fever. And a man from Capt. John Francis' Company D died as well, Tom believed, but he failed to recall the soldier's name.[172]

Opposite: Vicinity of Grahamville, S.C., during the Civil War. The Broad River tentacles leading into Boyd's Neck and Tenny's landings, which the 25th N.C. Troops were ordered to protect, can be seen on this map. The location of Camp Lee as well as the shortcut road that Tom and Walter Lenoir surveyed, northeast of Grahamville, have been added. *Library of Congress, Prints and Photographs Division.*

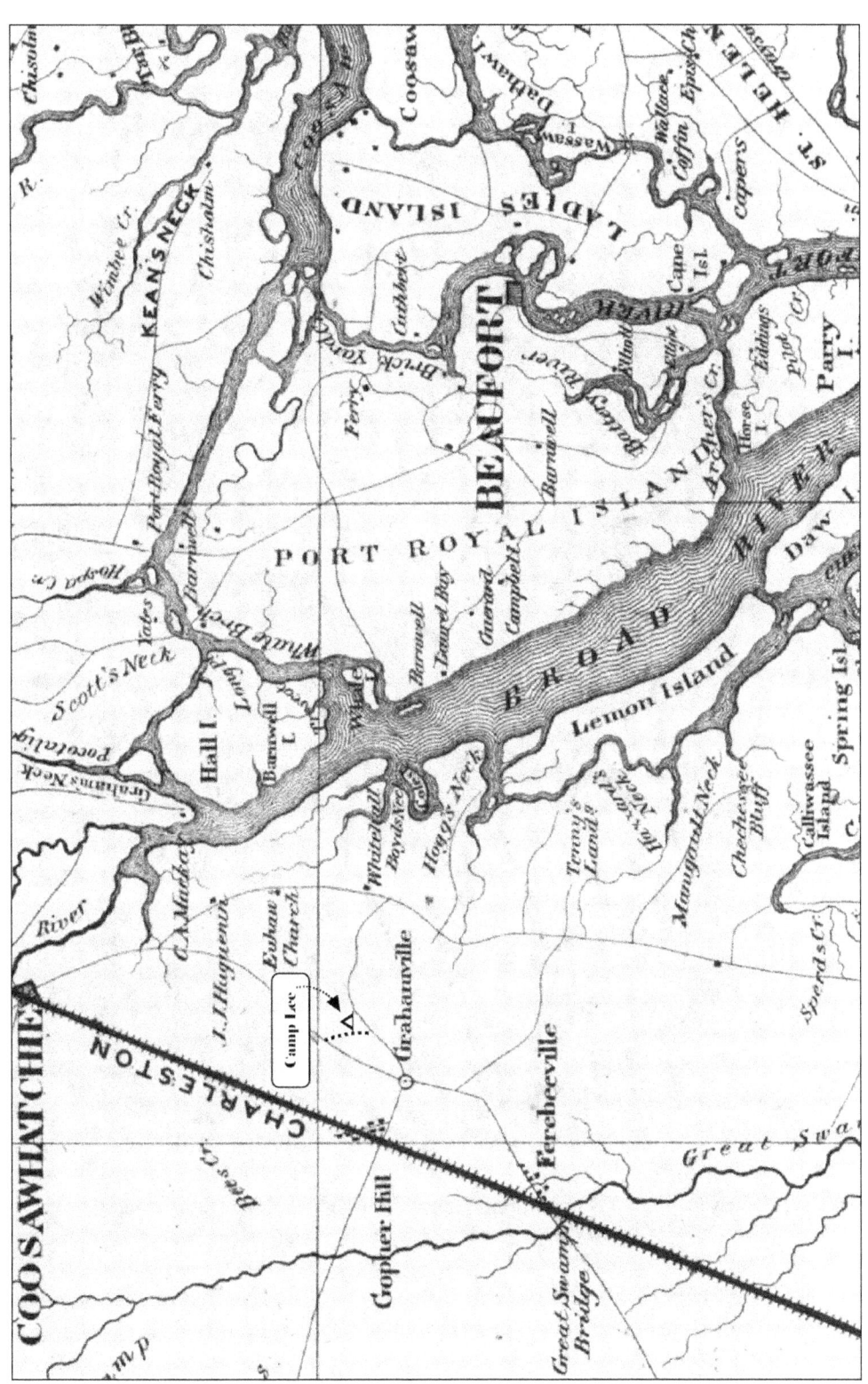

"Rebs Eating Corn-on-the-Cob." From Rod Gragg, *The Illustrated Confederate Reader* (1989).

February 1862

In the early morning hours, while Tom was on duty as officer of the day, he learned that two men from his own company were quite drunk and had to be replaced on the guard lines. The offending soldiers were privates Luther W. Murray and William (Columbus) Singleton, both merely young boys having only reached the age of seventeen when they enlisted the previous year. Tom's investigation uncovered the fact that Lt. Etheldred Blalock had procured a gallon of liquor from the assistant commissary of subsistence, Cap. John W. Walker, and told the captain it was "for the boys."

It seems that Murray and Singleton were not the only boys imbibing that evening. Several others were barely fit for duty. Although Tom only recorded the initials of their names, it is not difficult to determine that the other offenders were privates Roland Calloway Osborne, Henry Jackson Sorrells, Robert H. Hyatt, and William H. Hartgrove. Private Hartgrove, son of A. C. Hartgrove, who had been the overseer of the Lenoirs' East Fork farm for so many years, had just turned twenty-one years old the day before, and it is a reasonable presumption that he was celebrating his birthday with friends. Hartgrove would later overcome this lapse in judgment and be promoted to first lieutenant; and during the last months of the war he was, on occasion, tendered command of the Haywood Highlanders in the absence of his captain.

Tom reluctantly ordered Murray and Singleton to the guard tent for their foolhardiness but thought that some of the other older men likely bore more of the responsibility.

1862
February 1 – Saturday
Camp Lee

About 2 Oclock last night found out that L. W. Murray & W.A.S.C. Singleton were quite drunk and others had to take their places on The Guard lines

*Capt. Walker (Commissary) says that E. H. B. bought one gallon of liquor of him last night & said it was for the boys_ several others (R.C.O. & H.S_ & R.H.H. & W^m. H.) were barely fit for duty_ I ordered Murray & Singleton to the Guard tent, but think that several others (older) were more guilty than they_*

1862
February 2 – Sunday
Camp Lee, S.C.

*Sunday inspection & then made out an inventory of the effects of W^m. B. Rhodes, (made out 3 copies all) signed by L^t. Burnett, L^t. Cathey and myself_ His little pocket book contained, but $3.$^{50/100}$ including 5 postage stamps_ This $3.^{50} was handed to Serg^t. Cathey, & by him to Aaron Wright to be paid towards expenses of carrying his body to Haywood_ His clothes & other effects were boxed, labeled & handed over to M^r. Aaron Wright On yesterday (in presence of N.A. Pressley W^m. H. Hartgrove, & others) I paid Jas. M. Henderson ten dollars & fifty cents making (with one dollar in change which I had paid him at different times before 11.50 eleven dollars & fifty cents to be deducted from the money, which I rec^d. for him Immediately of inspection this morning had Murray & Singleton released from confinement_*

Sunday inspection did not come off as well as hoped. Tom found several men with dirty shirts and almost had them confined to the guard house. After the morning inspection and still harboring sympathy for the young boys he had dealt with so severely the day before, Tom gave orders for privates Murray and Singleton to be immediately released from confinement. There is no mention of a Sunday service in the record for this day. Instead Tom offers an inventory of the effects of Private Rhodes and names the witnesses that can vouch for his judicious handling and accounting of the sad affairs. Rhodes' "little pocketbook" contained but $3.50, including five postage stamps.

All of the money, clothes, and other personal belongings were carefully boxed, labeled, and entrusted to Aaron Wright, who was to accompany the body back to Haywood. Wright was not attached to Tom's unit or the 25th N.C. Troops. It is very possible that he was a civilian from the mountains who had brought supplies, foodstuffs, and other provisions from home to relatives and friends stationed at Camp Lee. Eighteen-year-old Pvt. William Wright was a Haywood Highlander, and it is plausible that Mr. Wright was either his father, brother, or other close kin.

Tom was very careful to record a transaction in which he turned over some of the pay that he had received and held for Pvt. James Henderson, who had endured, and thus far survived, a stubborn bout with typhoid fever. The journal entry for Nov. 24, 1861, documents that Tom sent ten dollars to Henderson's wife back home, and on this day he gave Henderson more of the money which had been held for him. Interestingly, Tom made sure that the transaction was made in front of others, and it appears that Private Hartgrove had sobered up and regained Tom's confidence to the extent that he was listed as a witness to this financial deal.

The men of Company F marched the short distance to Grahamville Station carrying the remains of Private Rhodes. The box with the body and another with the personal effects were loaded onto the train and entrusted to Mr. Wright, who was to see that this precious cargo arrived securely to awaiting family members at home.

Sounds of heavy cannon fire reached Camp Lee in the early afternoon from the direction of Bluffton. It was said that a Yankee gunboat had run aground and that a Confederate battery was attempting to destroy it. However, it is more probable that Tom was hearing the shelling from Yankee vessels running up New River near Red Bluff, just west of south below Bluffton. Confederate Gen. Thomas F. Drayton, commanding at Hardeeville, South Carolina, wrote to General Lee's headquarters about the Federal action on that day: "The enemy have shelled and burnt Box's and Lawton's houses, on New River. The obstructions from Red Bluff removed, and the sailors are sounding above it." He went on to state: "The shells from guns of steamers picked up 3 miles off."[173]

To General Lee this was an indication that the Yankees might be planning an advance from New River toward the Savannah River above the main Confederate fortifications protecting the important coastal city of Savannah. This would not do, Lee worried. To prepare for such an exigency he wrote to General Pemberton, who was in command of the forces around Grahamville and Coosawhatchie: "[Y]ou are desired to send to his support [Gen. Drayton's] such of your available force as might be necessary."[174] The course of subsequent events did not entail a Federal thrust at Savannah from the New River and, therefore, Colonel Clingman's 25th Regiment did not receive orders to vacate their breastworks in front of Grahamville and rush to General Drayton's support.

1862
February 2 [continued]

*Found several men with dirty shirts, & almost sent them to the Guard house_*

February 3 – Monday
Camp Lee, S.C.

Marched the whole Comp. out to R.R. Depot with the remains of W^m. B. Rhodes

Had the box containing his body, & the one containing his effects both put on board the cars in care of M^r. Wright

*Heard heavy firing in the direction of Bluffton which ceased about 2 or 3 oclock P.M._ It is rumored that it was Moore's Battery firing at a Yankee Ship which was aground_*

P.S. The yankee vessel broke in two & was lost, but our battery did nothing to help sink her

1862
February 8 – Saturday
Camp Lee

*My journal has been entirely neglected since Monday, but I do not now think of any very important occurrence connected with the Regt. which has transpired since that time_ Oh! I forget on last Tuesday a cavalry Company (pretty good looking) said to be from Lexington Dist. in this State passed this place & reported to Co^l. C. for orders & he sent them down about 4 miles to a place where some other cavalry had been stationed On Wednesday morning an hour or two before day a party of Yankees (supposed to be about 60) attacked a negroe quarters where four of our cavalry pickets (belonging to   [blank] were stationed, fired a great many shots at the dwelling house, the Negroe Cabins, etc_ killed the overseer, & wounded one of our men so severely that he died next day_ The Yanks were fired upon by two who were out watching with double barreled shot guns & it is supposed that some were killed_ The two pickets who were in the house did not fire_*

After a lapse of several days Tom resumed his diary accounts by writing that he could not think of any occurrences of importance related to the regiment. However, his memory quickly served him upon more reflection and he recalled that a "pretty good looking" cavalry company had reported to Colonel Clingman for orders. The colonel promptly dispatched the horsemen about four miles in advance of Camp Lee to cover the Broad River landings and to sound the alarm if enemy movements were afoot.

Also remembered was an enemy raid on a nearby negro quarters and overseer's house. Evidently, the four cavalry pickets stationed there were overwhelmed by a party of approximately sixty Yankees. After an exchange of gunfire Tom noted that the Yanks ran in one direction and the pickets in the other. Casualties on the Union side were only suspected, but not known. However, it was a certainty that the plantation overseer was killed in the midst of the confused action, as well as one of the Confederate cavalry pickets.

Tom notes that an artillery unit commanded by Captain Latham showed up below Camp Lee and reported to Colonel Clingman. This would have been Alexander C. Latham of the 1st Regiment N.C. Artillery, who had just been appointed commander of his light artillery company. The battery provided much-needed reinforcement for the Confederate defenders facing the Broad River and who remained on a high-alert level for the predicted Union thrust at the railroad.

The next couple of days seem to have been routine for Tom. He took an opportunity to read some in his Bible and wrote a letter to his "Lizzie Dear." During this same time Walter Lenoir wrote in a letter to their brother Rufus: "They have changed us from fresh beef to bacon, as the beef seems to be disagreeing with a portion of the men."[175]

The officer-of-the-day responsibility rotated to the company captains every ten days (since there were ten companies in the regiment). Tom served in that capacity on Feb. 10, having last had the obligation on Jan. 31—the same day when several of his boys got tight. He may have prevented another such occurrence when on this day he discovered a barrel of whiskey hidden under a pile of rice straw in the quartermaster's tent. Although Tom notes that it belonged to Lt. Lynch Dillard of Company B, he does not reveal whether he confiscated the whiskey, destroyed it, or simply left it buried where he found it.

As an afterthought, probably, he wrote that the "Ladies of Grahamville" had a concert that evening. Tom surely did not attend the performance due to his officer-of-the-day duties at the camp—although it is likely he would have passed on the opportunity to participate in yet another "frolic."

1862
February 8 [continued]

Then the Yanks ran & so did pickets
I am told
that on yesterday an
Artillery Company Commanded
by Capt. Latham
arrived two miles below this
*& reported to Co^l. C. for orders_*

February 9 – Sunday
Camp Lee

Nothing particularly to note
Read my Bible some &
*wrote to Lizzie Dear_*

February 10 – Monday
Camp Lee

*Officer of the Day_*
found a barrel whiskey
in Q.M. large tent, (among
the rice straw used for horse
food) which belonged to
L^t. Dillard_ Ladies of
Grahamville had concert tonight

1862
February 11 – Tuesday
Camp Lee, S.C.

*Went to the Hospital, we have only three sick now J.M. Henderson, Burton Henson & G.E Christopher, & they are all able to walk about the house After Dress Parade rode down with Co^l. Dearing (2 miles) & called on Capt. Latham of the Artillery & took supper with him & D^r. Pinkney, a L^t. & first Serg^t. They are to move up to the fortifications tomorrow_! Two Companies, (Capt. Blake's & Capt. Howel's) under Mag^r. Rutledge moved down to them this evening We heard of the loss of Roanoke Island today, & burning of E. City Bad news for N.C. & us_*

February 12 – Wednesday
Camp Lee, S.C.

*Co^l. Edmonston an T. L. Edwards Esq. & D. Burnett all arrived this evening from Haywood_*

Tom visited the Grahamville hospitals and found only three Haywood Highlanders among the patients: privates James Henderson, Burton Henson, and George E. Christopher. All seem to have been doing tolerably well and were able to walk about the house. Following the dress parade in the evening Tom and Lieutenant Colonel Dearing rode down toward the Broad River a couple of miles, where Captain Latham's artillery unit was posted. A call upon the captain earned the two infantry commanders a dinner invitation, which they readily accepted. Tom learned that Captain Latham had orders to move his artillery battery "up" to the fortifications on the next day and that Major Rutledge, along with companies H and I, had moved "down" to cooperate with him.

News had finally reached Grahamville of the capture of Roanoke Island by General Burnside's expedition. On Feb. 7 the superior Union vessels chased a rebel "mosquito" fleet away and landed about ten thousand Yankee troops on the island's western shore. The next day, Feb. 8, the amphibious forces overwhelmed the Confederate land-defense fortifications and forced the surrender of the beleaguered Confederate troops manning the works.

On the day after the capture of Roanoke, Federal warships trailed the mosquito fleet across Albemarle Sound and pursued it about twelve miles up the Pasquotank River, destroying it near Elizabeth City. Some of the town's citizens set their property on fire "to spite the Yankees," and when the Union soldiers disembarked a good portion of the town was ablaze.[176]

Tom records that three visitors from Haywood County arrived at Camp Lee, including Colonel Edmonston. It can only be supposed that this was Ninian Edmonston from Forks of Pigeon, who would have been approximately seventy-two years old at the time.

Edmonston was one of the early pioneers who helped establish the county in 1808 and in 1812 had volunteered and served in the second war against the British. He later forged a distinguished career in politics and became a successful farmer. The elderly man must have endured the arduous journey from North Carolina's western mountains to the coast of South Carolina to deliver much-wanted supplies to his two sons, privates Basil B. Edmonston of Company C and Benjamin F. Edmonston of the Haywood Highlanders.[177]

Cpl. Elisha Moore of Company D (not Company E as Tom noted) died of "fever" during the previous night. And the long missing Private Henry Bugg had returned from the mountains along with a new recruit, John Medford Meece, who was sworn in the next day. Tom notes that Bugg had been absent since Nov. 5, when the private had been too sick to travel with his regiment from Wilmington. But he was back now, and he would stay back. Bugg did not desert from the Haywood Highlanders as did so many in the years to come. He fought loyally and bravely through the entire war and was wounded at the Battle of the Crater in July 1864.

Captain William H. Bryson, the regiment's assistant quartermaster, also returned from Haywood with the others and brought good news for Tom. While in the mountains he had purchased for the army Tom's horse, Zeb, and four of his mules for $750—on credit! Bryson, at the relatively advanced age of forty-nine years, had enlisted in Company C as a private but was promoted to captain and assistant quartermaster about Sept. 1, 1861. The records show that he was discharged from the Confederate army on May 1, 1862, but the reason is not stated. It is possible that after the Confederate Conscription Act of 1862 was enacted, he became disaffected or simply elected to leave the service for reason of being over age.

1862
February 13 – Thursday
Camp Lee

Elisha Moore Co. E died last night
H. T. Bugg arrived
this evening just from
Haywood with Medford Meece
Bugg had been absent from
the 5th Nov^r._
Wm. H. Bryson Q.M. also
returned from the Mountains
today, & says that he bo^t.
my hosre Zeb. at $200.00 &
takes 4 of my mules at $550.
all to be paid for yet
Paid Capt. Walker for meal to be
distributed in Co. F = $ .50cents =.50

February 14 – Friday
Camp Lee

John Medford Meece was
sworn into the service of
the Confederate States
today by Co^l. Clingman

1862
February 15 – Saturday
Camp Lee

Co^l*. Ratcliff, Co*^l*. Mears Co*^l*. Clingman & Co*^l*. Dearing all called on me together today & found me asleep and quite unwell_*

February 16 – Sunday
Camp Lee

Took a dose of antibilious pills last night but am not any better today_ am not quite well enough to write to my Dear Wife

For the next two days Tom appears to have been bedridden with an unnamed malady. Concerned for his well-being, a cadre of colonels interrupted Tom's sleep as they looked in on him. Accompanying Colonel Clingman and Lieutenant Colonel Dearing on the sick visit were the commanders of the 18th Regiment N.C. Troops, Col. James Radcliffe and Lt. Col. Oliver Meares, whose unit was obviously still stationed nearby. Even a dose of "antibilious" pills failed to relieve Tom of the extreme discomfort he was feeling and provide the necessary vigor to write home to his wife.

During the interim while Tom was laid up and too sick to record in his diary, it seems that there was quite a scare in camp. On Feb. 20, while taking a break from guard duty, Walter Lenoir wrote in a letter home to a family member, "Since commencing this letter we have news that the Yankees are landing to-night at Boyd's Landing. We are ordered to cook a day's rations and may have a fight to-morrow. The issue is with the God of battles. May he be our strength and shield."[178] Whatever hope Tom or the other Haywood Highlanders held for getting the test they had been preparing for, they would be disappointed. There are no records of any associated hostilities with the landing Walter predicted. And it is a certainty that Tom would have made mention of any enemy engagements when he next picked up his diary to write. The "God of battles" saw fit to postpone the issue for another time.

A third Haywood Highlander, Pvt. George E. Christopher, succumbed to the ravages of typhoid fever, undoubtedly brought on by the poor sanitary conditions at Camp Lee. It was a stunning reversal, considering that just two weeks before Tom had recorded in his journal that Christopher, although sick, was able to walk around the house where he was being cared for.

Two days lapse before the diary accounts resume again, and they pick up on a sad note. Company F carried the remains of yet another of their mountain brethren to the railroad depot to be sent on the long trip back home. Packed in a wooden box as were the other fallen warriors, the body of George Christopher and his personal effects were loaded on one of the cars in the care of William Henry of Sulphur Springs, Buncombe County.[179] Henry had been the owner of the noted Sulphur Springs Hotel, a popular resort located a short distance west of Asheville that had just recently burned to the ground. He had journeyed out of the mountains to Grahamville in a wagon loaded with three thousand pounds of bacon for the soldiers of one of the Henderson County companies (either Company A or H).[180] Henry gave Tom his promise to see Christopher's remains safely to Haywood County and, after paying expenses, turn over the balance of cash to Christopher's widow.

1862
February 23 – Sunday
Camp Lee, S.C.

George E. Christopher died about 8 oclock tonight of typhoid fever in the Hospital at Grahamville S.C.

February 26 – Wednesday
Camp Lee

Went with the Company to the Depot to escort the remains of G. E. Christopher
Had the box containing his body, & also a small box containing his clothing etc. put on the cars in charge of William Henry of Sulphur Springs Buncomb
*He promised to see them safe to Haywood Co. and to pay over any bal. of cash left to C's. Widow_*

> Inventory of the effects of George E. Christopher late of Co. "F" 25th Regt. N.C. Vol. who died at Grahamville S.C. on the 23d day of Feb. 1862 —
> One coat, 1 overcoat, 1 blanket, 1 p. pants, 3 p. Shoes, 1 Bowie knife, 1 pocket knife, 1 padlock, 1 hat, 1 cap, 2 Shirts, 2 p. drawers, 2 cakes soap, 2 Spoons, 1 Comb, 13 Sheets letter paper, 9 envelops, 1 inkstand, 1 Testament, 1 Spelling book, 1 Pocket Memorandum book, 1 paper needles, a Small quantity of Sewing thread, & fifteen cents in Money
> We believe that the above list includes all the effects of any value left by George E. Christopher at Camp Lee & at the Hospital in Grahamville, S.C.
>
> Camp Lee S.C.   Thos. I. Lenoir
> Feb. 26th 1862   Capt. 25 Regt. N.C. Vols,
>   Comdg Co. "F"
>   Lt. E. F. Bulock
>   Lt. A. Barnett

An inventory of the effects of one of the Haywood Highlanders who perished from disease at Camp Lee was written in Captain Lenoir's hand and witnessed by his two lieutenants. *Lenoir Family Papers, Southern Historical Collection, Wilson Library, University of North Carolina at Chapel Hill; used by permission.*

On Feb. 18, 1862, Tom Lenoir wrote to his "Wee Bit Wife" from Camp Lee, reporting on the war, describing Haywood County visitors, and providing details of an accidental killing of a soldier. *Collection of Hugh K. Terrell and the late Emily Michal Terrell; used by permission.*

"Making Corn Meal during a Rest" by William L. Sheppard. *From* The American Heritage Century Collection of Civil War Art *(1974)*.

March 1862

Almost two months in arrears, the Confederate government finally paid the rebels serving with the Haywood Highlanders for the two months of service rendered from Nov. 1 through Dec. 31, 1861. Tom received $1,982 as the pay due to the noncommissioned officers and privates, and he paid it over to the men on that same day. He also accepted as his captain's salary $130 per month for the last two months, significantly more than the paltry $11 per month wages earned by the private soldiers.

Worrisome to Tom was the fact that the men who had died, or had been discharged, did not receive the pay due to them. A vague and complicated system was eventually established by the Confederate army whereby these ex-soldiers or their heirs could make application for the money owed. It required that administrators of these men's affairs make formal written requests for the funds to army bureaucrats in Richmond. The process was a long and involved one, often protracted for a year or more before the claims were satisfied or denied. All the while, widows, orphans, and whole families anxiously waited for the desperately needed cash that might have helped them survive through the difficult home-front circumstances created by the war.

Most assuredly the mountain boys would have been extremely anxious to receive the promised back pay for their military service. The previous day, March 4, represented just their second pay day since they joined up for the fight in July 1861. Most, if not all, of those Haywood Highlanders had loved ones back home who were dependent on the Confederate army pay to see them through the dark days until

1862
March 4
Camp Lee, S.C.

Camp Lee S.C
 Rec^d. of William H. Bryson Paymaster $1982 ^{00} as the pay due to the Non Com. Off. & Privates of Company F, from the 31st Oct. 1861 to Dec. 31st 1861 & paid it all over on the same day_ Those at the Hospital were paid after supper_ This did not include any pay due to discharged & dead men as The Paymaster refused to advance any money due the dead men them except to their Administrators, & the claims of the two discharged men A. Burnett & P.B. Franklin had been transferred to Lt. Burnett & also rec^d. $260.00 as my pay from Oct. 31st 1861 to Dec. 31st 1861

1862
March 5
Camp Lee

Serg^t. J.T. Cathey started home to carry money for the Volunteers, & to assist in procuring recruits_ He has permission to be gone 20 days

March 7
Camp Lee

Lt. Blaylock started this morning to Haywood on recruiting service & is to return in 20 days_ He borrowed $25.00 of me and gave his note_ Robert Poston also went with him on furlough his furlough is for 15 days

March 10 – Monday
Camp Lee, S.C.

Co^l. Clingman made a speech to the Reg^t. recommending reenlistment

their menfolk hurried back from the war—once the twelve-month enlistment periods ran out. It was for that very reason that Sgt. Joseph Turner Cathey started for Forks of Pigeon with his bags full of Confederate money. He was in effect acting as the company's courier by taking most of, if not all, of the soldiers' wages back to their families in Haywood. Cathey was given leave for twenty days to perform this essential and dangerous task as well as to assist in recruiting efforts for the regiment.

Lt. Etheldred Blalock was sent to Haywood, just as Sergeant Cathey had been the day before, to procure additional fighting men for the Confederacy. Pvt. Robert Poston, who was about thirty-eight years old at the time, accompanied Blalock on the trip, having been the fortunate recipient of a fifteen-day furlough.

Captain Lenoir makes reference in his diary to the fact that Colonel Clingman made a speech to the regiment recommending reenlistment. It likely was a most impassioned oration informing the men of the 25th Regiment of the new Bounty and Furlough Act adopted by the Confederate Congress in December 1861. This legislation provided that every soldier who reenlisted for a period of three years, or the duration of the war, could receive a bounty of sixty dollars and a furlough of sixty days.[181] The act was a drastic measure—one thought to be disastrous by many of the Southern military leaders, including Gen. Robert E. Lee—that was taken with the realization that the twelve-month enlistment periods of the early volunteers would soon be up. These men made up about one-half of the entire Confederate army.[182] It was suspected that a majority of them would simply hand over their muskets and melt back to their homes and families once their time ran out. Proving this suspicion accurate, Sgt. Garland Ferguson had written in a letter home the previous month: "The excitement about reenlisting has pretty much subsided. Not more than one sixth of the men have reenlisted."[183] Colonel Clingman's energies and promotions were directed to stir the excitement in the men once again and avert a looming disaster.

In contrast to the Confederate private soldier's $11 per month wages, captains such as Tom Lenoir received a monthly salary of $130, as his final payroll receipt for the period ending Apr. 30, 1862, illustrates (www.footnote.com, accessed 2009).

1862
March 14 – Friday
Camp Lee

About 2 oclock P.M. today we were ordered to be ready with provisions cooked for four days to start at 8 oclok to Newbern N.C_ afterwards we were told that we would probably get off at 11 Oclock & afterwards to go to bed & be up at five in the morning

March 15 – Saturday

Marched from Camp Lee at about 7 oclock A.M. & the train moved off at about 10 A.M. with men & baggage ------

After Union Gen. Ambrose Burnside's expedition had captured Roanoke Island in North Carolina on Feb. 8, it had also effectively chased off the Confederate navy's mosquito fleet and secured Albemarle Sound. However, Burnside's prize target, New Bern, North Carolina, which lay to the south along the lower reaches of the Pamlico Sound and a short distance up the expansive Neuse River, was still under Confederate control. In conjunction with Union Gen. George McClellan's landing of the Army of the Potomac on the Virginia peninsula opposite Richmond, Burnside launched another invasion on North Carolina soil. On Mar. 12 he sailed his Federal warships across the sound and up the Neuse, landing his Yankee forces just twelve miles below New Bern. The Northern invaders easily overwhelmed outlying Confederate defense works, and on Mar. 14 they opened an all-out attack against the rebel defenders arrayed in front of North Carolina's important port city.

The Confederate troops defending New Bern, led by Gen. Lawrence O'B. Branch, were routed in a short time and fell back in bad order to Kinston, located along the railroad about halfway between New Bern and Goldsboro, North Carolina. Over the next few days other Confederate troops located in Virginia and South Carolina were rushed to Kinston to unite with the remnants of Branch's command. There, at Kinston, they expected to oppose the next thrust by Burnside's bluecoats and protect the strategic railroad facilities at Goldsboro. Included in the reinforcements that were hustled to Kinston was the 25th Regiment N.C. Troops.

At 2:00 in the afternoon on Mar. 14, the same day that New Bern was attacked, Colonel Clingman received orders to be ready to start for New Bern at 8:00 that evening. These orders were subsequently revised, and the regiment was directed to get some sleep and be ready for an early start the next morning for North Carolina.

The Haywood Highlanders and the other companies of the 25th Regiment marched away from Camp Lee for the final time at 7:00 in the morning. The coastal guard duty they had performed at Grahamville had been relatively easy service compared to what they would experience later in the war. The countryside surrounding Port Royal had provided a bounty of food to eat and the winter weather had not been unseasonably cold—at least not per Tom's account. The Highlanders had participated in no minor or major fights while in South Carolina and most likely were anxious, and a little nervous, to test their mettle against Burnside's bluecoats in the anticipated battle for Goldsboro. After treading the short distance from Camp Lee to Grahamville's depot in the rain, the rebels loaded their baggage and other accoutrements and trappings of war on the train and embarked for New Bern at 10:00 a.m.[184]

Apparently it took almost eight hours for the locomotive to pull the train cars full of rebel soldiers from Grahamville to Charleston, a distance of approximately seventy-five miles. Arriving just before dark in the fire-scarred city where the war was birthed, the men were marched with their arms, accoutrements, and knapsacks across the Ashley River to a large passenger depot building belonging to the South Carolina Railroad. In one large room all ten companies, comprising around a thousand men, found shelter for the night. Tom explains that Lt. James Cathey spread his shawl on the dirty plank floor and, after pulling on their overcoats, the lieutenant, Tom, and Walter Lenoir lay down on it and tried to get some sleep. However, their rest was interrupted by several intoxicated men who had who gotten hold of some liquor in the streets of the city. Tom complained, "Drunken noisy men are particularly disgusting to others who are tired, hungry and sleepy."

1862
March 15 – [continued]

*The Regiment arrived at the Depot in Charleston just before dark, & finding that we could not get off before the next morning we were marched to a very large Depot belonging to the S.C. R.R. and all of the companies slept in one very large room_ Neither Walter W. Lenoir or my self had a blanket Lt. Cathey had a shawl, & after spreadin it on the dirty floor We put on our overcoats & would have slept pretty well if we had not been annoyed by drunk men_ Several of them climbed over a high wall, got into the street managed to get liquor & got drunk_ Drunken noisy men are particularly disgusting to others who are tired, hungry & sleepy_*

1862
March 16 – Sunday

*Slept but little last night Left Charleston about 8 oclock A.M.*_ ~~We w~~ *on two trains, right in front Were detrained several hours at Florence_ We all made a start on one train about 8 oclock P.M. but the engine stalled_ Then the train was divided & comp. "F" was on the 2ⁿᵈ train We spent the night in the cars*

March 17 – Monday

About nine oclock this morning the cars were stopped & it was said that a man had fallen from the top of the cars_ We examined the wheels and found blood on more than a dozen_ The engine was sent back & soon returned with him_ The wheels had passed across him just below the hips mangling him terribly_ He was not dead, but seemed to be insensible

After an uneasy sleep the men of the 25th Regiment boarded two trains of the Northeastern Rail Road and left Charleston at 8:00 in the morning for Florence, South Carolina. At Florence the regiment had to detrain, and after waiting several hours was embarked on a single train of cars belonging to the Wilmington & Manchester line. Getting a late start at around 8:00 that evening, they soon discovered that the locomotive engine could not pull the long train of cars. The train was divided, and Tom's Company F occupied the second train that lumbered through the night toward Wilmington, the crucial port town on North Carolina's coast.

The captain recorded that the cars were halted at about 9:00 in the morning. It had been reported that a man who was riding on top of a car, "in disobedience to orders," had fallen.[185] Upon examination of the train's wheels, blood was found on more than a dozen of them. The engine was uncoupled from the cars and sent back to search for the victim. Soon the lone engine returned with the unfortunate man aboard—still alive but badly mangled by the wheels of the train.

The name of the injured private solider was George H. Young, who was only eighteen years old when he enlisted in Cherokee County in June 1861. Although Tom records that he was attached to Captain Grady's company, he was actually one of John W. Francis's men of Company D. The unfortunate youth clung to life for the remaining passage to Wilmington but died in a hospital soon after reaching the port city. His tragic death was the second accidental fatality for the 25th Regiment since the war began. The other occurred one month earlier, on Feb. 18, 1862, when Pvt. Richard H. Sharp was "killed by accident by a sentinel on post."[186] Interestingly, Sharp had also been one of Captain Francis's men from Cherokee County.

Although the regiment arrived in Wilmington at about 10:00 in the morning the men did not get across the Cape Fear River until darkness had set in. Tom explains that first a boat ferried their baggage across and then returned for the regiment, which it transported in only one overly crowded load.

After eating their supper, the Haywood Highlanders and the rest of the regiment were again rustled into rail freight cars, these of the Wilmington & Weldon line. Clingman's army was then started for Goldsboro at 10:30 p.m., and Tom notes that he "slept but little" on the crowded car.

<u>March 17</u> – [continued]

We were 26 or 28 miles from Wilmington & he continued to breathe until we arrived at W. but he died soon after His name was George Young & he belonged to Capt. Grady's Company We arrived at Wilmington a little after 10 oclock A.M.

  *Geo. Young was carried to the Hospital & died soon after_*

  We did not cross the river until dark_ The baggage was all carried over first by the boat at one load_ & just about dark it came back for the Reg^t. & brought it all over at 1 load

  *After crossing the men [ate] some supper which had been prepared for them & we were then hurried into the cars _ started at 10 ½ oclock PM I was in a crowded car & slept but little_*

1862
March 18 – Tuesday

*Stopped a while this morning in Goldsboro & some crackers & boiled bacon was served to the men for breakfast then went on the same cars to Kinston in Lenoir County, passing over some beautiful country & in sight of M^r. John Washington's which seemed to be a pretty place_ At Kinston we met with Capt. Rankin, Co^l. Vance L^t. Co^l. Barbour, Willy Avery, & various other acquaintances We spread our tents in the Suburbs and got into them about dark_*

March 19 – Wednesday

*I forgot what happened on on that day except that Capt. Rankin took dinner with us_*

When the train reached Goldsboro in the morning hours it stopped for a while, and the men were served crackers and boiled bacon for breakfast. After the last bites of pork were consumed the soldiers boarded the same cars and resumed the train trip through Lenoir County and what Tom described as "some beautiful country." The namesake county was named in honor of Tom's grandfather, William Lenoir. The train passed within sight of John Washington's place, likely the same old and influential Kinston citizen who was a noted planter and a delegate to the North Carolina Secession Convention in May 1861, having voted in favor of secession.[187]

Colonel Clingman's regiment finally arrived at Kinston to join the other troops assembling there—four days after receiving orders for the movement to North Carolina. Tom notes meeting several acquaintances, including Lt. Col. William M. Barbour, 37th Regiment N.C., and the former Congressman from Asheville and future wartime governor of North Carolina, Col. Zebulon Vance, 26th Regiment N.C. Both of these men's regiments had been on the front defensive line at New Bern and were engaged in the thickest of the fighting. There undoubtedly was much to talk about, and Tom soon would have learned the sordid details of the Battle of New Bern. He would also have discovered that General Burnside had made no threatening moves out of his new stronghold as of yet. At the conclusion of these interesting discussions Tom and his Haywood Highlanders spread their tents in the "suburbs" of Kinston and "got into them about dark."

The following weekday was a routine one, apparently, and Tom could remember nothing worthy of note except having dinner with Capt. William R. Rankin of the 37th Regiment North Carolina Troops.

Tom sent the company's extra baggage back to Goldsboro to be stored, probably inside a railroad warehouse or other depot building.

In and around Kinston several training and bivouac camps sprouted during the war, including Camp Johnston, a few miles west of Kinston near Falling Creek, and Camp Ransom, to the east several miles and near Wyse Fork. Over the ensuing weeks the 25th Regiment N.C. Troops were marched back and forth through Kinston to one or the other of these camps and those on the outskirts of town.

As Tom notes, he became ill soon after arriving at Kinston and by the weekend did not feel well enough to leave his tent. He detailed Lt. James Cathey and brother Walter back to Goldsboro to check on Pvt. Fidellio W. Henson, who had been left there on the 18th due to sickness. However, Private Henson had seemingly recuperated and was already in route back to Kinston, passing the messengers of mercy on the way.

1862
March 20 – Thursday

*Rained some_ & we sent extra baggage back to Goldsboro_*

March 21 – Friday

Marched back through Kinston about seven miles to new encampment

March 22 – Saturday

I was too unwell for duty, & kept in my tent most of the day, and Lt. Cathey & W.W. Lenoir went to Goldsboro to see about F. W. Henson left sick there Henson returned, passing them on the way

1862
March 23 – Sunday

*Had a bad night last night cough very severe_ D^r. S. says that I must move to a house_ Walter W. Lenoir has succeeded in getting me a nice little room at Jesse H. Rouse's & I came to it this afternoon_*

March 28 – Friday

The 25th Reg^t. moved down to Kinston &

March 29 – Saturday

The Reg^t. move five miles below Kinston to to what I suppose is Camp Ransom

Captain Lenoir was feeling worse, apparently, and had not slept well during the night due to a very severe cough. With the realization that it would be very difficult for Tom to recover his health while living in a cold, damp, drafty tent, Dr. Satchwell advised him to seek a warm house of refuge to convalesce. Heeding the good doctor's counsel, Walter scavenged around and found a room for Tom at Jesse H. Rouse's place. Rouse was a planter, it is believed, because the records indicate that he sold fodder and corn to the Confederate army, delivering one shipment to Camp Johnston.[188] Tom was surely thankful for Walter's diligence and Rouse's generosity, and he wasted no time in moving into the room.

The captain's sickness would account for the several-day lapse in journal entries. Obviously he was in no shape to maintain his daily accounts. While still occupying his room in Rouse's home he resumed the journal record by noting the movements of the 25th Regiment the best that he could. On Mar. 28 the regiment moved back to Kinston from an outlying camp. And on the next day, Mar. 29, it marched to a camp some five miles below Kinston (toward New Bern). Tom believed that this was Camp Ransom, but clearly he was not certain.

Lt. Etheldred Blalock, who had been sent back to Haywood on a recruiting mission, returned to the regiment at Camp Ransom with three new men: James M. Singleton, Joshua A. Clark, and Francis M. Miller. Confederate records show that they were enlisted in Haywood County for a period of three years. All of those first enlistees who formed the Haywood Highlanders in the summer of 1861 had volunteered for only one twelve-month period. However, it was now obvious to all that the war was not going to be one of short duration, as was originally supposed by many Southerners. In fact, during this same time frame the Confederate government was deliberating a new legislative act that would make service in the Confederate army mandatory. Moreover, the law that was being contemplated would automatically extend the enlistment periods of all the one-year volunteers for an additional two years.

After a week of convalescence Tom finally felt fit enough to return to duty. Either in Goldsboro or somewhere between that town and Kinston, he waited by the side of the railroad tracks for the train to come along and carry him back to his men. While waiting for the cars Tom bumped into Charley Hickerson, who was either an acquaintance or old friend. After he visited a short while with this man the train arrived, and Tom hopped aboard and rode it to Kinston where it stopped just before 2:00 in the afternoon. He continued on the train for another five miles or so to a stop near the encampment (Camp Ransom, Tom believed), where the 25th N.C. Troops were stationed. There he disembarked and headed off in search of his Haywood Highlanders.

1862
March 30 – Sunday

*Lt. E.H. Blaylock arrived in camp with three recruits viz. James M. Singleton Joshua A. Clark & Francis M. Miller_*

March 31 – Monday

I left M^r. Rouse's today about half after twelve_ The cars came along soon after I got down to R.R. Saw Charley Hickerson a few minutes_ got on the cars & arrived at Kinston before two oclock_ & soon afterwards the cars brought me five miles further to (I suppose) Camp Ransom

"Confederate Sharpshooters" by Allen C. Redwood. *From Robert Underwood Johnson and Clarence Clough Buel, eds.*, Battles and Leaders of the Civil War *(1989), vol. 2.*

April 1862

Col. Joseph Cathey arrived at Camp Ransom from Forks of Pigeon on this first day of April. Accompanying him on the visit were two of his daughters.[189] Surely the trip was not as arduous as the one the colonel had made to Grahamville in the early days of November 1861. Reaching the western terminus of the railroad at Morganton after a wagon ride of at least two days, he and his daughters likely loaded crates and barrels of the scant supplies left over from the hard mountain winter onto the train. From there the locomotive conveyance would have transported the travelers almost to the picket line of Camp Ransom in eastern North Carolina. At that Confederate encampment, bristling with activity and on high alert for the next Yankee move out of New Bern, the Cathey brothers and other men from Company F and Company C would have received the visitors with overwhelming hospitality and joy.

Two of Lieutenant Blalock's new recruits from Haywood County—James Singleton and Joshua Clark—were sworn into the service of the Confederate States by Colonel Clingman. For some unknown reason this formality was not extended to the third recruit at the same time and on the same day. However, Francis Miller vowed his allegiance and loyalty to the South on the following day.

1862
April 1 – Tuesday

Col. Cathey arrived in camp_ His Daughters Miss Sallie & Mrs. Freeman came down with him.

April 2 – Wednesday

*James M. Singleton & Joshua A. Clark were this day sworn into the service of Confederate States by Col. T. L. Clingman in presence of Lt. E.H. Blaylock and myself_*

April 4 – Friday

*Francis M. Miller was this day sworn into the service of The Confederate States by Lt. Col. St. Clair Dearing in presence of Lt. E.H.B. and myself_*

1862
April 5 – Saturday

*Company F & the bal of the Right wing started on Picket duty at 12 oclk M Paid Capt. Walker eleven dollars & 25 cts = $11.25 which settled his accounts against Lt. Cathey, W.W. Lenoir & myself up to 1st of April 1862 and also settled accounts among ourselves to date_*

This day handed to Co^l. Cathey a letter directed to R.T. Lewis containing $300.00 in money & one directed to Co^l. J.C.H. containing a check on Bank of Charleston for $550.00 & also an order on Q.M. Maj^r. Hutson Lee of Charleston for $200.00_ He will leave the first in Morganton & mail the other at Hickory Station

At 12:00 midnight the Haywood Highlanders and the balance of what Tom referred to as the "right wing" went out on picket duty. While his company was thus posted, Tom managed to take care of some personal and army-related business matters that had undoubtedly been worrisome to him over the past weeks. He paid $11.25 to Capt. John W. Walker, the 25th Regiment's assistant commissary of subsistence, to settle army accounts owed by himself, Lt. James Cathey, and his brother Walter Lenoir. Walter had described in a letter home how he shared subsistence expenses with his compatriots: "[M]y rations are provided for by Tom and Lieut Cathey who draw what they please & pay for it, I bearing 1/3 of the expence [*sic*]."[190]

Tom also entrusted to the care of Colonel Cathey large sums of money and checks to carry back westward with him. Three hundred dollars in money was to be left at Morganton for a Mr. R.T. Lewis. And a bank draft and quartermaster's order totaling $750 issued to a Col. J.C.H. (possibly James C. Harper) was to be placed in the mail at Hickory Station, located along the rail line between Statesville and Morganton. Although no details of these payments are offered, it is surmised that they represent Confederate army reimbursements to private citizens, probably living in Caldwell County, for goods or services provided to the 25th Regiment N.C. Troops.

Tom had never fully recovered from the disease that first attacked upon his arrival back in North Carolina. If a diagnosis of the cause of the pneumonic symptoms and severe cough was rendered by the doctors, the malady or disorder is not named in Tom's journal. The former surgeon of the regiment, Dr. Solomon Satchwell, had been transferred to a hospital in Wilson, North Carolina, on Mar. 26, and it seems that the assistant surgeon, Dr. George Fletcher, was treating and caring for Tom. Fletcher, who had formerly been attached to Company H as a first lieutenant, sent Tom to the home of R. B. Vause, where a comfortable room more conducive to healing and recuperation was made available. Vause's place must have been located in the vicinity of Camp Ransom because Tom notes that he could look from his room at the men on dress parade.

Tom remained bedridden at Vause's for a week while Dr. Fletcher attended to him from time to time and nurtured the commander back to a reasonable state of health. It is obvious that Tom was too ill to see to his diary, and the entries only pick up again after a week's hiatus. It is not clear whether the captain moved back to the camp and his tent, or if he continued to occupy Vause's room while gradually easing back into the military routine. He notes that he "came" down to camp and drilled his men a little on one day and, on the next, "moved" down to camp and attended a battalion and company drill.

1862
April 9 – Wednesday

*Had a bad night in camp last night & coughed so badly that D^r. Fletcher sent me here to Mr. R. B. Vause' house where I have a comfortable room from which I can see the men on Dress parade_*

April 16 – Wednesday

Came down to camp & drilled a little

April 17 – Thursday

Moved down to camp & went out on Battallion & company drill

1862
April 18 – Friday

Paid R. B. Vause for
1 ½ bu. meal (for comp^y)   1.20
at 80 cts pr. bu. = 1.20
& also paid him for board
& washing up to date = $6.00
& he now owes me forty cents
*which is to be paid in washing_*
The Regt. was inspected
today by Maj^r. Case sent
*from Richmond_*

April 19 – Saturday
Regimental wash day
and I am now Off. Day
Guard mounted at 5 P.M.

April 28 – Monday

Held an election for
commissioned Officers for
Company "F" according
to an act of congress
making it necessary to
reorganizeng the whole Regt.
by again electing officers
Lt. James M. Cathey &
Lt. E.H. Blalock were
candidates for Captaincy
I told the Company that
I would not be a candidate
*for the following reasons_*

Over the next couple of days Tom settled his boarding and washing accounts to date with Mr. Vause and purchased some corn meal from him for the Haywood Highlanders. He records that an army officer from Richmond came down to inspect the regiment. It is presumed that Major Case discovered the appearance of the soldiers of the 25th Regiment and the cleanliness of their uniforms did not measure up to Confederate army standards. The very next day was declared "regimental wash day" and Tom, as officer of the day, got to oversee a thousand or more men laundering their clothes and cleaning themselves up.

In March 1862 the bloom of the early fervent days of war had long wilted and faded away for the South. An ever-strengthening and strangling naval blockade of the Southern port cities, Union advances into the Carolina coastal regions, Federal successes in the West forged by an obscure general named U. S. Grant, and an unfolding invasion of peninsular Virginia by Gen. George B. McClellan's powerful Army of the Potomac served to dampen the spirits and loyalties of many Southerners. Even Tom's overseer in Haywood County, A. C. Hartgrove, saw the difficulty that lay ahead for the South. He commented in a routine letter to Tom about the East Fork farming affairs: "[H]e [old Abe Lincoln] is making such progress in Tennessee I fear the south will have to do hard fighting before they gain there [*sic*] independence."[191] Consequently, the clamor from the Southern population for President Jefferson Davis and the Confederate government to do something grew louder and louder.

Making matters worse was the fact that the end of the one-year volunteer enlistment period for almost half of the Confederate army was fast approaching. With the support of General Robert E. Lee, President Davis and the Confederate Congress passed the first conscription law in American history. It declared that all able-bodied white male citizens between the ages of eighteen and thirty-five years—with certain special exemptions—be liable for army duty for three years. Furthermore, it obligated those early one-year volunteers, including most of the men belonging to the Haywood Highlanders, to remain in service for an additional two years, or the duration of the war.[192]

The new Confederate conscription law and the Bounty and Furlough Act forced a reorganization of the Confederate army at the end of April 1862. The men of the existing companies were compelled to re-elect new officers, including the captains. In turn, the regimental officers had to stand for reelection by the newly elected company commanders. Company F of the 25th Regiment was no exception. The men of the Haywood Highlanders would again have to decide whom they wanted to lead them into the battles that were certain to lay ahead.

Tom records without embellishment in his journal that lieutenants James Cathey and Etheldred Blalock were candidates for the captaincy of the Haywood Highlanders, omitting his own name from the abbreviated list. Actually, he himself had been forced by the exigencies of the Confederate reorganization to decide whether to continue to command his company as the war continued and, therefore, seek reelection. He decided to bow out. Interestingly, as early as Mar. 10 Walter Lenoir had written to Joe Norwood, their brother-in-law, that Tom "had not constitution enough for an active campaign, and he has decided not to re-enlist."[193] The hardships of military life in the field and the realization that he might not possess the necessary degree of callousness or hardness to lead certain mountaineers against their will were significant factors affecting Tom's judgment. He listed these in his diary along with the others given below as causes influencing his decision to quit the army:

• He thought his health was not sufficiently strong to fulfill the duties of a company captain, "as it should be done."

• He was convinced that nearly one-half of the men in his command were "impressed with the idea" that he was overly strict in discipline and would prefer to be commanded by some other officer.

• He did not like to command men who were dissatisfied with him.

1862
April 28 [continued]

*First that experience had proved that my health was such as to disqualify me, and prevent my fulfilling the duties of that office as it should be done_*
*Secondly I was convinced that a considerable portion of the Company (perhaps near half) were impressed with the idea that I was over strict in discipline_ & would prefer to be commanded by some other officer_*
*That I did not like to command men who were dissatisfied with me, & that I could not promise to be less strict until my notions of duty were very much changed that it was probable that I would become more strict from a sense of duty as I became better acquainted with the laws as contained in the General Regulations which had to be laws for us_*

1862
April 28 [continued]

That I could not electioneer for myself or any body else & would sooner go into the ranks as private than to electioneer for any office_ James M. Cathey was elected Capt. by a large majority on 28th April 1862 Thaddeus C.S. Hyatt was elected first Lie^t. also by a large majority James A. Blalock was elected 2nd Lieutenant There were so many candidates for the third Lieutenancy the we failed to make an election before dark and postponed it until the next Morning_ T. M. Green rec^d. 21 votes, J.T. Cathey 19 votes & John C. Singleton 19 votes

- He could not promise to be less strict, as his notions and senses of duty were likely to become even more rigid as he learned more of what was contained in the military regulations.
- He could not bring himself to "electioneer" for office and would sooner go into the ranks as a private soldier.

The men by large majorities elected Lt. James M. Cathey as their new captain and Cpl. Thaddeus C.S. Hyatt as the first lieutenant. Sgt. James A. Blalock was elected second lieutenant by a lesser degree of majority of the vote count.

There were apparently so many candidates for the third lieutenancy that a determination could not be reached on this first election day. Those receiving the highest number of votes on the first ballot were:

- Pvt. Thaddeus M. Green—21 votes (Green was only eighteen years old when he enlisted in June 1861)
- 1st Sgt. Joseph T. Cathey—19 votes
- 2nd Cpl. John C. Singleton—19 votes.

The election continued the next day at Kinston's Camp Ransom, where the races for the third lieutenancy and noncommissioned officers in Company F were still being contested. An ad hoc committee to run the elections was formed, comprising Captain Lenoir, Sgt. William Henderson, and Pvt. William Harrison Hartgrove. Tom reveals in his diary that at the last balloting for the third lieutenancy (there must have been at least one other) only two names were considered and voted on—Thaddeus M. Green and Joseph T. Cathey.

All across the encampment the other Confederate companies were holding similar elections, and the atmosphere throughout the regiment was surely one of highly-charged excitement. In Company F the voting was evidently close and contentious. There were eight more votes cast for the new third lieutenant than there were voters. However, the committee judged that Cathey had received a fair majority, since he had received eleven more votes than did Green. Therefore, Joseph T. Cathey was declared duly elected as third lieutenant.

1862
April 29 – Tuesday

This morning we finished the election for 3rd Lieu^t. At the last balloting only two names were voted_ Thaddeus M. Green and Joseph T. Cathey_ The election was held by William Henderson, William H. Hartgrove & myself, _ Henderson and Hargrove counted out the tickets & I scored_ There were six tickets rolled up together in one wad & Henderson & Hartgrove both say that they would be willing to swear that they were all for T. M. Green_ and we discovered that the number of votes cast was 8 more than the number of voters but as Cathey received 11 more than Green, it was evident that a decided majority had voted for him & he (J.T. Cathey) was declared duly elected 3rd L^t.

1862

April 29 [continued]

Then the following were elected

W^m. H. Hartgrove	1st Serg^t.
John C. Rogers	2nd Serg^t.
J. B. Meece	3rd D^o.
R. H. Hyatt	4th D^o.
W^m. T. Cathey	5th D^o.

and

Thos. F. Henson	1st Corp^l.
W^m. R. Clonts	2nd Corp^l.
Henry J. Sorrels	3rd D^o.
William Bonham	4th D^o.
John R. Jones	Drummer
John A. Smith	fifer
James E. Norton	Commissary

and I suppose that these elections for non Commissioned Officers were confirmed __

After the voting for the commissioned officers was settled, the attention turned to the noncommissioned officer positions in the company. The results of the balloting were as follows:

- 1st Sergeant—William H. Hartgrove
- 2nd Sergeant—John C. Rogers
- 3rd Sergeant—James B. Meece
- 4th Sergeant—Robert H. Hyatt
- 5th Sergeant—William T. Cathey
- 1st Corporal—Thomas F. Henson
- 2nd Corporal—William R. Clonts
- 3rd Corporal—Henry J. Sorrells
- 4th Corporal—William Bonham
- Drummer—John R. Jones
- Fifer—John A. Smith
- Commissary—James E. Norton.

Following the company elections the ten new company commanders and officers huddled to elect the regimental field officers. In that balloting Col. Thomas L. Clingman was unanimously reelected to command the 25th Regiment N.C. Troops, an obvious sign of his leadership capability and positive approbation from the company commanders. Maj. Henry Middleton Rutledge, only twenty-two years old, was elected lieutenant colonel with apparently about a dozen votes being cast for William McDowell (Rutledge would be promoted to colonel of the regiment on May 17, 1862, upon the promotion of Clingman to brigadier general.[194]) St. Clair Dearing, the former lieutenant colonel, retired from the command while under an anonymous charge of drinking too freely.[195] Capt. Samuel C. Bryson of Company C was elected major by a very small majority over Capt. Wesley N. Freeman, previously a second lieutenant in Company C and later acting adjutant for the regiment. The regimental field command after the April reorganization stood as follows:

Colonel—Thomas L. Clingman
Lieutenant Colonel—Henry M. Rutledge
Major—Samuel C. Bryson

Interestingly, of the original ten company commanders in the 25th Regiment N.C., only three of the "old captains of the regiment," as Tom put it, were reelected by their men. These were Capt. John W. Francis of Company D, Capt. William S. Grady of Company G, and Capt. Charles M. Roberts of Company K.

1862
April 29 [continued]

In the afternoon (Apr. 29th)
Capt. F. Johnstone
Capt. B. M. Edney and
myself held an election
for Field officers for
25th Regt. N. C. T.

Col. Thos. L. Clingman
was reelected unanimously

Majr. Henry Rutledge was
elected Lt. Col. having no
opposition_ A few votes
were cast for Wm. McDowell

Capt. Saml. C. Bryson
was elected Major by
a very small majority
*over Capt. W. S. Freeman_*

Only three of the old
Captains of the Regiment
were reelected_ viz.
Robards _ Grady & Francis

1862
April 30 – Wednesday

*The old officers commanded at Dress parade this morning, but were relieved from further duty by an order from Genl. Ransom which was read out at Morning dress parade_*
The new officers then took command at Muster and inspection which came off about 10 A.M.

*L^t. Co^l. Rutledge inspected_ The men transferred from our Company to another were mustered with their old companies & will not be considered transferred until tomorrow the 1st day of May At the request of Capt. Cathey I remain a few days to make out his Muster rolls etc. Walter W. Lenoir left us on day before yesterday (28th) for Caldwell County to help raise volunteers enough to complete another Company for Co^l. Zeb Vances Legion_*

Tom and the "old" company commanders presided at the regiment's morning dress parade. At the conclusion of the ceremony orders from Brig. Gen. Robert Ransom were read aloud relieving the several officers who were not elected, or did not stand for reelection, of further duty. The Confederate company records contain a notation which states that Capt. Thomas I. Lenoir was "honorably relieved from duty April 30, 1862" as approved by Gen. Robert Ransom.[196]

Tom wrote to Walter of Lieutenant Colonel Dearing's departure from the Confederate encampment: "Col. Dearing started today at two oclock. He mounted his horse. The drum was tapped a few times & in a few minutes nearly the whole regiment were around him to hear a speech. [H]e made a short address & a sight pretty one. Some of the men seemed to be almost ready to weep & he seemed a good deal affected also."[197]

Provisions contained in the Bounty and Furlough Act and the Conscription Act allowed all soldiers who reenlisted to transfer out of their existing companies to another of their choosing if they so preferred. The records reveal that only one of Tom's men, Pvt. Napoleon L. Glenn, transferred outside of Company F. He moved to Company I of the 25th Regiment. Company C contributed four transferred men to Company F: Pvt. Rufus L. Deaver, Pvt. William N. Deaver, Cpl. Thomas F. Henson, and Musician (Fifer) John A. Smith. Another man, Pvt. John C. Wilson, moved from the regiment's Company B into the Haywood Highlanders.

Even after being formally relieved of duty Tom could not escape having to fill out the company muster roll and payroll paperwork, those "troublesome institutions" with which he had been saddled for so long. Captain Cathey requested his assistance with the tedious work, and Tom had to be pleased to help his good friend. These clerical tasks would force the captain to remain in camp a few days longer to complete the assignment.

On Apr. 28 Walter W. Lenoir had bid his brother and the Haywood Highlanders good-bye at Camp Ransom during the confused time of the army's reorganization. With Tom's support and to the regret of many of the Haywood Highlanders, Walter returned to Caldwell County to raise another company of mountain men from that region for Zebulon Vance's command. In just a few weeks Walter and the Caldwell men he had rounded up returned to Kinston, where Vance was trying to assemble a legion—a military unit composed of two or three infantry regiments with supporting cavalry and artillery. However, not nearly enough men could be found to fill the ranks of Vance's army, and it was disbanded in July. To Walter's surprise, he was elected and appointed first lieutenant of Company C in the 37th Regiment N.C. Moreover, in a shockingly sudden turn of events he thereafter received the sobering news that the company's captain had resigned due to sickness and Walter was subsequently elected to command the company.[198] Soon his regiment was on the move northward from Richmond with the rest of the Army of Northern Virginia.

Walter's regiment was attached to Gen. A. P. Hills's Division of Stonewall Jackson's command and would participate in the Confederate victories at Cedar Mountain and Second Manassas in northern Virginia. Immediately following the fighting along the Bull Run on Sept. 1, Jackson's rebel army, which included Walter's regiment, again clashed with Union forces at Ox Hill near the Chantilly Plantation. In the fierce fighting that ensued Capt. Walter Lenoir was twice wounded in the right leg by two musket balls. Two days later his leg was amputated below the knee as he lay insensible on a table in a temporary field hospital.[199]

1862
April 30 [continued]

The men of Company "F" seem to be much attached to Walter & he was assured that he could have a Lieut^{cy}. in the Company if he would accept it_ but he thought it his duty to go & so did I __

"Rebs Roasting Corn," sketch by Alfred Rudolf Waud. *Library of Congress, Prints and Photographs Division.*

May 1862

The disastrous loss of New Bern by the North Carolina troops had been of considerable concern to the Confederate authorities. Changes were instituted in the state's high command, and Robert Ransom, Jr., then colonel of the 1st Cavalry North Carolina, was brought from Virginia to Kinston to take command of a brigade. The esteemed young general, known to be a strict disciplinarian, was a North Carolinian by birth and had graduated from West Point in 1850.[200]

The brigade that General Ransom formed was made up of four North Carolina regiments, including the 25th Regiment N.C. Troops. And it was to Brig. Gen. Ransom's headquarters that Tom headed off to draw the pay owed to him for his last four months of military service. He received from the brigade quartermaster a total payment of $520, or four months salary at $130 per month.

Again this day's entry documents that captains Lenoir and Cathey and Walter Lenoir—independent soldiers "fighting for nothing"—owed subsistence expenses to the regiment. Tom notes payment of a bill held against him and his comrades for food supplies. He handed $13.27 over to Capt. John Walker, the regiment's commissary of subsistence, as payment in full for provisions through May 1.

1862
May 3 – Saturday

Went over to Genl. Ransom's head Quarters & drew from the Brigade Q. M. Capt. Dewey (I believe was the name) my pay for the last four months ending April 30th 1862 = $520.00
 On Wednesday last paid to Capt. Walker his bill against Ja^s. M. Cathey, W. W. Lenoir & myself for provisions up to the first day of May 1862 Amounting to = $13.27 13.27

May 4 – Sunday

Cousin Edmund Jones & his son Capt. John T. Jones came to see me today _ John has just returned from a scouting trip of two weeks

1862
May 5 – Monday

I believe that I am nearly ready to start home expect to leave at six oclock in the morning So far as I know all my accounts with the army are settled or as nearly settled as they will probably ever be_ The $20.00 which was sent to me by W. S. Freeman from J. A. B. Fitzgerald of Haywood for the use of the sick & wounded of Company F was handed over to Capt. Cathey in presence of the company & there were no other funds in my hands belonging to the company_ I had not expended any of the 20.00 but kept it laid away for harder times_ & I never had in possession any other Company funds that I can now remember I sold my new Captain's coat to L^t. James A. Blalock at $45.00 my sash to J.T. Cathey at 2.50 & my pants to J.M.C. at 25.00 which were lower prices than they are now bringing in the Market and they were as good as new

Four days had passed since Tom was relieved of command at Kinston. His stay at Camp Ransom had been extended a while longer to assist Captain Cathey with the company muster and payroll paperwork and to close out some lingering personal affairs. He handed over to Captain Cathey the twenty dollars in cash that had been given by J. A. B. Fitzgerald of Haywood County to assist with the care of the sick and wounded. As far as he could remember, all other army matters were settled "as nearly … as they will probably ever be." And Tom sold off different elements of his captain's uniform—coat, sash, and pants—to some of the boys for what he judged to be less than market price.

The Cathey brothers purchased all of the cooking and tin ware that Tom and his servant, Uriah, had used over the past year at a bargain price, as far as he could figure. However, he could not let go of the "old case knife" he carried and had used for more than a decade back at Bachelor's Den in Haywood. Nor would he part with his sword, although several men coveted the weapon and had offered him fifty dollars for it. Finally, Tom dispensed with the remaining personal items he possessed, with the exception of what he wore, by giving away his bedclothes and a good pair of homemade shoes to some of the boys in need.

1862
May 5 [continued]

*I also let James & Turner Cathey have my cooking utensils, tin ware etc. at about half price & I only brought away one old case knife which I have used more than ten years at Bachelor's Den_*
I refused to sell my sword although offered $50.00 several times & by different persons
*I gave my Coverlid to J.T. Cathey_ a good blanket to D. S. Franklin _ & 1 D^o to R.H. Queen & a p^r. of good homemade shoes to Wiley Henson_*
*I am very sorry that I did not succeed in getting corrected some errors and omissions in making out the final statements for some discharged Soldiers, & also in making arrangements to draw the balance due to the families of the deceased soldiers_ Genl. Ransom says that the money due to deceased Soldiers' families can only be paid at Richmond & that powers of attorney are altogether useless, & that they will be paid upon the final statements_*

1862
<u>May 5</u> [continued]

*But these final statements have not been made out It was neglected by the whole regiment & I don't know who now is authorized to do it_ We enquired of Genl. Ransom_ He referred us to the Regulations, probably because he did not know how else to answer the enquiries I could find no officers in the 25th Reg^t. that seemed to know any thing about this matter of final statement for deceased Soldiers_ A few questions upon this subject were written down & sent to Ransom signed several captains & they were returned, without being answered & we were referred to the Regulations As I am now out of office I am probably not authorized to make out or correct any papers of the kind for discharged men or others_ Orders were received here tonight requiring the 25th Reg^t. to move at 8 oclk. A.M on tomorrow_ & we suppose that the whole Reg^t. will move towards Kinston_*

Of deep concern and regret to Tom was the fact that he was not able to arrange administrative matters so as to secure the pay due to the families of the deceased and disabled soldiers in his command. More than anything else, he surely would have hoped to carry this money back with him to the grieving and needy families in Haywood County. A letter he received from A. C. Hartgrove in early March included a query about the funds due Amos Reece (the young soldier who had died the previous Christmas) and is a good example of the type of issues that continually vexed the captain: "PS – David Reece requested me to ask you if you sent Amas [sic] Reeces money in his case. there none found when it was opened & he did not know whether it had been sent or not."[201] The Confederate Army's complicated system, administered in Richmond, was notoriously slow in disbursing funds to the rightful heirs of the fallen rebels. And Tom complains at length that none of the regiment's officers nor even General Ransom knew the details of how the process actually worked.

Surely adding to Tom's internal distress and worries was other news from home that he had recently received from Hartgrove. "I will now tell you something of the misfortunes at home. on last Saturday night some raugo [rogue] broke open your smoke house & stole three shoulders of bacon which would have weighed about 120 lbs. they pict [sic] the lock. it was the old pad lock that you left to the door. I hunted with three other men all day last Sunday to find the rascal but could [not] make any discovery." In a subsequent letter penned a few days later Hartgrove updated Tom on the bacon-theft business: "the rauges has stolen some of James Burnettes Bacon since they broke into your smoke house. I have a large steel trap kept in your smoke house & told the boys to keep a dog tied at the door."[202]

As a heavy rain beat down on the Confederate encampment the previous evening, Tom paid his final respects and bid the officers and men of the regiment farewell. The journal exposes a tender side to his former commanding officer, Lt. Col. Henry Rutledge. The young warrior invited Tom to the shelter of his tent and out of the rain, whereupon the colonel showed him a "likeness of his intended." Tom thought the girl (presumably Anna Maria Blake, whom Rutledge married soon after the war and, like the colonel, a resident of Flat Rock in Henderson County) was quite a pretty girl. Tom records his hopes for the couple.

The former captain arose quite early on this morning and rode over to R. B. Vause's house on "old Charlie," a horse loaned to him by Lieutenant Colonel Rutledge. At Vause's he made transportation arrangements for later that morning and then rode back to camp. Passes were needed to cross the picket lines, so Tom went over to General Ransom's headquarters to obtain one for himself and one for Vause. However, he evidently arrived a little too early to see the general in person. Ransom had not yet "made his appearance," so one of his staff officers wrote out the passes for Tom.

The Haywood Highlanders were up and stirring early on this morning as well. Tom took advantage of their roll call assembly to pass in front of the ranks and shake hands with each man. They were men to whom he felt an affinity and with whom he had developed close bonds over the past ten months or so. It is no wonder that he "felt quite sad at the idea of parting from the Boys."

1862
May 6 – Tuesday

Went early this morning to see R.B. Vause_ He agreed to take Uriah, myself & baggage to Kinston before 8 Oclock A.M. Would have gone to see him last night but it rained so very hard _

*Col. Rutledge carried me to his tent last night & showed me the likeness of his Intended she seems to be quite pretty & I hope that he will live to see many happy days with Her_ He loaned me "Old Charlie" to ride to Vause's, & then to Ransom's head Quarters to get a pass for Vause & myself_ Genl. Ransom had not made his appearance (perhaps he was asleep) & Majr. Barringer wrote the passes & signed Ransom's name to them_ His writing looks very much like Ransom's_*

Shook hands with Comp. "F" at Roll Call this morning & felt quite sad at the idea of parting from the Boys

1862
May 6 [continued]

*Vause came down quite early with his carriage this Morning & we started about half after six Oclock_ William M. Wright of Company "F" with us going to Goldsboro to see about the baggage belonging to Co. F We reached the Depot about ten minutes before the cars started & all got safe on board D^r. OHagan introduced me to Lt. Forester of 1st Reg^t. N.C. Cavalry_ He is a native of Wilkes Co. & is returning home on account of his health_ He looks very badly & the D^r. thinks that he has typhoid fever_ I got the benches fixed so that he could lie down, & then put my overcoat under his head & he seemed much more comfortable_ He seemed so weak that D^r. O.Hagan procured a private room at Goldsboro for him where he will have to remain until able to travel At Goldsboro, Wright & myself searched about among the baggage & found my trunk, mess-chest & three boxes_*

Vause was as good as his word and showed up promptly at camp at 6:30 in the morning with his carriage. It must have been a large hack to accommodate himself, Tom, Uriah, and their baggage, and a young private by the name of William M. Wright, who was being sent to Goldsboro to find the baggage belonging to Company F. Barely reaching the depot in time, Tom saw his small band on board safely just before the train left for Goldsboro.

Once inside the train cars Tom encountered the surgeon of the 35th Regiment N.C., Dr. Charles O'Hagan, who was escorting a patient to Goldsboro. Lieutenant Forester, the sick man, was from Wilkes County and attached to the 1st Regiment N.C. Cavalry. O'Hagan thought the man under his care was suffering from typhoid fever. Tom did his best, it seems, to rearrange the benches in the car so that the cavalryman could lie down. And he even placed his overcoat under the lieutenant's head to be used as a pillow.

Upon their arrival at Goldsboro Tom and Private Wright searched the depot for the company's baggage, which they eventually found. Included with it were Tom's own belongings, consisting of a trunk, a mess kit, and three boxes.

In Goldsboro the captain rid himself of two boxes made of poplar wood that contained few personal articles. The baggage that he kept—a large red box, his Augusta mess chest, and a trunk—he had loaded on the westbound train. While waiting in Goldsboro, Tom bumped into Col. James Radcliffe, who had commanded the 18th Regiment N.C. Troops at Grahamville. During their brief chat Tom discovered that the colonel had not been reelected during the April reorganization of the army and seemed to be quite miffed by the fact. The exclusion of Radcliffe was not unique at the time of the reorganization; numerous officers, good and bad, were ousted from the Confederate army. At the conclusion of the elections in late April Tom wrote to Walter reporting on the results and said that one new company captain had "a very green-looking set of Lieutenants." He continued and offered his opinion that it was evident that there had been some bad selections in the 25th Regiment.[203] Many of the displaced officers, however, were excellent professional soldiers, even graduates of West Point as was Radcliffe, who may have been deemed too strict or demanding by subordinate officers and the private soldiers.[204] In Colonel Radcliffe's case, Tom tended to sympathize, surmising there were "worse oficers in the Army than he."

On the Goldsboro-to-Raleigh leg of the journey Tom fell into company with a Captain Sloan of Greensboro. The captain, who was an assistant quartermaster, seems to have made a most favorable impression on Tom. The journal record indicates how pleased he was with Sloan and how much he liked the captain's looks. Such delightful company would have moderated the tedium on the train ride to the capital city, where they arrived at 5:00 in the afternoon.

1862
<u>*May 6*</u> *[continued]*

*I left the two poplar boxes as they had but few articles belonging to me in them_ & brought away the large red box, & my Augusta Mess-chest, & my trunk_ Saw Co^l. Ratcliff in Goldsboro & had some chat with him he seems to be hurt at the idea of his not being reelected Co^l. & I think it probable that there are worse officers in the Army than he_*

*Fell in company also with Capt. Sloan (James I believe) of Greensboro N.C. He is A Q.M_*

We traveled together to Raleigh & I was much pleased with him_ I first met him in Asheville in August last_ He has a son Thomas with Genl. Ransom, acting as Aid Clerk or something I like his looks very well also__ We go to Raleigh about 5 P.M (I believe

1862
May 6 [continued]

*Put most of my baggage in the Depot_ M^r. Sloan saw my mess-chest & at once proposed to buy it for some Maj^r. (Somebody) & I told him that as long as a frying pan & coffee mill 2 tin cups & 1 tin plate were missing out of it, he might have it for 25.00 and he at once agreed to take it. Went with boy Uriah to The Plantation Hotel to see Cousin E. W. Jones_ and found an empty bed in his room & got permission to occupy it_*
*He told me of the death M^{rs}. Rufus Patterson_ She was buried at Salem_*

May 7 – Wednesday

Went to some book--stores & bought some military books_ & then to the Capital, & looked around a while at the Members of the Convention Cousin Ed pointed out some of the most prominent

As Tom was storing his baggage at the Raleigh depot, the "Augusta" mess chest caught the eye of Captain Sloan. Sloan at once proposed to buy it for another officer acquaintance of his and was able to persuade Tom to part with it. But Tom made it clear that he would only let the chest go as long as a frying pan, coffee mill, two tin cups, and one tin plate "were missing out of it." Sloan at once agreed and paid $25.00 for the chest and took it off Tom's hands. The two men parted company at the Raleigh station, at which point Tom and his slave companion, Uriah, made their way to the Plantation Hotel where his cousin Ed W. Jones was staying. There was an empty bed in Jones's room, and he consented to let Tom stay overnight with him. Presumably Uriah found other, more rustic, accommodations for the night.

Tom's train from Raleigh to the western region of the state did not leave until the afternoon, so he and his Cousin Ed had all morning to roam the city streets. They visited a bookstore, it is recorded, and for reasons only known to him, Tom decided to buy some military books to haul back to the mountains. Or perhaps he obtained the books with intentions of giving them to Walter Lenoir, whose military career was taking off just as Tom's was ending. Afterward, Ed Jones guided Tom over to the capitol building and pointed out some of the more prominent legislators.

There were few orations on this day in the hall of North Carolina's state government, as Tom looked briefly on. Therefore, he sought out the Board of Claims, located somewhere nearby, and inquired about Haywood County's claim against the state for supplying materials to fashion tents and clothing, blankets, axes, pots and pans, and various other articles to outfit the Haywood Highlanders. The county had advanced a sum of $664.61 to purchase these items from Col. Joseph Cathey before the company left Forks of Pigeon. Now, almost a year later, Tom was seeking reimbursement from the state for the county's generous act of loyalty and support rendered to the Confederacy.[205] Almost certainly, Tom's queries roused little interest among the bureaucrats, nor did they provoke a resolution to the matter.

Tom also called at the state government's offices, where Cap. W. W. Pierce and Maj. John Devereux worked. Devereux was North Carolina's chief quartermaster and served in this vital capacity throughout the war, managing the procurement efforts to supply the North Carolina troops and the Confederate army with clothing, shoes, blankets, food, and various other necessities required by soldiers to wage war.[206] To these two quartermasters Tom made inquiries regarding the settlement of a lingering issue regarding clothing furnished to the men of the 25th Regiment N.C.

1862
May 7 [continued]

*There was but little speaking while I was in the Hall_*
  Then went down before the Board of Claims –
(or Committee on Claims)
I am not sure as to what it is called, & talked with them some about the Claim of Haywood County upon N. C. for furnishing tents, clothes etc. to the Haywood Highlanders
  Also called on Capt. Peirce Capt. Peirce A.Q.M. = W.W. Peirce & Maj^r. J. Devereux A.Q.M. and made some enquiries about clothing_ The over coats etc. etc.
  *Then saw Capt. Edney in the State House & he stated that he as agent for the 25th Reg^t. made an agreement with the Quarter M. Department which was written and signed stating that the reception of the overcoats at Camp Lee should be considered a final settlement of the clothing account of the 25th Reg^t. for the first six months_*

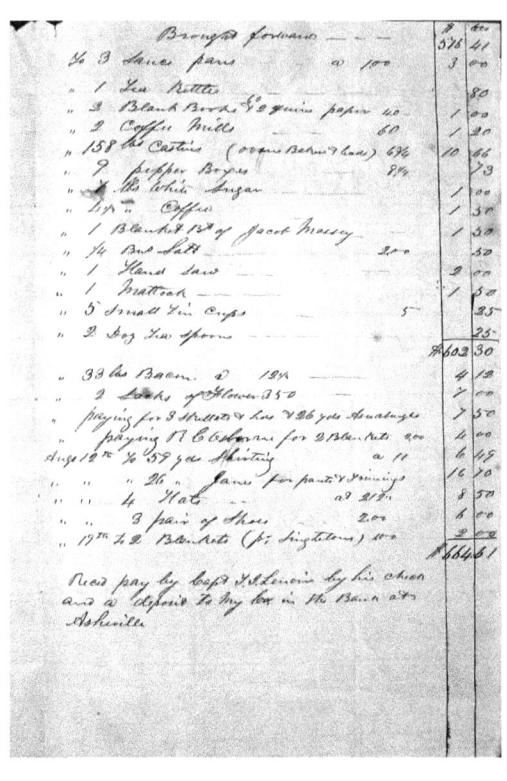

Above and opposite: A true copy of the bill Joseph Cathey submitted to Capt. Tom Lenoir for outfitting the Haywood Highlanders before the company left Forks of Pigeon in July of 1861. The county had advanced the sum of $664.61 to reimburse Cathey for the supplies, and in May 1862 Captain Lenoir was still trying to get the state of North Carolina to repay the county. *Lenoir Family Papers, Southern Historical Collection, Wilson Library, University of North Carolina at Chapel Hill; used by permission.*

I certify that the articles mentioned in the within bill were purchased for & applied to the use of "The Haywood Highlanders" (now) Company "F" of the Twenty fifth Regiment N. C. Volunteers, with funds advanced for that purpose by the County of Haywood North Carolina
Signed J. T. L.
Capt. H C V C

The above is a true Copy of the endorsement made by me on each of the Original bills sent to Raleigh
J. T. L.

Coppy J. Cathey's Bill to the Haywood Highlanders — $664.61

A true Coppy by J. T. Cathey

1862
May 7 [continued]

*Capt. E. also said that said agreement was left with Capt. Peirce_ I then went back & asked for said agreement but Capt. P. said that he knew of no such agreement_ & referred me to Maj^r. Devereux I then went up 3 p^r. stairs to Maj^r. D's office_ He said that he knew of no such agreement _ & that no body short of the Govr. had a right to make any such Agreem^t_ but upon searching a large book in which was recorded his correspondence with the Q.M. of the 25th Reg^t. we found a Copy (certified) of an agreement signed only by Capt. Edney stating that he as agent had agreed to take the overcoats as the bal. in full of the clothing for the first six months_*

*If the Q.M. Department at Raleigh did not agree ~~that~~ to such a settlement for the first six months, why was this agreement (signed by Capt. E.) recorded & certified to be correct ?? I will leave this matter to be settled by Maj^r. John Devereux_ Capt. W.W. Peirce & Capt. B.M.E_*

While prowling the halls of government in Raleigh, Tom encountered Capt. Balis M. Edney, former commander of the 25th Regiment's Company A from Henderson County. Like Tom, Edney had declined to stand for reelection during the April 1862 reorganization and was, in all probability, also making his way back to the western mountains. Edney explained to Tom that, as agent for the 25th Regiment, he had long ago settled the initial clothing account with the quartermaster's department. Moreover, he had signed a written agreement stating that the reception of overcoats by the regiment (in early January 1862) settled the accounting matter.

Armed with this new information, Tom returned to the quartermaster's department and again confronted Pierce and Devereux about the clothing account. Major Devereux adamantly denied an agreement had been made with the 25th Regiment, as Edney avowed. To prove it he opened his large book of correspondence and he and Tom pored through it in search of the document to which Edney had referred. Sure enough, they discovered Edney's signed agreement. Its existence must have come as a great surprise to Devereux, and Tom was understandably confused. If this executed contract was recorded and certified to be correct, then why did the quartermaster department of North Carolina maintain that the clothing account for the first six months was not settled? Tom could not discover the answer to this question nor, apparently, could he persuade the state in the regiment's favor. He reluctantly left the perplexing matter to Edney and the quartermaster department to work out. He had a train to catch.

Tom got away from Raleigh around noontime on the cars of the North Carolina Rail Road. Steaming by towns such as Hillsboro and Greensboro which had thus far escaped the warring armies of the North and South, he arrived in Salisbury at 1:00 in the morning. There he slept but little in the station depot, and after taking an early breakfast resumed his transit to Hickory Station.

George Harper, an acquaintance whom Tom bumped into at Salisbury, would have been welcome company on the ride to Hickory Station. Their conversation likely covered the gamut of political and social issues stemming from the crisis of war to matters of less significance and of a more personal nature. And the discomfort of the jolting and bumping ride along the tracks, accentuated by the car's hard benches, was lessened by the stimulation of animated companionship. They reached Hickory Station, about midway between Statesville and Morganton, just as the last hour of the waning morning approached.

Disembarking with their baggage, the men soon secured passage to Tucker's Barn on a hack owned by William Ballews. As the illumination of daylight quickly dimmed in the shadows of Caldwell County's low mountains, the small stagecoach arrived at Tucker's, or the town of Lenoir as it was better known. Living there at the time were close relatives who surely were overjoyed to see Tom and grateful for his safe return from the war. Included in the joyful reunion were undoubtedly sister Laura and brother-in-law Joseph Caldwell Norwood. And far more important, for the first time since marching away from Asheville in September 1861, Tom laid eyes on his own dear Lizzie, who was boarding with the Norwoods while attending Davenport Female College in Lenoir.

1862
May 7 [continued]

Left Raleigh in the after noon_ passed Hillsboro after sunset_ reached Salisbury after one Oclock A.M_ & slept only two or three hours_ Got an early breakfast, met with George Harper & started in cars to Hickory Station

May 8 – Thursday

Reached Hickory Station about 11 A.M. Took dinner at Link's _ & found Rev. John Mood & family there waiting for the hack to carry them to Lenoir_ & also a Miss Virginia Holton who was just from Lenoir & waiting for the down train to go to her home in Charlotte W^{m}. Ballews [?] came down with two hacks_ Mr. Mood's family occupied one hack & G. Harper & myself the other, We got to Tucker's Barn about dark_ I left a large box, & small trunk at H. Station to be sent by first opportunity

1862
May 9 – Friday

Arrived at Fort Defiance with Lizzie about sunset

May 10 – Saturday

*Went with W.W. Lenoir to Patterson to attend a muster_ Walter made a speech inviting them to enlist_ only two signed the document _ They were Edmiston brothers_*

May 13 – Tuesday

Started to Haywood with my wife in an old buggy which bought of W.W. Lenoir & driving Walter's horse Rip_ I am to send the horse back but [no] time was set for [it] to be sent back _

Tom and Lizzie's excitement to reacquaint themselves surely ran into the wee hours, they had so much catching up to do. Apparently the start for Fort Defiance was a late one. When finally their good-byes were expressed to friends and relatives in Lenoir, they began the passage over rough roads traversing the foothills to the famed plantation home of Tom's Lenoir ancestry. There were likely few silences in the couple's conversation along the way; and while chatting and rediscovering shared intimacies, they easily covered the nine miles or so to the "Fort" before darkness set in.

Fort Defiance was the current home to Captain Lenoir's mother, Selena (or Louisa), his sister Sarah, and his younger brother Rufus, and his family. Walter Lenoir was also still there; he had wasted little time after leaving the Haywood Highlanders at Kinston to start rousting the male citizenry of Caldwell County to join the Confederate army. On this day he and Tom made a trip over to Patterson, located approximately four miles as the crow flies to the west of Fort Defiance. At that small community an organized muster (probably of state militia troops which would later become the home guard) was underway, and Walter used the occasion to attempt to recruit men for Zeb Vance's Legion. After doing his best in delivering a speech to stir the loyalties of the assembled men, he apparently was only able to inspire two Edmiston brothers to enlist.

Tom and Lizzie stayed on at Fort Defiance for three days before packing up in an old buggy that Walter sold them and heading out for Haywood County. It was a small one-horse contraption and to pull it Tom secured the loan of Walter's horse, Rip.

Tom took advantage of the three days that he and Lizzie stayed over at Fort Defiance to settle a couple of notes that his mother, Mrs. Selena Louisa Lenoir, held upon him. The two notes combined amounted to $6,304 and were a considerable debt, and burden, that Tom was saddled with. On this day he paid his mother $1,379 and, including previous credits entered on one of the notes, his debt was reduced to $4,000. Selena Lenoir refused to accept interest, and Tom "lifted" the two old notes and gave her a new note for $4,000. Except for this large sum of indebtedness Tom figures his accounts to be squared with his mother.

1862
May 13 [continued]

While at Fort Defiance,
I paid to Mr^s. S.L. Lenoir
one thousand three hundred
and seventy nine dollar = $1379.00
which together with various
credits already entered on
a note due to her made
the sum of Twenty three
hundred & four dollars = $2304.00
which I have paid towards
two notes which she held
upon me, one of them was
for forty seven hundred dollars = $4700.00
& the other for one thousand
six hundred & 4 dollars = $1604.00
making together, $6304.00
She refused to receive interest & I
gave her a new note for $4000.00
*& lifted the two old notes_*
The one for $4700.00 was due
on Mar. 1st 1861 & on 18th May 1861
was credited by $205.00 & 27th Aug^t.
by $45.00 & on Dec. 28th 1861 c^r by
$125.00 f^r. W.W. Lenoir & Apr. 28th 1862
*by $550.00 f^r. Ja^s. C. Harper_*

1862
<u>*May 13*</u> *[continued]*

The other note was due Augt. 22nd 1861 & was given for $1604.00 & had no credits entered, & so my accounts are squared there except that I owe my one note to my Mother which was this day given for $4000.00 _

1862
<u>*May 14 – Wednesday*</u>

*Went to Nelson Powel's to have my buggy repaired & called on W^m. Ballews & paid my stage fare from Hickory Station_*

1862
<u>*May 15 – Thursday*</u>

Paid J.C. Norwood $10.00 for two p^r. shoes which he had made for me, & left one pair of these as a present for Ths. L. Norwood & also paid J.C.N. a 20.00 bill for Lizzie's board which he & Sister both refused at first but I insisted & he kept it

The first stop on the way to Haywood was Lenoir, where Tom had to have the old buggy repaired so that it could stand up to the long, hard trip into the mountains. While waiting for this maintenance work to be completed he looked up William Ballews and paid him for the previous week's stage fare from Hickory Station to Lenoir.

Tom and Lizzie stayed overnight at Lenoir, most probably again in the home of Laura and Joseph Norwood. It is apparent that Tom's brother-in-law, Joseph, had paid a cobbler to make a couple of pairs of shoes for him. He reimbursed Joseph for the shoes and made a gift of one pair to the Norwoods' son, Thomas. Moreover, Tom paid the Norwoods with a twenty-dollar bill (Confederate, no doubt) to cover Lizzie's boarding expenses with them.

Tom left his and Lizzie's baggage with Joseph Norwood, who was to haul it back to Hickory Station and send it by train to Morganton, where the rails terminated, and from there to Asheville by stagecoach. At midmorning the Lenoirs started for Haywood. Brother Walter accompanied them for a mile or two before having to reluctantly bid them good luck and farewell. Though the road was surely rough and rutted, it was little more than fifteen miles to Morganton. After crossing the Catawba River at Suddeth's Ferry they reached the railhead town at 4:00 in the afternoon. From there they went on to the home of one of Tom's Avery relations, Mr. C. M. Avery, where apparently he and Lizzie spent the night.

It must have been a long night of suffering and pain for Tom. He came down with a toothache, it seems, so he and Lizzie had to ride back to Morganton to find a dentist. Dr. Thomas Corpening "plugged" his tooth, his dentistry work rating only a "so-so" in Tom's estimation. More than likely the metric of "so-so" meant that the pain level induced by the good doctor's procedure was barely tolerable. While in Morganton Tom bumped into another Avery relative, "Uncle Avery," and had to apologize for not going by to see him. He justified his act of negligence with an explanation that the old buggy in which he and Lizzie were traveling rode too low to safely cross the river. After a short visit with Uncle Avery, the captain and his lady again headed west and rode on to the village of Marion, some twenty miles away.

1862
May 15 [continued]

*He had also paid 50 cents for hauling my baggage from H. Station & will now send it to Morganton to be sent to Asheville by stage_*

*Started for Haywood about 10 Oclock_ W.W. came a mile or two with us_*

*Crossed at Suddeth's Ferry Got to Morganton about four oclock P.M. & went on to C M. Avery's_*

1862
May 16 – Friday

*Went back to Morganton & got a tooth plugged by D^r. Thos. Corpening – so-so – Saw Uncle Avery & told him that we would have gone to see him but our buggy was too low to cross the river_ & then we went to Marion_*

1862
May 17 – Saturday

*Left Marion at 8 Oclock Called a few minutes at Pleasant Gardens, _ stopped about an hour at Genl. Burgins, & took a snack & gave Rip meal & water & then got to Alexanders before sun down_*

May 18 – Sunday

Came to Asheville for dinner, had head ache

May 19 – Monday

*Reached the Den about 7 ½ P.M. with my Dear little Wife & here she is leaning her head on my shoulder & reading as I write_*

To reach the Den required two long days of travel from Marion. The first stretch to Asheville was approximately twenty-five miles of winding road that passed through Pleasant Gardens and wound its way up the steep mountain slope, where it pierced the Blue Ridge range at the Swannanoa Gap. From the crest of that breach Tom and Lizzie followed the Swannanoa River as it flowed down into the Asheville vicinity. It was a familiar route to Tom—the same that he and the Haywood Highlanders had marched over on their way to eastern North Carolina the year before. They left Marion at 8:00 in the morning and reached Alexanders, located about twelve miles east of Asheville, at sundown after a grueling, bone-jarring ride of ten hours or more.[207]

On the Sabbath Tom was apparently suffering from another headache, yet he and Lizzie journeyed on into Asheville, where they took their dinner. It is not certain whether they continued on after their meal or found a place in Asheville to lodge overnight.

The next morning the reunited couple set out on the final leg of their journey home. The Den lay another twenty-five-mile stretch of treacherous turnpike and crude wagon paths ahead. From Asheville the Western Turnpike hugged the banks of Hominy Creek almost all the way to the village of Pigeon River (where present-day Canton is situated). At that juncture a rugged trace coursed up the Pigeon River to Forks of Pigeon and then alongside the East Fork a few final miles. It took all the daylight hours and then some for the Lenoirs to negotiate their way back home, arriving at the Den just after dark and utterly exhausted.

Although tired and weary and dirty from the day's long haul, Tom managed to pen a final entry in his journal that evening while his "Dear little Wife" leaned her head on his shoulder. And as suddenly as he had taken off his sword at Kinston and quit the army three weeks before, he closed out the diary record of his brief ten-month service in the Confederate army as captain of the Haywood Highlanders.

> (May 17
> Left Marion at 8 Oclock
> Called a few minutes at
> Pleasant Gardens,
> Stopped about an hour
> at Genl. Burgins, & took
> a snack & gave Rips
> Meal & water. & Then
> got to Alexanders before
> Sun down —
>
> Sunday
> May 18 Came to Asheville for
> dinner, had head ache
>
> Monday
> May 19 Reached The Den about
> 7½ P.M. with my Dear little
> Wife & here she is leaning
> her head on my shoulder, &
> reading as I write —

Finally home from the Civil War and comfortably situated in the old Den, Captain Lenoir closed out his wartime diary with this final entry while his "Dear little wife" rested her head on his shoulder." *Collection of Hugh K. Terrell and the late Emily Michal Terrell; used by permission.*

Early ploughing. *Harper's New Monthly Magazine*, vol. 61, June–Nov., 1880.

In War's Aftermath on the East Fork

After Tom Lenoir returned home from the war to his East Fork farm in May 1862 he resumed raising livestock and growing grain crops. The Den was surely a more pleasant and comfortable place to inhabit, and no longer deserved the name "Bachelor's Den." Lizzie was a co-occupant now and was able to offer Tom a sort of companionship and comfort that he had never before enjoyed; she helped share and bear the burdens of their difficult rural existence. As Tom reentered the everyday social and civil life of the community it must have been difficult to face the men and women whose sons he had led off to the war. These people, including some of his tenants, had expected Captain Lenoir to look after their cherished young men and teach them the rudiments of being soldiers. Now, here was the captain back amongst them, yet their loved ones either had fallen already from disease or were still away at the war front and most assuredly facing unknown dangers and extreme hardships.

Tom had realized, even before going off to war, that he was not physically constituted to withstand the privations and extreme exposure of an extended campaign in the field. Even the relatively easy duty on the coast of South Carolina had proved too strenuous for him. At an advanced age and afflicted with poor health, he had known that he was not the right man for the captain's job and had written so to his brother. Yet the captain's conscience must have been at ease that he had endeavored to do his duty in the Confederate army, had strived to perform beyond his physical capacity, and had made sacrifices that almost brought ruin to his body and to his Haywood farming enterprise.

No evidence has indicated that Tom dwelt hard on his inability to withstand the rigors of army life in the field. Almost immediately after returning home he was ordered

Rufus Theodore Lenoir, youngest brother of Thomas Isaac Lenoir, about 1875. Rufus was perhaps Tom's favorite correspondent and one with whom he shared his innermost feelings and discussed with relish farming affairs and livestock matters. Portrait by Johannes Oertel, oil on canvas, approx. 24" x 36". *Collection of the Fort Defiance Museum, Lenoir, N.C.; used by permission.*

Walter Waightstill Lenoir, younger brother of Thomas Isaac Lenoir, about 1843. Upon hearing that Walter had been wounded during the Civil War, Tom Lenoir rushed off to northern Virginia to find and retrieve him. *Collection of Ike Forester; used by permission.*

to lead local militia cavalry forces through the mountains to suppress the activities of Tories (Unionists) and Yankees and apprehend Confederate deserters. In late 1862 Tom led one such foray into East Tennessee against a plundering gang of Tories. Apart from killing one deserter and capturing a few Yankees the mission was largely unsuccessful. The operation had been carried out under wintry cold and rainy conditions over a two-week period, exacerbating Captain Lenoir's health problems; he returned home to the Den suffering with a fever and nearly incapacitated with a cold.[208] Throughout the duration of the war Tom served the Confederacy in this capacity, leading home guard troops in difficult and mostly futile efforts to rid the mountains of the hated and feared bushwhackers and outlying deserters.

Before the elder Thomas Lenoir died in 1861 he had divided his East Fork landholdings, comprising more than 4,000 acres, into a lower tract and an upper tract, just as Tom had advised. Tom inherited the lower tract, where his Den and farm buildings were located, and his younger brother, Walter, received the upper section. In the spring of 1863 Walter Lenoir, having lost his leg as a result of a battle wound the previous year, removed to Haywood to begin a farming career. Upon receiving the news of his brother's injury at the time, Tom had dropped everything and instantly rushed off to Virginia to find him, eventually collecting Walter just forty miles from Washington, D.C., and escorting him back to the family home in Caldwell County.[209]

Over a prolonged spell of convalescence and hobbling around on crutches and a prosthetic leg at the "Fort," Walter began to feel the need to demonstrate his worth and manly independence. He had to prove to himself and others that he could get on with his life and survive without the assistance and pampering of family and friends. After lengthy contemplation and introspection, he made the surprising decision to settle on his East Fork property near Tom. So Walt trekked to Haywood and moved into a vermin-infested cabin a couple of miles above the Den, promptly labeling his new quarters "Crab Orchard" after the styling given the property even before his father claimed it in 1806. There on a beautiful expanse of bottomland surrounded by steep, wooded mountain slopes and hard by the bold East Fork of Pigeon River he led a lonely existence, with only the African bondsmen for companions and an abundance of time for soulful meditation about his crippled condition and the South's deteriorating hopes.

When news of their mother's death in 1864 reached the Lenoir brothers in remote Haywood, Walt undoubtedly felt a deep sorrow over the loss, and experienced intense remorse to the utter depths of his being. He had not seen his mother since moving to Haywood County more than a year earlier. And Louisa had pleaded for her physically challenged son to return to Fort Defiance, even inquiring in a letter: "Was such a mind as yours bestowed to live the life of a Hermit? And will not its long continuance be detrimental in some ways, producing indifference, even selfishness [?]"[210] Unquestionably, Walter knew that his mother had died feeling that he had abandoned her and the family, and this would have been a heavy weight to bear along with the other farming burdens, slave affairs, and his pitiful physical condition.

The Lenoir brothers coped, as the war dragged on, with the severe shortages of foodstuffs and other supplies, such as leather and textile goods. When stretched for money to support his labor requirements Tom acknowledged to Walter the value possessed by these types of goods: "I could sometimes get work for such articles when folks won't look at money."[211] The mountaineers considered the rapidly devalued Confederate money practically worthless, and trade across the region was supported almost entirely with a barter economy. Salt, especially, was one of those critical items in short supply during the war. The people of Haywood County and throughout Western North Carolina experienced a severe deficiency of this important commodity, which was necessary for curing meats as well as seasoning cooked foods. Early on in the war Tom received a letter from a man in Waynesville attesting to its scarcity: "We are entirely out of salt at this time. [T]he court met last week and passed and [*sic*] order to have salt deposited at five localities in the County, and among them at Forks of Pigeon." The correspondent went on to offer encouraging news that a shipment was expected at any time from Wilmington through the railhead at Morganton.[212]

In addition to the deprivations suffered on the home front and the continued worry over the absence of loved ones fighting in the war, Tom and the other citizens of Haywood had to remain ever vigilant against thieving deserters and raiding Yankee cavalry units. Numerous raids were carried out from Union-controlled East Tennessee, a notorious hotbed of Unionist sentiment, against outlying western mountain settlements and homesteads. One such incident occurred during the waning days of the Civil War, in April 1865. Federal cavalry troops riding out of Asheville paid a visit to Tom and Walter's farms on the East Fork and confiscated everything that they could carry out of the valley. In a letter to younger Brother Rufus at Fort Defiance dated August 14, 1865, Tom bitterly related the unhappy event:

[A] company of Yankee thieves from Asheville came up South Hominy Creek and down Pisgah Creek. They took six of my horses and mules, rushed up to the house cursing and swearing with guns presented. Miss Laura Garrett [Lizzie's sister], Lizzie and myself were here. They threatened to kill Lizzie. Searched my pockets, took what gold and silver we had, some of Lizzie's jewelry, an old rifle, a Navy pistol, some of my clothes, my old silver watch, and other articles, including bacon, hams, flour, etc.[213]

Not mentioned but also included in the raiders' haul was Walter's horse, Rip—the same gentle beast Tom had borrowed to pull himself and Lizzie back to Haywood in May of 1862 at the conclusion of his brief Confederate army career.

Bitter partisan strife over who should dictate the fate of the emancipated slaves and control the reconstruction process divided the South and led to years of unrest, unlawfulness, continued suffering, and conflict in all the Southern states. Apparently, the flood of carpetbaggers from the North attempting to take advantage of the distressed situation in North Carolina did not overflow into the western mountains. What few Northerners found their way into the rugged highland recesses imposed little adverse impact on the mountaineers. And the reach of the organizations working to gain full civil rights for the former slaves, such as the Union League and the Freedmen's Bureau, did not extend into the territory surrounding Haywood County's Pigeon River.

In other areas of the state and across the South the Ku Klux Klan's white-hooded horsemen, riding in the night, kidnapped, horse-whipped, and, on occasion, hanged headstrong and enlightened freedmen. Their objective was to intimidate and frighten the former slaves away from participation in new societal roles established by the Radical Republican government. However, the range of the Klan's night rides seldom spread into the western mountain region of North Carolina. There were so few former slaves remaining in the county after the war that the attentions and efforts of these organizations were directed elsewhere, where greater populations of freedmen existed.

Prior to the war in 1860, the number of slaves residing and working in Haywood was 313, or only 5.4% of the entire county population.[214] At the conclusion of the war, when the freedom of these few men, women, and children had been guaranteed, their situation and immediate future prospects were ambiguous at best. That included the small clans of former slaves once owned and controlled by Captain Tom Lenoir on his farm along the East Fork of Pigeon River.

In May 1865, with the matter of the rebellion decided and the institution of slavery forever exterminated in the country, Captain Lenoir may not have been entirely certain how to deal with his newly freed bondsmen, but apparently Walter had no qualms. Walt gathered all his former slaves together in a meeting and simply informed them that he no longer needed their services. As a result, these emancipated men, women, and children moved into a rented cabin owned by Alfred Henson and located up the river a couple of miles, on Cold Creek. In fact, Walter was so anxious about their riddance that he "gave them his best cow, over a hundred pounds of bacon, 16 bu[shels] of corn, 3 hogs, some tools, etc." He justified his act of generosity to Joe Norwood, his brother-in-law, by simply offering that he desired to have "his hands washed of all further responsibility for the maintenance of Africans." Instead of hiring other poor farmers in the area or young men returning from army service to work in the fields and tend the livestock—a practice many former slaveowners resorted to—Walter leased his land to a local farmer, Jesse Anderson, Jr. The new Anderson tenant family moved into Walter's own cabin, while the crippled Confederate veteran relocated to a smaller cabin that had recently been built for a former slave family. Evidently a boarding arrangement was entered into, and Mrs. Anderson was contracted to cook for Walter, launder his clothes, and provide myriad other types of assistance.[215]

Captain Lenoir, on the other hand, was also pressed for laborers, but he opted to negotiate with his former slaves and enter into formal labor agreements with them. In the same Aug. 14, 1865, letter to his brother Rufus, Tom recorded his methods in dealing with the labor issue:

In the spring I told them if they would behave well and work faithfully and according to my directions until the corn was cribbed, I would give them one-third of it, half of the potatoes, buckwheat and molasses, their victuals and raw material enough to make the usual amount of clothing for the year. Wrote out two copies of agreement, signed before a witness. I have told them that they must not encourage others to come and settle around me, or I would cut loose from the whole concern.[216]

At the beginning of the war some eighteen slaves were owned and employed at Bachelor's Den. It is believed that most of this population remained on the farm in the immediate postwar period, and Tom's contract was evidently extended to all of them.

After the crops were harvested in the following year of 1866, Tom did not renew the contract with his former slaves. Walter reported to his folks at Fort Defiance that Tom "occasionally hires the negro men that used to belong to him, and sometimes Andy [one of Walter's former slaves], but generally hires white hands."[217] In March 1867 Captain Lenoir's entire family consisted of his "[w]ife, child, self, two young men ... & one young woman." These hired hands provided the necessary labor to replace that of the former slaves. Their services were absolutely required to carry on with the farming business and support the household. Yet in another letter to Rufus, Tom despaired over how he would raise sufficient cash to pay the salaries of his employees once their term of service was up. He greatly doubted that he could make enough by farming to pay their wages, support his family, and pay the debts he already owed. Tom had counted on a store of cotton in South Carolina that he had owned and a note held for $1,500 on an Asheville merchant, Mr. J. W. Patton, to pay his debts. Alas, "the cotton went up in smoke," and Patton's estate was insolvent and Tom considered the note "lost." The only items of value that could be sold to raise cash were the jacks (mules) and his bacon. However, Tom explained to Rufus that he needed these proceeds to put his farm in order—repair the fences and build a new hen house. In addition Tom confided his personal feelings regarding the loss of the institution of slavery and its impact on the

South, the Western North Carolina mountains, and himself:

> The evil effects of the destruction of our system of labor will of course be most apparent where it did most prevail—Consequently the western portion of N.C. will be less affected by it than the South generally, but even here it will be bad enough, & my anticipations of the future are not very flattering either for my County, my Clan, my Family, or Myself.[218]

Although Tom wrote that the western portion of North Carolina would be least influenced by the destruction of the Southern system of labor, he nevertheless was experiencing considerable difficulty caused by the loss of his slaves. Certainly the captain was not the only mountaineer feeling the effects of emancipation and reconstruction. His was not an uncommon problem; other large landholders were having to come to terms with it as well. Vast tracts of property and associated taxes, combined with the labor costs to support farming activities, tipped the balance sheets of landowners toward financial ruin. In the year following the end of the war Walter Lenoir opined in a lengthy epistle on the subject of land and the labor situation:

> We want to keep our lands if we can; and those of us who are fortunate enough to own much good land will, if we can keep it, have wealth enough for ourselves and our children. In order to keep it we must at least make it sufficient by production to support us and pay our taxes. To do this and to keep house we must hire labor, either colored, white native or foreign . . . . I take it for granted that you agree with me that we cannot get along for the present at least with colored labor. The negro will not be self supporting while he has access to the old crib and smokehouse. There is not enough of our native white labor to be hired; it will not be well affected to its new position, will be untrained and rather indolent and careless and will not take training kindly.[219]

Many of the wealthy landholders sold off their property, bit by bit, to cover their expenses and pay debts. Others resorted to harvesting and selling their timber, a practice Tom detested. He adopted neither of these measures. Realizing the impracticality of farming all of his vast acreage on the East Fork, and desperately needing income, Tom continued leasing tracts of land to tenant families in the postwar years. In 1866 he had at least nineteen tenants living and working on his land. A listing of these families and associated leased acres found in a memorandum book includes J. G. Burnett, J. Brookshire, F. Bennett, T. M. Crawford, B. Davis, Asb. Davis, F. Howel[l], J. M. Henson, I. Ivester, H. C. Ivester, N. Knight, G. W. Miller, L. F. Miller, Isaac Pless, W. P. Pless, L. Pless, R. Poston, D. T. Trull, and B. H. Trull.[220] Although Tom normally could not have expected to be paid for the use of his land in cash money, which was scarce even after the war had ended, he certainly could have required reimbursement in other forms.

Some of the renters provided vital services or labor, including watching his livestock, building fences and other facilities, working his fields, and collecting the fruits of the orchards. Additionally, those that rented tillable land would have been required to cultivate the ground and deliver over to him at the end of the harvest season a quarter or a third of the corn and other grain crops. All of this labor and product Tom used in some way to defray taxes and expenses on his East Fork landholdings. Leveraging the land with tenant contracts, raising cattle and other farm animals, and growing corn and wheat constituted the business model Tom had always used on his East Fork farm, in one variation or another. However, with the end of slavery he suddenly faced large expenditures for labor to support his farm and was hard pressed to meet expenses and support a growing family.

Three children were born to Tom and Lizzie Lenoir in the post–Civil War years: Mary in 1865, Laura in 1872, and Sarah in 1875. For much of the period spanning the childbirths and beyond Lizzie was afflicted with an eating disorder, and judging from the extant letters it was a very serious condition that greatly diminished her health. She wrote of her illness to Tom in 1866 while he was away on a trip to Kentucky to

Much of the land owned by Tom Lenoir on the East Fork of Pigeon River was occupied and worked by tenant families before and after the Civil War. An 1866 listing from Tom's memorandum book indicates tenants along with the acres leased to them. *Lenoir Family Papers, Southern Historical Collection, Wilson Library, University of North Carolina at Chapel Hill; used by permission.*

sell livestock: "I do wish I could overcome my abominable longing for something to eat. I know you are sorry for me but you can never know how to feel for me unless you are afflicted in same way."[221] Lizzie seems to have gone from one extreme of eating to another. In a letter from the year 1878 Tom wrote to his nephew, Walter Gywn, that Lizzie was "poorly and taking medicine—she weighs 90# [pounds] again."[222] Many other letters associated with the family during the post–Civil War era either make mention of Lizzie's poor health or reference her eating disorder. In consideration of this as well as Tom's age (past forty-five when Mary was born) and his own poor health, it seems remarkable today that the couple had the ability and good fortune to rear three girls.

In 1866 Tom and Walter worked to found an Episcopal church in Waynesville, signing their names to a formal application to the Episcopal Diocese of North Carolina.[223] After its establishment both Tom and Lizzie joined on Aug. 25, 1870, at which time Tom was baptized and the couple was confirmed.[224] In this same time frame Walter completely abandoned his Crab Orchard farm and Haywood lands and relocated to Watauga County. There he moved onto a large land tract, formerly owned by his brother William, that he had assembled by purchasing his siblings' inherited portions after William's death. Most of Walter's Haywood "upper" tract on the East Fork was purchased by his brother-in-law, James M. Gywn II, whereupon Gywn's son, also named James, and his wife, Amelia Harper Foster, moved to the property in about 1875.[225] They in short time changed the name of their pretty farm from "Crab Orchard" to "Springdale."

In May 1874 Tom was afflicted with a large skin infection on his neck, which doctors ultimately diagnosed as a carbuncle. He was bedridden for weeks. The foreboding news of his condition that reached the family in Caldwell County and filtered to Walter in Watauga left his recovery in doubt. Just as Tom had rushed to Walter's aid in Virginia during the war, the younger brother prepared to make the trip to Tom's bedside in Haywood. Walt excitedly scratched off a note inquiring one last time about Tom's condition: "[I]could hardly keep from starting to Haywood, and have been thinking constantly since about you, and about Middleburg [the northern Virginia town where Tom found Walter suffering in pain from a leg amputation during the war], and how I could hardly bear for you to be out of my sight when you came to me there." Walter confessed, "[I] could not return the kind nursing that you gave me, if I were with you, but I could read to you when you wished it, and help you about your accounts and such of your other business that I could see to."[226] But a timely letter from Tom, reporting that the older brother was indeed among the living and recovering, made a visit unnecessary. Tom's condition was greatly improved; he was then able to walk for a few minutes at a time. Surprisingly, at one time or another Tom had been attended to by three doctors, and still another had been called for but could not come.

Alas, his letter bore news of a much more distressing and somber nature. Tom reported on the death of his good friend and the most revered citizen in the community: "Oh that I could feel as thankful & as humble as I ought before a Merciful God who again raised me up, & spared my unprofitable life—But in his wisdom He has seen fit to take from our midst a much better & much more useful man—I allude to Col. Joseph Cathey." Cathey had died June 1 from some form of heart disease, and Tom was distraught at the loss of this man, who had lived a life which yielded such amazing accomplishment and utility for his community and county.[227]

In February 1876 Tom appears to have been building a mill. His brother Rufus wrote to him, "If you should <u>ever</u> start your mill I hope you will give me your mill experience in mill building."[228] Perhaps Tom was encouraged by Walter's labors in Watauga to construct and operate a water-powered mill. Although it is not certain when he completed and started up the facility, it was definitely in operation and taking orders for production by midyear 1879—that is, whenever the Good Lord was willing and provided sufficient water flow to drive the machinery. In that time frame a man wrote an order to Tom for six hundred feet of 1¼-inch planks and included in his note the following considerate request: "I am satisfied that you will treat Mr. Henson & myself as kindly as you can—If it should rain & thereby enable you to saw, please do so & this further obliges me etc."[229]

At the end of the decade of the 1870s, almost fifteen years after the conclusion of the Civil War and near the end of the Reconstruction era in the South, Tom's farming operations had not improved sufficiently for him to produce a profit. All of his hard work seems to have been to no avail, prompting Walter to remark in a letter: "[I]t adds to the gloom to find that a farmer as skillful, as attentive & as economical as you, & with such a farm, can't make his receipts equal his expenditures. We must do that much. If we can't bring up the receipts, we must bring down the expenditures." Not content with offering only these thoughts, which likely fell on unwelcome ears, Walter continued by conveying a deep concern for Tom's health:

> But I find myself still more discouraged about the state of your health than about the condition of your farming operations. You have been sick or in feeble health so much of the time during the fall & winter as to suggest the fear that either you are overtasked, and are overdoing yourself in the attempt to keep up with your business & your household cares, or that your general health is failing or disordered.

Walt also stressed how much more important Tom's life and health were to Lizzie and the girls than were the lands and stock and other property. He pleaded, "Think how utterly helpless they would be without you, a mother with ruined health, and three little girls, in a wild & lonesome neighborhood." Walter's sincere advice to his older brother conveys a genuine brotherly love and concern for Tom and his family.[230]

It also lays bare the utter futility of all of Tom's hard toiling over the years to produce livestock and grain crops in sufficient quality and quantity to cover his expenses, debts, and improvements. His father before him failed in that pursuit, and Tom was never able to turn his beautiful farmland situated along the East Fork of Pigeon River into a prosperous enterprise. He was only able to make do.

Nevertheless a Yankee visitor to Tom's farm at the time was so impressed during his stay on the East Fork that he wrote in a note of gratitude to his host: "It was the first time I ever caught trout in March; one of your apple trees had the diameter of a full yard—the largest I ever saw; and your cattle were the best I saw during those months travel at the South."[231]

Mary Lenoir, Tom and Lizzie's oldest daughter, known as "Mamie," was almost fifteen years old in January of 1880. At that time she corresponded with her Aunt Sarah at Fort Defiance to report on affairs at the Den. The young daughter's letter offers an inviting glimpse into the Lenoir farmstead. Mamie sympathetically wrote that her "mama" had been better than usual but had hurt herself lifting Sallie (Sarah, Tom and Lizzie's youngest). Following this incident Mamie indicated that her mama was not well "atall." However, she bragged: "I weigh twenty pounds more than Mama and can pick her up and carry her all about." Her father, Mamie wrote, was getting so old he could not do without his wooden-bottomed shoes to "go about in the mud." Tom seems to have instilled a little levity into the Lenoir household with the wood shoes that he fashioned. Mamie wrote that "[h]e finished a pair yesterday that weighed three pounds. [H]e calls them his pumps and sometimes he tries to dance with them on, and you don't know how funny he looks, they are a great help to him though. [T]hey keep his feet warm & dry."[232]

Sadly, tragedy crept across the Den's threshold toward the latter part of November 1880. A child was born to Lizzie at that time, and according to family lore some of the former slaves still residing in the area began dancing and chanting "Marse Tom's got a boy" upon hearing the good news.[233] But the celebrations were soon drowned out with sorrowful tears at the report that Tom's dear Lizzie did not survive the childbirth.

The baby's own feeble life flickered for only a short time after his mother's was snuffed out.[234] Tom was utterly devastated. A continuous stream of letters poured in from Lenoir family members in Caldwell County, offering to him their condolences and giving advice on what should be done with the girls. The folks at Fort Defiance (Rufus and his family and sister Sarah) as well as the Norwoods in Lenoir (Tom's sister Laura, and her husband, Joseph) generously suggested that they be allowed to take the youngsters into their care, feeling that Tom was in a peculiar situation to raise the girls alone. But Tom, apparently, would have none of it. The girls stayed with him in Haywood, and he determined to raise them the best that he could.

As events unfolded Tom and the girls lived only one more year at the Den. In December 1881 a hurried letter from Walter to Rufus reveals that Tom had taken sick and Walter had made the long journey from Watauga County to Haywood to be at his bedside. Tom was "very weak and despondent," observed Walter, and "his other symptoms are those of a mild form of typhoid fever." The Gwyns from Springdale, neighbors, and former slaves were visiting regularly and acting as nurses, doing what duty and love called for. Tom had to be helped out of bed frequently, and it took three good men taking hold of him to accomplish that feat. Afraid their well-intentioned aides might wear themselves out or become ill, Walter requested that Rufus send out his son, Tommy. He could take over Tom's farm work or help out in other ways that might be needed. Tom's outdoor business was in sad need of looking after, as Walt phrased it, and the corn was "ungathered" and the hogs had not been killed. Walter instructed that Tommy "take the Newfound Road from Asheville to Ford of Pigeon, turning down the river bank after crossing the bridge. The road up Hominy is in wretched condition & obstructed by the railroad work going on."[235] Tommy did not make it in time. Thomas Isaac Lenoir died in his Den on Jan. 5, 1882, at the age of sixty-four years, with his daughters and Walter at his side.

The three Lenoir girls were not left to the Haywood wolves, of course. Relatives retrieved them from the remote mountains soon after Tom was laid to rest beside Lizzie in a family plot near where the forks of the Pigeon River unite. Mamie was promptly sent away to Salem Academy in Salem, North Carolina (now Winston-Salem). The two younger daughters, Laura and Sallie, were taken in at Fort Defiance by their Aunt Sade (Sarah Lenoir) and the Rufus T. Lenoir, Sr., family. At the old "Fort" they romped through the halls and over the grounds graced by their famed great-grandfather and Revolutionary War hero, Gen. William Lenoir, and their highly respected and accomplished grandfather, Col. Thomas Lenoir. In due time Laura and Sallie were sent to boarding school as well. All three of Tom and Lizzie's daughters were afforded an education commensurate with their heritage—one that allowed them to meet the challenges of the industrial age and perpetuate the Lenoir legacy for generations to come.

Tom and his dear Lizzie lie peacefully today in a small family cemetery near the heart of the historic Forks of Pigeon community in Bethel, N.C. *Photo courtesy of Bill and Earlene Holbrook.*

PART II

History and Roster of the Haywood Highlanders

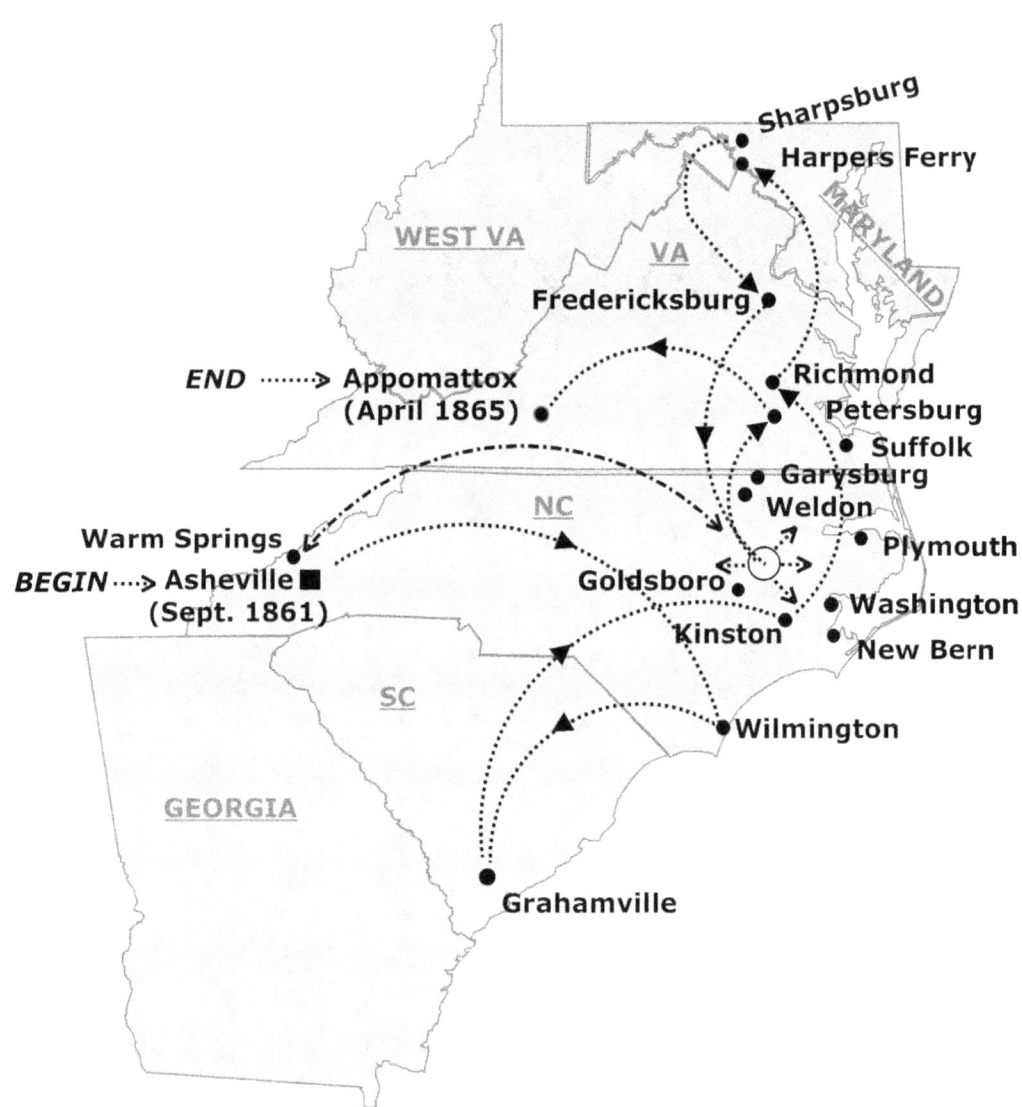

The journey of the Haywood Highlanders through the Civil War. *Map by Carroll C. Jones.*

⇛ THE AVERAGE ENLISTMENT AGE *of the soldiers who served with the Haywood Highlanders was 24.8 years.*

The Haywood Highlanders' Civil War Journey: The Last Three Years

IN THE EARLY MONTHS OF 1862 Gen. Ambrose Burnside's Union expeditionary force captured Roanoke Island and from there began methodically taking control of the sounds and towns along North Carolina's eastern coastal region. In mid-March the Yankees attacked New Bern and soundly routed the Confederate defensive forces posted there to protect the important port city. As a consequence of this battle, Colonel Clingman was ordered on March 14—the same day that New Bern was attacked—to move his 25th Regiment N.C. Troops to Kinston, North Carolina. There, interposed between New Bern to the east and the important Southern railroad facilities at Goldsboro to the west, Clingman's regiment joined up with other Confederate forces assembling in the area to fend against further enemy aggressions. Captain Lenoir's diary presents a vivid narrative of the movement of the regiment from Grahamville, South Carolina, by train to Kinston, via Florence, South Carolina, and Wilmington. Upon arrival at Kinston, the journal reveals, the regiment relocated several times from one Confederate camp to another, in and around Kinston, while anticipating another powerful assault by Burnside's forces. But the Union attack never materialized, and the Confederates took advantage of the lull to affect a general reorganization of its army triggered by drastic new laws intended to bolster the Southern fighting forces.

During this reorganization at Kinston in the final days of April 1862 Capt. Thomas I. Lenoir made a heartrending decision to resign from the service of the Confederate army. Upon his departure 1st Lt. James Madison Cathey was elected by the men of

Capt. James Madison Cathey was elected to command the Haywood Highlanders in April 1862 when Capt. Thomas Isaac Lenoir resigned from the army. Cathey was killed in the Battle of the Crater near Petersburg, Virginia on July 30, 1864. *North Carolina Department of Archives and History; used by permission.*

Company F to fill the captain's vacancy. Cathey's new officer's responsibilities were laden with no few issues at the time. The new Bounty and Furlough Act and Conscription Act forced the army to reorganize and, more important, compelled all of the twelve-month volunteers to reenlist for two additional years of duty. That applied especially to the Haywood Highlanders, almost all of whom had signed up to fight as one-year volunteers back in June and July 1861. It is a certainty that many of these rebel soldiers would not have been overjoyed with their new terms of enlistment nor have condoned such a manifestation of power by the Confederate government. After all, they had gone to war because of similar Northern antics, which threatened to take away certain of their inalienable rights and property. And Captain Cathey would have felt the brunt of his men's frustration and anger for not being allowed to return as anticipated to their mountain homes and families.

One of the officers of the 25th Regiment's Company A wrote in a letter at the time to his father: "There is a good deal of dissatisfaction in camp concerning the press [conscription] law, some say they are going home when their time is out regardless of consequences."[236] The men were doubtless dissatisfied, but Confederate service records disclose that not one of the Haywood Highlanders deserted during this time period.

Captain Cathey kept the mountain boys drilling and readying for the next enemy thrust out of New Bern toward Goldsboro's important Confederate railroad facilities. Moreover, a regimental command change in mid-May would have caused quite a stir in the ranks and occupied much of the men's idle time as they appraised a new colonel's swagger and style.

Colonel Clingman, who had led the mountaineers out of Asheville the previous year and directed their activities along the coast lines of the Carolinas, was suddenly made brigadier general and given an entire brigade to lead. Henry Middleton Rutledge, formerly a major and lieutenant colonel of the 25th Regiment and only twenty-two years old, was elected to take command of the ten mountain companies. The young Rutledge, a seasonal resident, with his father, of the Flat Rock community in Henderson County, was born into a wealthy rice-growing planter family from the low-lying coastal region bordering the South Santee River near Charleston. In a wartime letter he was described as being "tall, robust, well formed, and nimble, with a good eye and modest, self-possessed manner."[237] Shortly after the momentous capture of the United States government's Fort Sumter in April 1861 Rutledge wrote to the Confederate secretary of war, L. P. Walker, begging for a second or third lieutenancy. His words were in part: "I am aware that it is the plan of the government to appoint men who have received a military education rather than civilians but in the event of war it may be necessary to increase the army with those who feel a strong desire to serve the country even without that advantage."[238] It is manifest that Rutledge's heart bled for the South, and although lacking a military education he learned the step and maneuvers of the solider quickly and sufficiently impressed the 25th Regiment's company commanders that they elected him their colonel.

Even more organizational convulsions were in the wind for the Haywood Highlanders. The 25th Regiment N.C. Troops, to which the company was attached for the remainder of the war, was combined with three other North Carolina regiments to form the 2nd Brigade North Carolina (1st Brigade by some accounts) under the command of Brig. Gen. Robert Ransom. The West Point–trained officer, who had

A young man born to wealth and privilege in the South Carolina lowcountry planter society, Henry Middleton Rutledge succeeded Thomas L. Clingman as colonel of the 25th Regiment N.C. Troops in May 1862. *North Carolina Department of Archives and History; used by permission.*

served in the regular U.S. Army prior to the war, had been brought to Kinston after the disastrous loss of New Bern to assist with the army's reorganization and to take command of the troops assembling there. The 2nd Brigade, which would be styled Ransom's Brigade for the remainder of the war, was formed by the combination of the 25th, 26th, 27th, and 35th North Carolina infantry regiments. Additionally there were a couple each of cavalry companies and artillery batteries associated with the brigade

In April 1862 during the Confederate army's reorganization at Kinston, N.C., the Haywood Highlanders and the 25th Regiment North Carolina Troops were assigned to Brig. Gen. Robert Ransom's brigade. Ransom was a professional soldier and strict disciplinarian, and he very quickly managed to raise the ire of the mountain boys and alienate many of them. *Massachusetts Commandery Order of the Loyal Legion and the U.S. Army Military History Institute; used by permission.*

that were detached later in the war. The general was a professional soldier and strict disciplinarian who demanded much of his men. Evidence of this can be gleaned from a letter by one of the men of the 25th Regiment to his wife back home:

> "I want to see you verry bad[.] we hant had any fite yet and I don't think we will have[.] we are stationed 5 miles from Kinston and has got Chimneys to our tents and is doing tolerabel though it does look like that old ransom will drill us to death[.]"[239]

Walter Lenoir recorded in his own personal Civil War diary that the 25th Regiment was "put to drilling" five hours each day. Drilling, along with the two additional daily dress parades, kept the soldiers under arms about six hours every day.[240] "Old Ransom" might very well have drilled them to death, had circumstances in another theater of war not demanded the service of Ransom's Brigade and its Haywood Highlanders.

During the spring of 1862 any doubts that the men in the Haywood Highlanders company harbored of ever meeting and fighting the vile Yankee invaders quickly evaporated when they were ordered to Virginia and introduced to the "true music of war."[241] Robert E. Lee summoned the mountain boys, then stationed at Kinston, to Richmond to help beat back Union Gen. George McClellan's Army of the Potomac then advancing toward the Southern capital city. During the ensuing Seven Days' Battles, the men of Company F got their first taste of war in a clash with the Yankees at King's School House on June 25, 1862. Six days later, on July 1, they again fought the bluecoats at Malvern Hill and participated in Ransom's valiant charge up that slope against the Yankees' lethal artillery and musket fire. The mountaineers contributed their fair measure in General Lee's successful seven days' campaign to drive McClellan off the Virginia peninsula.

Approximately two months later the mountain boys again joined up with Lee's Army of Northern Virginia and marched northward, eventually crossing the Potomac River into Maryland, the enemy's homeland. After participating in the capture of Harpers Ferry, Virginia (now West Virginia), the Haywood Highlanders marched through the night to Lee's support on the banks of the slow-moving Antietam Run at Sharpsburg, Maryland. There, on Sept. 17, 1862, Company F was thrown into the line to halt fierce assaults made by their Northern adversaries in the West Woods, near where the little Dunker Church stood. The boys stubbornly held firm, resisting the furious blue storms rushing headlong into them, and did not quit the field. Although exposed to a deadly cannonade for much of the afternoon, they remained on the front line from ten in the morning until darkness settled over the battlefield. Only then, with the smoke and smell of exploded shell and musket fire lingering over the field and the pathetic moans and cries of the dying and wounded piercing the silent blackness, were the men of Company F able to hunker down and take respite from the furor and hell of war.

On the next day General McClellan refused to continue the battle beside Antietam Run, and on the day after that the Haywood Highlanders crossed back over the

Potomac River with Lee's Army of Northern Virginia. After spending the next two months recovering and refitting in the countryside surrounding northern Virginia's Shenandoah Mountains, the Haywood Highlanders led the van of Lee's army as it outraced Gen. Ambrose Burnside's Army of the Potomac to Fredericksburg, Virginia. At that beautiful old colonial town on Dec. 13, 1862, Captain Cathey's men fought off waves of Union attacks against the Confederate defenders arrayed around Marye's Heights. Company F aimed and fired their rifles first from the crest of the hill where the stately Marye house was located, then took up a position in front of the house along a sunken road with a low stone wall offering protection. From that strong lodgment wave after wave of brave bluecoats were slaughtered as they rushed toward the stone barrier and into a wall of hot lead thrown at them by the rebel defenders. On this day the Haywood Highlanders lent their hearts, their souls, their skills, and their stubbornness to help the Confederate army win its most glorious victory to date in the war for Southern independence.

After the Battle of Fredericksburg, Company F was ordered to eastern North Carolina in mid-January 1863. From that time until early May 1864 the Haywood Highlanders were stationed at various strategic locations in the eastern coastal region of the state as well as in southeastern Virginia. They engaged the enemy troops in several minor skirmishes and one battle during this fifteen-month span of the war. The company was surprised and routed from a fort at Gum Swamp on May 22, 1863; it helped repulse an enemy thrust at Richmond around July 4, 1863; a detail of men from the company and regiment skirmished with Tories near Warm Springs in Madison County on Oct. 26, 1863; it participated in a failed attempt to capture New Bern on Feb. 1, 1864; and it played an essential role in the successful Battle of Plymouth, where that important port town was wrested from Union control on Apr. 17–20, 1864.

Soon after the capture of Plymouth the Haywood Highlanders were hurried to Drewry's Bluff, near Petersburg, Virginia. The scant Confederate troops gathered there were desperately trying to defend Richmond from Federal Gen. Benjamin Butler's army, and Company F was thrown into the defense lines to bolster the skeletal

Confederate forces. For several days, beginning on May 12, 1864, the mountain boys and other meager assemblages of rebel soldiers and citizens under the command of Gen. Pierre G. T. Beauregard gave battle to the bluecoats and managed to keep them at bay. However, a month later the Union Army of the Potomac joined up with Butler's Army of the James. These combined forces of Gen. Ulysses S. Grant mounted one fierce assault after another at Beauregard's entrenched defenses in front of Petersburg. Barely holding back Grant's armies, the rebel defenders, including the mountain boys, were at last reinforced on June 18 by Gen. Robert E. Lee's Army of Northern Virginia. Thereafter, for nine long months the Haywood Highlanders manned the trenches protecting Petersburg during the Yankee besiegement.

While posted and living in the Petersburg saps the mountaineers of Company F endured hardships and dangers unfathomable today. For the lack of adequate food supplies they were forever hungry. For the lack of proper clothes and shoes they nearly froze to death during the cold winter months. For the lack of money they went unpaid by a depleted Confederate treasury unable to fund the army. Letters from Haywood County that reached the mountaineers during this period brought news of deprivations and horrendous conditions on the home front and were filled with pleas for the men to return to their homes. And that was not the worst of it. The Haywood Highlanders were exposed to deadly enemy sniper fire and incessant mortar barrages on a daily basis, day and night. The ranks were steadily thinned as the men who were slow to jump into their protective "bombproof" bunkers or carelessly exposed to the Yankee snipers were picked off one by one. Many were those who broke their oaths and deserted from the trenches. But others bore their miserable and thankless plight honorably and fought the enemy at the Battle of the Crater on July 30, 1864, at Globe Tavern on Aug. 21, 1864, at the Battle of Fort Stedman on Mar. 25, 1865, and finally at the Battle of Five Forks on Apr. 1, 1865.

The Confederate service records for the soldiers who fought with Company F reveal that no Haywood Highlanders were paroled with Lee's Army of Northern Virginia at Appomattox Court House on Apr. 12, 1865. The remnants of the company were either captured at Five Forks, caught while laid up in the Richmond hospitals, or apprehended while retreating along the Appomattox River between Five Forks and Appomattox Court House, where General Lee surrendered his army. As prisoners of war the Highlanders were held in various Federal prison camps until finally released at war's end after signing an oath of allegiance to the United States government. Then by boat, rail car, and wagon and on foot the last of the surviving Haywood Highlanders made the long treks back to their Haywood mountain hearths and to loved ones grateful for their return. The Civil War had come to an end at last.

"Rebels on the March." *From* The Illustrated Confederate Reader *by Rod Gragg (1989)*.

⇒ THERE WERE 131 MEN *who signed up to fight with the Haywood Highlanders. Out of this total force 25% were killed or died from disease, at least 23% deserted, and 18% resigned, were discharged, or transferred out of the company.*

A Closer Look at the Haywood Highlanders' Civil War Service

THE COMPANY'S FOUR YEARS OF SERVICE, which included lengthy stretches of relative easy duty interlaced with campaigns or work that involved hard fighting and extreme human hardships, comprised six distinct phases: Carolina coastal duty, Seven Days' Battle, Maryland campaign, Fredericksburg, North Carolina / Virginia coastal defense, and Richmond / Petersburg defense. The chapters that follow examine more closely the true service the Haywood Highlanders performed in each of these phases, with details of battles, engagements, and casualties.

⇒⇐

Carolina Coastal Duty
SEPTEMBER 18, 1861– JUNE 19, 1862

The Haywood Highlanders engaged in no actual conflicts with the Yankee expeditionary forces while stationed at Wilmington and Kinston, North Carolina, and Grahamville, South Carolina. The deadliest enemy the men faced was disease: four of them succumbed and died of sickness while serving in the eastern Carolinas. Also, one man was wounded by a deserter on June 10, 1862, and seven soldiers were lost from the company by reasons of resignation, discharge, and transfer. A list of casualties and other losses experienced over the first nine months is given below.

Casualties and Other Losses, Carolina Coastal Duty

Name	Date	Remarks
Killed (none)		
Died of Wounds (none)		
Wounded (1)		
1st Sgt. William J. Evans	6/10/1862	Wounded by a deserter.
Died of Disease (4)		
Pvt. George E. Christopher	2/23/1862	Died at Grahamville, S.C., of typhoid fever.
Pvt. Henry Christopher	5/30/1862	Died in hospital at Wilson, N.C., of disease.
Pvt. Amos M. Reece	12/25/1862	Died at Grahamville, S.C., of pneumonia.
Pvt. William B. Rhodes	1/31/1862	Died at Grahamville, S.C., of typhoid fever.
Captured (none)		
Deserted (none)		
Other (9)		
Capt. Thomas Isaac Lenoir	4/28/1862	Declined to stand for reelection and resigned.
1st Lt. Etheldred H. Blalock	4/28/1862	Defeated for reelection and resigned.
2nd Lt. James A. Burnett	4/28/1862	Declined to accept reelection and resigned.
Pvt. David Allen	3/8/1862	Discharged by reason of disability.
Pvt. Alfred Burnett	1/20/1862	Discharged by reason of disability.
Pvt. Perry B. Franklin	1/20/1862	Discharged by reason of disability.
Pvt. Napoleon L. Glenn	5/1/1862	Transferred to Co. I, 25th Reg. N.C.
Pvt. John W. Mahaffey	4/30/1862	Discharged by reason of disability. Reenlisted in the company on 8/15/1863 but later deserted.
Musician John V. Reece	9/14/1861	Discharged by reason of disability.

The Confederate army underwent a complete reorganization at the conclusion of this first phase of the war. At Kinston, North Carolina, the Haywood Highlanders elected new company officers, who in turn participated in the election of new commanders for the 25th Regiment N.C. Troops. The command structure at the end of the Carolina coastal defense phase is given below.

Ransom's Brigade (25th, 26th, 27th, 35th N.C. infantry regiments)
    Brig. Gen. Robert Ransom commanding

25th Regiment (Companies A, B, C, D, E, F, G, H, I, K)
    Col. Henry M. Rutledge commanding
    Lt. Col. Samuel C. Bryson (promoted from Co. C)
    Maj. John W. Francis (promoted from Co. D)

Company F (approximately 97 officers and private soldiers)[242]
    Capt. James Madison Cathey commanding
    1st Lt. Thaddeus C. S. Hyatt
    2nd Lt. James A. Blalock
    3rd Lt. Joseph T. Cathey
    1st Sgt. William H. Hartgrove
    2nd Sgt. John C. Rogers
    3rd Sgt. James B. Meece
    4th Sgt. Robert H. Hyatt
    5th Sgt. William T. Cathey
    1st Cpl. Thomas F. Henson
    2nd Cpl. William R. Clonts
    3rd Cpl. Henry J. Sorrells
    4th Cpl. William Bonham

Following pages: The draft copy of the Haywood Highlanders' April 1862 muster roll contains the names of the commissioned officers, noncommissioned officers, and private soldiers belonging to the company after the reorganization at Kinston, North Carolina. *Lenoir Family Papers, Southern Historical Collection, Wilson Library, University of North Carolina at Chapel Hill; used by permission.*

[Feb 27-1862?]

Cathey

1. Cathey James M. Capt.
2. Hyatt Thaddeus C. 1st Lt.
3. Blalock James A. 2nd Lt.
4. Cathey Joseph T. 3rd Lt.

1. Hartgrove William H. 1st Sgt.
2. Rogers John C. 2nd Sgt.
3. Mace James B. 3rd Sgt.
4. Hyatt Robert H. 4th Sgt.
5. Cathey William T. 5th Sgt.
*6. Cloud William R. 2nd Corp.
7. Bruce Henry J. 3rd "
8. Benhow William 4th "
9. Jones John R. Musician
10. Abbot Green B. Private
*11. Allman William N. "
12. Anderson Jasper N. "
13. Anderich Josiah M.D. "
14. Brookshire Humphrey "
15. Brockman John C. "
*16. Bagg Henry T. "
17. Bagg Jeremiah H. "
*18. Burnett John G. "
19. Byers William "
20. Chambers G. W. "
21. Christopher Henry "
22. Clark Joshua A. "
23. Collins Ebb Cutting Ell "
24. Crawford Amos A. "
25. Davis Joseph N. "
26. Elmerstone Benjamin F. "
27. Evans William J. "
28. Ferguson Ebed J. "

*Ferguson Garland S. Private
Ferguson Nathan J. "
Franklin David N. "
Franklin Henry J. "
33. Henn Napoleon L. "
34. Gordon Alson "
35. Green Samuel B. "
36. Green Thaddeus M. "
37. Hall George J. "
38.* Hall George R.* "
39. Harrald Ezekiel J. "
40. Henderson Harper "
41. Henderson James M. "
*42. Henderson William "
43. Henson Burton "
44. Henson Elijah L. "
45. Henson Fidelio W. "
46. Henson Henry J. "
47. Henson Wesley "
48. Henson Wiley "
49. Henson William "
50. Holland Humphrey R.
51. Holland Matthias "
52. Hood Pleasant B. "
53. Inman Joshua E. "
54. Inman Lewis H. "
55. Inman William D. "
56. Jones George W. "

57	Long Joseph A.	Private	
58	Mann Joseph B.	"	
59	Meece John M.	"	
60	Meece Morgan	"	
61	Meece William R.	"	
62	Mehaffey Francis M.	"	
63	Mehaffey John W.	"	
64	Miller Francis M.	"	
65	Murray Luther W.	"	
66	Norton James E.	"	
67	Osborne Roland C.	"	
68	Poston Robert	"	
69	Pressley Daniel N.	"	
70	Pressley Joshua A.	"	
71	Pressley Nelson A.	"	
72	Queen Robert H.	"	
73	Reece Isaac N.	"	
74	Reece Jonathan K.	"	
75	Reece William L.	"	
76	Roberson Isaac W.	"	
77	Rogers Matthew M.A.	"	
78	Singleton James A.	"	
79	Singleton James M.	"	
80	Singleton John C.	"	
81	Singleton William A.S.C.	"	
82	Starnes John	"	
83	Thomas John G.	"	
84	Thompson Joseph M.	"	
85	Thompson William	"	
86	Trull John W.	"	
87	Vance William P.	"	
88	Williams William H.	"	
89	Wright William M.	"	

"Rushing into the Mouth of Death on Malvern Hill" by Thure de Thulstrup. *From* The American Heritage Century Collection of Civil War Art *(1974)*.

> ➤ Only eleven Haywood Highlanders *were killed as a result of battle with the enemy. Twice that many—twenty-two—died of disease.*

Seven Days' Battles
June 20, 1862–August 25, 1862

At Kinston in early June 1862 General Ransom received urgent orders from Gen. Robert E. Lee to move his brigade to the vicinity of Richmond, Virginia. Lee, who had just recently relieved the wounded Gen. Joseph Johnston commanding the Confederate forces in Virginia, was frantically planning and preparing to defend Richmond from a formidable Union army approaching from the east. Heeding Lee's orders, Ransom's Brigade and its Haywood Highlanders started by train from Kinston on June 19 and arrived at Petersburg, Virginia, in the early morning hours of June 21. From there the troops marched a few miles to the north and encamped. During the brief time it was in the Petersburg vicinity, Ransom's Brigade was strengthened with the addition of the 48th and 49th North Carolina infantry regiments. On June 24 the brigade embarked again on the cars for Richmond, where they arrived around 10:00 that evening.

As daylight broke the next morning General Ransom was issued urgent orders to rush to the support of the Southern defenders occupying the extreme right of the Confederate line, which extended below (south of) the Chickahominy River. Upon Union General McClellan's orders to adjust the picket lines and test the enemy's strength the Yankees had launched an offensive in the area surrounding Seven Pines and the railroad junction at Fair Oaks. Among the Confederate Army's record of events for Company F is a firsthand report describing this initial military engagement of the Haywood Highlanders, presumably recorded a few weeks afterward by one of the company's officers:

> "We marched down the Williamsburg road five miles to where we found a heavy skirmish progressing into which by order of Brig. Gen [A. R.] Wright we were soon participating & give for our first time a check to the vile invaders of our homes by repulsing them twice & in which engagement Joseph M. Thompson was mortally wounded and died on 27. John A. Smith & J. M. Meece were severely wounded, Ben F. Edmonston & A. A. Crawford slightly wounded."[243]

Another participant in the action who penned a history of the 25th Regiment N.C. Troops some fifty years after the fight recalled the encounter slightly differently and with perhaps more flourish. Garland Ferguson of Company F was among the troops who double-quicked down the dusty Williamsburg Road toward the sound of musket and artillery fire.

> [B]y sunrise of the twenty-fifth it [the 25th Regiment] was on the march towards the front and to join the division of General Huger, which was then engaged at Seven Pines on the Williamsburg road. There was heavy fighting of artillery and musketry in front. It had at last come in hearing of the true music of war. About one-half mile from the line the regiment was ordered to double-quick. It was thrown in line on the immediate left of the Williamsburg Road, and when within range of the enemy the regiment halted, the front rank at the command fired and fell to the ground, the rear rank fired over them, then with bayonets fixed we raised the rebel yell and charged; the enemy gave way and the ground which had been lost in the morning had been retaken. The enemy opened a heavy fire of musketry and three times tried, without effect, to retake their lines. At 6 o'clock p.m. a heavy fire of grape shot was opened on the regiment without demoralizing or moving it. It was relieved at dark.[244]

It is clear from the accounts given by the two Haywood Highlanders that the battle was already in progress when the company was thrown into the line around 11:00 in the morning. Positioned on the left (north) side of the Williamsburg road, Company F repulsed at least two enemy attacks and withstood a fusillade of heavy grape shell until they were relieved. General Ransom's official report summarized the gallant and meritorious actions of the regiment: "This was the first time that this regiment (Twenty-fifth N.C.) was ever under fire, although in service for nearly a year. The regiment behaved admirably, and I am proud to bear witness to its unwavering gallantry."[245] Gen. Benjamin Huger, who commanded all of the Confederate forces committed to battle at King's School House, also commended the 25th Regiment and recommended to General Lee that the mountain boys be permitted to emblazon their banner with "King's School House." Only four other regiments were recognized in such a manner.[246]

⸻

After a series of battles along the Chickahominy River (the battles of Mechanicsville, Gaines' Mill, Savage's Station, and Frayser's Farm) Lee's Confederate Army managed to push McClellan's forces to the south side of the river, whereupon the Yankees bowed up and took an exceedingly strong position atop Malvern Hill. During this time the Haywood Highlanders continued to skirmish on a daily basis with the Yankees south of the Chickahominy.

> We skirmished more or less each day until July 1 our forces having overtaken the enemy on there [sic] retreat from before Richmond at Malvil [Malvern] hill. Our regiment was rushed into the battle about sunset which was then raging with violence & lasted for several hours. The following were the casualties of Co. F: J. [I.] N. Reece killed in action, J. M^c & J. N. Anderson, G. W. Chambers, W. P. Inman wounded. We followed the enemy to there [sic] gunboats on James River after which we returned to Drewry's Bluff where we stayed until July 30[.] we move near Petersburg, Va. where we are now encamped.[247]

As this company chronicler wrote, the mountain boys were again thrown into a raging inferno on the slopes of Malvern Hill. Not evident in the account is the fact that the Yankees were not budged from their elevated foothold on the hill and that they successfully fought off the attacking rebels by taking advantage of their superior artillery. The Haywood Highlanders twice charged into an impenetrable barrage of cannon and musket fire and were repulsed. In his account, Ferguson adds a little drama to the affair:

> On 2 July [July 1] at Malvern Hill late in the evening it [the 25th Regiment] made a charge, but for want of support and on account of a galling fire, it was ordered back, and with other regiments of the brigade, was reformed under cover by General Robert Ransom, and again advanced within one hundred yards of the enemy's guns and line, when the men raised a yell and charged in the face of a perfect sheet of fire from musketry and artillery, without wavering, to within twenty yards of the enemy's guns, some going even nearer. At this point General Ransom discovered that he was not supported and that the enemy were heavily massed, very greatly outnumbering his men. Unwilling to sacrifice his men in a hopeless charge and dark coming on he withdrew from the attack.[248]

A scant twenty yards from the enemy must have seemed miles. It was beyond human capacity to go further under the murderous fire. After General Ransom ordered the men back they moved to some woods, where they took cover and began licking their wounds. Darkness had settled over the battleground, and one Haywood Highlander had been killed and several wounded. "The wearied soldiers lay on their arms on the field that night"[249] and rested, surely dreading what might lie ahead of them the next day. However, when they arose from their grassy beds they learned that McClellan's forces had surprisingly retreated from their secure Malvern Hill roost and had indeed moved back to the James River. Their fleet of gunboats, with powerful naval guns, could easily protect them there and keep the Confederates at bay. In just a matter of several weeks McClellan embarked his troops aboard transport vessels and quit the Virginia peninsula.

After waiting a few days to observe the Yankees and divine their intentions, the Haywood Highlanders eventually made their way to Drewry's Bluff. At this naturally strong elevated position overlooking the James River approximately seven miles to the southeast of Richmond, the Confederates had installed heavy naval guns to protect the capital city from Union gunboats. The mountain boys stayed at Drewry's Bluff while working alongside slaves building fortifications to protect Richmond from future attacks. On July 30 the company marched by foot to Petersburg, Virginia. At that important Southern railroad juncture and manufacturing center the Highlanders resumed construction of earthworks and defenses to protect the city.

By the end of July reports of the Richmond battles had filtered back to the Forks of Pigeon community. Anxious friends and family would have learned that the Haywood Highlanders were finally in a fight and that the boys had held up well to the test. Captain Lenoir wrote to brother Walter to pass along the information he had received about their former company. In regards to the intense action at King's School House, he reported: "J. M. Meece was shot in the hand, John Smith in the mouth, (He [Smith] is at home but I have not seen him yet). He [Smith] said when he started to the war that he could catch all the bullets that the Yanks would shoot at him in his mouth." The captain obviously was impressed with the irony of Musician Smith's earlier bravado. He went on to offer further details regarding the fighting during both of the battles:

> The 25th was in two battles, on 25th June, & the great battle of Tuesday [Malvern Hill]. Capt. C. [Cathey] was in the first & had his canteen struck by a ball, but he was sick and not in the other. He is still quite sick at Richmond with fever, & his Father has gone to see him. Lieut. J. T. Cathey was in both fights, & his sword was shot from his side, but was only slightly

scratched. Joseph Anderson was shot in the shoulder while carrying his brother from the field.[250]

In a demonstration of bravery and brotherly devotion the young Joseph (Josiah) Anderson, only eighteen years old when he enlisted, was wounded and disabled for the rest of the war, and for life (although Captain Lenoir reported the injury as a shoulder wound, it is believed that Anderson was actually hit in the left leg). It is very likely that Lenoir obtained the above news from his friend Col. Joseph Cathey at Cathey's store. Cathey's oldest son, Joseph Turner, may have relayed the recent events to his father, including having his own sword shot from his side. Upon learning that his youngest son, Capt. James Madison Cathey, was seriously ill, Colonel Cathey apparently did not hesitate to set off for the front to see about him. The senior Cathey surely intended to do everything within his power to prevent his beloved boy from falling victim to disease, as so many Southern soldiers had.

While stationed at Drewry's Bluff and Petersburg the mountain boys were again attacked by the same deadly enemy that it had encountered on the coast of South Carolina—disease. "[I]t was here, in consequence of the exposure just gone through, that army sickness first made its telling effect on the regiment," recalled Garland Ferguson years later, perhaps forgetting the epidemic that had swept through Grahamville during the winter of 1861–62.[251] As he noted, camp dysenteries, illnesses more lethal than Yankee bullets—typhoid fever, measles, and cerebritis—again swept through the regiment in the aftermath of the Seven Days' Battles. Throughout the Civil War sickness accounted for a full one-third of all casualties; during the period of the Seven Days' Battles approximately seventy-six men from the 25th Regiment N.C. died of some form of disease. Company F suffered ten such deaths.

Casualties and Other Losses, Seven Days' Battles

Name	Date	Remarks
Killed (1)		
Pvt. Isaac N. Reece	7/1/1862	Killed at Malvern Hill, Va.
Died of Wounds (1)		
Pvt. Joseph M. Thompson	6/27/1862	Wounded at King's School House, Va.; died at Richmond, Va.
Wounded (8)		
Pvt. Jasper N. Anderson	7/1/1862	Wounded at Malvern Hill, Va.
Pvt. Josiah McDonald Anderson	7/1/1862	Wounded in leg at Malvern Hill, Va.; "disabled for life."
Pvt. George W. Chambers	7/1/1862	Wounded at Malvern Hill, Va.
Pvt. Amos A. Crawford	6/25/1862	Wounded at King's School House, Va.
Pvt. Benjamin F. Edmonston	6/25/1862	Wounded in the leg at King's School House, Va.
Pvt. William P. Inman	7/1/1862	Wounded at Malvern Hill, Va.
Pvt. John M. Meece	6/25/1862	Wounded at King's School House, Va., resulting in amputation of two fingers.
Musician John A. Smith	6/25/1862	Wounded in the jaw at King's School House, Va.
Died of Disease (10)		
Pvt. Green B. Abbott	7/21/1862	Died in hospital at Petersburg, Va., of "cerebro meningitis."
Pvt. George R. Hall	8/25/1862	Died at Drewry's Bluff, Va., of ulcers.
Pvt. Fidellio W. Henson	8/4/1862	Died in hospital at Petersburg, Va., of "cerebritis."
Pvt. George W. Jones	7/4/1862	Died in Buncombe or Haywood County of fever.
Pvt. Roland Calloway Osborne	8/5/1862	Died in hospital at Williamsburg, Va., of "febris typhoides."
Pvt. Joshua A. Pressley	8/24/1862	Died in hospital at Petersburg, Va., of "febris typhoides."
Pvt. Nelson A. Pressley	8/21/1862	Died in hospital at Petersburg, Va., of fever.
Corp. Henry Jackson Sorrells	7/30/1862	Died in hospital at Petersburg, Va., of "febris typhoides."
Pvt. John Stamey	6/25/1862	Died in hospital at Goldsboro, N.C., of fever.
Pvt. William Thompson	7/30/1862	Died in hospital at Petersburg, Va., of dysentery and/or fever.
Captured (none)		
Deserted (none)		

Other (11)		
Pvt. Humphrey P. Brookshire	7/16/1862	Discharged for being over age.
Pvt. John G. Burnett	7/16/1862	Discharged after providing a substitute.
Pvt. Eli Collins	7/16/1862	Discharged for being over age.
Pvt. Alson Gordon	7/16/1862	Discharged for being over age. Reenlisted in the company but was later wounded and retired to the Invalid Corps.
Pvt. Harper Henderson	7/16/1862	Discharged for being over age.
Pvt. William Henderson	7/16/1862	Discharged for being over age.
Pvt. Pleasant B. Hood	7/16/1862	Discharged for being over age.
Pvt. John M. Meece	8/2/1862	Discharged by reason of disability from wounds.
Pvt. Robert Poston	7/16/1862	Discharged for being over age.
Pvt. William A. S. C. Singleton	7/16/1862	Discharged for being under age.
Pvt. William P. Vance	7/16/1862	Discharged for being over age.

Opposite: The Peninsula Campaign, June 25–July 1, 1862. *Map by Peter Krafft, Florida State University.*

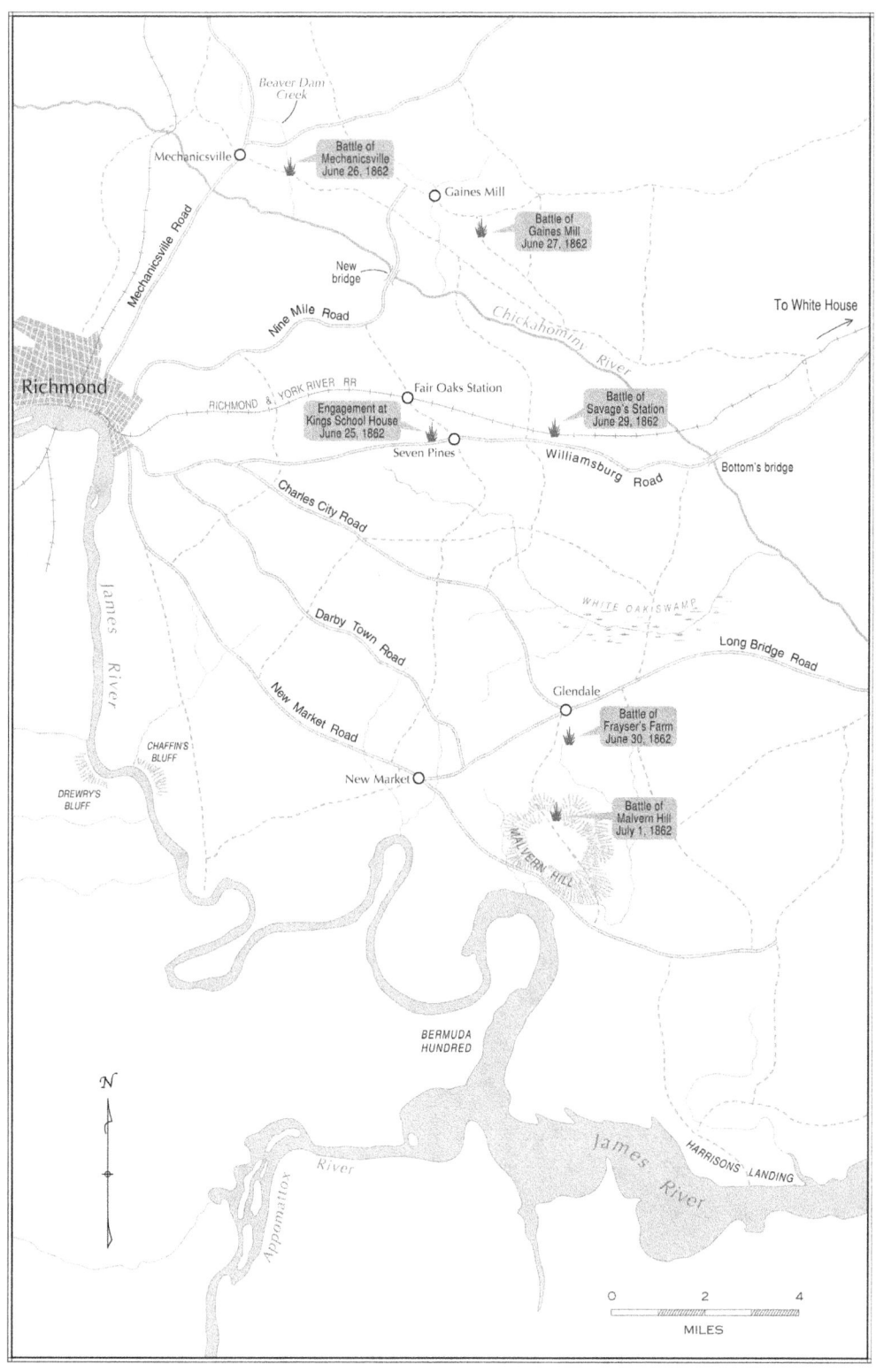

"Crossing the Potomac into Enemy Territory." Harper's Weekly, *Sept. 27, 1862.*

⇛ THE OLDEST SOLDIER *who served in Company F was Harper Henderson, who was 45 years old when he joined the company in Asheville on Sept. 17, 1861—the day before the company marched off to war. Private Henderson apparently got his fill of army life and fighting, because just two weeks after the Seven Days' Battles were concluded, near Richmond, Virginia, on July 1, 1862, he resigned by reason of being over age.*

Maryland Campaign
AUGUST 26, 1862–OCTOBER 31, 1862

IT WAS IN THE WEEKS FOLLOWING the Battle of Malvern Hill, while he watched and waited for McClellan's great army to move back to the North, that Gen. Robert E. Lee determined to take his army there as well. For strategic and political reasons and with the endorsement of President Jefferson Davis he gave orders for general movements toward the Potomac River, which divided the North and the South. While trekking into northern Virginia during the latter days of August, Lee's army, led by Gen. Stonewall Jackson, achieved a victory over the Federals at Cedar Mountain. Just days later, on Aug. 29, 1862, the Army of Northern Virginia battled with Gen. John Pope's Union forces near Manassas Station and Bull Run Creek (the battleground of the first grand Southern victory in July of 1861) and again defeated the Federals, forcing their retreat. The audacious Lee's strategy was playing out just as he had theorized. His strong, confident army was poised within striking distance of Washington, D.C., and maneuvered to ford the Potomac River into enemy territory.

Captain Cathey's boys did not play a role in these Confederate successes, however. The Highlanders moved from Petersburg back to the Richmond vicinity in mid-August 1862 and from there embarked on the cars of the Virginia Central Rail Road for Rapidan Station on Aug. 27. At that juncture they marched northward for about a week until they reached the Potomac River on or about Sept. 7. Ample time was afforded the Haywood Highlanders and the other mountain men of the 25th Regiment N.C. to become aware of the invasion plan to cross the Potomac and follow Lee's army onto enemy soil—and many did not like it. Garland Ferguson of Company F later described their reaction:

> When it was first made known to the men by General Lee's order that the army was to cross the Potomac there was a considerable murmur of disappointment in ranks. The men said they had volunteered to resist invasion and not to invade, some did not believe it right to invade Northern territory, others thought that the same cause that brought the southern army to the front would increase the Northern army, still others thought the war should be carried into the North; thus the men thought, talked and disagreed. This was the first dissension among the men of the regiment, but all were united in their confidence and love for Lee.[252]

Captain Cathey prodded his reluctant and unhappy men to wade across the Potomac on Sept. 7. Once ashore in Maryland they made their way to the town of Frederick, where they caught up with the Army of Northern Virginia. The company's report of events for September–October 1862 describes with scarce details the Haywood Highlanders' activities over the ensuing weeks as they engaged the enemy at Harpers Ferry, Virginia (now West Virginia), and at Sharpsburg, Maryland.

> The Co. with the Regt. left Rapidan Station on the 1 of Sept. marched each day until the 7. We cross[ed] the Potomac River into Maryland arrived near Frederick City on the 9 Sept. Were on detached service on 10. Recrossed the river on the 11. Arrived near Harpers ferry on the 13 & guarded that position until 15, that place being surrendered to our Forces. Our Brigade crossed the river again on the 16 & went into the Battle of Sharpsburg on the 17. drove the enemy from their position & held it until the 18. Recrossed the river again (J.A. Singleton & W.R. Clonts were slightly wounded on the 17) and came up near Martinsburg & encamped until Oct. 1.[253]

After their arrival at Frederick, the Haywood Highlanders were ordered with

Nestled alongside the Potomac River surrounded by commanding mountain heights, Harpers Ferry, Virginia (now West Virginia), was the scene in 1859 of John Brown's failed attempt to lead the local slaves to freedom. In Sept. 1862 the Haywood Highlanders participated with other Confederate troops led by Gen. Stonewall Jackson in the capture of this strategic river town. *Library of Congress, Prints and Photographs Division.*

Ransom's Brigade and Gen. John G. Walker's Brigade to proceed back to the confluence of the Monocacy and Potomac rivers to destroy an aqueduct of the Chesapeake and Ohio Canal. However, because of the "extraordinary solidity and massiveness of the masonry" the Confederate soldiers soon found that their tools were inadequate to drill holes for the explosives.[254] Failing in that task, they waded across the Potomac River and marched upstream along its south bank to Harpers Ferry, where a large part of General Lee's army, again led by Gen. Stonewall Jackson, was maneuvering to effect its capture. On Sept. 15 the Haywood Highlanders participated in the brief besiegement and cannonade of the important river town where a few years before the infamous John Brown had failed in his attempted slave insurrection. After enduring the Confederate cannon fire from the surrounding heights for little more than an hour the Union troops broke out a white flag and surrendered the town without much of a fight.

During this same time, however, at Sharpsburg, Maryland, which lay approximately fifteen miles to the northwest of Harpers Ferry, General Lee with the larger portion of his army had found trouble. By happenstance and luck General McClellan discovered an actual dispatch containing Lee's general orders to divide the rebel army and for a sizable segment of it to operate against Harpers Ferry. The usually cautious and methodical Union general engineered plans to cut Lee's forces in two and immediately gave instructions for the entirety of his army to march against that portion of Lee's army operating in Maryland and Pennsylvania. In a matter of a few days the two unevenly matched foes met at a small stream named Antietam Run near Sharpsburg and prepared to battle once again. A meager army of just 27,000 rebels faced a menacing and powerful array of 90,000 Yankees brimming with frustration and eagerness to appease a string of battlefield setbacks. This disparity in military strength would not do, and Lee knew it. He had earlier issued pressing orders to Jackson's army divisions at Harpers Ferry to come to him at once, and now he could only hope that they would reach him in time before McClellan launched his offensive.

At Harpers Ferry the Haywood Highlanders had little opportunity to enjoy the booty and bask in the successful venture in which they had participated. Learning of the trouble at Sharpsburg, they immediately marched to Shepherdstown, where they again waded across the Potomac River, and after marching through the night finally reached Sharpsburg just after the noon hour on Sept. 16.[255] The next morning, Yankee forces launched massive assaults against the left side of the Confederate defensive line. The Haywood Highlanders, along with the 25th Regiment and other regiments attached to Ransom's Brigade, were initially posted on the Confederate right. However, after the initial Federal onslaught aimed at the opposite end of the Confederate battle line, Ransom's Brigade was summoned to the action on the left. Garland Ferguson, a participant in the battle and at the time a private in Company F, summarized his regiment's contributions to the engagement:

> At Sharpsburg the regiment was put into action near the extreme left of Lee's line. Our troops were retreating in front of a determined charge of the

enemy, the men passed through the retreating troops, raised the yell, and charged with a determination that drove the enemy from the field to cover of his heavy works.[256]

As modest as Ferguson's description is, he still conveys a certain sense of excitement and danger as he and his brethren rushed through the beaten retreating rebels, hollered their fiendish, unearthly rebel yells, and drove the enemy back to the cover of their artillery. Another participant in the action that day wrote in much more vivid detail his recollection of the movements and actions of Ransom's Brigade during the morning hours of the battle:

> About an hour before day, on the 17th, our division began its march for the position assigned us on the extreme right, where we were to oppose the Federals in any attempt to cross either the bridge (since known as Burnside's) or the ford over the Antietam below it, near Shiveley's [Snavely's]…..On taking position, we immediately tore down the fences in our front which might obstruct the line of fire. About 9 a. m., a pressing order came to move to the left; this we did in quick time. As we were leaving our ground, I remember looking up the Antietam, the opposite bank of which was lined with Federal batteries. These were firing at the left wing of our army to the support of which we were moving. The Federal gunners could be seen with the utmost distinctness as they loaded and fired. Moving northwards, we were passing in rear of our line of battle and met constant streams of the wounded coming out. All this time there was the steady booming of the cannon, the whistling of shells, the pattering of fire-arms, and the occasional yell or cheer rising above the roar of battle as some advantage was gained by either side.
>
> Soon after passing the town the division was deployed in column of regiments. Around and just beyond the Dunker church, in the center of the Confederate left, our line had been broken and was completely swept away. A flood of Federals were pouring in; we were just in time—ten minutes', five minutes' delay, and our army would have ceased to exist. We were

The Haywood Highlanders were rushed with their regiment from one end of the Confederate battle line to the other to repulse a fierce Union charge in the vicinity of the Dunker Church, shown in this photograph taken after the battle. *Library of Congress, Prints and Photographs Division.*

marching up behind our line of battle, with our right flank perpendicular to it. As the first regiment got opposite to the break in our lines it made a wheel to the right and "went in." The next regiment, marching straight on, as soon as it cleared the left of the regiment preceding it, likewise wheeled to the right and took its place in line, and so on in succession. That is, we were marching north, and thus were successively thrown into line of battle facing east. As these regiments came successively into line they struck the Federal lines which were advancing; the crash was deafening. The sound of infantry firing at short distance can be likened to nothing so much as the dropping of a shower of hail-stones on an enormous tin roof.[257]

The work performed by the Haywood Highlanders that day in the West Woods near the little Dunker Church eclipsed all else they had rendered to that point in the war. General Ransom's report of the battle alluded to the tenacity and courage his men showed as well as the manner in which they beat back the enemy:

I cannot too highly compliment the action of the men and officers for their gallant behavior during the entire day. They formed, under a galling fire, and, in presence of our retiring troops, pressed forward and drove back a far superior force, and, three times afterward, repulsed determined attacks of the enemy and in largely superior numbers to our own; but the highest credit is due for the perfect staunchness exhibited during an eight hours' exposure to an unparalleled cannonade and within canister range.[258]

The Haywood Highlanders and North Carolinians held their position throughout the day as the enemy's heavy cannon fire continuously rained down upon them. The Yankees successively shifted the focus of their attack at the Confederate center and finally the right side of the rebel line. And surprisingly Lee's staunch Confederate forces, which eventually numbered some 40,000 rebels, were able to hold off against the fierce, yet disjointed and uncoordinated, attacks by McClellan's army. That night and throughout the next rainy day the Highlanders hunkered down on the field and awaited the Yankees to resume the hostilities, but the enemy declined to engage. On the night of Sept. 18–19 the Confederate forces quietly backed away from their defensive positions and retreated across the Potomac River to safer and friendlier environs. As the company record of events states, Company F "came up" near Martinsburg, Virginia (now West Virginia) and encamped until Oct. 1. Then they struck camp and marched to the vicinity of Winchester, Virginia, and remained there for a period of three weeks. On Oct. 23 the Highlanders again were on the move, this time to Paris, Virginia, where they encamped for a short time. Garland Ferguson offered this glimpse of the camping experience after the Battle of Antietam Run (Sharpsburg) in the northern Shenandoah Mountains:

> Camping equipments had been left behind at Richmond, and frequently on the march the men had to resort to ramrods for baking purposes and forked sticks for the roast; blankets and change of clothing had been left at Sharpsburg, and when the men recrossed the Potomac they were without

blankets and bare of clothing, this was late in September and the regiment did not receive new blankets till some time in October. The beds were roomy but cool.[259]

Partly because of these "roomy and cool" accommodations as well as the severe exposure they had gone through at Sharpsburg, several men in the 25th Regiment N.C. perished from disease in Virginia's Shenandoah Mountains—as did one Haywood Highlander. The Battle of Antietam Run, or Sharpsburg, has been called the bloodiest single day in the Civil War. However, the casualties suffered by Company F were inordinately light. Both of the wounded Haywood Highlanders returned to the company to fight another day. However, Pvt. John E. Brookshire, who died of fever while encamped in the Winchester, Virginia, area would never again see the mountain homeland that he surrendered his life to protect.

Casualties and Other Losses, Maryland Campaign

Name	Date	Remarks
Killed (none)		
Died of Wounds (none)		
Wounded (2)		
Pvt. William R. Clonts	9/17/1862	Wounded at Sharpsburg, Md.
Corp. James Anderson Singleton	9/17/1862	Wounded at Sharpsburg, Md.
Died of Disease (1)		
Pvt. John E. Brookshire	10/20/1862	Died at Winchester, Va., of fever.
Captured (4)		
1st Sgt. William J. Evans	9/14/1862	Captured at South Mountain, Md., and later exchanged.
Sgt. Wiley Henson	9/12/1862	Captured at Frederick, Md., and later paroled.
Pvt. William Henson	9/12/1862	Captured at Frederick, Md., and later paroled.
1st Sgt. Luther W. Murray	9/12/1862	Captured at Frederick, Md., and later paroled.
Deserted (1)		
Pvt. Amos A. Crawford	9/5/1862	
Other (none)		

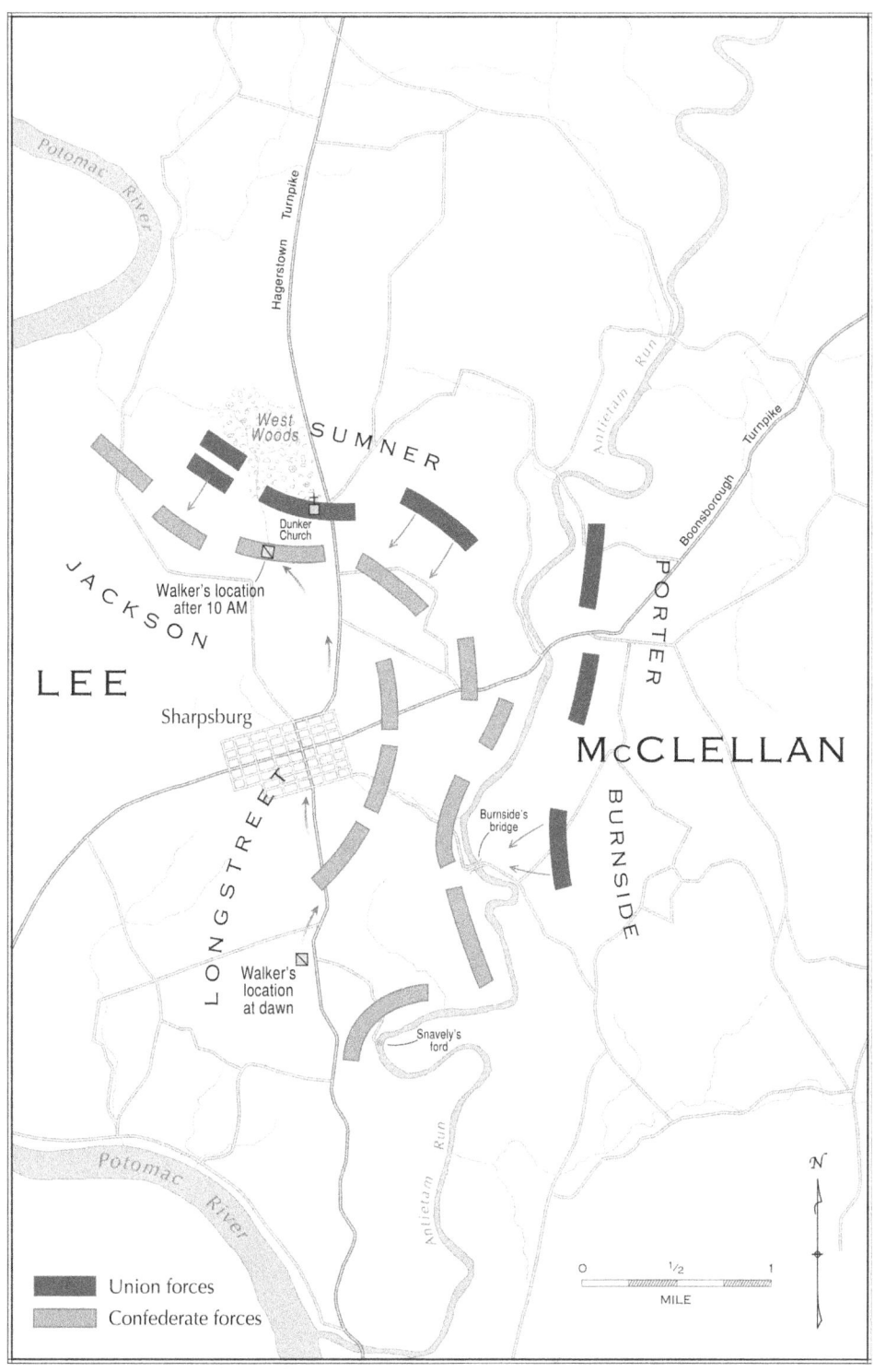

Battle of Antietam Run, Sept. 17, 1862. *Map by Peter Krafft, Florida State University.*

Before Marye's Heights. Illustration by Allen C. Redwood. *Library of Congress, Prints and Photographs Division.*

⇛ THE YOUNGEST SOLDIERS *to have fought with the Haywood Highlanders were Joshua A. Clark and Arthur Laughter, who were only sixteen years old when they joined the company in March and July of 1862 respectively. Five other youths enlisted at age 17: Robert J. H. Estes, George R. Hall, Luther W. Murray, John V. Reece, and William A. S. Columbus Singleton.*

Fredericksburg
NOVEMBER 1, 1862–JANUARY 3, 1863

THE HAYWOOD HIGHLANDERS CAMPED under the stars without blankets in the cool autumn air of northern Virginia for several weeks after the affair at Sharpsburg, Maryland. Their Confederate commanders were kept busy observing and trying to predict the next theater where their Union foes would choose to continue the conflict. Unbeknownst to them President Abraham Lincoln had chosen a new commander to head up the Army of the Potomac. Although McClellan had driven the Confederate army back across the Potomac River, Lincoln had been much displeased with his general's reluctance to continue the battle along Antietam Run on the second day and for not pursuing the escaping weaker Confederate army. For that seeming lack of aggressiveness and a host of other reasons, he replaced McClellan with Gen. Ambrose Burnside, whose expedition against North Carolina's eastern coastal region in the winter of 1862 had created so much havoc for the South. Burnside chose to assail Richmond from the north as a tactic to subdue the Confederates, and he started his army and supplies for Fredericksburg, Virginia. Upon watching and learning of his new adversary's movements on the north side of the Rappahannock River, General Lee gave orders for his army to move in that direction to oppose it. He hoped to steal the march on the Yankees and interpose on advantageous ground near Fredericksburg.

The Haywood Highlanders left Paris, Virginia, on Oct. 31 and marched via Culpeper Courthouse to Madison Courthouse, where they encamped for a few days. While bivouacked there the men were finally able to draw new uniforms and blankets. On Nov. 18 the company and the 25th Regiment were with the van of Lee's army, reaching Fredericksburg on or about Nov. 20 with Gen. James Longstreet's Corps. Immediately upon their arrival there the Confederates began taking up positions on the high ground overlooking Fredericksburg from the east. On the opposite side of Fredericksburg, across the Rappahannock River, Burnside's army was assembling and waiting on the arrival of pontoons to bridge the narrow but deep river. General Ransom's small division, which included his own and Gen. John R. Cooke's brigades, was assigned a position on top of Marye's Heights in rear of a stately old mansion known as the Marye house.

Garland Ferguson offered this firsthand account of the actions taken by the 25th Regiment N.C. leading up to and during the Battle of Fredericksburg, Dec. 13, 1862:

> On 11 and 12 December, 1862, the regiment was in position back of Marye's House. About 11 o'clock on the morning of the 13th, General Robert Ransom informed the regiment that General Cobb's men who were holding our line in front of Marye's House, were short of ammunition and must be reinforced, and that the undertaking was a dangerous one; the men fully understanding the importance and danger of the duty, moved forward with a firm and steady step, like patriots, to battle. On reaching the crest of the hill (the regiment having been divided so as to pass the house on either side) it met a fearful fire from the enemy two hundred yards off. In casting an eye along the line men could be seen falling like sheaves before the sickle. In less than two minutes the regiment's loss in killed and wounded was one hundred and twenty. It reached Cobb's line just as his men were emptying their last cartridge, and held the line, repelling six successive assaults, until relieved at nightfall.[260]

In response to General Ransom's orders to reinforce General Cobb's men and those of General Cooke the Haywood Highlanders rushed with the troops of the 25th Regiment N.C. around the Marye house and descended the slope of Marye's Heights toward the charging Union forces. Once reaching Cobb's position the Highlanders found themselves in a sunken roadbed with a stone wall offering protection from the enemy musket and artillery fire. It was an exceptionally strong lodgment, and Company F stood side by side with the other rebel defenders and fired with deadly effectiveness into the charging wall of bluecoats. Reportedly the attacks came every fifteen minutes and, as Garland Ferguson recorded, six successive assaults were repulsed. Each time the results were the same—hundreds of dead and wounded Yankees heaped and strewn across the field fronting the sunken road and wall. General Lee, upon observing the scene unfold before him, was reputed to have said: "It is well that war is so terrible—otherwise we should grow too fond of it!"[261]

General Ransom offered another account of the action occurring over the portion of the battlefield that was under his authority.

> The enemy now seemed determined to reach our position, and formed apparently a triple line. Observing this movement on his part, I brought up three regiments of my brigade to within 100 yards of the crest of the hills, and pushed forward the Twenty-fifth North Carolina Volunteers to the crest. The enemy, almost massed, moved to the charge heroically, and met the withering fire of our artillery and small-arms with wonderful staunchness. On they came within less than 150 paces of our line, but nothing could live before the sheet of lead that was hurled at them from this distance. They momentarily wavered, broke, and rushed headlong from the field. A few, however, more resolute than the rest, lingered under cover of some fences and houses, and annoyed us with a scattering but well-directed fire. The Twenty-fifth North Carolina Volunteers reached the crest of the hill just in time to pour into the enemy a few volleys at most deadly range, and then took position shoulder to shoulder with Cobb's and Cook's men in the road.[262]

And that was not all that Ransom allowed concerning the staunch action of the mountain men from Western North Carolina and Georgia: "While I do not disparage

The Haywood Highlanders were positioned in reserve behind the Marye house (above) at the beginning of the Battle of Fredericksburg. During the battle the Highlanders were ordered from Marye's Heights, where the house was located, to the sunken road at the foot of the Heights to reinforce the rebel defenders fighting from behind a low stone wall. *Library of Congress, Prints and Photographs Division.*

any, I cannot fail to mention the splendid and dashing action of the Twenty-fifth North Carolina Volunteers, Lieutenant Colonel (Samuel C.) Bryson commanding [Colonel Rutledge was recovering from the effects of typhoid fever], in going into battle." The 25th Regiment N.C. was the only regiment out of the eight under Ransom's command at Fredericksburg that he singled out for praise. Several years after the war the general looked back on that shining victory at Fredericksburg and wrote of the superlative performance turned in by his North Carolinians.

> I may be pardoned for remembering with pride that among the Confederate troops engaged on the *whole* battlefield of Fredericksburg, Va., December 13, 1862, none were more honorably distinguished than the sons of North Carolina, and those of them who, with brother soldiers from other States, held the lines at Marye's Hill against almost ten times their number of as brave and determined foes as ever did battle, can well trust their fame to history when written from truthful official records.[263]

The Confederate victory was so overwhelming and complete that a devastated Burnside would refuse to continue the battle over the following days. Winter weather forced both combatants to the warm hearths of the encampments, and they would cast wary eyes across the Rappahannock River at each another until the sap rose again in the trees. Following the battle the Haywood Highlanders camped in the vicinity of Fredericksburg until the end of the year. To protect themselves from the freezing temperatures, snow, and ice the mountaineers fashioned shelters from pine brush and built log fires to keep warm. They were also able to draw another supply of blankets and clothing in addition to what they received from home.[264] In consideration of Ferguson's gruesome, though inflated, report of some one hundred and twenty men from the 25th Regiment N.C. falling within a two-minute period around the Marye house, the casualty report for Company F that follows seems minimal—especially when compared to the 15,000 casualties inflicted on the Union forces. All three of the company's wounded later reported back for duty.

CASUALTIES AND OTHER LOSSES, FREDERICKSBURG

Name	Date	Remarks
Killed (none)		
Died of Wounds (none)		
Wounded (3)		
Pvt. Francis M. Mahaffey	12/13/1862	Wounded in the arm at Fredericksburg, Va.
Pvt. John W. Trull	12/13/1862	Wounded in the left foot at Fredericksburg, Va.
Pvt. John C. Wilson	12/13/1862	Wounded in the left hand at Fredericksburg, Va.
Died of Disease (none)		
Captured (none)		
Deserted (none)		
Other (none)		

From a position behind the low stone wall running along the sunken road under Marye's Heights the Haywood Highlanders helped stave off wave after wave of Union attacks during the Battle of Fredericksburg. *Library of Congress, Prints and Photographs Division.*

Opposite: Battle of Fredericksburg, Dec. 13, 1862. *Map by Peter Krafft, Florida State University.*

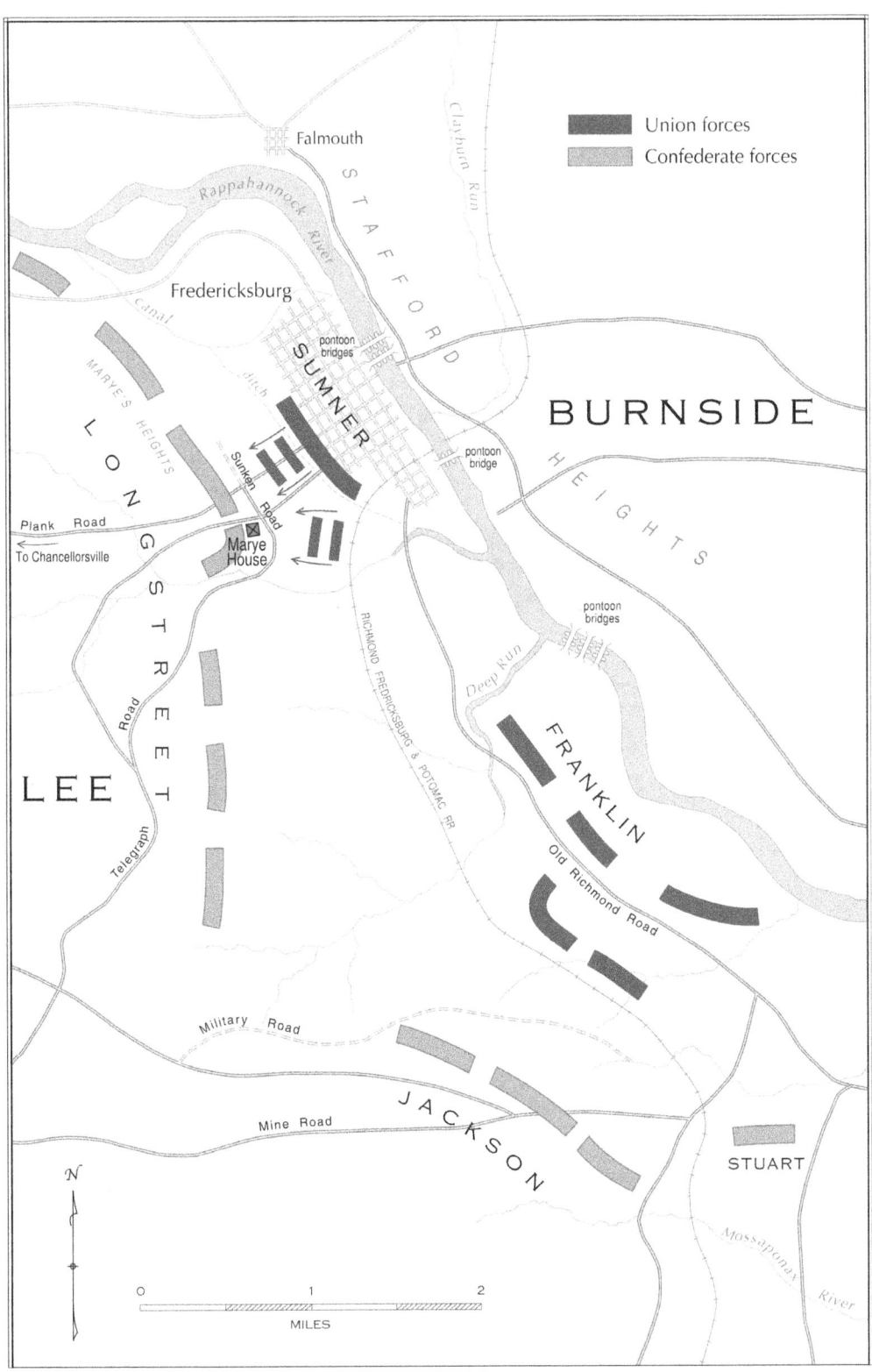

"*C.S.S. Albemarle* Under Construction in a Corn Field," by M. H. Hoke. *From* The American Heritage Century Collection of Art *(1974)*.

> ⇛ At least thirty Haywood Highlanders *deserted from the company, never to return.*

North Carolina / Virginia Coastal Defense
January 4, 1863—May 6, 1864

During the winter months of 1862–63 Robert E. Lee's Army of Northern Virginia held General Burnside's Army of the Potomac in check across the icy waters of the Rappahannock River around Fredericksburg. At the same time the Yankees were still active and threatening Confederate towns and facilities in eastern North Carolina. Kinston had been ransacked, and a crucial railroad bridge at Goldsboro was destroyed by marauding Federals on Dec. 17, 1862. Moreover, troop and transport concentrations were observed in southeastern Virginia, and it was thought that another large expedition was soon to descend on Wilmington, North Carolina, or some other Carolina coastal target. Secretary of War James Seddon wrote to Lee on Jan. 1, 1863, warning of this possibility: "I have information that there is in Hampton Roads a large fleet, said to be one hundred transports. General [Gustavus W.] Smith has just returned from North Carolina; apprehends very seriously invasion on a large scale in that State."[265]

Wilmington's vital port facility was one of the last remaining safe havens for Southern blockade runners ferrying their treasures of much-needed military arms and supplies as well as domestic and manufacturing necessities. Also, the rich low-lying countrysides along eastern North Carolina's coastal river networks were covered with valuable food- and stock-growing plantations that were desperately needed to support the Southern armies in the field as well as the North Carolina populace. Gov. Zebulon Vance of North Carolina worked zealously to effect the turnout of militias, exempt men, and others over forty-five years of age to protect his state's coastal area. General Lee, who was anxiously waiting for Burnside's dormant army to make a move, was beleaguered by dispatches warning of the pending disaster in North Carolina and requesting that he send North Carolina troops there. He finally relented and on Jan.3, 1863, gave orders for General Ransom and his two brigades (Ransom's and Cook's) to start toward Richmond.

So it was that the Haywood Highlanders were uprooted from their pine shelters in the cold and snow at Fredericksburg and herded off on foot to more comfortable southern environs. One of the rebel soldiers attached to Ransom's Brigade recounted that march away from Fredericksburg and the men's reaction when they finally learned their true destination:

> The men started to march, ostensibly, for a new camp. The men started out loaded down with camp impedimenta and winter quarters fixings, but marching past the site selected for the camp, we halted only after a fifteen mile march. As we marched, one by one, the planks, breadtrays, stools, water buckets, etc., etc., were grudgingly discarded until at the end of the day's march, while our impedimenta was gone, our hearts were light with the hope that we were on the way to North Carolina. This proved to be true, for after marching through Richmond we took the cars at Petersburg for Kenansville, N. C., our destination.[266]

About Jan. 7 the Highlanders reached Petersburg, Virginia, where they encamped until the Confederate generals confirmed that the threat in North Carolina was real and the boys were needed there. On Jan. 17 they boarded the cars of the Petersburg-Weldon Railroad and disembarked one day later at Warsaw Station, near Kenansville, North Carolina. For the next sixteen months the Haywood Highlanders performed their military labors at various hot spots throughout eastern North Carolina and southeastern Virginia. While this coastal guard duty was light in the sense that Company F participated in very little battle action or skirmishing with the enemy, the work was

Above: Gen. Matt W. Ransom, formerly colonel of the 35th Regiment North Carolina Troops and older brother of Gen. Robert Ransom, took command of Ransom's Brigade after the younger Ransom was promoted to major general in May 1863. *From* Histories of the Several Regiments and Battalions From North Carolina in the Great War, 1861–1865.

Above right: In the early spring of 1864 Confederate Gen. Robert F. Hoke led a rebel force composed of three brigades, two regiments, and the river gunboat CSS *Albemarle* to wrest Plymouth, N.C., from Union control. The Haywood Highlanders company participated in the capture of this important port town. *North Carolina Department of Archives and History; used by permission.*

Right: Maj. Gen. Daniel Harvey Hill, shown in this carte de visite by George S. Cook, commanded all troops in North Carolina during 1863, including the Haywood Highlanders. *South Caroliniana Library, University of South Carolina, Columbia; used by permission.*

surely tedious, tiring, and trying to the men's souls as they were ordered time and time again to strike camp at a moment's notice and rush to one after another perceived threat. On as many as fifty occasions during this period (as can be seen in Appendix C at the end of this work) the company was moved to various North Carolina locales such as Kenansville, Wilmington, Topsail Sound, Goldsboro, Warm Springs, Kinston, Trenton, Washington, Weldon, Garysburg, New Bern, Tarboro, and Plymouth. Also, the company's watch included many marches by foot and rail to Richmond and Petersburg in southeastern Virginia, where they parried enemy intentions or intrusions at Drewry's Bluff, Seven Pines, the Blackwater River area, Franklin, and Suffolk.

In addition to sending Ransom's brigades to North Carolina, Secretary of War James Seddon, with the support of General Lee, appointed Gen. Daniel Harvey Hill, a North Carolinian, to command all military operations in the state. The recent setbacks at Kinston and Goldsboro and the imminent threat on the coastline had encouraged an earlier suggestive query from Lee that was routed to Gov. Zebulon Vance by Secretary Seddon : "[Lee] seeks to know whether the presence of one of his most distinguished generals (General D.H. Hill of your State) might not prove advantageous in rousing and stimulating the people and in counseling and cooperating with the State authorities."[267] Vance obviously was taken with the idea of a native North Carolinian commanding the ever-increasing number of Confederate forces in his state. Almost immediately Hill issued an inflammatory message exhorting his troops in the field to perform their solemn duty in checking the enemy:

> "Soldiers! Your brutal and malignant enemy is putting forth efforts unexampled in the history of the world. Having failed to subjugate you, he is maddened with the thirst for vengeance, and is pushing forward his foreign mercenaries to plunder your property, and lay waste your homes."[268]

Hill did not mince words in describing his hated Northern adversary. And as further encouragement for the infantry forces under his command, such as the Haywood

Highlanders, he added: "The infantry have to bear the brunt of every battle and to endure special hardships in every campaign . . . . If our liberty ever be won it will be due mainly to the indomitable pluck and sturdy endurance of our heroic infantry."[269] How the Highlanders reacted to their new leader's rhetoric is not known, although the service records reveal that at least seventeen of them deserted during this phase. However, it is manifest that a majority of the men bore up under the defensive load placed on them in eastern North Carolina. The service rendered by the Highlanders during this stretch of time did not reach the level of the heavy duty they had performed the year before; it included only one pitched battle and many smaller actions against the Yankees and Tories. The following survey of the company's activities during this sixteen-month period, while not exhaustive in detail, demonstrates the notable service that it performed and the important events in which it was associated.

Gen. D. H. Hill's Siege of Washington

As it turned out Federal designs were not toward Wilmington, but targeted instead Charleston, South Carolina, in March and April of 1863. Nonetheless, the aggressive General Hill was not prone to let the considerable number of troops under his control in North Carolina (approximately 30,000) stand around idle. Therefore he schemed to take back control of the coastal port town of Washington, which had fallen during the Burnside expedition in March 1862. On Mar. 30, 1863, Hill's Confederate forces surrounded the town, located at the confluence of the Tar and Pamlico Rivers, and effectively corralled the Yankees garrisoned there and cut them off from their gunboats. General Hill's purpose was not only to harass the Yankees and possibly capture the town, but also to get out food supplies from the low-lying country to feed the Confederate army, and to create a diversion to delay or hamper ongoing Federal operations against Charleston. However, after sixteen days of close besiegement two Yankee supply boats eluded the Confederate guns and succeeded in reaching and supplying the town, forcing Hill to abandon the siege.[270]

The Haywood Highlanders and the 25th Regiment N.C. Troops are not believed to have directly engaged the enemy during this time frame. But they operated in and around the vicinity of Washington from April 7 until after the siege was lifted around April 17. While the exact nature of their role is unknown, the absence of reports of killed or wounded men during this time frame may indicate that their role was one of backup or guarding key corridors where Union reinforcements might have been routed.

⇒⇐

Embarrassing Affair at Gum Swamp

On Apr. 29, 1863, shortly after the failed siege at Washington, North Carolina, and about the same time that Robert E. Lee's Army of Northern Virginia was fighting and winning the Battle of Chancellorsville, Virginia, Company F along with the 25th Regiment N.C. was marched about nine miles southeast of Kinston to a remote Confederate outpost. There, in an inhospitable area known as Gum Swamp, a fort had been constructed of circular earthworks to guard the rail line leading into Kinston from Union-occupied New Bern. The mountain boys were garrisoned with the 56th Regiment N.C in this rustic, lonely fort in swampy environs with orders to guard against another Yankee raid toward Kinston. At daylight on May 22 three Union regiments drove in the rebel pickets in front of the fort and commenced to attack the works. Unknown to the Southern defenders, two more enemy regiments had stolen through the thick cover of the swamp, with the aid of a native guide, to the rear of the outpost to cut off their escape. Around 10:00 a.m. these Yankee troops opened fire and advanced against the surprised rebels.

The official records contain reports of the action at Gum Swamp recorded by the Union commanders involved that day. Gen. J. G. Foster proudly described the surprise rear attack:

> On arriving in the rear of the enemy's position Colonel Jones deployed such portions of his command as could be used to advantage, opened fire,

and advanced. The enemy fired a few desultory volleys, then broke and fled in great confusion, taking to the swamps and escaping by paths known only to themselves.[271]

The Union forces rushed into the vacated fortifications and succeeded in capturing 165 of the rebel defenders and almost took Gen. Robert Ransom, who inopportunely was at the post when the attack occurred. Also included in the booty taken from the rebels that day were 28 horses, 10 mules, 2 baggage wagons, 3 ambulances, 10 sets single harness, 6 artillery harness, 11 saddles, 3 saddles (artillery), 9 bridles, 80 muskets, 80 sets of equipments, 11,000 rounds of ammunition, and one 12-pounder howitzer with limber.[272] All of these trappings of war were of immense value to the Confederate army, which could ill afford to lose them.

At dusk that same evening Gen. D. H. Hill reached the outpost with the remaining regiments of Ransom's and Cooke's brigades and pushed the enemy out of the Confederate works, chasing them back to their fortifications near New Bern. Most of the rebels taken prisoner on that day were from the 56th Regiment. The Haywood Highlanders and other soldiers of the 25th Regiment escaped, for the most part, with only a blemish on its service record. General Lee commented in a note to General Hill: "I regret to hear of the occurrence reported by you [Gum Swamp], and fear that the regiment allowed itself to be surprised. I am gratified, however, that you drove the enemy back so promptly to his intrenchments and did all in your power to retrieve the disaster."[273] Even General Lee termed the events at Gum Swamp a "disaster," and it is understandable that the original historian of the 25th Regiment (Garland Ferguson) would omit a recounting of this embarrassing episode.[274]

Old Ransom's Brigade Becomes New Ransom's Brigade

In the latter days of May 1863 Brig. Gen. Robert Ransom was promoted to the rank of major general and assigned a new division elsewhere. In his place another Ransom, his older brother, Col. Matt W. Ransom of the 35th Regiment N.C., took command of Ransom's Brigade on June 15. Matt Ransom had been a highly respected lawyer in North Carolina before the war and had served as attorney general of his state and as a member of the legislature. He was enthusiastically recommended to fill his brother's vacancy by the commanding officers of the 25th, 49th, and 35th regiments. They wrote to the Confederate Secretary of War James Seddon: "For this command we respectfully beg leave to recommend Col. Matt W. Ransom 35 Regt. N.C. Troops. . . . We have been associated with him since our organization as a Brigade and can bear testimony to his merit and ability as an officer & a gentleman—his efficiency as disciplinarian & his skill & intrepidity on the field of battles."[275] President Davis and Secretary Seddon were likely swayed by the regimental officers' impassioned plea, and it was thus that the old Ransom's Brigade became the new Ransom's Brigade.

Skirmish with Tories at Warm Springs

Following their unfortunate experience at Gum Swamp, Captain Cathey's Haywood Highlanders embarked on the cars at Kinston for the Petersburg and Richmond, Virginia, area. Around July 4 they were stationed near Seven Pines (where they had first battled the Yankees one year earlier) and helped repulse an enemy thrust at Richmond near Bottom's Bridge on the Chickahominy River. Two weeks later the Highlanders found their way back to North Carolina and were posted in the Weldon and Garysburg region, where they could protect these important rail centers and check enemy advances in the surrounding country. During this time frame a detachment of soldiers from the 25th Regiment led by Lt. Col. Samuel C. Bryson was ordered to the Western North Carolina mountains to recruit fresh soldiers and help the local home guard and Confederate troops combat a large gang of Yankees and Tories operating in the Madison County area. The heavy Unionist sentiment in east Tennessee boiled over the state border into Madison, where raids, robberies, and other acts of terror were being regularly carried out against the local populace by the so-called Tories.

No details of the detachment's activities or their actions in combating the Tories can be found in the Confederate records. Garland Ferguson of Company F wrote only the following short account regarding the detachment's service in his regimental history: "In October, 1863, a detachment of the regiment under Lieutenant-Colonel Bryson, had an engagement at Hot Springs, in Madison County, North Carolina. The enemy outnumbered them twenty to one, and the loss of the detachment in killed and wounded was heavy, including Lieutenant Hyatt, of Company F, who was killed on the field."[276] Although details are sparse in the military records of this skirmish at Hot Springs (or Warm Springs), other scarce civilian accounts offer clues to what actually might have occurred. From them the following version of events has been reconstructed:

On Oct. 26 Brig. Gen. Robert Vance, brother to the governor and commander of the local militia forces and a scattering of regular troops in the Western District of North Carolina, launched a two-pronged attack against the Tories who held Warm Springs.[277] Regular troops detached from the 25th Regiment were sent to the head of Spring Creek and instructed to proceed cautiously down the creek road to Warm Springs. At the same time General Vance was to lead another column of his own troops and approach Warm Springs along the Buncombe Turnpike, which followed the French Broad River. When General Vance received information of the enemy's strength and position he determined that the river approach was impracticable and immediately dispatched a courier to countermand the Spring Creek expedition. However, the messenger did not reach the 25th Regiment's force in time. The Yankees, apparently being informed of the rebel movement down the creek, were well positioned and primed to attack the Confederate force, which is believed to have numbered approximately one hundred or more men. The small contingent of Haywood Highlanders and mountain boys from the 25th Regiment N.C. was soundly defeated.

A contemporaneous diary kept by Mrs. Cornelia Henry of Sulphur Springs in Buncombe County records: "We lost 5 killed & 2 wounded. Our forces fought well. . . . The men who did most of the fighting were a detail from the 25th N.C. Reg. as brave men as ever drew a trigger. They were under the immediate command of Lt.

Welch of Haywood ... they fought hand to hand, knocked each other down with their muskets."[278] Mrs. Henry's diary reveals that Lt. William Pink Welch from Haywood County's Company C held immediate command of the 25th Regiment's troops as they descended the Spring Creek road into the ambuscade. The diarist's casualty information may be misleading, however, as regimental service records document that three men were in fact killed, three more were wounded (one by bayonet), and two were captured.[279] A casualty that is not in dispute is Haywood Highlander Lt. Thaddeus Hyatt, who received a mortal wound, perhaps in the close-quarter fighting, and fell dead on the field. No other Haywood Highlanders are known to have been lost or wounded at the engagement in Madison County's Warm Springs on Oct. 26, 1863.

The defeat at the hands of the Tories excited fears among the citizenry of Asheville and Buncombe County. Most folk expected that at any time the Tories and Yankees would march up the French Broad River and lay waste to their fair town and surrounding country. However, that did not transpire. The Tories vacated Warm Springs just days after the Oct. 26 clash and receded back into the mountain fastnesses to terrorize remote homesteads and helpless families whose men were off fighting on either side. General Vance apparently felt that he had the Unionists stymied for the time being, because just a couple of weeks later he wrote to Governor Vance that he had "raided Cocke County [Tennessee]..., and brought out safely 800 hogs and some horses and cattle" and that he was "not only saving property for the Government, but threatening the enemy on his lines."[280] Yet the woes for the mountain dwellers were far from over. The bushwhacking element composed of Tories, draft evaders, and deserters would continue to wreak havoc and terror across the Western North Carolina mountains until the war's end.

General Pickett's Bungled Assault on New Bern

During the last several months of 1863 Captain Cathey's men remained in and around Weldon and Garysburg, protecting the railroads and nearby manufacturing centers and plantations. For a brief two-week stint in early December they moved up to Petersburg, Virginia, and on Dec. 20 moved to Franklin, Virginia, abruptly returning to Weldon two days later. Commanding the movements of the Haywood Highlanders and all the troops then located in North Carolina was Maj. Gen. George E. Pickett. This Virginian, who less than three months previously had led a failed desperate charge against a strong Union position atop Cemetery Ridge at Gettysburg, had assumed command of the Department of North Carolina on Sept. 23, 1863.[281] His appointment was preceded by the assignment of generals James Longstreet and D.H. Hill to support Braxton Bragg's Army of Tennessee in the western theater. On the recommendation of Gen. Robert E. Lee, whose Army of Northern Virginia was then in winter quarters along the line of the Rapidan River in Virginia, an offensive was plotted to drive the Federals from New Bern. Lee wrote to President Davis just after the new year of 1864 arrived: "The time is at hand when, if an attempt can be made to capture the enemy's forces at New Bern, it should be done." He knew that he could spare troops for the endeavor and believed that the country surrounding New Bern could provide much needed sustenance and supplies for his army.[282]

General Pickett himself was selected to conduct the New Bern campaign, and he divided his force of 13,000 men into three columns. The ambitious plan that was hatched called for the individual columns to launch joint surprise attacks against the Federal defenses at New Bern. Also, fourteen naval cutters at his disposal were to descend the Neuse River and attempt to capture the enemy's gunboats. Three regiments from Ransom's Brigade, including the 25th Regiment N.C. and Captain Cathey's Highlanders, were attached to Gen. Seth M. Barton's column that marched out of Kinston on Jan. 30, 1864, toward New Bern. The Company F record of events simply states that "[t]he company with the Regt left Camp near Weldon N.C. & arrived in the immediate vicinity of Newbern on 1 of Feb. besieged the town for two days & returned to Kinston on 5."[283]

The fate of this expedition met with similar results to those of General Hill's siege of Washington in April 1863. After General Barton reached his intended point of attack, along with General Matt Ransom and other Confederate officers he reconnoitered the enemy's formidable defense works behind Brice's Creek. Barton later wrote in his official report: "I was ... unprepared to encounter obstacles so serious, and was forced to the conviction that they were insurmountable by any means at my disposal."[284] Gen. Robert F. Hoke led the only column, out of the three spearheads aimed at New Bern, that actually engaged and struck the enemy and mounted any serious effort to fulfill Pickett's orders. After learning of Barton's situation and losing the element of a coordinated surprise assault on three fronts, General Pickett abandoned his ill-fated plan to capture New Bern.[285] The 25th Regiment N.C. and the Haywood Highlanders received orders on Feb. 3, 1864, to march back to Kinston.

Capture of Suffolk, Virginia

Soon after the unsuccessful expedition against New Bern the Haywood Highlanders found themselves on the rail cars bound for Weldon, where they arrived on Feb. 6, 1864. After encamping at Weldon for almost three weeks the mountain boys boarded the cars again on Feb. 25 and marched (by rail) to Franklin, Virginia. From that point they set out on foot eastward through the North Carolina counties of Gates and Pasquotank and reached South Mills (near Elizabeth City) on Feb. 29. General Matt Ransom's regiments trudged northward from South Mills and on Mar. 9 moved against Suffolk, Virginia. They handily drove off the Federal forces then occupying the town and in the process captured a piece of artillery and quartermaster's stores of much value.[286] The Haywood Highlanders were surely participants in this exciting action, in which they engaged against black Union soldiers for the first time in the war.

Capture of Plymouth

The final service rendered by the Haywood Highlanders during their sixteen months of primarily coastal defense duty involved their participation in an attack affecting the capture of Plymouth, North Carolina. General Robert F. Hoke, still bitter and smarting over the bungled Confederate assailment of New Bern two months earlier, was given overall command responsibility to reduce the defenses of Plymouth and recapture that port town. The forces he had available to him were his own and Kemper's brigades, the 8th and 43rd North Carolina regiments, and Matt Ransom's Brigade (minus the 49th Regiment, which was on detached duty.) Additionally, he anticipated the support of the CSS *Albemarle,* then under construction in a cornfield along the Roanoke River. On Apr. 12, 1864, General Ransom started his men on the cars from Weldon to Tarboro and by Apr. 15 was marching with Hoke's other forces toward Plymouth. Over a two-day period, Apr. 19–20, the Confederates' well-positioned artillery and a pair of rifle guns mounted on the *Albemarle* unleashed an incessant barrage of cannon fire on the Yankee forts at Plymouth. A final infantry assault initiated at the break of dawn on the last day involved severe house-to-house fighting, which resulted in the capture of approximately 2,000 prisoners.

The first historian of the 25th Regiment, Garland Ferguson, had very little to say about the battle for Plymouth. He only offhandedly mentioned that "[i]n April, 1864, the regiment participated in the assault and capture of Plymouth, N.C."[287] No further details are offered to illuminate the regiment's actions, or the service that its Company F might have rendered in the successful venture. However, from other sources and a map credited to one of the men from the 56th Regiment of Ransom's Brigade, it is possible to glean much more information.[288]

After forming at Tarboro, Hoke's forces marched through the towns of Hamilton, Williamston, and Jamesville, North Carolina, and arrived in the vicinity of Plymouth at nightfall of Apr. 17. From Ransom's Brigade the 25th Regiment and four other detached companies were thrown out in a skirmish line and pushed forward nearly to the enemy's entrenchments. For most of the next day the rebel forces waited on the *Albemarle* to descend the Roanoke River and support an assault against the Union defenders forted up in the town. Although the Confederate gunboat failed to arrive, a strong demonstration was launched at sundown with Ransom's Brigade positioned on the right, or south side, of the town. Gen. Matt Ransom was conspicuous on the field as he kept his mount throughout the several hours' action and led his men in the attack. Undeterred, the enemy replied with great spirit from the forts and their several gunboats maneuvering in the Roanoke River beyond the town. Ransom's line was able to push the defenders back into their breastworks but no further. However, on the rebels' left side of the field of battle Hoke's Brigade was able to overwhelm and take the Yankees' outlying 85th Redoubt, otherwise known as Fort Wessells.[289]

The next day, Apr. 19, saw the arrival of the *Albemarle* to the theater. After avoiding the Union's big guns, Capt. James W. Cooke and his crew wasted little time in dispatching the Yankee cutters. One, the USS *Southfield*, was quickly sunk, and three other vessels fled down river to safety. During the evening hours, while the *Albemarle's* guns and Hoke's considerable number of artillery batteries played on the enemy's fortifications, Ransom's Brigade moved to a new position on the downriver (east) side of town. Their move was affected only after making a difficult crossing of the deep Conaby Creek over felled timbers and an improvised pontoon bridge. Once in position, with a skirmish line thrown out, the men of the brigade—including the 25th Regiment—slept in the line of battle.[290]

At sunup on the 20th the men began stirring out of their blankets along the rebel line east of Plymouth. Excited and tense about the looming fight, the soldiers began making hurried preparations and girding for battle. One of the men from Ransom's Brigade who arose early before Plymouth on that morning recalled the scene:

> At the first break of day Ransom was again in the saddle, and his ringing voice came down the line: 'Attention, brigade!' Every man was upon his feet instantly, and the adjusting of twisted blankets across the left shoulder and under the belt at the right hip was only the work of another moment; the line of battle was formed, 'Fix bayonets, Trail arms! Forward march!' and the charge began. The alignment was as follows: The Fifty-sixth on the right, flanked by Company I, as sharpshooters, (resting on the Roanoke and near the *Albemarle*, then engaged, as it had been at intervals through the

The CSS *Albemarle*, shown in this photograph taken after the Confederate river gunboat was sunk by the U.S. Navy and then raised, played a vital supporting role in the Confederate army's capture of Plymouth, North Carolina, in April 1864. *United States Naval Historical Center; used by permission.*

night, with Battery Worth on the river face of the town), and Twenty-fifth, Thirty-fifth, Eighth and Twenty-fourth successively on to the left.[291]

Ransom's Brigade, with the support of the *Albemarle*'s guns and the artillery units, slowly began winning back the town and taking the fortifications along the river. The men fought furiously house-to-house up Columbia and Water Streets, which paralleled the river. They initially used a herd of cattle to screen their movement and waded through a canal and swamp that impeded their way. In concert with Ransom's movement on the east, the brigades of Hoke and Kemper moved against the enemy from the west. As one Yankee fort or gun battery after another fell there eventually was only one Union stronghold left to reduce. Holed up in Fort Williams, the last Union bastion, were Gen. Henry W. Wessells and the remnants of his forces—still actively fighting and defiant. A barrage of Confederate cannon fire was directed at the fort until finally, at mid-morning, a white flag was raised over the parapets and the fort surrendered. Wessells later justified his action by explaining:

> This terrible fire had to be endured without reply, as no man could live at the guns.... This condition of affairs could not be long endured without a reckless sacrifice of life; no relief could be expected, and in compliance with the earnest desire of every officer I consented to hoist a white flag, and at 10:00 AM of April 20 I had the mortification of surrendering my post to the enemy with all it contained.[292]

One report in a Richmond newspaper stated that the capture of Plymouth netted for the Confederacy some 2,500 prisoners, 28 artillery pieces, 500 horses, 5,000 stands of small arms, and masses of ammunition. With Federal control of Plymouth finally relinquished, the portal city once again was opened to blockade runners laden with extremely critical food and war-making supplies.[293]

The 25th Regiment N.C. Troops suffered casualties numbering as high as three men killed and another twenty wounded, per one accounting.[294] However, the service records for Company F reveal that not one soldier was injured in the capture of Plymouth. Overall, the company's coastal guard duty in eastern North Carolina and Virginia exacted a heavy toll in troops from the Haywood Highlanders. As can be seen in the table below, it was during this time that desertion first raised its ugly head within the company. Seventeen of the Highlanders simply gave up the fight and left their brethren behind. Some of them turned themselves over to the enemy and signed an oath of allegiance to the United States government. The rest simply hid out in the mountains or elsewhere and eluded the home guard and regular troops sent to capture them until the war was over.

Casualties and Other Losses, North Carolina/Virginia Coastal Defense

Name	Date	Remarks
Killed (2)		
1st Lt. Thaddeus C.S. Hyatt	10/26/1862	Killed by Tories at Warm Springs in Madison County.
Pvt. George W. Chambers	6/10/1863	Killed by deserters (William L. Reece of Company F) while on detached duty.
Died of wounds (none)		
Wounded (none)		
Died of disease (6)		
3rd Lt. Joseph T. Cathey	9/8/1863	Died in hospital at Wilson, N.C., of "febris typhoides."
Pvt. Eli Collins	2/9/1863	Died at Guinea Station, Va., of typhoid fever.
Pvt. Jasper N. Anderson	5/12/1863	Died in hospital at Goldsboro, N.C., of "febris typhoides."
Pvt. William R. Meece	3/31/1863	Died in Farmville, Va., of pneumonia and/or diarrhea.
Pvt. Francis M. Miller	4/1/1863	Died in hospital at Wilson, N.C., of typhoid fever.
Pvt. James M. Singleton	1/4/1863	Died in hospital at Petersburg, Va., of typhoid pneumonia.
Captured (none)		

Deserted (17)		
Pvt. William N. Allman	2/24/1864	Deserted.
Pvt. William R. Clonts	2/24/1864	Deserted.
Pvt. Rufus L. Deaver	2/1/1864	Deserted on the march and went over to the enemy. Paroled at Knoxville, Tenn., around 5/22/1864.
Pvt. William N. Deaver	2/1/1864	Deserted to the enemy and paroled at Knoxville, Tenn., around 5/22/1864.
Pvt. Samuel B. Green	8/14/1863	Went over to the enemy and paroled at Knoxville, Tenn., around 5/25/1864.
Pvt. Burton H. Henson	11/29/1863	Deserted on the march and went over to the enemy. Paroled at Knoxville, Tenn., around 5/22/1864.
Pvt. Elijah L. Henson	3/1864	Deserted to the enemy after February 1864. Paroled at Knoxville, Tenn., around 5/25/1864.
Corp. Thomas F. Henson	1/28/1864	Deserted on the march and went over to the enemy. Paroled at Knoxville, Tenn., around 5/25/1864.
Sgt. Wiley Henson	2/22/1864	Deserted.
Pvt. Matthias Holland	3/1864	Deserted to the enemy after February 1864. Paroled at Knoxville, Tenn., around 5/22/1864.
Pvt. John W. Mahaffey	1/28/1864	Deserted on the march and went over to the enemy. Paroled at Knoxville, Tenn., around 5/22/1864.
Pvt. James Bradford Meece	1/1864	Deserted to the enemy after December 1863. Paroled at Knoxville, Tenn., around 5/22/1864.
Pvt. Daniel N. Pressley	3/1864	Deserted to the enemy after February 1864. Paroled at Knoxville, Tenn., around 5/22/1864.
Pvt. Robert H. Queen	8/17/1863	Deserted.
Musician John A. Smith	3/27/1863	Deserted.
Pvt. John G. Thomas	11/27/1863	Deserted on the march and went over to the enemy. Paroled at Knoxville, Tenn., around 5/25/1864.
Pvt. William H. Williams	6/1/1863	Deserted in front of the enemy.
Other (2)		
2nd Lt. William M. Wright	2/23/1864	Resigned for unreported reason and relieved of duty.
Pvt. Samuel P. Singleton	6/1863	Discharged by reason of disability.

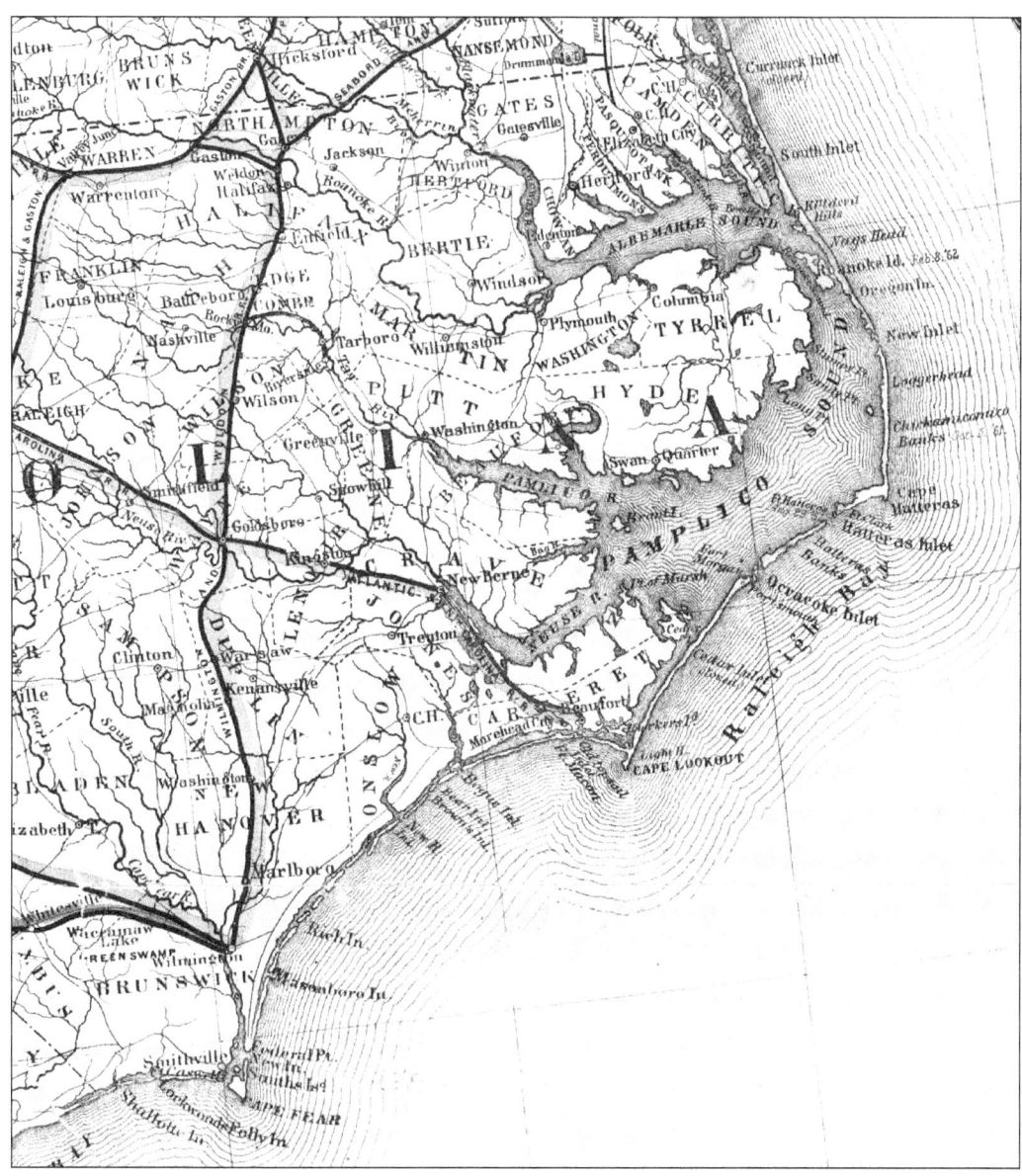

For almost the entirety of 1863 the Haywood Highlanders were on the march from one hotbed of activity to another, protecting the important coastal towns, railroads, and plantations of eastern North Carolina. *Library of Congress, Maps Division.*

"A Dangerous Occupation." Harper's Weekly, *Sept. 24, 1864.*

≋ One soldier who had deserted *from the company was executed on Feb. 18, 1864—not as a consequence of the act of desertion, but for murdering a fellow Haywood Highlander, Pvt. George W. Chambers, on June 10, 1863.*

Richmond / Petersburg Defense: The Last-Ditch Effort
May 7, 1864—April 9, 1865

At the onset of spring, with weather conducive for the movement and logistical supply of great armies in the field, Gen. Robert E. Lee's Army of Northern Virginia resumed the campaign against the Army of the Potomac. In central Virginia, Lee engaged the Union forces led by Gen. Ulysses S. Grant in a series of murderous running battles along the Rapidan, North Anna, and South Anna Rivers. At places such as the Wilderness, Spotsylvania, North Anna, and Cold Harbor, the two great armies clashed, each time with similar results—thousands and thousands of dead soldiers and Lee still interposed between the Federals and Richmond. While Lee was thus distracted, Union Gen. Benjamin F. Butler schemed to attack Richmond. He proceeded to assemble and transport some 30,000 Federal troops up the James River, and on May 5, 1864, and landed his Army of the James midway between Richmond and Petersburg at Bermuda Hundred. From there Butler directly threatened the railroad linking Petersburg and Richmond. Additionally, he could move on Richmond, which lay approximately fifteen miles to the north; or he could descend southward some ten miles against Petersburg, an important manufacturing center and a hub for the key railroads connecting with North Carolina and the Deep South states.

Meanwhile in North Carolina, the capture of Plymouth was being hailed all across the state as a great triumph and feat of arms. A resolution proclaiming the victory and commending General Hoke and those under his command for their magnificent conquest was passed by the North Carolina legislature. However, the Haywood Highlanders would not have long to relish their success at Plymouth. Butler's expedition up the James presented a grave danger to the Confederacy and forced the officials in Richmond into a crisis-management mode. Troops in and around the Confederate capital were insufficient to successfully oppose this new enemy threat. North Carolina's mountain boys were needed there—and needed quick. Just as General Hoke and his forces were preparing to besiege New Bern, only days after taking back Plymouth, Hoke received urgent orders to cease all operations in North Carolina and proceed with his command to Petersburg.

Battle of Drewry's Bluff

The Haywood Highlanders left Kinston on May 8, 1864, and because of railroad disruptions caused by Yankee cavalry raids did not reach Drewry's Bluff until May 11. On the very next day Captain Cathey's men engaged in a fierce struggle with an advance portion of Butler's army. Garland Ferguson of Company F gave the following account of this action: "The regiment was engaged at Drewry's Bluff 12 May, 1864, in which engagement Company F lost Lieutenant Ebed J. Ferguson, killed, and six non-commissioned officers and privates wounded."[295] General Hoke's dispatches during this precarious period maintained that the fighting was continuing in his front on May 13 and that he had not sufficient forces to fill up the entrenchments.[296] Another soldier from Ransom's Brigade who was a participant in the skirmishing later confirmed this account: "On 13 May, 1864, while occupying the outer line of works defending Drewry's Bluff, Ransom's Brigade was attacked by Butler's advance with overwhelming force. After gallantly repulsing these attacks, though flanked on the right and in the rear, the brigade held its own and during the night withdrew to the main line of defenses."[297]

On May 14 Gen. P. G. T. Beauregard, whose command was extended from North Carolina to that portion of Virginia lying below the James River, arrived at Drewry's

Bluff.[298] Like a knight errant sent to save the beleaguered Confederacy, he immediately took charge of the resistance operations against Butler's onslaught. And just two days later, May 16, the main Battle of Drewry's Bluff came off. The Haywood Highlanders fought in a fierce struggle alongside of Hoke's other troops and those of generals Robert Ransom and Alfred H. Colquitt, and were successful in driving General Butler's Union forces back. Yet in the ensuing days the fighting continued in the vicinity of Ware Bottom Church and Bermuda Hundred. Finally, on May 20, the Confederates attacked Butler's Bermuda Hundred line and were able to push the Yankees back into a neck formed by the James and Appomattox Rivers. Butler was effectively bottled up between the rivers, and the Haywood Highlanders were employed for the next few weeks manning the fortified Confederate Howlett Line to keep the Yankees "corked."

Old Bory's Petersburg Defense

Old Bory, as General Beauregard was affectionately known to the troops serving under him, diligently worked the military and political chains of command to reinforce his skeletal forces below the James River. Even Confederate War Department clerks were pressed into service to man the defense works, which extended in a semicircular fashion from Drewry's Bluff on the James River southward around the eastern side of Petersburg and to a point just south of that town. Unbeknownst to either Old Bory or General Lee was the fact that General Grant had determined to move the greater portion of the Army of the Potomac around Lee's right flank and across the James River to affect a junction with Butler. In a wide flanking movement the Federals secretly sidled around the Army of Northern Virginia's eastern outposts and on June 14 began crossing over pontoon bridges spanning the James. Immediately the two Union armies—the Army of the Potomac and the Army of the James—began maneuvering and making preparations for an all-out attack against Old Bory and his meager forces occupying the Confederate entrenchments before Petersburg.

Captain Cathey and the Haywood Highlanders worked to keep the Yankees bottled

For the entirety of the time that the Haywood Highlanders occupied the trenches before Petersburg (June 1864–March 1865), the company and the 25th Regiment N.C. Troops were attached to a division commanded by Gen. Bushrod R. Johnson (above, left).
Library of Congress, Prints and Photographs Division.

In May 1864 Confederate Gen. P. G. T. Beauregard (above, right) was rushed from North Carolina to take command of the meager defense forces protecting Richmond and Petersburg, Virginia. The Haywood Highlanders were counted among Beauregard's scarce troops that were charged with protecting the important Southern cities from the onslaught of Union armies.
Library of Congress, Prints and Photographs Division.

up at Bermuda Hundred until June 4, when they were relieved. The company with its regiment and Ransom's Brigade then marched up the James to Richmond and out to the rebel defensive positions east of the capital between the Chickahominy River and Chaffin's Bluff (a fortress located on the James River opposite of Drewry's Bluff). For more than a week, in the same swampy woods where they had first clashed with the enemy two years before, the Haywood Highlanders guarded Richmond from attack. The mountaineers were presumably unaware that Grant was in the process of stealing around their position at that very moment to affect a crossing of the James and unite with Butler below the river. On June 15 the Highlanders received urgent orders to rush to the support of General Beauregard, who was just learning through intelligence sources of the combination of Federal armies in his front near Petersburg.[299] A catastrophe was certain to fall on the Confederacy if Old Bory, who by then had managed to scrape together approximately 5,400 men, could not stave off the enemy hoard numbering almost 50,000 Yankees.[300]

After an all-night march Company F reached the outskirts of Petersburg on June 16 with the 25th Regiment N.C. and the other regiments of Ransom's Brigade. Upon their arrival the North Carolina boys were instantly thrown into the rebel lines to repel the ferocious Federal assaults already underway. One of the combatants from Ransom's Brigade later recalled, "Arriving in sight of the inner line of the works defending Petersburg the enemy were seen advancing upon the same. At a run, through a storm of shot and shell, the Confederates succeeded in getting to the works just in time to meet the enemy's charge and drive them back."[301] Garland Ferguson, who was also a participant in the action, later recorded: "On 16 June, 1864, the regiment crossed to the South of the Appomattox for the defence of Petersburg and entered at once into the fight in front of Avery's House, and checked the advance of the enemy who was driving back the Petersburg militia, the only protection to the city at that time."[302]

Beauregard's thin gray line held back the bluecoats that day, but just barely. During the night Old Bory gave orders to fall back to a new, shorter defensive line of entrenchments closer to Petersburg. Early the next morning of June 17 the hard fighting was renewed near Avery's house, and Beauregard's stubborn, ragtag defenses continued to repel assault after assault made by a relentless enemy throughout the day. Finally, as darkness began settling over the field, the Confederate line was pierced, and as a countermeasure Gen. Archibald Gracie's Brigade was moved up to contain the thrust. A noted historian of Lee's army described the final hours of that long difficult day:

The next few hours were decisive. Beauregard had received no relief from the attacks that had begun disastrously at dawn of June 17. Toward evening the assaults became more furious. About dusk a desperate attack by a Division of the IX Corps breached another section of the line and took Battery 14, which had been held by part of Wise's command. The arrival of Archibald Gracie's Brigade prevented deep penetration, but a necessary counter-attack by Matt Ransom's North Carolina Brigade cost it many lives. By the time Ransom's men threw the Federals out of the salient they had taken, Beauregard was poised for a withdrawal to new positions.[303]

On the following day General Lee arrived with the main body of the Army of Northern Virginia, whereupon he began to place his veteran troops between Petersburg and the enemy. Lee assumed command of all the Southern forces opposing Grant's armies, finally relieving General Beauregard of the enormous responsibility that he had borne over the past month. Yet, Old Bory must surely have been content with himself and the service he had rendered for his beloved South. He and his scarce rebel defenders, including the Haywood Highlanders, had done their job. They had miraculously managed to hold off a force more than five times their size and in so doing saved Petersburg from immediate domination by the blue-coated forces of the United States Government. General Lee's engineers immediately set about staking new defense entrenchments to be dug for the continued defense of Petersburg. It was in those trenches that the Army of Northern Virginia, including the Haywood Highlanders, would live and fight for the remaining nine months of the war.

Battle of the Crater

For several weeks following their mid-June 1864 battles to defend Petersburg, the Haywood Highlanders applied themselves to digging and fortifying the entrenchments protecting the city. The division they were attached to, Gen. Bushrod R. Johnson's, was given responsibility and care of a section of the defensive line extending from the

Appomattox River to the Jerusalem plank road.[304] Despite a scarcity of digging tools, the mountaineers worked diligently to excavate enormous quantities of red soil. For protection from the incessant mortar fire of the enemy they constructed bombproof shelters and burrowed "gopher" holes into the walls of the dirt embankments. The Highlanders also threw up a timber abatis to obstruct and slow down enemy frontal assaults. This effective defensive measure was constructed by installing rows of felled trees and crossed tree laps with sharpened points. Any charging Yankee troops attempting to negotiate this dangerous wooden maze would be greatly hindered and slowed, making themselves easy targets for the rebel sharpshooters. Opposite the rebel trenches the Federal soldiers were mirroring their foes' work with earth entrenchments and fortifications of their own. General Grant, known for his propensity for ordering men to make murderous bloody charges against strongly fortified positions, chose to demonstrate a more patient course to weaken Petersburg's Confederate defensive works.

Grant effectively besieged the city, knowing well that he could feed and supply his own army and being confident that his counterpart, Lee, did not have sufficient resources to support and sustain the Army of Northern Virginia for an extended duration. So the two sides settled into their respective earthworks, shot minié balls and fired artillery rounds at their foes, and watched each other through rifle slits across narrow open spaces separating the lines. With plentiful ammunition, the Yankees continuously rained mortar shells down on the Confederate trenches, and their vigilant infantry forces maintained a deadly sniper fire to force the rebels underground. By contrast, the Southern soldiers were forced to husband their ammunition, to the indignation of the officers and men, because it was in such scarce supply.

During this late July time frame Sgt. Garland Ferguson wrote home informing friends and family back in Haywood that North Carolina's sitting governor, Zebulon Vance, had received a large majority of the regiment's vote in the gubernatorial election of 1864.[305] Perhaps the weary soldiers were buoyed by Vance's stirring speeches as he made a campaign swing into Virginia to reach the North Carolina soldiers serving in

Lee's Army of Northern Virginia and defending Richmond and Petersburg. Speaking the language of the common soldier, he shouted out to the crowds of Tarheels that surrounded him, "Boys, you must fight till you fill hell so full of Yankees that their feet will stick out the windows."[306] However, in Ferguson's own company such fiery rhetoric and warmongering did not assuage the longings for home and bitter sentiments harbored by many of the weary mountaineers. Vance won by only a slight majority of the vote in the Haywood Highlanders company. Ferguson reported that seventeen men cast their votes in favor of Vance and thirteen voted for the peace candidate, William Woods Holden. Obviously, almost half of the company's diminutive force of approximately thirty men who were fit for duty were anxious for a swift end to the war and thought Holden's aggressive peace policies might just offer the solution to gain that end. In his letter the young Sergeant Ferguson, a Vance supporter himself, offered an optimistic hope that "all the voters of Crabtree will go to the election and vote for Vance and the Vance ticket." The sergeant's fervent political promotions were rewarded during the August 1864 balloting when Governor Vance was reelected by an overwhelming majority of the state's populace.

This same letter penned by the hand of Sergeant Ferguson also bore news unrelated to politics. The sergeant allowed that he had "been detailed on a working party—work of a night throwing up Batterys and rest of a day." And of a much more somber note was the report that "Thos. [Thomas] Holland died of a wound received the 24th or the 25th. he was a good Soldier and well liked by all the boys. He leaves a wife and one child to mourn his loss." To wrap up his short letter Ferguson concluded with an idiom apparently common to the mountaineers then and one still familiar today, "Tell all the family howdy for me."[307]

On July 21 one of Gen. Bushrod Johnson's brigade commanders heard curious digging sounds at some depth under the ground in his front and requested an engineer to come and investigate.[308] Although the engineer failed to discover the source of the mysterious sounds, little could he or the rest of General Johnson's troops, including the Haywood Highlanders, have known that a Yankee plot was unfolding deep under the

Union Lt. Col. Henry Pleasants' Pennsylvania miners plant the powder charges under the rebel entrenchments at Petersburg. The detonation of this mine on the morning of July 30, 1864, initiated the Battle of the Crater. Sketch by Alfred Rudolf Waud. *Library of Congress, Prints and Photographs Division.*

ground at that very time. The clever Yankees were attempting to tunnel under a salient in the Confederate line with the notion of planting a mine, or bomb, under the rebel forces occupying the position. The idea was hatched in the minds of Lt. Col. Henry Pleasants and his regiment of Pennsylvania soldiers, many of them coal miners by profession, and was fully endorsed by General Grant. In theory a devastating explosion would breach the Southern defenses, and the Union forces, waiting in anticipation,

Union officers observe the explosion of the mine under the rebel entrenchments at Petersburg on July 30, 1864. Capt. James Madison Cathey of the Haywood Highlanders was killed in the battle that ensued. Sketch by Alfred Rudolf Waud. *Library of Congress, Prints and Photographs Division.*

could rush through the opening and overwhelm the surprised troops who may have survived the blast. The tunneling work began in late June and, when completed on July 28, measured 511 feet long and contained approximately 8,000 pounds of powder packed into the end of the tunnel.[309]

On July 30, 1864, at 4:55 in the morning the mine was detonated. The results were more terrible than the Yankees could have ever hoped. The huge explosion blasted open a crater 170 feet long, 60 to 80 feet in width, and 20 feet deep, and instantly killed or buried 278 men of Gen. Stephen Elliott's brigade.[310] However, the Union forces who rushed into the breach were poorly prepared for the mission and lacked inspired leadership. As a result a thousand or more bluecoats found themselves confined, as if in a fishbowl, and unable to maneuver. General Grant would later report after the battle,

"It was the saddest affair I have witnessed in the war. Such opportunity for carrying fortifications, I have never seen and do not expect again to have."[311]

Located immediately adjacent and to the Confederate left of Elliott's salient were Ransom's Brigade and the Haywood Highlanders. From that vantage point Garland Ferguson offered the following description of the scene and the action that he watched unfold:

> The position of the regiment on 30 June [30 July], 1864, was on the right of Ransom's brigade and to the left of Elliott's South Carolina brigade. The explosion of Grant's Mine was in the line occupied by the left regiment of the South Carolina brigade. Immediately after the explosion the Twenty-fifth regiment, then numbering about two hundred and fifty men moved from the trenches and formed a new line in the rear of the trenches occupied by the South Carolinians, which had been taken at the time of the explosion and which were then occupied by the enemy. The regiment, with a remnant of the Sixth South Carolina, was the only force between the enemy and the city, at that point. The enemy massed his troops in our trenches in front of us until he had sixteen regimental flags in our works. He made several attempts to move forward and force our line, but was successfully repulsed and held in check for several hours, until reinforcements arrived. The regiment led Mahone's men in the charge which retook the works. In retaking the works the fight was hand to hand, with guns, bayonets, and swords, in fact anything a man could fight with. One sixteen year old boy had his gun knocked out of his hands and picked up a cartridge box and fought with that.[312]

Another soldier of Ransom's Brigade who witnessed the charge to retake the works later recorded his admiration for the gallantry demonstrated on that day by the 25th Regiment N.C. Troops, including the Haywood Highlanders: "I saw the Twenty-fifth Regiment as they came dashing up the hill towards the Crater. How we cheered them! They rushed up the Crater which was full of the enemy, white and black, fired one volley and then turning the butts of their guns, they let them fall, crushing the skulls . . . at every blow."[313] The divisions commanded by Bushrod Johnson and William Mahone took back the trenches that were held so briefly by the Union troops. But the sacrifices that were made in blood and casualties on the Confederate side were extreme. Johnson reported the losses in Ransom's Brigade to be 14 men killed, 68 wounded, and 8 missing. The 25th Regiment had approximately two hundred fifty men engaged in the Battle of the Crater, per Garland Ferguson's historical account. He reported in a letter to the home folks after the battle that the regiment's casualties were 7 killed, 31 wounded, and 8 missing—approximately one-half of the casualties suffered by the entire brigade.[314] From the small band of 25 to 30 Haywood Highlanders who participated in the battle 2 men were killed, 2 were wounded, and at least 2 were captured.

Counted among the dead on that cruel day was Capt. James Madison Cathey, who had led Company F for more than two years since being elected in April 1862. He was "[c]ut down in the bloom of his young manhood, in the discharge of defending the Sunny South from invasion" as his obituary sadly stated.[315] The twenty-five-year-old commander would be sorely missed by the Haywood Highlanders, all of whom held an immense amount of respect for Cathey and most of whom were his close companions.

Engagement at Globe Tavern

About two weeks after the Battle of the Crater, 1st Lt. James Blalock was appointed to fill the captain's vacancy in Company F, and it would not be long before his mettle was tested. To the south of Petersburg, Union forces had managed to seize a portion of the Petersburg-Weldon Railroad near Globe Tavern and Ream's Station. The railroad provided an essential link to eastern North Carolina and the vital food and military supplies the state offered. It was of such strategic importance to General Lee's Army of Northern Virginia that he instantly commanded Beauregard to take a healthy contingent of rebel forces to regain control of the railroad. On Aug. 20 Captain Blalock received orders with the rest of Ransom's Brigade to move out of the trenches and

Upon the death of Capt. James Cathey at the Battle of the Crater on July 30, 1864, 1st Lt. James Allen Blalock was appointed to fill the captain's vacancy in the Haywood Highlanders. Captain Blalock posed for this photograph with his three new captain's bars. *North Carolina Department of Archives and History; used by permission.*

march to the southern end of the Confederate defensive line below Petersburg. There they would encounter the Weldon railroad leading southward; the Globe Tavern was within a couple of miles of the rebel defenses. The next day, Aug. 21, one of several battles to control the railroad was fought in the vicinity of Globe Tavern.

Near Globe Tavern on the east side of the railroad the Federals had dug in and formed a lodgment close by a farmhouse owned by the Davis family. The position was heavily fortified behind seemingly impenetrable undergrowth and timber obstructions. Orders were given to the several brigades maneuvering in front of the enemy, including Ransom's Brigade, that assaults were to be mounted through the jumbled tree laps to get at the enemy. When the bugle sounded as the sun peeked over the eastern horizon the Haywood Highlanders rose up and lurched forward into a wall of timber and enemy lead. "They had to charge some distance through an abatis of felled trees," was the way one of Ransom's men remembered the charge. "The men had to pick their way through the interlaced timbers and advance without regard to company or regimental formations."[316]

Garland Ferguson penned two accounts of the engagement. The first was a recap of the day's fierce fighting, which he recorded two days after the event in a letter to his older brother, Nathan—also a Haywood Highlander but unaccountably home at the time:

> We had a fight with Yankees on the Weldon Railroad. Our Brig. moved up near them on the 20th, and threw out pickets, on 21st, at sunup we were in motion and moved in line across Davis Corn field. Cooks Brig. formed on left and Kirklands on the right and A.P. Hill with his brigades still further to the right.
>
> The Enemy were behind a work in a very thick undergrowth. We charged them out with a yell loosing [sic] but very few, and captured a good number of prisoners. We then without falting [sic] crossed work, and charged through a very bad blockaded way[,] the undergrowth being cut down, and the enemys batterys playing heavily on us. We charged up near their batterys and would have carried them but for want of the Troops coming up on our right and left. We then fell back to the works we had captured.... Segt. Hawkins carried the colors acting very brave. Old Co. 'F' acted as gallant as any men ever did. We are in the ditches at our original positions. The Yankees still hold the railroad. Lieut. Hargrove is gone home on furlough of 30 days. Co. 'F' reports 9 men for duty, the Regt. 171 total for duty[;] quite small is it not."[317]

Quite small indeed was the Haywood Highlanders' ability to muster only "9 men for duty" after the clash on the Weldon railroad!

Ferguson's second record of the action at the Davis house near Globe Tavern was contained in his nine-page regimental history written more than thirty-five years after the sounds and smoke of the guns had settled. Recalling from memory, and possibly referencing his old letter, the historian painted the exciting scene and action nearly as he had before, although with fewer details:

> The enemy had entrenched himself behind heavy earthworks and had felled the timber in front, crossing the laps of the trees and sharpening the limbs. In order to reach their works the timber had to be removed so as to make

a passway for the men. During this time the enemy kept up a constant fire until our men reached the works. The color-bearer of the regiment [25th N.C. Troops] was shot down and Sergeant J. B. Hawkins, of Company C, caught the colors, rushed forward and placed them on the works. The works were taken and the enemy driven back under cover of his heavy artillery. The loss of the regiment was heavy in killed and wounded.[318]

Common threads in both of these battle descriptions were the charge made through difficult barricades thrown up by the enemy, Yankee cannons playing upon the vulnerable rebel attackers, and the valor displayed by Ensign John W. Hutchison of the regimental color guard (formerly attached to Company A) and Sgt. Joseph B. Hawkins of Company C as they carried the regiment's colors and led the men forward.[319] The Haywood Highlanders followed the flag bearers to the top of the enemy's works and drove the Yankees to the rear under cover of their heavy artillery. Ransom's Brigade was tactically successful in taking the Federal lodgment at the Davis house, but they did not achieve their overall mission of wresting control of the railroad from the Union forces. On Aug. 24 and 25 more battles were fought a few miles south of Globe Tavern at Reams Station. There a larger army of Confederate soldiers, not including Ransom's Brigade, managed to take back a portion of the railroad for a brief period of time. However, the stronger Union forces were soon able to gain complete control of the critical Weldon railroad, forcing the Confederates to offload supplies some twenty miles away and haul them by wagon around the Union's left flank to Petersburg. Rebel casualties were heavy at Globe Tavern. The regiment lost two killed, twenty-seven wounded, and seven missing.[320] Company F lost one soldier who died of wounds, Pvt. James Martin Henderson, and approximately four mountaineers were wounded, including Garland Ferguson.

Even though he was wounded in the right shoulder, the tender responsibility of writing a letter to Private Henderson's widow with the news of her husband's tragedy fell to 2nd Lieutenant Ferguson, as 1st Lt. William Hartgrove had gone home on a

Bombproof shelters such as the ones captured in this photograph were the living quarters of the soldiers manning the entrenchments at Petersburg. Note the wooden barrels which topped off the log and mud chimneys of the soldiers' "hearths." *Library of Congress, Prints and Photographs Division.*

thirty-day furlough. Ferguson wrote to the woman that he was near the unfortunate Henderson when the soldier was shot through the body and fell. A short time after the private was moved to the rear in an ambulance Ferguson stated, "[H]e told me farewell, said that he would die. [H]e told me to tell his loving wife that he was prepared to die & that he wanted her to meet him in Heaven." Ferguson also avowed that "James was a Good Christian Soldier, a good friend of mine, and much beloved by all the boys."[321]

Winter of 1864–65

The Haywood Highlanders fought no more major battles during the hard winter of 1864–65 at Petersburg. They remained holed up in the trenches protecting that section of the Confederate line which ran from the Appomattox River to the Jerusalem Plank Road. Living conditions were abominable, with little to eat; winter clothing and shoes were in short supply; and firewood for their crude hearths was always scarce and difficult to come by. Moreover, the men were not receiving pay for their hazardous army service because the Confederacy was bankrupt, its treasury coffers long depleted. Consequently, the soldiers could not send money home to their families, who were in many cases suffering even greater privations.

On the home front, flour and meal for making breads, and sugar and salt for spicing basic fare, were not just scarce but in many instances impossible to obtain. Horses and stock were impressed by Confederate officials for the use of the army, and many needy homesteads, with men absent at war, had little means to provide sustenance for their inhabitants. In addition, lone women and children living in remote cabins in the Western North Carolina mountains were being terrorized by roaming gangs of bushwhacking Tories, deserters, and other men running from army service. The terrorist bands threatened and robbed vulnerable families of what little money, food, and livestock they might have possessed. News of these atrocities and the dire circumstances at home reached the mountaineers in the Petersburg ditches through letters from wives and children and parents. Pitiful were their pleas for help. And these sorrowful appeals urging the men to come home just added weight to the burden of the soldiers—a burden that many could simply not bear.

The miserable conditions in the Petersburg saps and the pressures from home caused many of the Confederate soldiers to desert, and they fled the rebel lines for their homes in epidemic numbers during the winter of 1864–65. In February 1865 Gen. Robert E. Lee wrote of the desperate situation in a letter to the Confederate Secretary of War, John C. Breckenridge:

> Sir: I regret to be obliged to call your attention to the alarming number of desertions that are now occurring in the army.... The desertions are chiefly from the North Carolina regiments, and especially those from the western part of that State. It seems that the men are influenced very much by the representations of their friends at home, who appear to have become very despondent as to our success. They think the cause desperate and write to the soldiers, advising them to take care of themselves, assuring them that if they will return home the bands of deserters so far outnumber the home guards that they will be in no danger of arrest.[322]

One of the North Carolina regiments that Lee referred to was surely the 25th Regiment N.C. Troops to which Company F, the Haywood Highlanders, belonged. Over the entire course of the Civil War the regiment lost more than 275 soldiers through desertion, the Haywood Highlanders accounting for at least 30 of those instances (an attrition rate of 23 percent when compared with the total number of Haywood Highlanders, 131, who served throughout the war). As General Lee noted, the mountaineers fled in higher numbers from the army than did others fighting for the South. Overall, the desertion rate for soldiers from the state of North Carolina was approximately 12 percent and for the Confederacy as a whole 14 percent (for the North the rate was 10 percent). However, the research performed by one noted historian indicates that approximately 24 percent of all the men who enlisted from the mountains deserted.[323] Not surprisingly then, the desertion rate of the Haywood Highlanders, although seemingly high, is comparable with the desertion frequency for all the Carolina highlanders who signed up to fight in the Civil War.

The honorable men who remained with Captain Blalock through the difficult winter at Petersburg suffered more than the deprivations previously mentioned and the feelings of guilt for the dire circumstances of loved ones back home. They also struggled to survive the incessant barrages of enemy mortar fire and the increasingly effective work of the enemy snipers. Day after day they endured the incoming mortar rounds by seeking the protection of bombproof shelters or jumping into convenient gopher holes

The hideous red trenches of Petersburg were protected by sharp-pointed, wooden-pole abatis. *Library of Congress, Prints and Photographs Division.*

dug into the trench embankments. And on a daily basis men were receiving wounds from exploding shell fragments and Yankee sharpshooter bullets aimed at anything that moved. Throughout the last few months of 1864 and the first two months of 1865 the Union siege of Petersburg continued. During this bleak period the remaining few Haywood Highlanders dutifully manned the trenches, dodged lethal enemy projectiles, ate meager rations of corn meal and bacon, and reflected on their circumstances in the field and those at home.

＝＝

Battle of Fort Stedman

By March 1865 the situation for the South was grave indeed. With the exception of the dwindling troops of Lee's Army of Northern Virginia confined to the Petersburg and Richmond trenches, the Confederate armies that remained in the field were either defeated or powerless to offer significant offensive threats. Union Gen. William Tecumseh Sherman's Army of the Tennessee had burned Atlanta, had cut a destructive swath through Georgia and captured Savannah, and was making its way northward through the Carolinas to join up with Grant's forces. The intent of these two highly capable Union generals was to finally surround the Confederate army at Petersburg and destroy it or force its surrender. And the wily General Lee was fully aware of the threat that the junction of the two Federal armies would pose. He had determined to take his weakened army and unite with the remaining Southern forces gathering in North Carolina. But before affecting such a maneuver he had to escape Grant's tight clutches at Petersburg.

In an effort to loosen Grant's stranglehold and open up sufficient ground to disengage and make an escape to the West, Lee and Maj. Gen. John B. Gordon planned and organized an attack against a heavily fortified point in the Union's siege lines. Fort Stedman, as the Yankee stronghold was known, opposed a salient in the rebel defenses manned by Gen. Bushrod Johnson's division. It was located on Hare's Hill just across from the position held for the previous nine months by Ransom's Brigade and the Haywood Highlanders. The objective of the mission was to surprise the Federals occupying Stedman and capture those works. Once that goal was accomplished, the attack was to continue toward fortifications on both flanks and in the rear of Fort Stedman, where imposing Yankee artillery batteries were positioned. If adequately

Col. Henry M. Rutledge of the 25th Regiment North Carolina Troops described the fighting during the Battle of Fort Stedman as the "hottest fight" of his war experience. Harper's Weekly, *Apr. 15, 1965.*

supported by additional Confederate cavalry and Gen. George Pickett's infantry forces, the breakthrough of the Federal defenses around Hare's Hill might be exploited with follow-up strikes against the rear of the Union lines.

Even a partial success could possibly allow the Confederates to seize and hold the commanding ground in the enemy's rear. In that case, Lee and Gordon surmised, the Union besiegers would almost certainly be forced to recall the forces on their left and deploy them defensively against the Southern assailants lodged securely in their newly won fortifications. Thus afforded with opportunity to maneuver beyond his hard-pressed right flank south of Petersburg, Lee's desperate desire for a junction with the Confederate forces in North Carolina might still be affected. The westward roads and rail facilities would be opened for a brief interlude to facilitate the safe movement of either a portion of his army or a general withdrawal of the entirety of the Army of Northern Virginia from the Richmond–Petersburg theater of war. That was the Confederate plan.[324]

Early on the morning of Mar. 16, 1865, Captain Blalock's troops, with Ransom's Brigade, moved out of the trenches and marched to the southern extremity of the Confederate defensive line. At Hatcher's Run, southwest of Petersburg, the mountain boys spent a few days in some huts built by the army and were able to briefly escape the doldrums of the saps. Their respite was short-lived, however. On Mar. 24 the brigade was rushed suddenly back to its old position in the entrenchments, arriving there during the evening hours. Upon their arrival the Haywood Highlanders soon learned of General Lee and General Gordon's plan to attack Fort Stedman and discovered that their own role in the scheme was to be vital.

During the night of Mar. 24–25 Gordon's rebel forces captured Fort Stedman without firing a shot. However, the rest of the grand plan was not successful, and after a few hours of holding Stedman the Confederate soldiers were forced to give up their tenancy when General Gordon ordered a retreat back to the safety of the rebel defensive lines. The Haywood Highlanders, along with the other men from the 25th Regiment N.C. Troops, were compelled to make their way back to the trenches across an open field under heavy artillery fire. As a result the unit suffered many casualties, and all of their planning and sacrifice was for naught.

Years later Col. Henry Rutledge of the 25th N.C. described "the storming of Fort Stedman" as "the hottest fight in his entire war's experience."[325] Garland Ferguson of Company F had even more to say about the fierce fighting that night:

> On 25 March, 1865, a detail of ten men from each regiment of Ransom's brigade, under Lieutenant Burch, was placed in charge of Lieutenant J. B. Hawkins, of Company C, Twenty-fifth regiment, who received his orders from General Robert Ransom [Matt Ransom, in fact] in these words: "I

order you to take Fort Stedman, not attack it." Lieutenant Hawkins quietly executed this order and had the fort in possession without the firing of a gun.

The Twenty-fifth was moved forward to the left of Fort Stedman and nearly in front of the position it had occupied in the ditches through the winter; drove in the enemy's pickets, took their first works and held them. The fort of the enemy in the field on the left was not taken, and the enemy from that point poured a fearful enfilading fire into the regiment. Several unsuccessful efforts were made from the front to dislodge the regiment. After the enemy retook Fort Stedman and was advancing in front and while the regiment was suffering the effects of an enfilading fire from the left, the Colonel walked along the line of his regiment with his cap on sword, shouting to his men, 'Don't let them take our front, Twenty-fifth, the Twenty-fifth has never had her front taken.' At this time orders were received from General Gordon to fall back to our line of works.[326]

Such were the memories of the young colonel and the gallant Ferguson of the failed attack. Lieutenant Hawkins of Company C was ordered to "take Ft. Stedman, not attack it," and he was manifestly successful in accomplishing that critical part of the plan. Although the means that he used to capture the fort are not completely clear, it has been suggested that the lieutenant and his cohorts feigned to be Confederate deserters in order to gain access unmolested to the fort's interior. Once inside they were able to easily surprise and subdue the small enemy garrison. It should be noted that this is the same extraordinary Haywood County soldier who as a sergeant on Aug. 21, 1864, had gallantly taken up the regiment's fallen colors and led the 25th North Carolina Troops to the top of the Yankee works at the Davis house near Globe Tavern.

Overall the Confederate army suffered 5,000 casualties—almost one-fifth of the troops available to General Lee—in the failed attack against the Union stronghold, Fort Stedman. Ransom's Brigade lost approximately 1,364 soldiers, and four Haywood Highlanders were wounded. Among the injured was Garland Ferguson, who suffered a fractured left leg caused by a gunshot wound. In addition four Highlanders, two of whom were wounded, were taken as prisoners of war.

Battle of Five Forks

However desirous General Lee was to take his army to North Carolina, the ruinous Battle of Fort Stedman did not win sufficient maneuvering space or time to safely and orderly retract his troops from Petersburg and Richmond. Instead Grant forced the Southern general's hand on Mar. 26, 1865, by continuing his clockwise sidling movement around the Confederate right flank. He ordered a corps of infantry and a powerful cavalry force led by Gen. Philip Sheridan to turn Lee's right flank, and by Apr. 1 the Union forces had cornered a portion of the Confederate army led by Gen. George Pickett at a crossroads southwest of Petersburg called Five Forks. Outnumbered three to one, Pickett's 10,000 troops hurriedly threw up defensive measures and awaited an onslaught by the bluecoats. Forming the extreme left flank of the Confederate line, Ransom and Wallace's brigades established a refused flank line to resist an anticipated enemy turning movement.[327] Thus, Ransom's Brigade, with its 25th Regiment North Carolina and the remnants of Company F, was precariously positioned in the air and vulnerable to envelopment by a strong enfilading attack.

The Federals sensed the weakness presented on their right and launched an assault of such magnitude and force that it was irresistible. Ransom and Wallace's brigades were quickly rolled up and scattered in retreat. General Pickett, who had been miles to the rear of the front line at a shad bake, arrived in sight of the battle action in time to see the retreating left. Years later, with perhaps a more romantic memory of the day's battle, Col. Henry Rutledge wrote:

> At Five Forks I was more proud of the regiment than I had ever been before, and that is saying a great deal. I have thought of them and compared them to the "Stonewall" of Manassas. They were surrounded on three sides

Photographs taken just after the Civil War show the interior of Union Fort Stedman's formidable defenses. *Library of Congress, Prints and Photographs Division.*

by many times their own numbers, but there they stood, a solid mass of mountain men, broad sides from the enemy being poured into them, and there they stood like the rock of Gibraltar.... Yes, there stood the gray line, the only line that stood that day, that I saw, and finally, after combating five different and separate times over the same field, pine thickets, broom grass, old fields, all sorts of a place, I was going to win. I was attempting to whip the enemy with the Twenty-fifth North Carolina, and I knew I could do it. I thought I was getting along finely, until I happened to look to front, left and right, and saw we were surrounded with but a small loop hole to get through. We backed through that, emptying into their faces the last cartridge we had.[328]

The 25th Regiment's mountain men, including the Haywood Highlanders, backed their way out through the small loophole that Colonel Rutledge found and scattered to the rear with the other Confederate forces. The rebels who had escaped the field in panic either were rounded up by the Federal cavalry or continued to flee from their pursuers. More than 5,000 Confederate troops were captured at the Battle of Five Forks on that day and the next.[329] A check of the Haywood Highlanders' service records indicates that at least four mountaineers were taken prisoner at Five Forks. They included Pvt. Francis Mahaffey and 1st Sgt. Luther Murray as well as 1st Lt. William Hartgrove and his uncle, Pvt. Rufus Hartgrove.

It was the end of the journey for Haywood County's Haywood Highlanders. Those mountaineers not apprehended at Five Forks were picked up in the days immediately following that battle by Union cavalry and infantry forces sweeping in to capture Petersburg and the Southern capital, Richmond. However, Gen. Robert E. Lee's Army of Northern Virginia had managed to evacuate those cities just in time and fled westward along the banks of the Appomattox River. After running for a week from Grant's hounds, the Army of Northern Virginia was brought to bay at Appomattox Courthouse. General Lee surrendered his army to Grant on Apr. 9, 1865; three days later the surviving soldiers of the Army of Northern Virginia stacked their muskets, were paroled, and started on the long roads to home. From the ten companies that made up the 25th Regiment North Carolina, Company F was the only company not represented at the Appomattox surrendering ground. The luck and endurance of the Haywood Highlanders had simply run out.

Casualties and Other Losses, Richmond/Petersburg Defense

Name	Date	Remarks
Killed (3)		
Capt. James Madison Cathey	7/30/1864	Killed at Battle of Crater at Petersburg, Va.
3rd Lt. Ebed J. Ferguson	5/16/1864	Killed at Drewry's Bluff, Va.
Cpl. William Bonham	2/17/1865	Killed in trenches by a shell at Petersburg, Va.
Died of wounds (4)		
Pvt. Benjamin F. Edmonston	7/30/1864	Wounded in head at Battle of Crater and subsequently died.
Pvt. James M. Henderson	8/21/1864	Wounded in lung at Globe Tavern, Va., and died in hospital at Petersburg, Va., two days later.
Pvt. Thomas Holland	7/26/1864	Hospitalized at Petersburg, Va., with a shell wound of the right thigh and died same day.
Musician John R. Jones	8/13/1864	Died of wounds.

Wounded (17)		
2nd Lt. Garland Sevier Ferguson	5/14/1864	Wounded at Drewry's Bluff, Va.
	8/21/1864	Wounded in the right shoulder at Globe Tavern.
	3/25/1865	Wounded in left leg at Battle of Fort Stedman.
Pvt. William M. Baggett	12/1/1864	Wounded prior to Jan. 1, 1865.
Pvt. Rodom C. Best	10/12/1864	Wounded in the back and left hand at Petersburg, Va.
Pvt. Henry Tilman Bugg	7/30/1864	Wounded in leg at Battle of Crater.
Pvt. Jeremiah H. Bugg	3/25/1865	Wounded in right arm at Battle of Fort Stedman.
Pvt. William F. Francis	3/25/1865	Wounded in neck and/or right breast at Battle of Fort Stedman.
Pvt. Alson Gordon	8/21/1864	Wounded in leg near Petersburg, Va., and leg amputated above the knee.
Sgt. Wesley Henson	5/20/1864	Wounded at Drewry's Bluff, Va.
Pvt. William Henson	5/11/1864	Hospitalized at Richmond, Va., with gunshot wound to right thigh.
	3/25/1865	Wounded in left shoulder at Battle of Fort Stedman.
Pvt. William P. Inman	8/21/1864	Hospitalized at Richmond, Va., with gunshot wound of the neck.
Pvt. Joseph F. Long	8/21/1864	Hospitalized at Petersburg, Va., with gunshot wound of left hand.
Corp. Joseph B. Mann, Sr.	7/30/1864	Broke right arm at Battle of Crater.
Pvt. Morgan Meece	7/1/1864	Wounded in unspecified engagement between Mar.—Dec. 1864.
Died of disease (1)		
Pvt. Nathan Ferguson	8/1864	Died at home of disease.

Captured (16)		
1st Lt. William Harrison Hartgrove	4/1/1865	Captured at Battle of Five Forks. Paroled on 6/18/1865.
2nd Lt. Garland Sevier Ferguson	4/3/1865	Presumably captured in a hospital at Petersburg, Va. Paroled on 8/2/1865.
Pvt. Jeremiah H. Bugg	3/25/1865	Captured at Battle of Fort Stedman. Paroled on 8/14/1865.
Pvt. John C. Evans	7/30/1865	Captured in trenches at Petersburg, Va. (presumably at Battle of Crater). Paroled on unspecified date.
Pvt. William F. Francis	3/25/1865	Captured at Battle of Fort Stedman. Paroled on 7/7/1865.
Pvt. Leonard Godwin	7/30/1865	Presumably captured at Battle of Crater. Paroled and later exchanged on 11/15/1864.
Pvt. Rufus P. Hartgrove	4/1/1865	Captured at Battle of Five Forks. Paroled on 6/14/1865.
Sgt. Wesley Henson	3/25/1865	Captured at Battle of Fort Stedman. Paroled on 6/14/1865.
Pvt. William Henson	4/3/1865	Presumably captured in a hospital at Petersburg, Va.
Pvt. Ambrose House	?	Paroled at Farmville, Va., around 4/11/1865.
Pvt. Isaac W. Jones	3/25/1865	Captured at Battle of Fort Stedman. Paroled on 6/28/1865.
Pvt. Francis M. Mahaffey	4/2/1865	Captured near Petersburg, Va. (presumably in aftermath of Battle of Five Forks). Paroled on 6/29/1865.
Pvt. John C. Moore	4/3/1865	Captured in hospital in Richmond, Va. Paroled on 4/18/1865.
1st Sgt. Luther W. Murray	4/2/1865	Captured near Petersburg, Va. Paroled on 6/15/1865.
Pvt. J. R. Tindle	?	Paroled at Farmville, Va., around 4/11/1865.

Deserted (12)		
Pvt. George H. Blalock	3/1865	Reported absent without leave after Jan.–Feb. 1865.
1st Sgt. William J. Evans	2/4/1865	Deserted while absent on furlough.
Pvt. David N. Franklin	11/1864	Deserted before 12/31/1864, when he was paroled in eastern Tenn.
Pvt. David W. Gaddis	1/26/1865	Deserted while absent on furlough.
Pvt. Thaddeus M. Green	1/26/1865	Listed as a deserter.
Pvt. George Hall, Jr.	2/4/1865	Listed as a deserter.
Pvt. Ezekiel T. Harrell	11/3/1864	Listed as a deserter.
Pvt. Lewis Hezekiah Inman	8/1/1864	Went over to the enemy. Paroled in eastern Tenn. in December 1864.
Pvt. William P. Inman	11/2/1864	Deserted after release from hospital at Raleigh, N.C., and went over to the enemy. Paroled in eastern Tenn. in December 1864.
Pvt. Arthur Laughter	2/28/1865	Deserted to the enemy. Paroled at Washington, D.C., around 3/6/1865.
Pvt. Matthew McA. Rogers	12/1864	Transferred out of regiment but deserted before reporting to new unit. Paroled at Knoxville, Tenn., around 3/10/1865.
Pvt. John C. Wilson	2/28/1865	Deserted to the enemy. Paroled at Washington, D.C., around 3/6/1865.
Other (2)		
Pvt. Dillard T. Luther	9/30/1864	Discharged "by civil authority."
Pvt. James P. Scott	1/1/1865	Promoted and transferred to regimental field & staff.

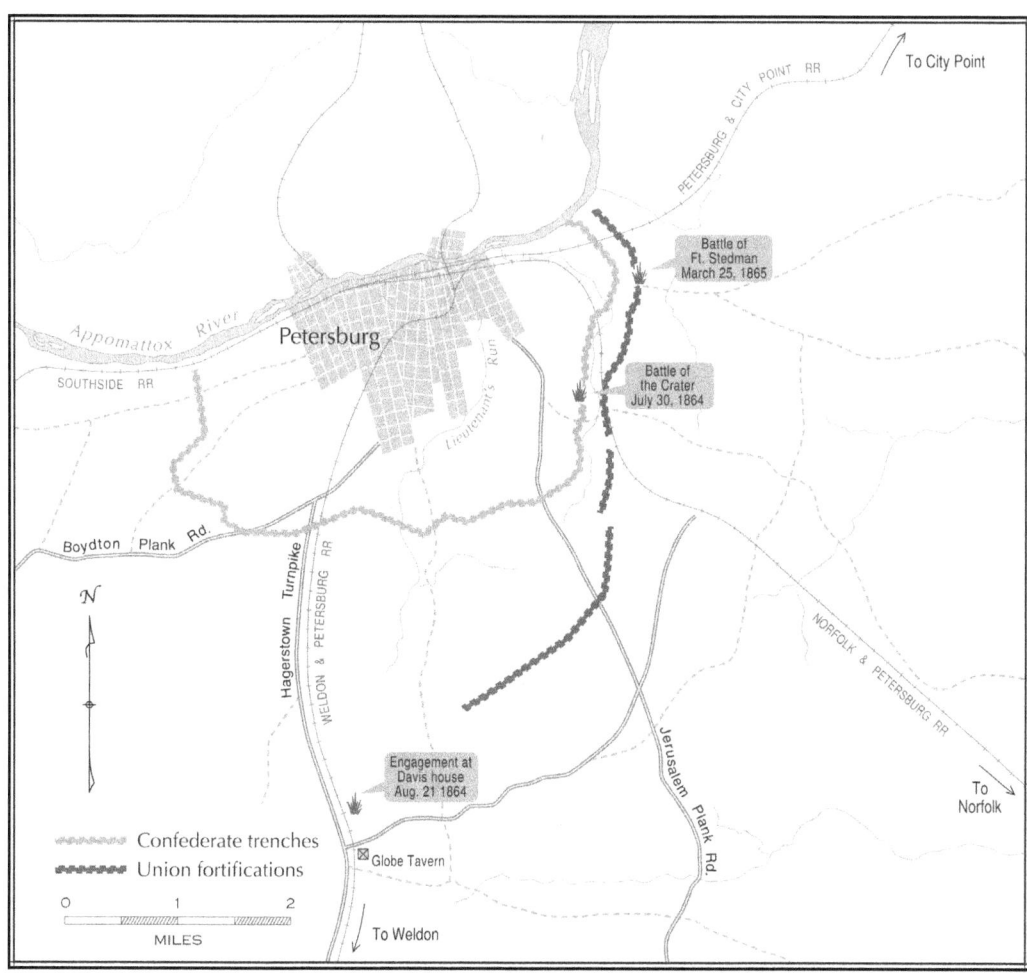

Siege and battles of Petersburg. *Map by Peter Krafft, Florida State University.*

"As Brave a Man As Ever Met the Enemy" by Walton Taber. *From* The American Heritage Century Collection of Civil War Art *(1974).*

⇒ THERE WERE NO HAYWOOD HIGHLANDERS *who surrendered with Gen. Robert E. Lee's Army of Northern Virginia at Appomattox Court House in April 1865.*

Lifting the Shroud of Time

TODAY IT IS EXTREMELY DIFFICULT to determine the specific deeds that individual Haywood Highlanders performed or the degree of valor they might have displayed on the Civil War battlefields. Certainly no audio or video recordings of their actions exist, and there are very few written testimonies by the Company F soldiers themselves to enlighten modern-day historians writing of their exploits. Primary source materials, although extremely scarce, have survived in the forms of diaries and wartime letters and are indeed helpful in looking back on the time and developing some sense of what it might have been like to fight in such a horrific war. Additionally, there are the soldier's service records that the North Carolina State Department of Archives and History as well as the National Archives have compiled over the years using company muster rolls, payrolls, rosters, hospital registers, prison registers, parole registers, state records, pension records, and a variety of other contemporaneous records. The lists of casualties and losses suffered by the Haywood Highlanders presented in this work were gleaned from these excellent sources. And upon close perusal of the compiled service history for each of the Highlanders it is possible to comprehend to some degree their military contributions and soldierly capacity.

My study of the Haywood Highlanders' service records has led to the discovery of interesting information and tantalizing coincidences, as well as certain conclusions regarding the soldiers from Company F. For example, there are several instances in which three brothers served together in the company, and many other cases of siblings and close relatives who fought alongside each other. At least one soldier deserted three times from the company, and another was executed for taking the life of a fellow

Highlander. A compilation of some of these intriguing findings is given below, along with service sketches of a few selected soldiers whose conduct was conspicuous beyond all others.

Brothers in Arms

There are many cases of brothers and close relatives who served together with the Haywood Highlanders. An attempt has been made to identify all of these sibling occurrences and a few other examples of father–son and uncle–nephew relationships within the company ranks. This accounting is as comprehensive as possible under the circumstances; it is a highly difficult proposition to verify after so many years blood relationships among the soldiers in a Civil War Company. While census records provide valuable clues, spelling of both surnames and given names is inconsistent. Census enumerators sometimes misspelled names (especially when attempting to spell phonetically), or simply misrecorded facts, and their script handwriting sometimes proves illegible today. Complicating the matter still further, spelling variants are common in company muster rolls. Nevertheless, by consulting the census data for the years 1850 and 1860 as well as family genealogy information and by other documentary evidence, many cases of familial connections among the Haywood Highlanders have been revealed.

Jasper N. Anderson, aged 22, and his brother, **Josiah McDonald Anderson**, 18, enlisted together in the Haywood Highlanders on June 29, 1861. Both of these sons of Jesse and Elizabeth Anderson were wounded on the same day, July 1, 1862, in the Battle of Malvern Hill near Richmond, Virginia—the first major battle in which Company F was engaged.[330] Pvt. Josiah Anderson was wounded in the left leg and disabled for the rest of his life as he was carrying his brother from the field.[331] For reasons unknown he was not discharged from service, and the records report his absence as "wounded" through February of 1865. Pvt. Jasper Anderson was able to rebound from his wounding and rejoined the company two months later. However, in the spring of 1863 Jasper was afflicted with typhoid fever and had to be hospitalized at Goldsboro, North Carolina. On May 12, 1863, he succumbed to the ravages of that deadly disease.

Jeremiah H. Bugg, 20, and **Henry Tilman Bugg,** 18, enlisted together on June 29, 1861. The brothers were the sons of Henry and Naoma Bugg of Forks of Pigeon.[332] The pages of Captain Lenoir's diary contain numerous references to Pvt. Henry Bugg's illness and reveal the captain's concern for the young soldier (for a fuller account of Bugg's plight, see pp. 84, 106, 146). On Nov. 5, 1861, when the company was first ordered to Charleston, South Carolina, Bugg was then unwell and had to be left in Wilmington, North Carolina. The diary pages indicate that the private was still sick in Wilmington on Nov. 21 and Captain Lenoir was holding his pay. More than a month later, on Dec. 29, Lenoir sent a transportation ticket to a Confederate railroad agent so that Bugg could rejoin the company at Grahamville, South Carolina. However, the young private had disappeared from the Wilmington hospital and Captain Lenoir was at a loss as to his whereabouts. He gave the following account of the singular disappearance in a letter that he wrote to his wife at the time:

> "He [Bugg] was considered well enough to be sent on to us & would have been in a few days. But his mind still seemed to be a little deranged, & he seemed to think he had a discharge & was at liberty to go home & about two weeks ago, with his gun & accoutrements left the hospital in Wilmington, & we have not been able to hear from him since. . . . He had no money but possibly may beg his way along on the R.Road."[333]

Private Bugg had, in fact, begged his way back home to Haywood County, and it would not be until Feb. 13, 1862, that he returned to duty at Camp Lee.

This inauspicious beginning to Henry Bugg's military career belied the commendable service he would eventually render to the Confederacy. The youth served with his company through all of the heavy fighting and light action leading up to the occupation of the trenches protecting Richmond and Petersburg, Virginia, in May 1864. At the Battle of the Crater on July 30, 1864, Private Bugg was wounded in the right leg. However, he was able to return to duty prior to the end of the year and subsequently was present and accounted for until February 1865, when the accounts of his military service are forever silent.

Brother Jeremiah Bugg, also a private, had no less a solid and lengthy career as a rebel soldier. He too served through the war until receiving a gunshot wound in the right elbow during the furious fighting at the Battle of Fort Stedman on Mar. 25, 1865. Jeremiah was taken prisoner during that battle and spent a brief period aboard a Union hospital steamer ship, the *State of Maine*, before being imprisoned at Old Capitol Prison in Washington, D.C., and later at Elmira, New York.

Another pair of brothers were **Joseph Turner Cathey** and **James Madison Cathey**, sons of Col. Joseph and Nancy Hyatt Cathey of Forks of Pigeon.[334] Colonel Cathey and his two sons helped raise the Haywood Highlanders in May and June of 1861, and both young men enlisted at the same time on June 29, 1861. Joseph Turner entered the army as first sergeant at the age of 26, and James Madison was appointed third lieutenant upon his enlistment at the age of 23. During the Confederate army's reorganization in April 1862 Sgt. Joseph Cathey was elected third lieutenant and Lt. James Cathey was elected captain by the soldiers of Company F. Joseph Cathey served honorably through the first two years of the conflict but died on Sept. 8, 1863, of typhoid fever in a hospital in Wilson, North Carolina. Captain James Cathey gallantly led his mountaineers through the perils of war until the Highlanders entered the Petersburg, Virginia, trenches in mid-1864. Captain Cathey was killed on July 30, 1864, at the Battle of the Crater as he charged with his boys into the confused masses of black and white Union soldiers occupying the Confederate trenches.

Brothers **Henry Christopher** and **George Eleanor Christopher** signed up together with the Haywood Highlanders on June 29, 1861 at the relatively ripe ages of 43 and

33 respectively. Both were from Forks of Pigeon and were memorialized in Captain Lenoir's diary when he wrote in November 1861 that Eleanor had to be placed under guard for fighting with his brother (see p. 83). Both men's Civil War experience was brief and tragic. Pvt. Eleanor Christopher died of typhoid fever on Feb. 23, 1862, while stationed at Grahamville, South Carolina. Within just three months his brother, Pvt. Henry Christopher, perished on May 30, 1862, from disease in a hospital at Wilson, North Carolina.

Hiram Clark and his son **Joshua Clark** were a father-son duo who served with the Haywood Highlanders. While on a recruiting trip back home in the mountains Lt. Etheldred Blalock persuaded the sixteen-year-old Joshua to join the Haywood Highlanders on Mar. 22, 1862. However, it was a different story for Joshua's father, Hiram Clark. Exempt from service in the army by reason of being over age in 1862 when Joshua volunteered, Hiram Clark at age 38 became obligated to serve in 1863 when the press (conscription) law's age limits were expanded. Before being drafted, however, he joined up with Joshua's Company F on May 1, 1863, and both father and son served at least through February 1865, when they were last accounted for in the muster rolls. Joshua was apparently a fine young soldier and was promoted to corporal in 1864. Neither of their names appears in the casualty records, so it is believed that both father and son survived the war.

Brothers **William N. Deaver,** 21, and **Rufus L. Deaver**, 19, sons of Eli and Mary Deaver of Forks of Pigeon, joined Haywood County's Company C of the 25th Regiment N.C. Troops on May 31, 1861.[335] At Kinston, North Carolina, during the reorganization of the Confederate army, both brothers chose to transfer into Company F on May 1, 1862. However, their military careers ended ingloriously in early 1864 when both deserted and eventually made their way to eastern Tennessee. At Knoxville they went over to the enemy, and both brothers signed an oath of allegiance to the United States on the same date, May 22, 1864.

Clockwise from upper left: 3rd Lt. Joseph Turner Cathey; 1st Lt. William Harrison Hartgrove; 2nd Lt. Garland Sevier Ferguson. *North Carolina Department of Archives and History; used by permission.*

Nathan J. Ferguson, 29, and **Garland Sevier Ferguson,** 18, were the sons of William and Ruth Gibson Ferguson of the Crabtree Township in Haywood County.[336] These brothers, living far removed from Forks of Pigeon, enlisted nevertheless with the Haywood Highlanders on June 29, 1861, along with the very first fervent mountaineers joining the company. Pvt. Nathan Ferguson served without injury or wound until February 1864. At that point his military career is somewhat of a mystery as there are no other Confederate records that indicate his status or presence. However, a family letter reveals that Nathan died at his home in August 1864, presumably from disease.[337]

For younger brother Garland, on the other hand, bountiful records bear testimony to the stellar military career that he forged. He fought in the several severe battles in which Company F was engaged during 1862, with the exception of Antietam, when he was laid up in a Petersburg, Virginia, hospital with "febris remittens."[338] He helped protect eastern North Carolina from Yankee intrusions in 1863. And at Beauregard's desperate defense of Richmond, Virginia, against Gen. Benjamin's Butler's attacking army, Ferguson was apparently wounded in the shoulder on May 14, 1864, and hospitalized. After returning to duty the following month he was promoted to second lieutenant just before being wounded again. This time he was hit in the right shoulder at the hard fighting that occurred near the Globe Tavern on the Weldon Railroad below Petersburg on Aug. 21, 1864. Before the end of the year Lieutenant Ferguson returned again to the Petersburg trenches for duty. On Mar. 25, 1865, he participated in the last desperate Confederate action to push the Yankees out of their fortifications around Fort Stedman near Petersburg. In that fiercely contested battle, Ferguson was wounded for yet a third time when a minié ball shattered his left thigh bone. Ferguson, who later gave credit to 1st Lt. William Hartgrove for saving his life, was helped back to the rebel lines and transported to a Petersburg hospital where, on Apr. 3, 1865, he was captured by Union troops entering the city.[339] Not until four months later, after the war had ended, was Garland Ferguson healed and fit to leave the hospital. He was released on Aug. 2, 1865, presumably after taking an oath of allegiance to the United States, and started on the long road back to Haywood's Crabtree community.

William Harrison Hartgrove and his uncle, **Rufus P. Hartgrove**, were ages 20 and 33 respectively when they joined the company's ranks. William's father, Augustus Columbus Hartgrove, and Rufus were the sons of William Manson Hartgrove, who had first entered Haywood County and settled at Forks of Pigeon around 1823. William Harrison was an original enlistee who mustered into Captain Lenoir's company on July 18, 1861, the very day the Highlanders marched out of Haywood for Asheville,

North Carolina. Rufus was apparently not possessed of such fervent conviction as his younger nephew. He did not enlist in the army until Sept. 1, 1863, when obligated to do so by the Confederate Conscription Law. An obvious reason for Rufus's late entry into the war was the fact that he was married when the war broke out and had three young children to protect and support. Both of these Hartgrove warriors served in the Confederate trenches until the end. At the Battle of Five Forks on Apr. 1, 1865, near Petersburg, Virginia, 1st Lt. William Hartgrove and Pvt. Rufus Hartgrove were both captured by Union forces and sent off to Northern prisoner-of-war camps.

William Henson and **Wesley Henson,** joined the Haywood Highlanders as original enlistees. William was 26 years old and Wesley 21 when they both pledged an oath to the Confederacy on June 29, 1861. These two Henson Highlanders were the sons of Aaron and Elizabeth Henson, and the documentary evidence seems to show that they were stalwart soldiers, serving until the last month of the war.[340] Early on in the war Pvt. William Henson was captured at Frederick, Maryland, on Sept. 12, 1862, but was later exchanged, whereupon he loyally returned to his company and brethren in arms. His brother, Wesley Henson, was promoted to the rank of sergeant in 1864, a good indication of the respect that his peers held for him and his soldierly abilities. Interestingly, both brothers were wounded in the fighting around Drewry's Bluff near Richmond, Virginia, in May 1864. However, they returned to duty before the year was out. On Mar. 25, 1865, the brothers participated in the Battle of Fort Stedman near Petersburg, Virginia, reputedly the hottest action that Company F and the 25th Regiment N.C. Troops experienced during the war. Pvt. William Henson was wounded in the left shoulder during that action and hospitalized at Petersburg. Sgt. Wesley Henson was captured during the same fight by the Union forces and imprisoned at Point Lookout, Maryland.

Burton H. Henson, 26, and **Wiley Henson,** 19, sons of Daniel and Mary Henson, enlisted together on June 29, 1861, in Captain Lenoir's company.[341] Burton later deserted on the march and went over to the enemy, signing an oath of allegiance to the United States on May 22, 1864. Brother Wiley Henson's career ended in a similar manner, although his service seems to have been more eventful. Captured at Frederick, Maryland, during Lee's first Maryland invasion in September 1862, Private Henson was confined at Fort Delaware, Delaware, until being exchanged in November 1862. He subsequently returned to duty and was promoted to sergeant—a sure sign of his capacity for soldiering—before the year 1863 was out. Then, for some inexplicable reason not recorded in the Confederate records, Wiley deserted from his company in February 1864 while stationed near Weldon in eastern North Carolina.

Thomas F. Henson, Fidellio Henson, and **Elijah L. Henson,** sons of Nathaniel and Catherine Henson, represent another of several instances in the history of the Haywood Highlanders in which three brothers served together.[342] Fidellio, 22, and Elijah, 20, joined the company on June 29, 1861 as original enlistees. The oldest brother, Thomas, transferred from Company C to Company F at Kinston, North Carolina, on May 1, 1862, the same day that he received a promotion to corporal. He was 31 years of age at the time. Pvt. Fidellio Henson did not survive the war. While constructing protective fortifications in the vicinity of Richmond and Petersburg, Virginia, he was hospitalized and died on Aug. 4, 1862 of "cerebritis." Thomas and Elijah both deserted from the company ranks in early 1864 while stationed in eastern North Carolina. They went over to the enemy and swore an oath of allegiance to the United States on the same day at Knoxville, Tennessee.

Joshua E. Inman, 23, **William Pinkney Inman,** 22, and **Lewis Hezekiah Inman,** 19, sons of Joshua and Mary Polly Smith Inman of Forks of Pigeon, enlisted with the Haywood Highlanders on June 29, 1861.[343] Pvt. Joshua Inman was present or accounted for until February 1864, and from that period on there are no further records of his service with the company. Pvt. Lewis Inman's service records indicate that he deserted from Company F on three separate occasions, the last from the trenches of

Petersburg, Virginia, in August 1864. He evidently made his way back to east Tennessee where he took an oath of allegiance to the United States in December of 1864.

The third brother, Pvt. William Pinkney Inman, also deserted from Confederate service, an experience upon which Charles Frazier's novel *Cold Mountain* is loosely based.[344] In actuality Pinkney was wounded twice during the war. He was slightly injured on July 1, 1862, at the Battle of Malvern Hill near Richmond, Virginia, but was able to return to duty two weeks later. During the battles for the Weldon Railroad Pvt. Inman received a flesh wound in the neck on Aug. 21, 1864, in the engagement at Globe Tavern near Petersburg, Virginia. He was admitted into General Hospital at Petersburg the same day and on Sept. 30, 1864, was transferred to a hospital in Danville, Virginia. Then on Oct. 3, 1864, Pinkney was moved from the Danville hospital to Pettigrew General Hospital No. 13 in Raleigh, North Carolina, with a complaint of chronic diarrhea. In a week's time his health had improved sufficiently for the Raleigh doctors to release him for duty. However, instead of returning to the Petersburg trenches where the Haywood Highlanders were holed up, Pinkney determined to hightail it back to the mountains.

Eluding the Confederate troops and home guard units who were prowling the state in search of deserters, Inman made his way back to the mountains and eventually into east Tennessee. He gave himself up to the enemy at Knoxville, and in late December 1864 took an oath of allegiance to the United States, whereupon he was released from confinement. However, Inman did not make good on his escape from Confederate army service. As he and a friend made their way through the Pigeon Gap between Waynesville and the Forks of Pigeon community, just a few miles from their homes, they were shot and killed by a posse of home guardsmen.[345]

Brothers **Morgan Meece**, **John Medford Meece**, and **James Bradford Meece** served together in the Haywood Highlanders, and were the sons of Peter and Nancy Meece.[346] Morgan, 24, and James Bradford (Bradford), 19, were original company enlistees signing up on June 29, 1861. John Medford (Medford), 21, rode the trains with Captain Lenoir's patient, Pvt. Henry Bugg, from Haywood County to Grahamville,

South Carolina, and was sworn into the Confederate army on Feb, 14, 1862. Bradford eventually deserted to the enemy and on May 22, 1864, took an oath of allegiance to the United States at Knoxville, Tennessee. Morgan and Medford were both wounded during the war. Medford was shot in the hand on June 25, 1862, at the engagement at King's School House near Richmond, Virginia. As a result his index and middle fingers were amputated and he was discharged from the army on Aug. 2, 1862, by reason of disability from his wounds. Morgan was hit at an unspecified place and time in 1864 and was reported absent wounded through February 1865.

Siblings **Daniel N. Pressley**, 23, **Nelson A. Pressley**, 21, and **Joshua A. Pressley**, 18, joined the Haywood Highlanders on June 29, 1861. It is a certainty that their parents, Thomas and Jemima Pressley, were filled with pride as the three sons marched off to Asheville on July 18, 1861.[347] But they would also have borne unspoken apprehensions, not knowing what grave dangers their sons were treading toward and realizing that their offspring might not survive the perils of war. And if they did indeed harbor such fearful sentiments, then, as it turned out, they were justified. In the latter days of August 1862 privates Nelson and Joshua Pressley both died of sickness—likely typhoid fever—just two days apart. The records indicate that the brothers were patients at different hospitals in Petersburg and nearby Drewry's Bluff, Virginia. The eldest brother, Daniel, survived the plagues of deadly disease and storms of enemy bullets and returned to his waiting parents at Forks of Pigeon. However, he made his escape from the war front by deserting to the enemy in early 1864 and taking an oath of allegiance to the United States at Knoxville.

Of the five soldiers with the surname "Reece" who served with the Haywood Highlanders it is believed that at least two were brothers. According to census records **Jonathan K. Reece**, 23, and **Isaac N. Reece**, 21, who joined the army as original company enlistees, appear to have been sons of Samuel and Lucinda Reece.[348] Pvt. Isaac Reece was killed on July 1, 1862, at the Battle of Malvern Hill near Richmond, Virginia. His older brother, Jonathan, served through the war with no extended spells of sickness, no periods of absence without leave, or any indications that would hint of desertion, a remarkably steady and sound record of exemplary service. During the darkest hours of the Confederacy Pvt. Jonathan Reece was still guarding the approaches to Petersburg, Virginia, when he was present and accounted for through February 1865. After that period in time the records fail to demonstrate further the admirable military career compiled by this fine soldier from Forks of Pigeon.

All three brothers, **John C. Singleton**, 26, **James Anderson Singleton**, 21, and **William A.S.C. (Columbus) Singleton**, 17, nicknamed the "three musketeers" by at least one historian, joined up with the Haywood Highlanders at Camp Patton in Asheville, North Carolina. The published tales of the Singletons' wartime experiences were, perhaps, embroidered to the extreme. The youthful Columbus was discharged from the army in July 1862 for reason of being under age. Before leaving the front, however, he at least had his taste for battle whetted during the Seven Days' Battles which occurred in the vicinity of Richmond, Virginia: at King's School House on June 25, 1862, and at the Battle of Malvern Hill on July 1, 1862. When asked after the war to describe that week's inferno, one of the brothers quipped: "The Minié balls were flying so thick about us that if it were possible I could have put out my hand and caught it full."[349] After the Seven Days' Battles the older Singleton brothers were not discharged, nor did they desert. Anderson was wounded at the Battle of Antietam at Sharpsburg, Maryland, on Sept. 17, 1862. He was able to return to duty by the end of the year and in 1864 was promoted to the rank of corporal. Both Anderson and John, original company enlistees, fought it out to the end and were present or accounted for through February 1865.

William Thompson, 28, and **Joseph M. Thompson**, 21, sons of Alexander and Isabella Thompson of Forks of Pigeon, enlisted together on June 29, 1861.[350] Both of these Haywood Highlanders fought in the engagement at King's School House near

These three Singleton brothers served with the Haywood Highlanders. Pictured here some sixty years after the conclusion of the Civil War are (left to right) William A. S. Columbus Singleton, John C. Singleton, and James Anderson Singleton. *Collection of Charles Cathey; used by permission.*

Richmond, Virginia, on June 25, 1862, where Joseph received a severe wound and died two days later. As events transpired, William would survive his brother for only one additional month. He succumbed to sickness—fever or dysentery—in a Petersburg, Virginia, hospital on July 30, 1862.

Conspicuous Beyond All Others

IN ADDITION TO THE EXEMPLARY MILITARY CAREERS CITED ABOVE— those of men such as Capt. James Cathey, Lt. Garland Ferguson, brothers William and

Wesley Henson, privates Jonathan Reece and Henry T. Bugg, brothers Anderson and John Singleton, and Lt. William Hartgrove—others from Company F stand out for one reason or another upon analysis of the army records and documentation compiled in various archives. For example, conspicuous might a soldier's record be if he served bravely through the entire war and suffered one or more wounds. Equally noticeable, on the other hand, is a man whose service information is spotted with references to multiple desertions or that includes evidence of the commitment of a crime against a fellow soldier from the company. Although the abbreviated service records of all the Haywood Highlanders are appended to this work and can be scrutinized, those men who compiled less honorable or perhaps shameful army careers will go unnamed and unjudged in this examination. However, a few selected Haywood Highlanders whose service records are indeed conspicuously noteworthy have been pulled from the darkness and obscurity of the old archives and are further illuminated below.

James Allen Blalock, an original enlistee with the Haywood Highlanders, was appointed third sergeant when he joined the company on June 29, 1861, at the age of 22 years. Blalock's military career outshines most and is notable for the fact that he served through the entirety of the war without injury or wounds or extended absences from the company due to sickness. During the reorganization of Company F in April 1862 at Kinston, North Carolina, Sergeant Blalock was elected second lieutenant by the men of the company. Around November 1863 he was appointed to replace 1st Lt. Thaddeus Hyatt, who was killed on Oct. 26, 1863, in a skirmish with Tories at Warm Springs in Madison County. Eight months later, when Capt. James Cathey was killed at the Battle of the Crater near Petersburg, Virginia, on July 30, 1864, Lieutenant Blalock was appointed captain of the Haywood Highlanders. He commanded the mountaineers, entrenched at Petersburg, for the rest of war. The records reveal that the day after the Battle of Five Forks on Apr. 1, 1865, Captain Blalock was admitted into a Farmville, Virginia, hospital suffering with pneumonia. Three days later Blalock was apparently able to escape capture by the Union cavalry and infantry troops swooping into Petersburg. He was moved by the Confederate army to a hospital in Danville, Virginia, and admitted with a complaint of "debilitas," a contemporary term for weakness of the body. Because no further records are found for Captain Blalock it cannot be determined definitively how the war ended for him. It is very probable, however, that he was apprehended and taken prisoner by the Yankees while a patient in the Danville hospital, as were many other rebel soldiers.

A young man by the name of **William Bonham** joined Captain Lenoir's Haywood Highlanders on June 29, 1861, while still only 18 years old. He must have been an extraordinary youth by any measure, one sturdy and mature beyond his years. No other soldier from Company F is thought to have compiled a service record as clean as Bonham's or performed his army duties continuously without some period of absence due to sickness or furlough. However, Bonham did just that until he met his end in the trenches of Petersburg, Virginia, in 1865. Upon the company's reorganization at Kinston, North Carolina, in April 1862 Private Bonham was elected by the men of the company as their fourth corporal. He was present at every major and minor engagement that the Haywood Highlanders was involved in up to, and likely including, the skirmish with the Tories at Warm Springs on Oct. 26, 1863. He survived that fracas and returned to the company in November–December 1863, whereupon he helped with the capture of Plymouth, North Carolina, in early 1864 and then followed his commanders to the saps of Richmond and Petersburg. Sadly and tragically, Corporal Bonham was the unlucky victim of a well-aimed Yankee shell exploding within the Confederate trenches on Feb. 17, 1865. It was a sudden end to the life of a loyal and dedicated young Confederate soldier, one who managed to forge an honorable and exemplary record, the equal of which no other Haywood Highlander surpassed.

Besides the Ferguson brothers previously mentioned, Haywood County's Crabtree Township contributed another Ferguson to the Haywood Highlanders when **Ebed J.**

Ferguson joined up on June 29, 1861, at the age of 25. This original enlistee served dutifully and rose from the ranks to sergeant on June 23, 1863, and was appointed third lieutenant in December 1863. Sadly, Lt. Ferguson was killed at Drewry's Bluff, Virginia, around May 16, 1864, during Beauregard's spirited defense of Richmond.

The career of **Alson Gordon** is a good example of the impact of the Confederate Conscription Law on the Southern manhood during the Civil War. Alson joined the Haywood Highlanders as an original enlistee on June 29, 1861, when he was 36 years old. After serving for a year and fighting with his company at the Seven Days' Battles, Private Gordon took advantage of the new conscription law and resigned by reason of being over the maximum age of 35. However, before the year 1862 was out the Confederate Congress had revised the highly unpopular impressment law to obligate all men between the ages of 18 and 45 years to serve in the army. Therefore, on Aug. 15, 1863, Alson Gordon reenlisted with the Haywood Highlanders while Lt. James Blalock was in the Haywood County mountains on a recruiting mission. Private Gordon served loyally for the next year, but during the fight at the Davis house near the Globe Tavern on Aug. 21, 1864, he was severely wounded in the left leg. After surviving an amputation of his leg above the knee, Alson was honorably retired on Dec. 30, 1864, to the Invalid Corps.

Henry Henson, Jr., one of the original enlistees, signed up to fight with the Haywood Highlanders on June 29, 1861, at the age of 25. It is not believed that he was a brother to either of the other sets of Henson brothers who served with the company. Pvt. Henry Henson's record is one that does not stand out when first reviewed. He was not wounded at any time during the war, nor did he advance in rank beyond that of a private soldier. However, the word "desertion" does not appear in his record, which is both solid and enduring. Henson served from the very beginning of the war until his records simply end with the muster for January–February 1865 when he was present and accounted for. It appears that he suffered a bout with a disease the doctors diagnosed as "icterus," or jaundice, which caused him to miss the battles of Sharpsburg and Fredericksburg in the latter several months of 1862. However, it is likely that he participated in the skirmish with Tories at Warm Springs, since he was listed as absent on detached service during that period. And it is significant to note that he manned the trenches at Richmond and Petersburg through the last, darkest days and hours of the Confederacy.

Humphrey P. Holland signed up with the Haywood Highlanders on June 29, 1861, at the age of 23. This original enlistee was soon made a color corporal and served in that capacity through 1863. As a color corporal he was a member of the regimental color guard and entrusted to carry the flag of the regiment into battle. Usually this honor was bestowed on men of undoubted courage and who held the respect of their peers in arms. Color Corporal Holland was surely no exception. The records indicate that he was assigned to detached duty from July until sometime in November–December 1863. Therefore it is very likely that he was involved with other detached troops from the 25th Regiment N.C. in a fight with Tories at Warm Springs on Oct. 26, 1863. In the first month or two of 1864 Humphrey Holland was reduced to the ranks as a private soldier for an unspecified reason. He served as a private for the rest of the war until the records of his service abruptly end in January–February 1865, when he was still present or accounted for.

Robert H. Hyatt joined Captain Lenoir's Haywood Highlanders at Asheville, North Carolina, on Aug. 5, 1861, at the age of 21 years. This original enlistee was elected to the rank of fourth sergeant by the men of his company during the Confederate army's reorganization at Kinston, North Carolina, in April 1862. It is apparent from reading the records that Sergeant Hyatt was a good soldier and respected by his peers. He participated in all the heavy fights of 1862 including the Seven Days' Battles, the Battle of Antietam Run, and the Battle of Fredericksburg. In 1863, when the company moved to eastern North Carolina, Sergeant Hyatt spent a substantial amount of time on detached service. For an unspecified reason or infraction Hyatt was reduced to the ranks on June 23, 1863. However, he still worked on detached duty and even fulfilled the demanding role of courier for General Ransom. The records show that he returned from detached service to the Haywood Highlanders in January–February of 1864 and afterward dutifully followed his company to the earthworks around Richmond and Petersburg. There Hyatt fought from and slept in the trenches through the winter of 1864–65 while receiving little nourishment and no pay. The January–February 1865 company muster lists Pvt. Robert Hyatt as being present for duty and still a loyal Haywood Highlander.

Thaddeus Constantine Sebastin Hyatt was 23 years old when he joined the Haywood Highlanders on June 29, 1861, as an original enlistee. Appointed third corporal, he served in that capacity until the company's reorganization at Kinston, North Carolina, in April 1862. At that time the men of the company demonstrated the high esteem they held for Hyatt by electing him with a large majority of votes to the first lieutenancy of the company. The records show that at various times 1st Lieutenant Hyatt commanded the company in Capt. James Cathey's absence through the year 1862. After the company moved away from the Fredericksburg, Virginia, front back to eastern North Carolina in early 1863, Hyatt was evidently separated from his company on detached service for several months on end. On Oct. 26, 1863, he fought with a detachment from the 25th Regiment N.C. Troops (one hundred or so men) against a large contingent of Tories and Yankees who had taken over Madison County's Warm Springs in Western North Carolina. Lieutenant Hyatt was killed in the fierce fighting where it was reported that the Tories outnumbered the rebels twenty to one.

Francis M. Mahaffey enlisted with the Haywood Highlanders at Asheville on Sept. 10, 1861, just one week before the company broke camp and marched out of the mountains. He was 33 years old and managed to endure the hardships of the army while fighting throughout the entire conflict. During the Battle of Fredericksburg on Dec. 13, 1862, Private Mahaffey was wounded slightly in the left arm but was able to return to duty before year's end. From that midpoint in the war he moved with his company to eastern North Carolina in 1863 and then back to Virginia in 1864 to fend off the Yankees at Richmond and Petersburg. Private Mahaffey was finally captured by the enemy on Apr. 2, 1865, the day after the Battle of Five Forks.

A youthful **Luther W. Murray** began a notable military career when he joined the company as an original enlistee on June 29, 1861, at the tender age of 17. Early in the war at Grahamville's Camp Lee, Captain Lenoir had Murray and young Columbus Singleton placed in the guard tent for being drunk (see pp. 171–72). Just a boy at that time, Private Murray was forced to grow up quick. He soon fought the bluecoats for the first time at the Seven Days' Battles around Richmond in the last days of June 1862. And the records reveal his capture at Frederick, Maryland, on Sept. 12, 1862, just days prior to the involvement of Company F in the important actions at Harpers Ferry, Virginia (present-day West Virginia), and Sharpsburg, Maryland. Within two months, however, Murray was exchanged at Aiken's Landing on the James River in Virginia, whereupon he returned to duty by the end of 1862. In 1864 Private Murray was promoted to sergeant and in the first months of 1865 was promoted once again to first sergeant. Sergeant Murray was captured for a second time on Apr. 2, 1865, as the Union cavalry forces rounded up the disoriented and straggling Confederate soldiers after the Battle of Five Forks on the previous day. Murray was confined at Point Lookout, Maryland, until being released on June 15, 1865, after taking the oath of allegiance to the United States.

Isaac W. Roberson was 21 years old when he enlisted with the Haywood Highlanders on June 29, 1861. The original enlistee served for the duration of the war, although the records indicate that he was sick in hospitals and on leave for extended periods, as were many soldiers at one time or another during the Civil War. In early July 1862 Private Roberson was admitted to a Richmond hospital with the complaint of "haem," or parasites in the blood.[351] However, he was released after a week's time and returned to his company to follow the Army of Northern Virginia to Sharpsburg, Maryland, and Fredericksburg, Virginia. Again, from the records, it appears that Roberson was hospitalized for several months in 1863 of some unspecified disease. In the latter months of 1864 Private Roberson worked as a teamster for the Confederate army and was subsequently present or accounted for in the last muster record of February 1865.

John W. Trull was 21 years of age when he enlisted with the Haywood Highlanders at Forks of Pigeon on June 29, 1861. The original enlistee appears to have been absent sick when Company F participated in its first action at the Seven Days' Battles. However, he returned to the company in time to participate in the major battles at Sharpsburg, Maryland, and Fredericksburg, Virginia, in the latter part of 1862. At Fredericksburg, Private Trull was "slightly" wounded in the left foot, as was noted in the company record of events. By March 1863 Trull had returned to his company and served until January–February 1865 when he was listed as "absent on sick furlough."

Judge Garland S. Ferguson (above, left), wounded three times during the Civil War, overcame the scars of the Rebellion and became a respected politician and jurist in Waynesville, North Carolina. In 1901 Ferguson penned a brief history of the 25th Regiment North Carolina Infantry Troops. *Digital collection, Haywood County Public Library.*

William Hartgrove (above, right), or "Captain Hack" as he was more commonly known, forged a worthy postbellum public service and professional career in Haywood County. He served for many years as a county commissioner and surveyor and represented the county in the state's General Assembly. *Collection of Carroll C. Jones.*

"Rebel," sketch by Alfred Rudolf Waud. *Library of Congress, Prints and Photographs Division.*

⇛ THERE IS EVIDENCE IN THE RECORDS *that at least one Haywood Highlander deserted from the company three times. On the final act of desertion he went over to the enemy in east Tennessee and took the oath of allegiance to the United States.*

The Last Highlanders Standing

NOT ONE HAYWOOD HIGHLANDER, as has been noted previously, surrendered at Appomattox Court House with the seventy-four rebels from the 25th Regiment N.C. Troops and the remnants of Robert E. Lee's Army of Northern Virginia.[352] Surprisingly, only *twenty-seven* men from Company F, who were not counted as deserters or listed as "absent sick" or "absent wounded" in the service records, survived the hazards and hardships of the Petersburg saps beyond February 1865. Surely these remaining Highlanders must have realized that the cause was lost and the end of the struggle was drawing near. To those last few survivors the end of the war came in several different fashions. One unfortunate soul was killed in the trenches by an exploding shell. Four mountaineers, two of whom were wounded, were captured at the Battle of Fort Stedman on March 25. Additionally, two others who received wounds in that battle were later apprehended in a Petersburg hospital. Six more Highlanders were captured at the disastrous Battle of Five Forks on Apr. 1, or in its aftermath when the Union army swarmed in and took control of Petersburg and the Confederate capital.

Straggling soldiers from Company F were rounded up, and those wounded and sick and confined to the hospitals were captured and counted as prisoners of war. It is not known how many Haywood Highlanders remained with the 25th Regiment N.C. after the Battle of Five Forks, with the exception of two who were captured and paroled at Farmville around Apr. 11. Although the details and circumstances associated with how these two resilient men were caught are not clear today, they very well could have been fleeing with Lee's van and have been captured in one of the fierce running engagements with the Union's cavalry and infantry forces along the banks of the Appomattox River.

At least thirty Haywood Highlanders, like these Confederate solders depicted going up" or "going over" to the enemy, deserted and never returned to their company." Harper's Weekly, *July 16, 1864.*

A story is told of one such North Carolinian who was captured in Lee's flight—and it could very well have been one of these two Highlanders. Upon hearing his Federal captors call out to him, "Surrender, surrender, we've got you!" the ragged and famished Johnny Reb hollered back as he dropped his gun: "Yes, you've got me, and the hell of a git you've got!"[353]

The Confederate records do not account for the fates of the remaining eleven or so Haywood Highlanders. Instead, the service information that has been extracted from the various archival sources simply offers the tantalizingly empty words "present or accounted for through February, 1865." Or in the singular case of Capt. James Blalock, listed as a patient in a Farmville, Virginia, hospital on Apr. 2, 1865 and then transferred three days later to another hospital in Danville, it can only be presumed that he was hospitalized after the Battle of Five Forks and then probably taken prisoner in the Danville hospital by the Union forces pursuing Lee's retreating army toward Appomattox Court House.

Just twenty-seven men remained—out of a total of 131 Haywood Highlanders whose names once filled the rolls of the company—and fought from the earthen trenches during the last three or four months of the Civil War. There were, of course, many other brave mountaineers who had battled to rid their homeland of the Yankee foe and consequently fell as casualties of war. And many more were the Highlanders whose service was not in all cases respectable or commendable, those who lost their fervor or lacked the strength or determination or courage to continue the battle for Southern independence. These souls either resigned from the army because of age or disability or simply turned their backs to brethren and battlefields and deserted.

At least thirty men can be counted as deserters from the company's service records, yet it is a surety that there were even more cases that are not evidenced in the archives. The motivating factors that influenced the South's soldiers to desert were numerous and powerful—simply more than many mortals, brave and other, were able to resist. The desertion rate within the ranks of the Haywood Highlanders climbed to a staggering rate of 23%.

Another large grouping (approximately twenty-four men) left the service of the Confederate army for sundry reasons including resignation, transfer, disability, and providing a substitute. Taken together all of these contributing causes—casualties of war, desertion, resignation, and a variety of other factors—served to diminish the size of the company by 75%.

In 1865, as dark clouds enveloped the Confederacy and the blue Yankee hordes began maneuvering for the final surges to win Petersburg, the remaining Haywood Highlanders manned the trenches to fight with Lee's diminished and weakened army. These warriors who fought it out until the bitter end have, for the most part, escaped special consideration in this work. That last contingent of twenty-seven rebels left battling with the remnants of Lee's Army of Northern Virginia at Petersburg were the brave, the stalwart, the resolute, and the fortunate. They were the following Haywood Highlanders:

* Blalock, James A., Captain
* Ferguson, Garland Sevier, 2nd Lt.
* Hartgrove, William Harrison, 1st Lt.
* Bonham, William, Corporal
* Bugg, Henry Tilman, Private
* Bugg, Jeremiah H., Private
  Christopher, McDaniel, Private
  Clark, Joshua A., Corporal
  Francis, William F., Private
  Hartgrove, Rufus P., Private
* Henson, Henry, Jr., Private
* Henson, Wesley, Sergeant
* Henson, William, Private
* Holland, Humphrey P., Private
  House, Ambrose, Private
* Hyatt, Robert H., Private
  Jones, Isaac W., Private
* Mahaffey, Francis M., Private
  Mahaffey, Joseph H., Private
  Moore, John C., Private
* Murray, Luther W., 1st Sergeant
* Reece, Jonathan K., Private
* Roberson, Isaac W., Private
  Scott, James P., Private
* Singleton, James Anderson, Corporal
* Singleton, John C., Private
  Tindle, J. R., Private

    * original enlistee

A large group of rebel prisoners of war taken at the Battle of Five Forks on Apr. 1, 1865, wait to be processed. More than 5,000 Confederate soldiers were captured, including six men from the Haywood Highlanders. *Library of Congress, Prints and Photographs Division.*

It should be noted that almost one-half of this group were conscripts and served in the war for less than two years. Their service was for the most part compelled by Confederate laws and army officers sent into the western mountains and other regions to round up more men to fight for the cause. On the other hand, the original enlistees who mustered in with the company before it left Asheville in September 1861 have been so identified—and for good reason. They were the first to volunteer to protect their homeland, and they served for the entire duration of the war. No conscript laws or home guardsmen were required to coerce these men into uniform. They perceived the threat to take away their inalienable rights and reacted almost instantly when the call was made at Forks of Pigeon for volunteers to form a company. For all who read the names above which have "original enlistee" branded to the side there can be no uncertainty as to the sort of men they were and no doubt that they gave their due for the Southern cause. Whether the righteous cause for which they so stubbornly and gallantly fought was worthy of their exertions and sacrifices was certainly a matter of debate and war then, and is still arguable today. However, the heroic service and character of those last "original enlistee" Haywood Highlanders is unassailable.

"Hobbled Rebel" by Edwin Forbes. Library of Congress, Prints and Photographs Division.

≡ ONLY ONE SOLDIER *joined the company as a substitute. Pvt. Arthur Laughter was discharged from Company A of the 25th Regiment N.C. Troops, by reason of being under age, on July 16, 1862. On the same day the enterprising sixteen-year-old Laughter enlisted in Company F as a substitute for Pvt. John G. Burnett. No record has been found indicating the compensation that Laughter received for relieving Burnett of his military obligation.*

Afterword

Following Gen. Robert E. Lee's surrender at Appomattox, the remaining Confederate armed forces across the South threw down their arms in short order. Troops in Waynesville, North Carolina, under the direct command of Col. William Holland Thomas and Lt. Col. James R. Love, surrendered to the Federals in May 1865, ending all formal hostilities in the state. The capitulation of the Army of Northern Virginia at Appomattox Court House on Apr. 9, 1864, officially ended the war for the soldiers attached to Company F (Haywood Highlanders) of the 25th Regiment N.C. Troops. Certainly it had concluded many months before for most of the mountaineer rebels who served in the company. Thirty-three Highlanders who had lost their lives to either enemy bullets or disease would never again embrace their families or grace the warm firesides of rustic cabins. Some of the soldiers had hobbled back to the mountains wounded and forever maimed physically and mentally from their Confederate army service. There were also many others who had skulked away from the battle fronts and found their way back to the mountains to either hide out around their homes or give themselves over to the enemy in east Tennessee or other places of Union refuge. Yet, for the remaining few active Haywood Highlanders, resilient and loyal beyond all others, it was the final duty and battles around Petersburg, Virginia, in the spring of 1865 that signified the closure of their military careers.

Slowly, these men began finding their way back to their mountain homeland. From the Union prisoner-of-war camps across the North and the hospitals around Richmond and Petersburg the Highlanders started on their long journeys back to Haywood County. Lt. William Harrison Hartgrove, a captive in an officer's prison on

Johnson's Island, near Sandusky, Ohio, was released on June 18, 1865, after pledging and signing an oath of allegiance to the United States. Hartgrove immediately set out on his trip home, which included conveyance on stock boats and trains to the terminus of the railroad at Morganton, North Carolina. From that point it is presumed he trekked by wagon and on foot to ascend the Blue Ridge and make his way to Forks of Pigeon and his waiting family. Overall, three weeks were consumed in his travels from northern Ohio. Midway into the grueling odyssey, nonetheless, Hartgrove stopped off in Petersburg to check on friends still confined in the city's hospitals. One of the patients that he visited was 2nd Lt. Garland Ferguson, whose left thigh bone had been shattered at the Battle of Fort Stedman nearly three months earlier. For eleven days Hartgrove waited and whiled away his time at Petersburg in hopes that Ferguson would be released, and so he could escort his wounded friend home. However, after almost two weeks of lingering around the hospital and upon learning that three more weeks of hospitalization were required before travel would be possible, Lieutenant Hartgrove decided to continue his journey back to the mountains alone.[354] It was not until Aug. 2, 1865, that Ferguson was freed from hospital confinement and permitted to start out for Haywood's Crabtree Township. Still in a severe crippled condition and having to limp along on crutches over crude mountain roads for much of the way, he surely found the passage painful and difficult.

Lieutenants Ferguson and Hartgrove, Capt. James Blalock, Sgt. Luther Murray, Cpl. Anderson Singleton, Pvt. Jonathan Reece, Pvt. John Singleton, and all the other surviving diehard warriors trudged along the washed-out turnpikes and roadways leading into Haywood County. They negotiated rutted wagon traces hugging the Pigeon River and its tributaries and climbed narrow pathways coursing up to the ridgetops. And they eventually found their way back to the cabins and hearths they had vacated years before and into the waiting arms of kindred. Joyful reunions these surely were, as the Highlanders feasted their eyes on loved ones and accustomed their senses once again to the sights and sounds and smells of families and homesteads. And after these homecomings little time would have transpired before the men took notice of the deplorable conditions surrounding them.

Missing roof shakes, blown or rotted away, left the cabin interiors vulnerable to the rains. Unfilled chinks in the log walls allowed the elements and critters to gain easy entrance into the homes through gaping holes. Outbuildings and fencing were in varying states of disrepair. Washed and scoured wagon roads and footpaths were barely passable. The livestock so critical to the mountain families was in short supply, having been either impressed by the Confederacy, exchanged for tax obligations, or taken away by raiding Yankee cavalry troops or bushwhacking gangs of deserters, Tories, and other men avoiding army service. Unplowed fields that lay fallow were spotted with eroded scalds and elsewhere were grown over with wild grasses and briars. The modest areas still under cultivation could not possibly produce sufficient grain and corn crops to sustain families, much less afford an income. Vital food ingredients such as grain, salt, and sugar had been extremely scarce during the war and remained so in the months following the cessation of hostilities. As the last of the Haywood Highlanders finally arrived back in their communities and gazed around at the countryside in neglected ruin, they could immediately see the impact of the war and their forced absence on the mountain habitat. And the men could see that there was much work to be done.

―――

The two lieutenants who had developed such strong bonds through almost four years of hard Confederate army service, William Hartgrove and Garland Ferguson, had been just young boys when Captain Lenoir took them under his wings. During the early days at Camp Lee near Grahamville, South Carolina, the captain was forced to discipline Hartgrove, a lowly private at the time, for a lapse in judgment. On his twenty-first birthday the private and several friends celebrated and imbibed ardent spirits in excess, and Hartgrove was the target of Captain Lenoir's ire. Garland Ferguson was only eighteen when he enlisted with the Haywood Highlanders, being one of the few volunteers who was not an inhabitant of the Forks of Pigeon community. However, he was as determined and as tough as any of the older Highlanders—having survived three wounds on separate occasions—and proved himself time and time again in battle.

Both Hartgrove and Ferguson were able to shake off the physical and mental scars from their army experience, although surely with much difficulty. They determined to make something of themselves after the war and set out on divergent paths and very different careers. William Hartgrove taught schools and began farming around Forks of Pigeon in the immediate postwar years. Later he began a long career as a county surveyor and entered into the realm of politics, in which he was able to forge a notable record of public service, serving several terms as a county commissioner and representing Haywood County in the lower house of the State General Assembly. Although occupied with these commendable pursuits, he nonetheless was able to work a short stint as the first agent of the Western North Carolina Railroad in the village of Pigeon River (later Canton) and helped to found and publish two local newspapers. At the end of "Captain Hack" Hartgrove's life an obituary author described him as being a "useful citizen" and contemporaries hailed him as Canton's "first citizen."[355]

Garland Ferguson, on the other hand, chose as a professional career the study and practice of law. Still hobbling on crutches as a result of his most recent wound, Ferguson successfully ran for clerk of superior court in 1866. He was able to read law under the tutelage of different Waynesville jurists while fulfilling the obligations of the clerk's office. Remarkably, the young man obtained his license to practice in 1867, and by 1871 had established a law partnership with his brother in Waynesville. From that start his professional career carried him to the halls of the North Carolina State Assembly as a senator representing Haywood County and to the bench of the Sixteenth Judicial District, serving two decades as a jurist.[356]

Capt. Thomas Isaac Lenoir came to the mountains of Haywood County out of a sense of familial duty and respect for his father. He was left alone to learn the fundamentals of farming and to manage his father's resources, which included a small company of slaves and extensive tracts of land along the East Fork of Pigeon River.

When elected to command the Haywood Highlanders at the beginning of the Civil War, he accepted that responsibility knowing he was not the right man for the job. However, because of what he described as his "peculiar situation" and out of a sense of duty to his neighbors, he led the volunteers from Forks of Pigeon to war. His upbringing and rich Lenoir heritage would allow nothing less. Tom was reared to do his duty and to be a leader of people. Although not persuaded toward politics as were his father and grandfather, he led by example in his community and through a hard-won respect gained from the work ethic and integrity he demonstrated. And Tom Lenoir learned the practice of farming well. While his work did not earn for him prosperity and riches, it earned the esteem of his neighbors and the citizens of Haywood County. He became known throughout the western Carolina mountains as a first-rate cattle man and a person of unquestionable moral character worthy of his famed Lenoir heritage.

Appendix A
Haywood Highlanders—Roster and Service Records

Captains

Blalock, James Allen. Enlisted June 29, 1861, at age 22 in Haywood County. Enlisted as sergeant and elected 2nd Lt. Apr. 28, 1862. Appointed 1st Lt. in November 1863 and promoted to captain Aug. 16, 1864. Present or accounted for through Apr. 7, 1865, when listed in a hospital in Danville, Va. with "debilitas."

Cathey, James Madison. Enlisted June 29, 1861, at age 23 in Haywood County. Appointed 3rd Lt. June 29, 1861, and elected captain Apr. 28, 1862. Killed at the Crater near Petersburg, Va., July 30, 1864.

Lenoir, Thomas Isaac. Enlisted June 29, 1861, at age 43 in Haywood County. Appointed captain June 29, 1861; declined to accept reelection as captain Apr. 28, 1862.

Lieutenants

Blalock, Etheldred H., 1st Lt. Enlisted June 29, 1861, at age 44 in Haywood County. Appointed 1st Lt. June 29, 1861, and served until defeated for reelection Apr. 28, 1862.

Burnett, James A., 2nd Lt. Enlisted June 29, 1861, at age 24 in Haywood County. Appointed 2nd Lt. June 29, 1861; declined to accept reelection as 2nd Lt. of this company Apr. 28, 1862. Later served as 2nd Lt. of Company I, 62nd Regiment N.C. Troops.

Cathey, Joseph Turner, 3rd Lt. Enlisted June 29, 1861, at age 26 in Haywood County. Enlisted as 1st Sgt. and elected 3rd Lt. Apr. 28, 1862. Died in hospital at Wilson, N.C., Sept. 8, 1863, of "febris typhoides."

Ferguson, Ebed J., 3rd Lt. Enlisted June 29, 1861, at age 25 in Haywood County. Promoted to sergeant June 23, 1863, and appointed 3rd Lt. around Dec. 4, 1863. Killed at Drewry's Bluff, Va., on or about May 16, 1864.

Ferguson, Garland Sevier, 2nd Lt. Enlisted June 29, 1861, at age 18 in Haywood County. Enlisted as sergeant but reduced to ranks Apr. 28, 1862. Promoted to sergeant in Sept.–Oct. 1863. Wounded at Drewry's Bluff, Va., May 14, 1864; returned to duty June 1864. Appointed 2nd Lt. around Aug. 16, 1864. Wounded in the right shoulder near Globe Tavern, Va., Aug. 21, 1864; returned to duty prior to Jan. 1, 1865. Wounded in the left leg at Fort Stedman, Va., Mar. 25, 1865, and hospitalized at Petersburg, Va., where he was presumably captured Apr. 3, 1865. Released from Richmond, Va., hospital Aug. 2, 1865, after taking Oath.

Hartgrove, William Harrison, 1st Lt. Enlisted July 18, 1861, at age 20 in Haywood County. Promoted to sergeant Apr. 28, 1862, and later appointed 1st Lt. Aug. 16, 1864. Captured at Five Forks, Va., Apr. 1, 1865 and confined at Old Capitol Prison, Washington, D.C., until transferred to Johnson's Island, Ohio, Apr. 9, 1865. Released June 18, 1865 after taking the Oath.

Hyatt, Thaddeus C. S., 1st Lt. Enlisted June 29, 1861, at age 23 in Haywood County. Enlisted as 3rd Cpl.; appointed 1st Lt. Apr. 28, 1862. Killed at Warm Springs, N.C., around Oct. 26, 1863.

Wright, William M., 2nd Lt. Enlisted Aug. 22, 1861, at age 18 in Buncombe County. Promoted to sergeant May 14, 1863; appointed 2nd Lt. Sept. 10, 1863. Resigned for unreported reason and relieved from duty Feb. 23, 1864.

Noncommissioned Officers and Privates

Abbott, Green B., Private. Enlisted June 29, 1861, at age 21 in Haywood County. Died in hospital at Petersburg, Va., around July 29, 1862, of "cerebro meningitis."

Allen, David, Private. Enlisted July 18, 1861, at age 27 in Haywood County. Discharged Mar. 8, 1862, by reason of disability.

Allman, William N., Private. Enlisted June 29, 1861, at age 19 in Haywood County. Enlisted as musician but reduced to ranks Apr. 28, 1862. Deserted Feb. 24, 1864.

Anderson, Jasper N., Private. Enlisted June 29, 1861, at age 22 in Haywood County. Wounded at Malvern Hill, Va., July 1, 1862, and returned to duty on Sept. 22, 1862. Promoted to corporal Sept. 22, 1862, but reduced to ranks Feb. 17, 1863. Died in hospital at Goldsboro, N.C., May 12, 1863, of "febris typhoides."

Anderson, Josiah McDonald, Private. Enlisted June 29, 1861, at age 18 in Haywood County. Wounded in the left leg and "disabled for life" at Malvern Hill, Va., July 1, 1862. Reported absent wounded through February 1865.

Baggett, William M., Private. Enlisted June 10, 1864, in Moore County. Wounded prior to Jan. 1, 1865, and reported absent wounded or absent sick through February 1865.

Best, Rodom C., Private. Enlisted Sept. 1, 1863, in Haywood County. Wounded in the back and left hand at Petersburg, Va., and hospitalized at Petersburg Oct. 12, 1864. Furloughed for sixty days Dec. 9, 1864.

Blackburn, William P., Private. Enlisted June 10, 1864, in Lincoln County. Present or accounted for through February 1865.

Blalock, George H., Private. Enlisted Apr. 7, 1863, at age 41 in Haywood County. Present or accounted for until January–February 1865, when reported absent without leave.

Bonham, William, Corporal. Enlisted June 29, 1861, at age 18 in Haywood County. Promoted to corporal Apr. 28, 1862. "Killed in the trenches by a shell" near Petersburg, Va., Feb. 17, 1865.

Brookshire, Humphrey P., Private. Enlisted Sept. 18, 1861, at age 44 in Buncombe County. Discharged July 16, 1862, for being over age.

Brookshire, John E., Private. Enlisted June 29, 1861, at age 18 in Haywood County. Died at Winchester, Va., Oct. 20, 1862, of "fever."

Bugg, Henry Tilman, Private. Enlisted June 29, 1861, at age 18 in Haywood County. Wounded in the right leg at the Battle of the Crater near Petersburg, Va., July 30, 1864. Returned to duty prior to Jan. 1, 1865, and present or accounted for through February 1865.

Bugg, Jeremiah H., Private. Enlisted June 29, 1861, at age 20 in Haywood County. Wounded in the right arm and captured at Fort Stedman, Va., on Mar. 25, 1865. Confined at various Federal hospitals until confined at Old Capitol Prison, Washington, D.C., Apr. 24, 1865, and then Elmira, N.Y., May 1, 1865. Released at Elmira Aug. 14, 1865, after taking the oath.

Burnett, Alfred, Private. Enlisted Aug. 14, 1861, at age 26 in Buncombe County. Discharged Jan. 20, 1862, by reason of "physical disability."

Burnett, John G., Private. Enlisted June 29, 1861, at age 29 in Haywood County. Enlisted as corporal but reduced to ranks Apr. 28, 1862. Discharged July 16, 1862, after providing a substitute. Later served in Company I, 62nd Regiment N.C. Troops.

Byers, William, Private. Enlisted June 29, 1861, at age 18 in Haywood County. Present or accounted for through February 1864. No further records.

Cathey, William Turner, Sergeant. Enlisted June 29, 1861, at age 22 in Haywood County. Enlisted as a fourth sergeant and elected as fifth sergeant on Apr. 28, 1862. Present or accounted for through February 1864. Believed to have died afterward during the war of unknown cause.

Chambers, George W., Private. Enlisted June 29, 1861, at age 22 in Haywood County. Wounded at Malvern Hill, Va., July 1, 1862, and returned to duty Sept. 6, 1862. "Killed . . . by deserters" June 10, 1863, while absent on detached duty.

Christopher, George E., Private. Enlisted June 29, 1861, at age 33 in Haywood County. Died at Camp Lee near Grahamville, S.C., Feb. 23, 1862, of "typhoid fever."

Christopher, Henry, Private. Enlisted June 29, 1861, at age 43 in Haywood County. Died in hospital at Wilson, N.C., around May 30, 1862, of disease.

Christopher, McDaniel, Private. Enlisted May 1, 1864 in Haywood County. Present or accounted for through February 1865.

Clark, Hiram, Private. Enlisted May 1, 1863 at age 38 in Buncombe County. Present or accounted for through Feb. 1865.

Clark, Joshua A., Corporal. Enlisted Mar. 22, 1862, at age 16 in Haywood County. Promoted to corporal in March–December 1864 and present or accounted for through February 1865.

Clonts, William R., Private. Enlisted June 29, 1861, at age 18 in Haywood County. Promoted to corporal May 1, 1862, and reduced to ranks in September–October 1862. Wounded at Sharpsburg, Md., Sept. 17, 1862, and returned to duty prior to Nov. 1, 1862. Deserted Feb. 24, 1864.

Collins, Eli, Private. Enlisted Aug. 14, 1861, at age 33 in Buncombe County. Discharged July 16, 1862, for being over age. Reenlisted in this company on an unspecified date (probably in January 1863) and died at Guinea Station, Va., Feb. 9, 1863, of "typhoid fever."

Crawford, Amos A., Private. Enlisted June 29, 1861, at age 26 in Haywood County. Wounded in the hand at King's School House, Va., June 25, 1862, and returned to duty prior to Sept. 1, 1862. Deserted Sept. 5, 1862.

Davis, Joseph N., Private. Enlisted Mar. 22, 1862, at age 23 in Haywood County. Present or accounted for through February 1865 but reported absent sick during much of this period.

Deaver, Rufus L., Private. Previously served in Company C of this regiment and transferred to this company May 1, 1862. Deserted on the march Feb. 1, 1864, and went over to the enemy. Took the oath at Knoxville, Tenn., around May 22, 1864.

Deaver, William N., Private. Previously served in Company C of this regiment and transferred to this company May 1, 1862. Deserted to the enemy on an unspecified date and took the oath at Knoxville, Tenn., around May 22, 1864.

Edmonston, Benjamin F., Private. Enlisted June 29, 1861, at age 25 in Haywood County. Wounded in the leg at King's School House, Va., June 25, 1862, and returned to duty in July–August 1862. Mortally wounded in the head at the Battle of the Crater July 30, 1864.[357]

Estes, Robert J. H., Private. Enlisted Feb. 28, 1863, at age 17 in Haywood County. Present or accounted for through February 1864. No further records.

Evans, John C., Private. Enlisted Oct. 10, 1863, in McDowell County. Deserted on the march Feb. 1, 1864, and returned to his home in McDowell County, where on June 19, 1864, he assisted two escaped Federal prisoners of war by acting as their guide in crossing Swannanoa Valley. On the morning of June 27, 1864, "his house was surrounded [by Confederate soldiers] . . . and he [was] captured and sent to jail in Asheville, North Carolina where he remained 11 days with his hands tied behind his back." Then sent under strong guard to Petersburg, Va., to work in the trenches. Captured in the trenches July 30, 1864, and confined at Elmira, N.Y., through Sept. 30, 1864. Released on an unspecified date after taking the oath.

Evans, William J., 1st Sergeant. Enlisted June 29, 1861, at age 18 in Haywood County. Wounded "by a deserter" June 10, 1862, and returned to duty prior to July 1, 1862. Captured at South Mountain, Md., Sept. 14, 1862, and confined at Fort Delaware, Del. Exchanged at Aiken's Landing, James River, Va., Nov. 10, 1862, and returned to duty prior to Jan. 1, 1863. Promoted to third sergeant around Nov. 30, 1863, and promoted to first sergeant in March–September 1864. Deserted Feb. 4, 1865, while absent on furlough.

Ferguson, Nathan J., Private. Enlisted June 29, 1861, at age 29 in Haywood County. Present or accounted for through February 1864. Died at home in August 1864.

Francis, William F., Private. Enlisted June 10, 1864, in Caswell County. Wounded in the neck and/or right breast and captured at Fort Stedman, Va., Mar. 25, 1865. Confined at various Federal hospitals until confined at Old Capitol Prison, Washington, D.C. Apr. 24, 1865, and then transferred to Elmira, N.Y., May 11, 1865. Released at Elmira July 7, 1865, after taking the oath. (Federal hospital records dated March 1865 give his age as 18.)

Franklin, David N., Private. Enlisted Mar. 22, 1862, at age 30 in Haywood County. Promoted to corporal May 23, 1863, but reduced to ranks subsequent to Feb. 29, 1864. Deserted to the enemy on an unspecified date and took the oath in eastern Tennessee Dec. 31, 1864.

Franklin, Henry J., Private. Enlisted June 29, 1861, at age 32 in Haywood County. Deserted around Sept. 23, 1862, and returned to duty in March–June 1863. Present or accounted for through February 1864.

Franklin, Perry B., Private. Enlisted Aug. 14, 1861, at age 25 in Buncombe County. Discharged Jan. 20, 1862, by reason of disability. Later served in Company I, 62nd Regiment N.C. Troops.

Gaddis, David W., Private. Enlisted Feb. 28, 1863, at age 37 in Haywood County. Deserted Jan. 26, 1865, while absent on furlough.

Glenn, Napoleon L., Private. Enlisted June 29, 1861, at age 18 in Haywood County. Present or accounted for until transferred to Company I of this regiment May 1, 1862.

Godwin, Leonard, Private. Enlisted June 10, 1864, in Sampson County. Captured near Petersburg, Va., July 30, 1864, and confined at Point Lookout, Md., until transferred to Elmira, N.Y., Aug. 8, 1864. Paroled at Elmira Oct. 11, 1864, and exchanged at Venus Point, Savannah River, Ga., Nov. 15, 1864.

Gordon, Alson, Private. Enlisted June 29, 1861, at age 36 in Haywood County. Discharged July 16, 1862, for being over age but reenlisted in the company Aug. 15, 1863. Wounded in the leg near Petersburg, Va., Aug. 21, 1864, and left leg amputated above the knee as a result of wounds. Reported absent wounded until Dec. 30, 1864, and then retired to the Invalid Corps.

Green, Samuel B., Private. Enlisted Aug. 14, 1861, at age 23 in Buncombe County. Deserted Aug. 14, 1863, and went over to the enemy. Took the oath at Knoxville, Tenn., around May 25, 1864.

Green, Thaddeus M., Private. Enlisted June 29, 1861, at age 18 in Haywood County. Enlisted in Company C, Infantry Regiment, Thomas Legion, in June 1862. Failed to report for duty with that unit and continued to serve in this company through February 1864. Wounded in action on an unspecified date. Reported absent wounded or absent sick until Jan. 26, 1865, and then listed as a deserter.

Hall, George, Jr., Private. Enlisted June 29, 1861, at age 25 in Haywood County. Present or accounted for through February 1864 but reported absent sick during most of that period. Reported absent without leave in November–December 1864 and then listed as a deserter Feb. 4, 1865.

Hall, George R., Private. Enlisted June 29, 1861, at age 17 in Haywood County. Elected musician (fifer) Oct. 16, 1861, but reduced to ranks Apr. 28, 1862. Died at Drewry's Bluff, Va., around Aug. 25, 1862, of "ulcers."

Harrell, Ezekiel T., Private. Enlisted June 29, 1861, at age 18 in Haywood County. Deserted Sept. 24, 1862, but returned to duty Jan. 26, 1863. Furloughed on an unspecified date after February 1864 and failed to return to duty. Dropped from the rolls of the company and listed as a deserter Nov. 3, 1864.

Hartgrove, Rufus P., Private. Enlisted Sept. 1, 1863, at age 33 in Haywood County. Deserted on an unspecified date after February 1864 but returned to duty prior to Jan. 1, 1865, after an unauthorized absence of seven months. Captured by the enemy near Petersburg, Va., Apr. 1, 1865, and confined at Point Lookout, Md. Released June 14, 1865, after taking the oath.

Henderson, Harper, Private. Enlisted Sept. 17, 1861, at age 45 in Buncombe County. Discharged July 16, 1862, for being over age.

Henderson, James Martin, Private. Enlisted June 29, 1861, at age 25 in Haywood County. Wounded in the left lung near Globe Tavern, Va., Aug. 21, 1864, and died in hospital at Petersburg, Va., two days later.

Henderson, William, Private. Enlisted June 29, 1861, at age 38 in Haywood County. Enlisted as sergeant but reduced to ranks Apr. 28, 1862. Discharged July 16, 1862, for being over age.

Henson, Burton H., Private. Enlisted June 29, 1861, at age 26 in Haywood County. Deserted on the march Nov. 29, 1863, and went over to the enemy. Took the oath at Knoxville, Tenn., around May 22, 1864.

Henson, Elijah L., Private. Enlisted June 29, 1861, at age 20 in Haywood County. Deserted to the enemy on an unspecified date after Feb. 1864. Took the oath at Knoxville, Tenn., May 25, 1864.

Henson, Fidellio W., Private. Enlisted June 29, 1861, at age 22 in Haywood County. Died in hospital at Petersburg, Va., Aug. 4, 1862, of "cerebritis."

Henson, Henry, Jr., Private. Enlisted June 29, 1861, at age 25 in Haywood County. Present or accounted for through February 1865.

Henson, Thomas F., Corporal. Previously served in Company C of this regiment and transferred to this company May 1, 1862, with the rank of corporal. Deserted on the march Jan. 28, 1864, and went over to the enemy. Took the oath at Knoxville, Tenn., around May 25, 1864.

Henson, Wesley, Sergeant. Enlisted June 29, 1861, at age 21 in Haywood County. Promoted to sergeant on an unspecified date in 1864. Wounded at Drewry's Bluff, Va., around May 20, 1864, and returned to duty prior to Jan. 1, 1865. Captured at Fort Stedman, Va., Mar. 25, 1865, and confined at Point Lookout, Md. Released June 14, 1865, after taking the oath.

Henson, Wiley, Sergeant. Enlisted June 29, 1861, at age 19 in Haywood County. Captured at Frederick, Md., Sept. 12, 1862, and confined at Fort Delaware, Del. Exchanged at Aiken's Landing, James River, Va., Nov. 10, 1862, and returned to duty prior to Jan. 1, 1863. Promoted to sergeant around Nov. 30, 1863. Deserted Feb. 22, 1864.

Henson, William, Private. Enlisted June 29, 1861, at age 26 in Haywood County. Captured at Frederick, Md., Sept. 12, 1862, and confined at Fort Delaware, Del. Exchanged at Aiken's Landing, James River, Va., Nov. 10, 1862, and returned to duty prior to Jan. 1, 1863. Hospitalized at Richmond, Va., May 11, 1864, with a gunshot wound to the right thigh. Furloughed for sixty days May 26, 1864, and returned to duty prior to Jan. 1, 1865. Wounded in the left shoulder at Fort Stedman, Va., around Mar. 25, 1865, and hospitalized at Petersburg, Va., where he was presumably captured by the enemy Apr. 3, 1865. No further records.

Holland, Humphrey P., Private. Enlisted June 29, 1861, at age 23 in Haywood County. Enlisted as color corporal but reduced to ranks in January–February 1864. Present or accounted for through February 1865.

Holland, Matthias, Private. Enlisted June 29, 1861, at age 21 in Haywood County. Deserted to the enemy on an unspecified date after February 1864. Took the oath at Knoxville, Tenn., around May 22, 1864.

Holland, Thomas, Private. Previously served in Company I, 62nd Regiment N.C. Troops, and enlisted in this company Sept. 4, 1863. Hospitalized at Petersburg, Va., July 26, 1864, with a shell wound of the right thigh and died in Petersburg hospital the same day.

Hood, Pleasant B., Private. Enlisted June 29, 1861, at age 35 in Haywood County. Discharged July 16, 1862, for being over age. Later served in Company I, 62nd Regiment N.C. Troops.

House, Ambrose, Private. Paroled at Farmville, Va., around Apr. 11–21, 1865.

Hyatt, Robert H., Private. Enlisted Aug. 5, 1861, at age 21 in Buncombe County. Promoted to sergeant Apr. 28, 1862, but reduced to ranks June 23, 1863. Present or accounted for through February 1865.

Inman, Joshua E., Private. Enlisted June 29, 1861, at age 23 in Haywood County. Present or accounted for through February 1864. No further records.

Inman, Lewis Hezekiah, Private. Enlisted June 29, 1861, at age 19 in Haywood County. Deserted Sept. 5, 1862, but returned to duty Nov. 19, 1862. Deserted again on an unspecified date after February 1863 but returned to duty Apr. 27, 1863. Deserted for third time around Aug. 1, 1864, and went over to the enemy. Took the oath in eastern Tennessee in December 1864.

Inman, William Pinkney, Private. Enlisted June 29, 1861, at age 22 in Haywood County. Wounded at Malvern Hill, Va., July 1, 1862, and returned to duty July 15, 1862. Deserted Sept. 5, 1862, but returned to duty Nov. 19, 1862. Hospitalized at Petersburg, Va., Aug. 21, 1864, with a gunshot wound of the neck. Deserted from hospital at Raleigh, N.C., around Nov. 2, 1864, and went over to the enemy. Took the oath in eastern Tennessee in December 1864 and subsequently was shot and killed by the home guard as he made his way home.

Jones, George W., Private. Enlisted Aug. 12, 1861, at age 29 in Buncombe County. Died in Buncombe or Haywood County July 4, 1862, of "fever."

Jones, Isaac W., Private. Enlisted June 10, 1864, in Johnston County. Captured at Fort Stedman, Va., Mar. 25, 1865, and confined at Point Lookout, Md. Released June 28, 1865, after taking the oath.

Jones, John R., Musician. Enlisted June 29, 1861, at age 21 in Haywood County. Appointed musician Apr. 28, 1862. Died of wounds Aug. 13, 1864. Place and date wounded not reported.

Laughter, Arthur, Private. Previously served in Company A of this regiment and enlisted in this company in Henderson County July 16, 1862, as a substitute. Reported under arrest in January–February 1864 for unknown reason. Confined at E.D.M. Prison in Richmond, Va., until released in May 1864 after volunteering to serve in the defense of Richmond against the Sheridan raid. Deserted to the enemy Feb. 28, 1865, and confined at Washington, D.C. Released around Mar. 6, 1865, after taking the oath.

Long, Joseph F., Private. Enlisted June 29, 1861, at age 22 in Haywood County. Deserted Jan. 28, 1864, but returned to duty on an unspecified date. Hospitalized at Petersburg, Va., with a gunshot wound of the left hand received on Aug. 21, 1864. Reported absent wounded or absent sick through February 1865.

Luther, Dillard T., Private. Enlisted May 1, 1864, in Haywood County. Present or accounted for until discharged "by civil authority" Sept. 30, 1864.

Mahaffey, Francis M., Private. Enlisted Sept. 10, 1861, at age 33 in Buncombe County. Wounded in the arm at Fredericksburg, Va., Dec. 13, 1862, and returned to duty prior to Jan. 1, 1863. Captured near Petersburg, Va., Apr. 2, 1865, and confined at Point Lookout, Md. Released June 29, 1865, after taking the oath.

Mahaffey, John W., Private. Enlisted June 29, 1861, at age 27 in Haywood County. Discharged Apr. 30, 1862, by reason of disability. Reenlisted in the company Aug. 15, 1863. Deserted on the march Jan. 28, 1864, and went over to the enemy. Took the oath at Knoxville, Tenn., around May 22, 1864.

Mahaffey, Joseph H., Private. Enlisted Sept. 1, 1863, at age 42 in Haywood County. Deserted on the march Feb. 1, 1864, and returned to duty prior to Jan. 1, 1865. Present or accounted for through February 1865.

Mann, Joseph B., Sr., Corporal. Enlisted June 29, 1861, at age 18 in Haywood County. Promoted to corporal Sept. 10, 1862. Broke his right arm at the Battle of the Crater July 30, 1864. Reported absent on furlough through February 1865.

Mann, William B., Private. Enlisted Aug. 15, 1863, at age 41 in Haywood County. Reported under arrest in January–February 1864 for unknown reason. Confined at E.D.M. Prison in Richmond, Va., until released May 1864 after volunteering to serve in the defense of Richmond against the Sheridan raid. No further records.

Meece, James Bradford, Private. Enlisted June 29, 1861, at age 19 in Haywood County. Promoted to sergeant Apr. 30, 1862, but reduced to ranks around Nov. 30, 1863. Deserted to the enemy after Dec. 1863. Took the oath at Knoxville, Tenn., around May 22, 1864, and was sent to Indiana.

Meece, John Medford, Private. Enlisted Feb. 14, 1862, at age 21 at Grahamville, S.C. Wounded at King's School House, Va., around June 25, 1862, resulting in amputation of index and middle fingers. Reported absent wounded until Aug. 2, 1862, when he was discharged by reason of disability from wounds.

Meece, Morgan, Private. Enlisted June 29, 1861, at age 24 in Haywood County. Wounded in an unspecified engagement in March–December 1864. Reported absent wounded through February 1865.

Meece, William R., Private. Enlisted June 29, 1861, at age 18 in Haywood County. Died at Farmville, Va., Mar. 31, 1863, of "pneumonia" and/or "diarrhoea."

Miller, Francis M., Private. Enlisted Mar. 17, 1862, at age 25 in Haywood County. Died in the hospital at Wilson, N.C., Apr. 1 or Apr. 10, 1863, of "typhoid fever."

Moore, John C., Private. Enlisted June 10, 1864, at age 20 in Moore County. Captured in hospital at Richmond, Va., Apr. 3, 1865. Paroled around Apr. 18, 1865.

Murray, Luther W., 1st Sergeant. Enlisted June 29, 1861, at age 17 in Haywood County. Captured at Frederick, Md., Sept. 12, 1862, and confined at Fort Delaware, Del. Paroled and exchanged at Aiken's Landing, James River, Va., Nov. 10, 1862. Returned to duty prior to Jan. 1, 1863. Promoted to sergeant in March–December 1864 and promoted to first sergeant in January–February 1865. Captured near Petersburg, Va., Apr. 2, 1865, and confined at Point Lookout, Md. Released June 15, 1865, after taking the oath.

Norton, James E., Private. Enlisted June 29, 1861, at age 23 in Haywood County. Present or accounted for through Feb. 1865 but reported absent sick during most of that period.

Osborne, Roland Calloway, Private. Enlisted June 29, 1861, at age 24 in Haywood County. Died in hospital at Williamsburg, Va., Aug. 5, 1862, of "febris typhoides."

Poston, Robert, Private. Enlisted June 29, 1861, at age 38 in Haywood County. Discharged July 16, 1862, for being over age.

Pressley, Daniel N., Private. Enlisted June 29, 1861, at age 23 in Haywood County. Deserted to the enemy on an unspecified date after February 1864. Took the oath at Knoxville, Tenn., around May 22, 1864.

Pressley, Joshua A., Private. Enlisted June 29, 1861, at age 18 in Haywood County. Died in hospital at Petersburg, Va., around Aug. 24, 1862, of "febris typhoides."

Pressley, Nelson A., Private. Enlisted June 29, 1861, at age 21 in Haywood County. Died in hospital at Petersburg, Va., Aug. 21, 1862, of "fever."

Queen, Robert H., Private. Enlisted Mar. 17, 1862, at age 25 in Haywood County. Deserted Aug. 29, 1862, but returned to duty July 1, 1863. Deserted again Aug. 17, 1863.

Reece, Amos M., Private. Enlisted June 29, 1861, at age 20 in Haywood County. Died in hospital at Grahamville, S.C., Dec. 25, 1861, of "pneumonia."

Reece, Isaac N., Private. Enlisted June 29, 1861, at age 21 in Haywood County. Killed at Malvern Hill, Va., July 1, 1862.

Reece, John V., Musician. Enlisted July 13, 1861, at age 17 in Haywood County. Enlisted as musician and present or accounted for until discharged around Sept. 14,

1861, by reason of "disability caused by an old cut on his foot." Later served as corporal in Company I, 62nd Regiment N.C. Troops.

Reece, Jonathan K., Private. Enlisted Aug. 6, 1861, at age 23 in Buncombe County. Present or accounted for through February 1865.

Reece, William L., Private. Enlisted June 29, 1861, at age 25 in Haywood County. Deserted Aug. 29, 1862, but returned to duty on an unspecified date. Deserted again around Mar. 27, 1863, and reported under arrest in July–August 1863 and later confined at Castle Thunder Prison, Richmond, Va., in September–October 1863. Reported under arrest at Weldon in November–December 1863. Executed Feb. 18, 1864, "for murdering G. W. Chambers" while a deserter.

Rhodes, William B., Private. Enlisted June 29, 1861, at age 24 in Haywood County. Died at Grahamville, S.C., Jan. 30 or 31, 1862, of "typhoid fever."

Roberson, Isaac W., Private. Enlisted June 29, 1861, at age 20 in Haywood County. Enlisted as corporal but reduced to ranks Apr. 28, 1862. Present or accounted for through February 1865.

Rogers, John C., Private. Enlisted June 29, 1861, at age 23 in Haywood County. Promoted to second sergeant Apr. 30, 1862, but reduced to ranks Sept. 30, 1862. Present or accounted for through February 1865 (on sick furlough).

Rogers, Matthew McA., Private. Enlisted July 18, 1861, at age 22 in Haywood County. Present or accounted for through June 1863 but reported absent sick during much of that period. Listed as a deserter and dropped from the rolls of the company July 8, 1863. Returned to duty Sept. 21, 1863. Transferred to Company A, 19th Regiment N.C. Troops Nov. 16, 1864, but deserted prior to reporting to new unit. Took the oath at Knoxville, Tenn., around Mar. 10, 1865.

Scott, James P., Private. Enlisted June 10, 1864, at "Pearson." Appointed sergeant major Jan. 1, 1865, and transferred to the field and staff of this regiment.

Singleton, James Anderson, Corporal. Enlisted Aug. 14, 1861, at age 21 in Haywood County. Wounded at Sharpsburg, Md., Sept. 17, 1862, and returned to duty in November–December 1862. Promoted to corporal in March–December 1864. Present or accounted for through February 1865.

Singleton, James M., Private. Enlisted Mar. 18, 1862, at age 20 in Haywood County. Died in hospital at Petersburg, Va., Jan. 4, 1863, of "typhoid pneumonia."

Singleton, John C., Private. Enlisted July 30, 1861, at age 26 in Buncombe County. Promoted to corporal Oct. 16, 1861, but reduced to ranks Apr. 30, 1862. Present or accounted for through February 1865.

Singleton, Samuel P., Private. Enlisted Apr. 1863 at age 24 in Haywood County. Discharged in June 1863 by reason of disability.

Singleton, William A. S. C., Private. Enlisted Aug. 14, 1861, at age 16 in Haywood County. Present or accounted for until discharged July 16, 1862, for being under age.

Smith, John A., Musician. Previously served as Private in Company C of this regiment and transferred to this company and appointed musician (fifer) May 1, 1862. Wounded in the jaw at King's School House, Va., June 25, 1862, and returned to duty Oct. 11, 1862. Deserted Mar. 27, 1863.

Sorrells, Henry Jackson, Corporal. Enlisted June 29, 1861, at age 23 in Haywood County. Promoted to corporal Apr. 28, 1862. Died in hospital at Petersburg, Va., July 30, 1862, of "febris typhoides."

Stamey, John, Private. Enlisted June 29, 1861, at age 21 in Haywood County. Died in hospital at Goldsboro, N.C., around June 25, 1862, of "fever."

Thomas, John G., Private. Enlisted June 29, 1861, at age 31 in Haywood County. Deserted on the march Nov. 27, 1863, and went over to the enemy. Took the oath at Knoxville, Tenn., around May 25, 1864.

Thompson, Joseph M., Private. Enlisted June 29, 1861, at age 18 in Haywood County. Wounded at King's School House, Va., June 25, 1862. Died of wounds at Richmond, Va., June 27, 1862.

Thompson, William, Private. Enlisted June 29, 1861, at age 28 in Haywood County. Died in hospital at Petersburg, Va., July 30, 1862, of "dysentery" and/or "fever."

Tindle, J. R., Private. Paroled at Farmville, Va., around Apr. 11–21, 1865.

Trull, John W., Private. Enlisted June 29, 1861, at age 21 in Haywood County. Wounded in the left foot at Fredericksburg, Va., Dec. 13, 1862, and returned to duty in March 1863. Present or accounted for through February 1865.

Vance, William P., Private. Enlisted July 23, 1861, at age 35 in Buncombe County. Discharged July 16, 1862, for being over age.

Williams, William H., Private. Enlisted June 29, 1861, at age 20 in Haywood County. Deserted "in front of the enemy" June 1, 1863.

Wilson, John C., Private. Previously served in Company B of this regiment and transferred to this company May 1, 1862. Wounded in the left hand at Fredericksburg, Va., Dec. 13, 1862, and returned to duty in January–February 1863. Deserted to the enemy around Feb. 28, 1865, and confined at Washington, D.C. Released around Mar. 6, 1865, after taking the oath.

APPENDIX B

Haywood Highlanders—Casualties of War

The table below presents the casualty statistics for the Haywood Highlanders during the Civil War.

Period of Service		Killed	Died of Wounds	Wounded	Died of Disease	Deserted
Theater	Date					
Carolina Coastal Duty	9/18/1861–6/19/1862	0	0	1	4	0
Seven Days' Battles	6/20/1862–8/25/1862	1	1	8	10	0
King's School House	6/25/1862	0	1	4		
Malvern Hill	7/1/1862	1	0	4		
Maryland Campaign	8/26/1862–10/31/1862	0	0	2	1	1
Fredericksburg	11/1/1862–1/3/1863	0	0	3	0	
N.C./Virginia Coastal Defense	1/4/1863–5/6/1864	2	0	0	6	17
Richmond/Petersburg Defense	5/7/1864–4/9/1865	3	4	16	1	12
TOTALS		6	5	30	22	30

Note: One man (William Reece) was executed, for murdering G. W. Chambers. Chambers' death is included in the above statistics; however, Reece's death is not counted.

Appendix C

Haywood Highlanders—Every Move They Made

CAROLINA COASTAL DEFENSE			
Date	Location	Movement	Remarks
9/18/1861	Asheville, N.C.	Marched by foot to Morganton, N.C., arriving about 9/20.	Morganton was the railroad's western terminus in North Carolina during the Civil War.
about 9/25/1861	Morganton, N.C.	Marched by train to Raleigh, N.C., stopping for a couple of days to be outfitted with uniforms. Entrained again on 9/27 and marched by railroad to Wilmington, N.C., arriving 9/28.	Encamped at Camp Davis near Wilmington.
11/5/1861	Wilmington, N.C.	Marched by train to Charleston, S.C., arriving on 11/7.	
11/8/1861	Charleston, S.C.	Marched by train to Coosawhatchie, S.C., arriving the same day.	Encamped in vicinity of Fort Beauregard.
11/14/1861	Fort Beauregard	Marched by foot about 9 miles to Grahamville, S.C., arriving the same day.	Encamped at Camp Lee.
3/15/1862	Grahamville, S.C.	Marched by train to Kinston, N.C., arriving on 3/18.	
3/21/1862	Kinston, N.C.	Marched by foot about 8 miles west toward Goldsboro, N.C.	Encamped at Camp Johnston near railroad.
3/23/1862	Kinston, N.C., vicinity	Marched by foot back to Kinston, N.C.	Encamped for 2 nights and performed guard duty.

Date	Location	Movement	Remarks
3/25/1862	Kinston, N.C.	Marched by foot back to camp, arriving same day.	Encamped near Kinston.
3/28/1862	Kinston, N.C., vicinity	Marched by foot back to Kinston, N.C., arriving same day.	
3/29/1862	Kinston, N.C.	Marched by foot about 5 miles in direction of New Bern, N.C.	Encamped at Camp Ransom.
5/2/1862	Camp Ransom	Marched by foot to Kinston, N.C.	
6/1/1862	Kinston, N.C.	Marched by foot about 8 miles west toward Goldsboro, N.C.	Encamped at Camp Johnston.

SEVEN DAYS' BATTLES

Date	Location	Movement	Remarks
6/19/1862	Kinston, N.C.	Marched by train to Petersburg, Va., arriving on 6/21/1862. Marched by foot 2 miles north and encamped.	Encamped near Petersburg.
6/24/1862	Petersburg, Va., vicinity	Marched by foot to vicinity of Richmond, Va., arriving on 6/25.	Haywood Highlanders rushed down Williamsburg Road to participate in the engagement at King's School House, Va., on 6/25/1862.
6/26/1862 to 7/1/1862	Richmond, Va., vicinity	Haywood Highlanders fought several skirmishes with the retreating enemy forces on the south side of the Chickahominy River. On 7/1/1862 the Haywood Highlanders fought in the Battle of Malvern Hill and subsequent to that action followed the enemy to Harrison's Landing on the James River. At that safe harbor the Union gunboats kept the pursuing Confederate army and the 25th Regiment's troops at a distance.	Participated in the final hours of the Battle of Malvern Hill.
7/6/1862	Richmond, Va., vicinity	Marched by foot to Drewry's Bluff, Va., arriving by 7/7.	Encamped at Drewry's Bluff.

| 7/30/1862 | Drewry's Bluff, Va., | Marched by foot to below Petersburg, Va., and encamped. | Encamped near Petersburg. |
| 8/19/1862 | Petersburg, Va., vicinity | Marched to the vicinity of Richmond, Va. | |

MARYLAND CAMPAIGN

Date	Location	Movement	Remarks
8/27/1862	Richmond, Va.	Marched by Virginia Central Railroad to Rapidan Station, Va., arriving on 8/28.	
8/31/1862	Rapidan Station, Va., vicinity	Marched by foot toward Maryland via Culpeper, Jefferson, Warrenton, and Leesburg, Va. Crossed the Potomac River on 9/7 and reached Frederick, Md., on 9/9.	Encamped near Frederick.
9/10/1862	Frederick, Md., vicinity	Marched by foot back across the Potomac River at Point of Rocks on 9/11 and continued march until reaching Harpers Ferry, Va., on 9/13.	Haywood Highlanders participated in the siege and capture of Harpers Ferry 9/13–9/15/1862.
9/16/1862	Harpers Ferry, Va., vicinity	Marched by foot across the Potomac River at Shepherdstown, Va., and arrived late on the night of 9/16 at Sharpsburg, Md.	Haywood Highlanders participated in the Battle of Antietam Run (Sharpsburg) on 9/17/1862 and played a key role in the Confederate victory.
9/18/1862	Sharpsburg, Md.	Left the battlefield on the night of 9/18–9/19 and marched by foot back across the Potomac River at Shepherdstown, Va., to the environs of Martinsburg, Va., arriving there about 9/20.	Encamped near Martinsburg.

Date	Location	Movement	Remarks
10/1/1862	Martinsburg, Va., vicinity	Marched by foot to Winchester, Va.	Encamped near Winchester.
10/23/1862	Winchester, Va., vicinity	Marched by foot to Paris, Va., arriving on 10/25.	Encamped near Paris.

HEIGHTS OF FREDERICKSBURG

Date	Location	Movement	Remarks
10/31/1862	Paris, Va., vicinity	Marched by foot via Culpeper Courthouse, Va., and encamped briefly.	Encamped at Culpeper Courthouse.
11/8/1862	Culpeper Courthouse, Va.	Marched by foot to Madison Courthouse, Va., and encamped for a few days.	Encamped at Madison Courthouse.
11/18/1862	Madison Courthouse, Va.	Marched by foot to the vicinity of Fredericksburg, Va., arriving there about 11/20.	Encamped in the Fredericksburg vicinity until the end of the year 1862. On 12/13/1862 the Haywood Highlanders participated meritoriously in the Battle of Fredericksburg.

EASTERN NORTH CAROLINA COASTAL DEFENSE

Date	Location	Movement	Remarks
1/3/1863	Fredericksburg, Va.	Marched by foot to Petersburg, Va., via Hanover Junction and Richmond, Va. arriving about 1/7.	Encamped near Petersburg.
1/17/1863	Petersburg, Va.	Marched by Petersburg & Weldon Railroad and Wilmington & Weldon Railroad to Warsaw Station, N.C., located 40 miles below Goldsboro, N.C., arriving on 1/18.	Encamped near Warsaw Station.
1/20/1863	Warsaw Station, N.C., vicinity	Marched by foot 10 miles southeastward to Kenansville, N.C., arriving same day.	Encamped near Kenansville.

2/22/1863	Kenansville, N.C., vicinity	Marched by foot 8 miles to train depot at Magnolia, N.C. Entrained there and marched by Wilmington & Weldon Railroad to Wilmington, N.C., arriving same day.	Encamped at Wilmington.
2/24/1863	Wilmington, N.C.	Marched by foot approximately 2 or 3 miles east of Wilmington, N.C.	Encamped near Wilmington.
2/27/1863	Wilmington, N.C., vicinity	Marched 9 miles north of Wilmington, N.C., to railroad bridge over Northeast Cape Fear River, arriving same day	Encamped at Northeast River Station, N.C., and guarded the railroad bridge.
3/7/1863	Northeast River railroad bridge	Marched by foot to camp below Wilmington, N.C., arriving same day.	Encamped near Wilmington.
3/10/1863	Wilmington, N.C., vicinity	Marched by foot to Topsail Sound, N.C.	Encamped at Topsail Sound.
3/25/1863	Topsail Sound, N.C.	Marched by foot to Wilmington, N.C. Entrained there and marched by railroad to Goldsboro, N.C., arriving at night on 3/28.	
3/29/1863	Goldsboro, N.C.	Marched by train to Kinston, N.C., arriving on same day.	
3/30/1863	Kinston, N.C.	Marched by foot about 7 miles in the direction of Trenton, N.C.	Encamped near Trenton.
4/1/1863	Trenton, N.C. vicinity	Marched by foot to Kinston, N.C.	
4/2/1863	Kinston, N.C.	Marched by foot to the vicinity of Washington, N.C., arriving on 4/5.	Encamped near Washington.
4/7/1863	Washington, N.C., vicinity	Marched by foot to Swift Creek, N.C., approximately 13 miles south of Washington, N.C., arriving the same day.	Encamped at Swift Creek.

4/8/1863	Swift Creek, N.C.	Marched by foot to Cross Roads, 8 miles above Washington, N.C., arriving same day.	Encamped near Washington. Haywood Highlanders participated in Confederate Gen. D. H. Hill's ill-fated siege and attempt to capture Union-held Washington.
4/9/1863	Washington, N.C., vicinity	Marched by foot and crossed over to the north side of the Tar River near Washington, N.C.	Encamped near Washington.
4/10/1863	Washington, N.C., vicinity	Marched by foot and re-crossed to the south side of the Tar River near Washington, N.C.	Encamped near Washington.
4/17/1863	Washington, N.C., vicinity	Marched by foot in the direction of Greenville, N.C., eventually arriving in Kinston, N.C., on 4/20.	Encamped near Kinston.
4/29/1863	near Kinston, N.C.	Marched by foot to Gum Swamp, about 9 miles southeast of Kinston, N.C., and arrived same day.	Encamped in fort at Gum Swamp. On 4/30/1863 the 25th Regiment repulsed a small force of enemy troops at Gum Swamp. However, on 5/22/1863 a larger Union assault surprised and routed the 25th and 56th regiments stationed at Gum Swamp.
5/27/1863	Kinston, N.C.	Marched by railroad to Petersburg, Va. arriving on 5/28.	

5/28/1863	Petersburg, Va.	Marched by railroad to Richmond, Va. arriving on same day.	
6/2/1863	Richmond, Va.	Marched by railroad to Petersburg, Va., and then on to Ivor Station near the Blackwater River in Virginia.	Encamped in the vicinity of Ivor Station, near the Blackwater River.
6/12/1863	Ivor Station, near the Blackwater River in Va.	Marched by railroad to Petersburg, Va., and then on to a point near Drewry's Bluff, Va., arriving the same day.	Encamped at Drewry's Bluff.
6/17/1863	Drewry's Bluff, Va.	Marched by railroad to Petersburg, Va.	Encamped near Petersburg.
6/21/1863	Petersburg, Va.	Marched by railroad to a point near Drewry's Bluff, Va.	Encamped at Drewry's Bluff.
6/25/1863	Drewry's Bluff, Va.	Marched by foot via pontoon bridge to north side of James River and then on to the vicinity of Seven Pines, Va.	Encamped near Seven Pines.
7/12/1863	Seven Pines, Va., vicinity	Marched by foot and railroad to Petersburg, Va.	Encamped near Petersburg.
7/20/1863	Petersburg, Va.	Marched by railroad to Weldon, N.C.	Encamped near Weldon, N.C.
7/22/1863	Weldon, N.C.	Marched by railroad back to Petersburg, Va.	
7/28/1863	Petersburg, Va.	Marched by railroad to Garysburg, N.C.	
7/29/1863	Garysburg, N.C.	Marched by foot to Jackson, N.C., arriving on 7/30.	Encamped 3 miles west of Jackson, N.C.
8/1/1863	Jackson, N.C., vicinity	Marched by foot to Garysburg, N.C.	Encamped at Garysburg, N.C.
8/3/1863	Garysburg, N.C.	Marched by foot to camp 2 miles west of Garysburg, N.C.	Encamped 2 miles west of Garysburg, N.C.

Date	Location	Movement	Notes
10/16/1863	Weldon, N.C., and Garysburg, N.C., vicinity		A large detachment of troops from the 25th Regiment was deployed to Western North Carolina to combat a band of Tories near Warm Springs, N.C.
11/9/1863	Weldon, N.C., vicinity	Marched by foot 13 miles on scout below Jackson, N.C., and returned to Weldon, N.C., on 11/11.	Encamped near Weldon.
11/29/1863	Weldon, N.C.	Marched by railroad to Petersburg, Va.	
12/16/1863	Petersburg, Va.	Marched by railroad back to Weldon, N.C.	
12/20/1863	Weldon, N.C.	Marched by railroad to a point near Franklin, Va.	
12/22/1863	Franklin, Va.	Marched by railroad to Weldon, N.C.	Encamped near Weldon.
1/28/1864	Weldon, N.C.	Marched by railroad to Goldsboro, N.C., arriving the same day.	
1/29/1864	Goldsboro, N.C.	Marched by railroad to Kinston, N.C., arriving the same day.	
1/30/1864	Kinston, N.C.	Marched by foot to the vicinity of New Bern, N.C., arriving on 1/31.	Haywood Highlanders participated in Confederate Gen. George Picket's unsuccessful attempt to retake New Bern from Federal forces on 2/1—2/2/1864.
2/3/1864	New Bern, N.C.	Marched by foot back to Kinston, N.C., arriving on 2/5.	
2/6/1864	Kinston, N.C.	Marched by railroad to Weldon, N.C., arriving same day.	Encamped near Weldon.

2/25/1864	Weldon, N.C.	Marched by railroad to Franklin, Va., arriving same day.	Encamped near Franklin.
2/27/1864	Franklin, Va.	Marched by foot through Gates and Pasquotank counties (N.C.) on 2/27 and 2/28 and marched to South Mills, N.C. (near Elizabeth City, N.C.), on 2/29.	Haywood Highlanders participated in the Confederate action at Suffolk, Va., on 3/9/1864, in which the Federals were driven out of the town.
3/12/1864	Suffolk, Va., vicinity	Returned to Weldon, N.C.	
4/12/1864	Weldon, N.C.	Moved to vicinity of Tarboro, N.C.	
4/15/1864	Tarboro, N.C., vicinity	Marched to Plymouth, N.C., arriving about 4/17/1864.	Haywood Highlanders participated in Confederate Gen. Robert F. Hoke's capture of Plymouth, N.C., on 4/17–4/20/1864.
4/21/1864	Plymouth, N.C.	Marched by foot to Washington, N.C., and then on to New Bern, N.C.	Haywood Highlanders participated in General Hoke's plans to retake these important Confederate towns. However, Hoke received orders on 5/6/1864 to come with his troops to Petersburg, Va., to fend off a pending Union assault on Richmond.

RICHMOND AND PETERSBURG DEFENSE			
Date	Location	Movement	Remarks
5/7/1864	New Bern, N.C., vicinity	Marched by foot to Kinston, N.C., arriving on the morning of 5/8.	
5/8/1864	Kinston, N.C.	Marched by railroad via Goldsboro, N.C., and Weldon, N.C., to a point where the railroad was interrupted some 20 miles south of Stony Creek Station, Va. Marched by foot around the interruption and through the night to Stony Creek Station. Entrained there on 5/10 and marched by railroad to Petersburg, Va., arriving on the same day.	
5/10/1864	Petersburg, Va.	Hurriedly marched to Swift Run Creek, Va., and then on to Drewry's Bluff, Va., arriving on 5/11/1864.	Haywood Highlanders immediately engaged in continuous fighting around Drewry's Bluff for the ensuing several days and then were assigned to keep Union Gen. Benjamin F. Butler's forces bottled up at Bermuda Hundred.
6/4/1864	Drewry's Bluff, Va., vicinity	Marched by foot to Bottom's Bridge, near Richmond, Va.	Encamped near Bottom's Bridge.
6/9/1864	Bottom's Bridge, near Richmond, Va.	Marched by foot to Chaffin's Farm, Va., located across the James River from Drewry's Bluff, Va.	Encamped near Chaffin's Bluff.

6/15/1864	Chaffin's Farm, Va., on the James River	Marched by foot through the night crossing the pontoon bridge over the James River and reaching Petersburg, Va., on 6/16.	Haywood Highlanders were instantly thrown into furious fighting then taking place on 6/16 and 6/17/1864, as Confederate Gen. P. G. T. Beauregard defended Petersburg, Va., from heavy Union assaults.

After successfully defending against the Union attacks on Petersburg, Virginia, on June 16 and June 17, 1864, the 25th Regiment N.C., and its Company F, or Haywood Highlanders, remained in the Petersburg area for the rest of the war. The troops dug, fortified, and manned the "hideous red" trenches protecting the city throughout the hot summer of 1864 and the bitter cold winter of 1864–65. Deprivations, danger, homesickness, and hunger would be constant companions of the mountaineers from Western North Carolina, and many were those who could not bear the suffering and hardship and chose to return to their families and the seclusion of the Carolina highlands. The men of Company F who remained in the ditches participated in the great battles and lesser engagements that were waged during the long Petersburg siege, including the battles of the Crater, Weldon Railroad, Fort Stedman, and Five Forks.

Appendix D
Selected Excerpts from the Lenoir Letters

THOMAS ISAAC LENOIR AND HIS FAMILY were prolific letter-writers, as were many during the nineteenth century before the telephone and, much later, electronic mail provided instant long-distance communication. Tom wrote from the lonely confines of his log cabin, the comfortable Fort Defiance plantation home, a crowded New York barroom, noisy general stores, his boarding school, the university, a county courthouse, and other sundry places that offered brief respite and refuge. Information gleaned from hundreds of Lenoir family letters has been incorporated into this volume. Excerpts from a few of these are presented in this section so that readers can gain an appreciation for the appearance, style, structure, and content of letters—some scratched out using quill and ink—recorded more than one hundred and fifty years ago.

Unless otherwise noted, letters are from the Lenoir Family Papers, Southern Historical Collection, Wilson Library, University of North Carolina at Chapel Hill, and used by permission.

Morganton Sept 16th 1806

Dear Sir

Mr Gambill informs me that he is to call by the Fort, to see you about your taxes due in Ashe. I should have put money in the hands of Mr Gambill to pay the Tax on my land there, had I not expected to have seen you what title I have got, to bear my expences to Buncombe &C. I should therefore be glad if while paying for yours, you would pay for mine also.

Louisa has a wish to go to Buncombe, and to gratify her curiosity I have consented to go with her. We have appointed to start the day after tomorrow, and shortly after we return, we intend going to Wilkes —

It does not afford me much pleasure to reflect on the unprofitable manner in which I have spent so much time in the prime of life, and to think of my present situation, that I am without a home, without any flattering prospects of getting one that will be agreable, and without any apparent means of rendering society the service, or my friends that satisfaction I could wish, causes me much uneasiness.

I think it highly necessary for me to change my present manner of living, and promise myself much benifit from your advice and

Thomas Lenoir to General William Lenoir (Thomas' father), Sept. 16, 1806, page 1 of 3: A dejected Thomas Lenoir communicates that he has consented to take his wife, Louisa, to Buncombe County (present-day Haywood County) to see the land her father, Waighstill Avery, desires to endow to her.

time, & he had gone home — The Superintendt of the Deaf & Dumb Asylum spoke very favour-ably indeed of him — Said that he was one of the best boys that he ever saw &c.

We stayed one night at Sam:l Finley's, where we were made quite at home, & very kindly treated — He gave us a letter of introduction which was of some service to us —

In Staunton, we visited the Deaf & Dumb, the Blind, & Lunatic Asylums — & were much pleased with those institutions —

From Staunton, we went to Wiergers & Weats Caves — Then through Strasburg & Winchester, &c. to Harper's Ferry — We did not get to see any of Mr Stewart's folks —

At Harper's Ferry we stayed about a day & half then walked by the side of the Canal 61 miles to Washington City — This canal appeared to us, to be a stupendous work — The aqueducts across the Monocacy & Catoctin are splendid — The Monocacy is near 200 yd wide where the aqueduct crosses —

Our expenses so far have been fully as great as I expected — In the country is costs us just about $1.75 p. day for both — In the towns it is more — At the White Sulphur Springs they charged $1.75 each p. day — Here it is $1.50 each — Too trifling!!!

Tom Lenoir to Thomas Lenoir (Tom's father), Aug. 10, 1843, page 2 of 3: After arriving in Washington City, Tom writes to his father describing how he and brother Walter had walked sixty-one miles along side of the Chesapeake and Ohio Canal. Tom allows, "This canal appeared to us, to be a stupendous work."

East Fork January 3rd 1846

Dear Sir these lines will inform you that we are all well at present & that we have plenty to eat but I do not believe it will be a common thing in this country next summer I wrote to you in my last letter that I had killed 14 head of hogs but had not weighed them they weighed 2486 lbs & I killed 6 yesterday that weighed 1260 lbs the Berkshire stag weighed 365 lbs the whole amount of pork killed is 4086 lbs & there is 5 hogs to kill yet your stock of all kinds are doing very well I have not finished gathering corn yet I have both big cribs full & about 300 bu to gather yet I mentioned to you in my last letter that I did not expect to continue with you any longer than my time was out but I have arranged my business so that I could stay until next fall if you want me & if you wish to employ until next fall I would be glad you would send me word if you do not expect to come out in a short time the reason I want know is that I have contracted for a piece of land & have a chance of renting it next summer & I cannot rent but until I know whether I stay any longer with you or not the neighbours & friends are generally well so nothing more at present but remaining your friend &c

Col. Thomas Lenoir   A C Hartgrove

A. C. Hartgrove to Thomas Lenoir, Jan. 3, 1846: Hartgrove, Thomas Lenoir's overseer of his Haywood farming enterprise, apparently having contracted for his own piece of land to work in Haywood, communicates that he will no longer continue to work for Lenoir.

Thomas Lenoir to Tom Lenoir, March 28, 1846, page 2 of 2: After leaving Tom in charge of the Haywood County East Fork farming enterprise the senior Lenoir offers some last-minute words of advice and direction to his son regarding his duty. Tom is also instructed to write every two weeks and "oftener in case of unexpected occurrences."

to tame some wild shoats, & I have been regretting ever since that I was not at home — for about that time they had a great frolic here, & I would not have missed it for all the wild shoats —

Some of the boys were setting up coal wood, & one of them standing in the shop, when a large bear came pacing along on the track of the hogs with his head down, & passed between them and the orchard fence without appearing to notice them, & went on to the cabbage patch where he seemed disposed to climb the fence & take hold of my berkshire, but some of them called the dogs, & he turned back & jumped into the orchard & met the dogs, (for they all (four) happened to be at the house,) & they turned him toward the cribs & he jumped into the yard, & the dogs fought him around the cribs & all over the garden, & across the creek — When he would attempt to climb the fences or trees they would pull him back until they worried him almost down — One of the boys shot him 3 times, & another beat him with a hand spike, but he was still able to travel a little, & seized Bruce by the head & was biting him cruelly, when one of them fell upon with an axe & put an end to him —

He was almost too poor for pork, but was as long a bear as I ever saw, & a real old hog thief no doubt —

Tom Lenoir to Thomas Lenoir, Feb. 13, about 1847, page 3 of 3: Tom tells a "bear tale" about how his "boys" killed a bear on the farm. It was "almost too poor to pork," Tom writes, "but was as long a bear as I ever saw, & a real old hog thief no doubt."

The Den Oct 16th 1852

Rufus T. Lenoir Esq.
Fort Defiance
N.C.

Dear Brother

A fellow that was noted for his eloquence & ingenuity in swearing, once drove a wagon loaded with large turneps up a long steep hill — When he reached the top he looked back & discovered that the gate of his wagon had just dropped off, & all his turneps were scampering down the hill like so many frightened rabits — He sprang from his horse, & threw down his hat, intending to let off one of his best effusions — But upon reflecting a moment, he declared that it was no use to try, for said he "I cant do it justice"

Well I went down to the Post office yesterday evening expecting to meet you, but when I found your letter there instead of yourself, I thought of that Turnep Man, said confound it, & came to a full stop —

You ought to have come — It is the right time to take those cattle if they are going — You have got me in a fix, & I dont know what to do — but think that I will start at the time appointed with the sheep, & will take Rover to Mr. A. W. Finley — Poor Erve will be disappointed now, for if you come for the cattle, it will not suit for him to go with you, for there will be nobody with him coming back &c. &c. I think you may expect me about the first day of Nov. & you must be ready to start back with me very soon thereafter —

I havent time to write any more, & I am glad of it — Your disconsolate brother Tom

Tom Lenoir to Rufus T. Lenoir (Tom's brother), Oct. 16, 1852: In a typical letter from Tom to brother Rufus, his favorite correspondent, he relates a joke.

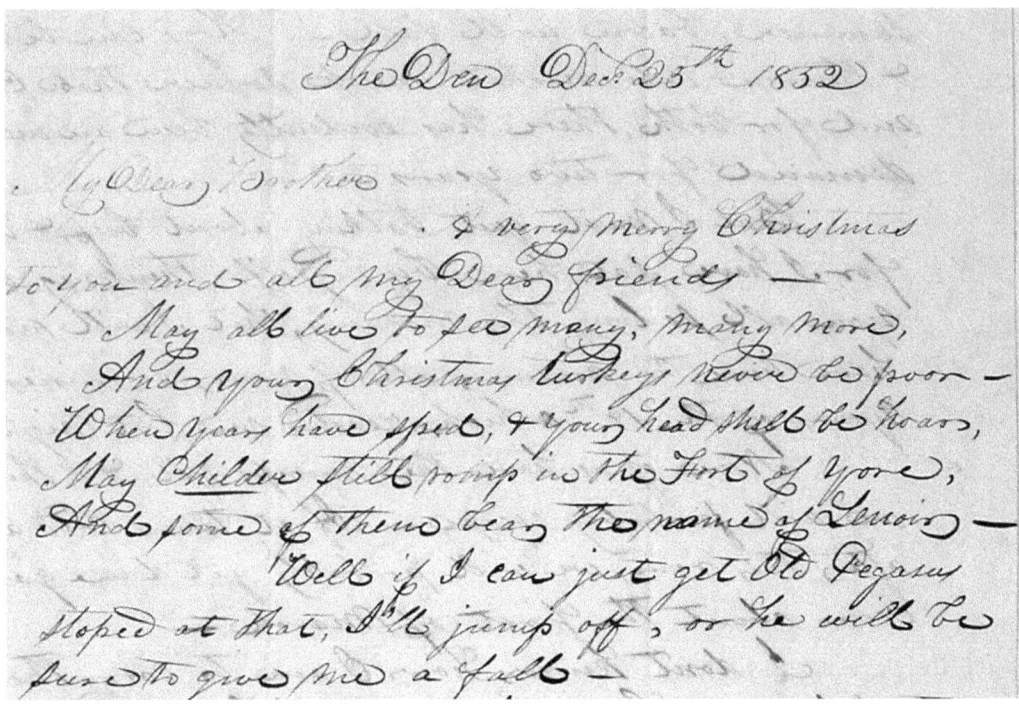

On Christmas day in 1852 a lonely Tom Lenoir sat before the hearth in his Den and penned a letter to Rufus and the folks at Fort Defiance. The excerpt shown above and transcribed below reveals the East Fork farmer's poetic side.

> A very merry Christmas to you and all my Dear friends.
> May all live to see many, many more,
> And your Christmas turkeys never be poor.
> When years have sped, & your head shall be hoar [gray],
> May Children still romp in the Fort [Defiance] of yore,
> And some of them bear the name of Lenoir.

Pages 415–17: Tom Lenoir to Rufus T. Lenoir, Jan. 14, 1854, pages 1, 2, and 3 of 4: Tom relates a story to Rufe of two grannys who had come to Bachelor's Den (Tom's cabin) to care for the sick slave woman, Patsy. They borrowed a teaspoon of gunpowder from Tom and commenced to make their patient some "gunpowder tea." Tom declares to Rufe, "Did you ever! Who knows what important bearings it may have upon our commercial intercourse with the ancient Empire of China."

"Bachelordom" Jan'y 14th 1854

Dear Brother

You requested me to send the pedigree of Young Leviathan, but I am sorry that I can't give it more fully —

His sire was sired by Buncomb, and Buncombe by imported Emancipation — Buncomb's dam was Betsy Ruffin, & she is said to have been a thorough bred mare Owned by Dr. Hott —

Young Leviathan's Dam is Cholera — Maberry's celebrated racer — Cholera was sired by imp'd Leviathan, & Cholera's dam was John McGhee's noted Old Mare called Firetail —

We can get Betsy Ruffin's pedigree of D.H. & by writing to Ten. I can learn something more of Old Firetail — & when I see Mr. Patton I can get the pedigree of his grand dam on the sire's side — & from here I fear that he has inherited a wee drop of plebeian blood —

Well Rufe I must cut this communication short, & if you knew just how I've been fixed this morning, you would not blame me for feeling a little crusty, & in a bad mood for writing

A few hours before day this morning Patsy sent out for the Granny, & behold two came, & here they have been in my room a good part of this morning entertaining me with interesting discourses connected with changes of the weather. Moon 4646.

One says she wants no better almanic than her Guinea chickens, for when they holler all night she knows what to look for — & when she hears the fire treading snow she knows what is coming — The other says she looked in her almanic tother day & "saw that Markary was close to Jubiter & that is a sign of cold weather" —

But thank the stars (whether Jubiter & Markery, or The Seven Stars) they are out just now — I asked one of them a while ago how her Patient was, & she replied "She keeps sorter poorly & dauncy but wont get quite bad enough" but as one of them was in here a few minutes ago for a teaspoonful of gunpowder, I think its about time for me to decamp — for I have read of some horrible explosions lately — but after all it may turn out to be but a flash — but I will order my horse, & start to the Post Office —

I still think of going to Columbia, & starting next Tuesday or Wednesday — Be sure to write me immediately & direct to Columbia S.C. —

I believe I wrote to you upon this subject before but am not sure, but I certainly did to Father —

I lately bought a little mare of T. Byers, the man that bought Boomer & Rheta — She is small but quite handsome — I did not want her, but as he was owing me just $400.00, I thought it most prudent to try to collect part of it — When I come back I will sell her if I can — & would take her down the country but am told that horses are lower there than here — She is too small for my use —

If I thought you would let any body else see this, I would feel like ~~writing~~ you some of the same experience —

Love to all

Your affectionate bro.
Tom

P.S.

That old woman has come in again, and says that she put the powder in some tea for Petey — Did you ever! Well I have heard of Gunpowder tea ~~before~~, but never before of tea made of the real genuine Brimstone Gunpowder — Isn't it an important discovery? Who knows what important bearings it may have upon our commercial intercourse with the Ancient Empire of China —

Attend to it Ye Importers! Ye Politicians! Ye Statesmen! Ye Grannies! Truly this is a progressive age — The march of Science seems onward & with a rapid pace — And when considered as an inseperable adjunct to that

I was in Waynesville yesterday but did not see one case of intoxication, but I am sorry to know that the only reason was that they couldn't get the critter — The place had been drunk dry — The cause of temperance seems to make but slow progress in this County —

Something like Cholera Morbus has been prevailing a good deal in this Country, but seems to be disappearing — We are all as well as usual here, & I do not hear of any bad cases near us —

Mrs. John Sellers died about a week ago — It is thought that her death was caused by over exertion while cutting grain with a cradle — She was fifty or sixty years old — What do you think of that? Of course she was Dutch —

I suppose that Walter told you of the death of Spencer Bird — He had been afflicted a long time with something like liver complaint — He seemed to be a worthy man, & consistent Christian —

On yesterday a letter was read to the Crowd in town from Wm. H. Thomas stating that some Engineer had agreed to make a R. Road Survey from the Tennessee River to French Broad, if each County through which it passes will pay him $100.00 — Subscriptions were called for, & in a short time amounted to $130.00 — Mr. Thomas writes that Macon & Jackson will do their parts — & so we will probably have a survey, if we never get a R. Road —

Tom Lenoir to Rufus T. Lenoir, Aug. 5, 1854, page 2 of 4: Tom reports to brother Rufe that he has been in Waynesville the day before and not witnessed one case of intoxication—"probably because they could not get the critter." He also says that a letter from W. H. Thomas was read to the crowd stating that an engineer has agreed to make a railroad survey from the Tennessee River to the French Broad if each county through which it passed would pay the surveyor $100."

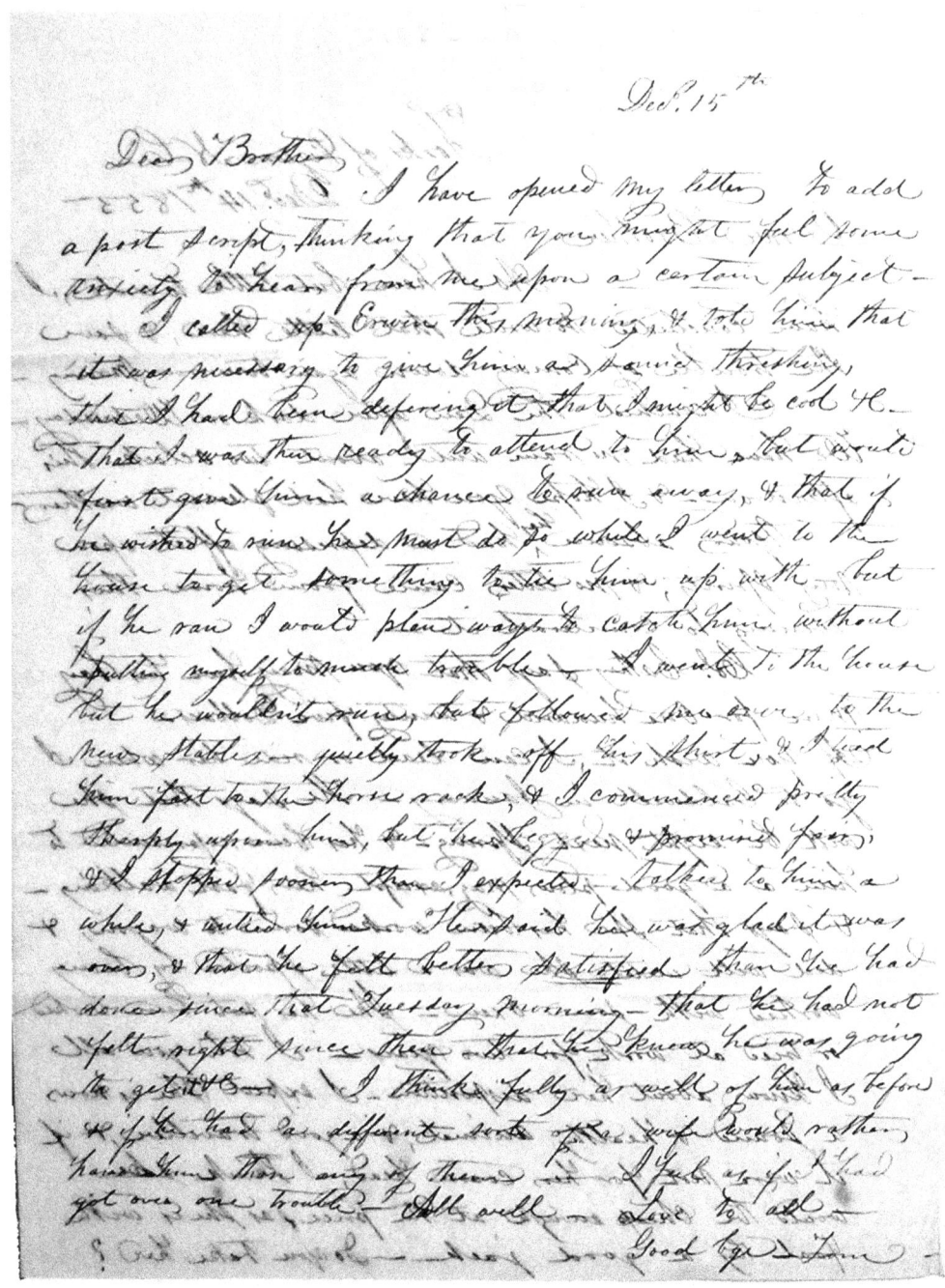

Tom Lenoir to Rufus T. Lenoir, Dec. 15, 1855, 1 of 2 pages: Although this letter is difficult to read because of the thinness of the paper and the bleed-through, Tom describes in painful detail how he has disciplined the slave, Erwin. After the cruel job was done, he writes, Erwin "was glad it was over, & that he felt better satisfied…"

do not consider myself smart enough to run much in debt for land, & then make the money by farming soon to pay for it — This would be contrary to my experience so far, & to what I have observed in others —

Upon examining the map, I find that the West line of your Black Walnut Bottom tract if extended North & South across your lands would only split one tract — & according to my calculation (just made for the first time) would only lack about sixty acres of dividing your lands into two equal parts — The upper part consisting of 17½ tracts & containing 2280 acres — & the lower part including 16½ tracts & covering 2340 acres —

It is probable that the average of the soil on the upper half is a good deal better than that on the lower half — but I would value the lower half much the highest on several accounts — Because it contains more level land — more cleared land (although some of it is worn out) & because I would have less fear about the titles, & feel much more at home at the Old Den — If I were to own much land here, I would expect to have to sell my interest in the Town of Patterson — & I intend to sell my little tracts in Watauga — There are also four negroes here that I would like to own, Isaac, Patsy, & her two children Col. C. still owns her husband, & he seems to think a good deal of his children Now my Dear Father if I have suggested any thing contrary to your wishes, I hope you will excuse it & not think me inclined to dictate to you — or obstinate in my planning — I think I can submit as willingly to have my plans modified, or completely changed, as most men can, & grieve about it as little — Your affectionate Son Tom

Tom Lenoir to Thomas Lenoir, Oct. 19, 1860, page 4 of 4: In this long letter to his father, who did not have much longer to live, Tom suggests his idea on how the senior Lenoir's immense East Fork property could be divided into two parts, an upper and a lower tract. Tom offers that he would prefer to have the lower half where the "Old Den" is located.

through Spartanburg to see Lipscomb. I must either go or come that way — I sent the bay and Meg both down by Branch late in Nov. He made a quick trip but I can't judge yet as to his success —

If I were sure of getting a good safe buggy horse in Caldwell, perhaps I would ride the mule there, & ride him back — What do you think of it?

My buggy is just standing here rusting & rotting, & I have nothing to work to it — I don't believe that any thing has been hitched to it in twelve months —

I promised Mr. Garrett that, if he would take his Daughter back to School, I would bring her back to Haywood, & I must do so, but where the horse is to be had I don't know —

Tom Lenoir to Rufus T. Lenoir, Dec. 14, 1860, page 2 of 3: Tom reveals to Rufe a promise made to Mr. (William) Garrett to pick up Garrett's daughter, Lizzie, at the female college in Lenoir and bring her home. Just a few short months later Tom would marry the young Lizzie Garrett.

Lenoir, NC 1861
[Thos. I. Lenoir]

May 23rd 61

My Dear Brother

Doubtless, you will be surprised to see a letter from me, and if I had known of one you received before you left here I should have said what I have to say to you then, but the fact is I did not realize that you seriously intended to get up that company until May told me about that letter you got from Turner Cathey. — Now my dear brother I am decidedly of opinion that you can serve your country better by staying at home and making bread and meat for our soldiers to eat than by going to be a soldier yourself at this stage of the game. There

Laura Lenoir to Tom Lenoir, May 23, 1861, page 1 of 3: When Tom's sister, Laura, heard that he was seriously considering taking the command of a volunteer company from Forks of Pigeon she was incredulous. On this page Laura begins to state her opposition to such a move by Tom and writes that he could better serve his country by "making bread and meat for the Southern soldiers."

& not unite with the other Company & from what I hear there is no probability of their selecting any body else to command them & no man could think of declining under such circumstances — I don't believe that I am the right man but of course can't say so now, & feel that it will be my duty to pitch in whenever they ask me —

My health is only tolerable, & I have some doubts as to the effect of Camp life upon me, but perhaps it will improve me —

My business is very much neglected, & it seems as if I had done nothing at all since I came back from Caldwell —

Romeo's leg seems a little better just now — the second blister is still running but Dr Allen says that it it is probable that he will never be well —

Frank has been quite sick for several days — his pulse at 120 this morning — but I think is probably only worms —

Tom Lenoir to Rufus T. Lenoir, June 10, 1861, page 3 of 4: Tom informs Rufus of the pending marriage with Lizzie Garrett, and that he does not believe he is the right man to captain the Haywood Highlanders but feels it his duty. *Collection of Hugh K. Terrell and the late Emily Michal Terrell; used by permission.*

The Den June 18th 1861

Dear Brother
It is currently reported about here that Tom Lenoir was married on last Thursday & strange as it seems, I am sometimes inclined to believe it. But whether it be true or not, it is certain that a very nice young Lady came home with him, & was seen riding behind next day on his big bay horse over the river to the Strawberry patch, & then he took her down to preaching last Sunday in his buggy, & was rather late (of course that wasn't his fault) & every body was grinning at him & he grinned back at them — Now don't all that look rather suspicious? It is true they behaved very well away from home but I guess it would be right hard to find out how they carry on in The Den —

I just don't believe that he can think much about any thing except that little flax headed Gal — He is pretending to be studying Military Tactics, but it's not my opinion that he is making much progress in that or any other kind of Tactics — It is thought that a Volunteer Company will be made up for him to Command immediately after harvest, but there is some doubt about it's being completed so soon as he has only fifty at present — But I think it will be made up after a while, & hard as it will be, he must leave his little wife — He talks of taking her back to Asheville but she will not agree to that as yet —

Tom Lenoir to Rufus T. Lenoir, June 18, 1861, page 1 of 2: Tom cannot wait to report to Rufus that his wedding with Lizzie Garrett has come off as planned. On this page he also writes that only about fifty men had signed up for his volunteer company." *Collection of Hugh K. Terrell and the late Emily Michal Terrell; used by permission.*

The Dew July 2d 1861

W. W. Lenoir Esq.
Dear Brother
Our Volunteer Company meets this morning at 10 Oclock to drill & elect Officers — If you still think of going with us, I wish you could be here — We now number Seventy one, & will probably be increased some to day — We will be apt to start somebody (maybe Col. Cathey) to Raleigh this evening if he can get off in time to reach Asheville tonight, that he may go on in the Morganton Stage tomorrow, to offer the services of the Company to the Gov'r. — Get Commissions, instructions &c. —

If he gets off today he will, I suppose, pass Hickory Station on Thursday —
I suppose we will be ordered to Asheville for the present — I wrote to Bro. Joe. last Saturday asking if he could board Lizzie again & two other daughters of Mr. Garrett — I wish Lizzy to return to School & I think she will consent —

You said something about my taking Uriah w. me, but unless you go yourself I would not quite feel willing — He says he would like to go — But if we remain at Asheville a month

Tom Lenoir to Walter Lenoir, July 2, 1861, page 1 of 3: Tom records that his volunteer company numbers seventy-one men. He mentions the possibility of taking the slave, Uriah, to the war with him and also writes that Col. Joseph Cathey was going to make a trip to Raleigh on behalf of the company.

I was told this morning that another Company arrived at Camp Patton before day this morning having traveled in the night to beat some other Company there — This last make ten for they have another Reg't mustered in & several Companies expected soon — I could get no information concerning the time of the election of their officers.

We have no arms yet — It is said that we will meet Col Clingman as we go to Raleigh. We know nothing as to where we will go next from Raleigh — We had some little trouble in the Camp Friday night — but I think the worst of it is past — Some members of some Companies were trying to get up a rebellion alledging as the reason that the discipline was such as they would not submit to — None of my Company were engaged in it — The ring leaders were arrested & are now in jail in Asheville, three of them —

But I must close
Love to all
Your affectionate brother
Tom

I have not rec'd a line from you yet —

Tom Lenoir to Walter Lenoir, Sept. 15, 1861, page 2 of 2: This page from a letter written by Tom at Asheville's Camp Clingman relates news of the Haywood Highlanders and the 25th Regiment N.C. Troops. The regiment has not yet been issued arms and a few disgruntled men have even tried to get up a rebellion because of the harsh discipline at the Asheville training camps.

R.T.L. Ho Ho Augt 14th 1865

My Dear Brother

Chum of ox? That, he will
start early in the morning & I must try
to write a little to night, but these nights
are so short that bed time will soon be here
for it is after 8 oclock now—

I have almost forgotten how to write,
having written but one or two letters since
last April — and I don't like to begin.
I wish I could be with you a week &
talk instead of writing —

Walter wrote a very long letter a few
days back to Bro. Joseph & sent it to
Asheville by Dr. Sahuney & I expect that
contains more general news than I could
remember to write — for I am sorry to find
that my memory has failed very much —

About the last of April a Company of
Yankee Thieves came from Asheville up
South Fleming & down Pisgah Creek, stopped
at Walters, took Old Rip & one of his Mules
& his bacon hams — Came on here & were
in the yard before we saw them or heard
of their approach — The boys were plowing

Tom Lenoir to Rufus T. Lenoir, Aug. 14, 1865, page 1 of 6: In this very long letter Tom describes, among other matters, a Yankee raid along the East Fork and the manner in which he has been dealing with his newly emancipated slaves.

United States engages soon in any foreign war — & that the institution of Slavery has been finally abolished in the United States, by those who have mismanaged & abused the best government on earth (for an honorable, just, & generous people) Not from any real desire to benefit the Negro, or truly philanthropic motives, but were instigated by avarice, envy, hatred, & malice — And that this success of the wicked has been permitted by the Great Ruler of the Universe, not that he has changed his edict, uttered prophetically through Noah concerning the children of Ham, but because the institution of Slavery had been abused — & perhaps not alone by individuals, but by the different State Governments, in allowing individual abuse, or by unjust & improper legislation —

The evil effects of the destruction of our system of labor will of course be most apparent where it did most prevail — Consequently the Western portion of N. C. will be less affected by it than the South generally, but even here it will be bad enough, & my anticipations of the future are not very flattering either for my Country, my State, my Family or Myself —

I must let Walter tell you the neighborhood news, & I must confine my few further remarks to my little family, farm & stock

Tom Lenoir to Rufus T. Lenoir, Mar. 27, 1866, page 2 of 4: Tom offers his political philosophy on the destruction of slavery and states that the effects would be felt less in Western North Carolina than elsewhere.

My family now consists of Wife, Child, self, two young men. One hired until 1st January & the other, until 1st Aug't (one at 10 & the other at 8. dollars pr. Month) & one young woman until 1st Jan'y at 75.00 pr. Year & one D. D. at one dollar pr. week for no particular period — all to be paid at the end of their terms of service in U. S. paper currency unless sooner otherwise paid — I am right well pleased with three of those hired, the other has not been with us long — But I often feel much doubt and misgiving as to my ability to make enough by farming to pay such prices, & support my family & pay the debts which I already owe. If I were out of debt I would not feel as I do about it — I relied mostly on my Cotton in S.C. & my note on J. W. Patton which amounted at his death to about 1500.00 to pay my debts, but the Cotton went up in Smoke & I consider the note lost as the estate is said to be insolvent — & I have no other notes that will probably help me much to pay debts, & nothing to sell except jacks & about 1000 ℔ bacon — The jacks don't bring money, & the proceeds of the bacon will be all needed to put my farm in order It would take it all to repair the fences & build a hen house —

Tom Lenoir to Rufus T. Lenoir, Mar. 27, 1866, page 3 of 4: Tom writes that he feels considerable doubt and misgivings about his ability to make enough by farming to support his family and pay his debts.

[W. W. Lenoir
Hickory Tavern, N.C.]

The Den June 10th 1874

Dear Brother,

Yours of 29th May came by last mail —. I hope you have received Lizzie's second & third letters — If you have, you will not leave Watauga at present on my account, for I was much better when she wrote the 3d letter, & I would be very sorry for you to be hurried off just in the midst of Mill building on my account; but I wished very much to see you about the time Lizzie first wrote for I thought then that my friends here considered my recovery doubtful, & I longed to see my distant friends — But my neck is much better, healing nicely & I am getting well as fast as I ought. — & am now able to walk for a few minutes at a time without help, & am gaining both flesh & strength —

Oh that I could feel as thankful & as humble as I ought before a Merciful God who again raised me up, & spared my unprofitable life —

But in his wisdom He has seen fit to take from our midtst a much better & much more useful man — I allude to Col. J. Cathey —

Tom Lenoir to Walter Lenoir, June 10, 1874, page 1 of 2: Tom writes to inform Walter that he is much better and his neck is healing. Additionally, he reports the sad tidings that God "in his wisdom … has seen fit to take from our midtst [sic] a much better & much more useful man … Col. J[oseph] Cathey."

at uncle T's loss, felt that I ought not to complain.

The people on East Fork have been troubled a good deal about milling. It was a long time before Cathey's started, & it has was been stopped again for several weeks, to repair the dam while the water was low— one corner of the mill house was sunk about 15 inches. Pless's mill is about ready to start again. There has been some wheat threshed in the country— the crop is said to fall short of peoples expectations. The present prospect for corn on East Fork is very poor I think; & I hear bad accounts from other portions of the county, of corn, & very bad of oats. Hay is very fine I think. I am about 2/3 done mowing— the "turn out" is better than last season. Uncle T. has not cut much. Mack A. has

J. M. Gwyn to Walter Lenoir, July 30, 1876, one page of 6: Walter and Tom Lenoir's nephew, James M. Gwyn (who moved to Walter's farm on the East Fork of Pigeon River and promptly styled it Springdale) writes to his uncle about a freshet which has devastated property along the East Fork. He reports that the "people on East Fork have been troubled a great deal about milling," with mills shut down for weeks to effect repairs.

that I can barely live, I make a few scratches towards preparing my land for nephews & nieces who will none of them have it in the wild state that I will leave it in when I die. The fault will be in them, not in the land. But our government so burdens us with debt & mad extravagance that it is no longer easy to live by farming, & I dont wonder that so few of the rising generations of educated people have the heroism to try it. It is a gloomy subject to reflect on, and it adds to the gloom to find that a farmer as skillful & attentive & as economical as you, & with such a farm, cant make his receipts equal his expenditures. We *must* do that much. If we cant bring up the receipts, we must bring down the expenditures. As I wrote to Wat Gwyn, he who doesn't pay his way as he goes is somebody's pauper, and he who does, is the freest of the free. We had better wear our own rags, & be free, than wear somebody else's broadcloth.

Walter Lenoir to Tom Lenoir, Feb. 11, 1879, page 2 of 4: This page of a letter written by Tom's brother Walter at Shull's Mills in Watauga, N.C., offers some business advice to Tom. "If we can't bring up the receipts," he writes, "we must bring down the expenditures."

> June 20th 1879
>
> Capt. T. I. Lenoir
>
> Dear Sir, I will be pleased to take your 600 feet of 1¼ plank, And pay Six dollars on your Tax for The Year 1879 as you wish me to do—
>
> I am satisfied that you will treat both Mr. Henson & myself as kindly as you can — If it should rain & thereby enable you to saw, Please do so & thus farther oblige me &c
>
> Yours as Ever &c
>
> R. V. Welch

Mr. R. V. Welch to Capt. T. I. Lenoir, June 20, 1879: Tom Lenoir has built a water-powered sawmill on his East Fork farm, and this letter from a customer reveals a serious flaw in Tom's mill design—it can only operate after periods of significant rainfall. Welch writes, "If it should rain & thereby enable you to saw, Please do so & thus further oblige me, etc."

W. B. Gwyn Esq.,   The Den Dec. 12th 1879

Dear Nephew, I have rec'd yours of 3rd inst. inclosing rec't. which is herewith returned without my signature, but will sign & inclose a blank rec't. for you to fill up, as I think you intended to write $141.47 instead of $122.30 — ⁕ I saw Jim yesterday & he said all well at his house — We are about as usual here — My cough not quite so bad for a week past — ⁕ Is there any probability of my ever getting any thing from Patton or McDowell, upon that old debt? A financial crisis is now impending — I am called upon as surety to pay $275.00, which will probably be a clear loss, except the lesson which it teaches, & it would seem that any old fogy ought learn that in less time than 62 years, one will not seek his acquaintance beware of Jesse Holms, if he happens to pass this way.

Your affectionate Uncle Tom —

Received of W. B. Gwyn one hundred and _____ dollars in full of claims against R. R. Jones and L. E. Wilson, less 10 p'cent Commission on the same, and five dollars fee for Miles Lenoir, retained by the said W. B. Gwyn — This Sept. 24th 1879.

T. L.

Tom Lenoir at the Den to W. B. Gwyn, Esq., Dec.12, 1879. The sixty-two year old Tom Lenoir (his handwriting markedly less careful than in his younger years) wrote to his nephew, an Asheville attorney, to ask if there was a chance to collect old debts owed by Patton or McDowell. It seems that Tom needs the money to forestall an impending financial crisis in which he owes $275 as a surety.

herself the other night lifting Sallie and is not well atall. I weigh twenty pounds more than Mama and can pick her up and carry her all about. — I will soon have use for my strength will soon have to take my place in the kitchen department our girl who has been with us most of the time for five years is to be married before long.

Papa says he is getting so old he can't do with out wooden bottom shoes to go about in the mud with he finished a pair yesterday that weighed three pounds he calls them his pumps and some times he tries to dance with them on, and you

Mamie (Mary) Lenoir to Aunt Sade, Jan. 12, 1880, page 3 of 4: Tom Lenoir's oldest child, Mamie, reports to Tom's sister, Sarah, at Fort Defiance that she weighs twenty pounds more than her mother and describes her father's wooden-bottomed shoes, or pumps, as he refers to them.

[to Thos. I Lenoir
Springdale, N C]

Shull Mills, Watauga co N C 27 Nov 1880

Dear Brother

Two postals from Springdale have told me of the death of sister Lizzie, & of the poor little babe whose feeble life flickered for so short a time after its loving kind hearted mother's went out. We are prone to try to speak words of comfort to those we love best, when they are bowing under the weight of such heavy affliction; but alas! they are of but little avail. It is superfluous for me to say to you, who have practiced it so much better than I, that the best comfort for those who sorrow is to be found in the discharge of duty. The mother still lives to you in the daughters. May they do all they can to console & comfort you, & to promote your happiness; for they bring to you a heavy weight of care & responsibility. Mary is at an age when she needs, greatly

Walter Lenoir to Tom Lenoir, Nov. 27, 1880, page 1 of 4: When Tom's wife, Lizzie, and newborn child died in November 1880, the letters flooded in to the Den from family members. In this one Walter offers his sympathy and reminds Tom that "The mother still lives to you in the daughters."

[Rufus T. Lenoir
Patterson, NC]

Forks of Pigeon Haywood co N C 19 Dec 1881
Dear Brother
 I have just written to sister Laura, giving her a fuller account of brother Tom's sickness & its present condition than I can repeat in time for the mail which will leave Springdale in the morning. So I have asked her to forward the letter to you. You will see in that letter that brother Tom is very weak and very despondent, & that his other symptoms are those of a mild form of Typhoid fever. He has been so far well supplied with good nurses. Romy is in constant attendance. Mr Bennum has been here more than a week & has no time set for leaving. He is a most affectionate watchful skillful nurse. Jamie Gwyn is here every day, & sits up all night every other night. Laura Gwyn is here prompt gentle & skillful, always on duty, at the bedside, in the dining room, in the kitchen, every where that duty calls, shrinking from nothing that love or duty suggests. And now Mary is here & I am glad to see how well she begins to do her part. The neighbors too have been very kind & their visits so far have been well timed, not coming in crowds, & not all failing to come any night.

Walter Lenoir to Rufus T. Lenoir, Dec. 19, 1881, page 1 of 4: From Tom's bedside Walter writes to their brother Rufus of Tom's dire condition. The symptoms were those of typhoid fever, and Walter remained at Tom's side until his brother's passing two weeks later.

> We expected to start Tommie about a week or ten days ago, but we had high water and I not well — his throat seems to trouble him considerably & I fear will be a great drawback to his usefulness — We expect him to start to Icard in the morning if the weather will admit of it — I do not know when he will reach you — After he has been with you a few days you can tell better how long it would be well for him to stay — If you think best to send him back with the little girls I guess he will take good care of them — You & cousin James & Laura can judge better how soon they had better start — I think like you that Mary ought to go to Salem. The sooner the better — Laura & Sallie can both come here & if it should be thought best for Laura to go to Sister Annie's there will be passing frequently —

Rufus T. Lenoir to Walter Lenoir, Jan. 8, 1882, page 2 of 3: After learning of Tom's death Rufus writes to Walter, who is still in Haywood County taking care of his brother's estate and family matters. On this page of the letter Rufus addresses the issue of taking care of Tom's girls.

Notes are numbered continuously throughout this work. The first instance of each citation contains full bibliographical details; subsequent citations employ a shortened form.

Citations to *The War of the Rebellion, Official Records of the Union and Confederate Armies,* are styled as O.R., with references to series, volume, and chapter given in arabic numbers. Where a volume is in more than one part, the reference will be to a part, chapter, and page (O.R. 1:11, part 2, chap. 23, p. 792.).

Introduction

1. James M. McPherson, *Battle Cry of Freedom: The Civil War Era* (New York: Oxford Univ. Press, 1988), p. 274.

Part I: Thomas Lenoir's East Fork Legacy
Thomas Lenoir, Haywood County Pioneer

2. Letter dated Sept. 16, 1806, from Thomas Lenoir at Morganton, N.C., to Gen. William Lenoir at Fort Defiance, Wilkes County, N.C., Lenoir Family Papers, Southern Historical Collection, Wilson Library, University of North Carolina at Chapel Hill (hereafter cited as Lenoir Family Papers).

3. "I John Patton Surveyor of said County [State of North Carolina, Buncombe County] do herby authorize and Defend [?] Thomas Lenoir to survey a tract of land on the East Fork of Pigeon River for Waighstill Avery by virtue of Warrant issued to said Avery the 20th Day of October 1792. Given under my hand this 21st day of August 1806. [signed by] John Patton Esq.," document, Lenoir Family Papers.

4. Thomas Lenoir, "Memorandum of Tenants on E. Fork of pidgeon [*sic*] River 1806," collection of Lenoir letters and documents held by Ike Forester of Lenoir, N.C. (hereafter cited as Forester Collection).

5. A letter signed by Louisa Avery Lenoir in December 1804 narrows the date of her marriage to Col. Thomas Lenoir to the year 1804 (collection of Hugh K. Terrell and the late Emily Michal Terrell of Bethel, N.C., hereafter cited as Terrell Collection). The Lenoir family's plantation, Fort Defiance, was located in present-day Caldwell County.

6. Letter dated June 25, 1807, from Thomas Lenoir at Asheville, N.C., to Walter R. Lenoir at Morganton, Burke County, N.C., Lenoir Family Papers.

7. Ora Blackmun, *Western North Carolina: Its Mountains and Its People to 1880* (Boone, N.C.: Appalachian Consortium Press), 165.

8. U.S. Census Records for North Carolina, 1810. Quotations and population statistics are from Thomas D. Love's summation of his census enumeration labors in Haywood County in 1810 and addressed to Beverly Daniel esquire, Marshal North Carolina, Nov. 6, 1810. Love described the vastness of the county and asked "for such additional allowance [reimbursement of expenses] as may be covered by the Act of Congress."

9. W. C. Allen, *The Annals of Haywood County North Carolina, Historical, Sociological, Biographical, and Genealogical* (Raleigh: North Carolina State Library, 1935; repr., Spartanburg, S.C.: Reprint Company, 1977), 33.

10. John Preston Arthur, *Western North Carolina: A History (from 1730 to 1913)* (Asheville, N.C.: Edward Buncombe Chapter of the Daughters of the American Revolution of Asheville, North Carolina, 1914; repr., Johnson City, Tenn.: Overmountain Press, 1996), 168.

11. Letter dated July 2, 1809, from Thomas Lenoir at East Fork of Pigeon to Gen. William Lenoir at Fort Defiance, Wilkes County, N.C., Lenoir Family Papers.

12. Letter dated May 11, 1812, from Thomas Lenoir at East Fork of Pigeon to General William Lenoir at Fort Defiance in Wilkes County, N.C., Lenoir Family Papers.

13. Letter dated Mar. 3, 1815, from Thomas Lenoir at Asheville, N.C., to his brother, William, at Mouth of Holston in Tennessee, Lenoir Family Papers; W. Clark Medford, *The Early History of Haywood County* (Asheville, N.C., Miller Printing Co., 1961), 55.

14. Original official commission document dated Dec. 19, 1818, Lenoir Family Papers.

15. Emily Terrell and Hugh K. Terrell, "Thomas Lenoir," pp. 17–18 in Evelyn M. Coltman, *Legends, Tales, & History of Cold Mountain: A Pigeon Valley Heritage Collection* (Waynesville, N.C.: Richard L. Coltman, 2008), Book 3, 2007.

16. The six children born to Thomas and Selina Louisa Avery Lenoir in Haywood County were William Avery (1808–1861), Selina Louise (1813–1836), Laura Leah Carolina (1815–1894), Thomas Isaac (1817–1882), Mary Ann (1819–1898), and Sarah Joyce (1821–1899). After moving to Wilkes County the couple had two more children: Walter Waightstill (1823–1890) and Rufus Theodore (1825–1912). The loss in 1812 of their infant daughter Ann Eliza devastated the parents, as can be seen in a letter that a distraught Thomas Lenoir wrote to his father on May 11, 1812: "Oh! my Dear Father, to describe the feeling of (Perhaps too fond) a parent, on this occasion, is too great a task for my feeble pen. I shall not attempt it; but will endeavour to become more resigned to the will of the wise disposer of the universe, and not improperly lament the death of an infant, who never could have got rid of the troubles of this wicked world in a better time, than before she knew good

from evil, and of course, never could have incurred the displeasure of an all wise and just Creator" (Lenoir Family Papers).

17. Letter dated May 26, 1816, from Thomas Lenoir at East Fork of Pigeon to his brother, William, Lenoir Family Papers.

18. Letter dated Oct. 10, 1821, from Thomas Lenoir at East Fork of Pigeon to Gen. William Lenoir at Fort Defiance, Wilkes County, N.C., Lenoir Family Papers.

19. 1820 U.S. Census information for Haywood County, N.C., lists 35 slaves.

20. Terrell and Terrell, "Thomas Lenoir," in Coltman, *Legends, Tales, & History of Cold Mountain*, Book 3, 2007, p. 17; letter dated May 26, 1816, from Thomas Lenoir at East Fork of Pigeon to his brother, William, Lenoir Family Papers.

21. Letter dated Oct. 4, 1821, from Thomas Lenoir at Asheville, N.C., to Gen. William Lenoir at Fort Defiance in Wilkes County, N.C., Lenoir Family Papers.

Thomas Isaac Lenoir: A Son's Coming of Age

22. Letter dated Nov. 21, 1829, from Thomas H. Hill in Burke County, N.C., to Col. Thomas Lenoir at Fort Defiance, N.C., Lenoir Family Papers.

23. William L. Barney, *The Making of a Confederate: Walter Lenoir's Civil War* (Oxford and New York: Oxford University Press, 2008), 27.

24. Letter dated May 30, 1839, from Thomas I. Lenoir at Chapel Hill, N.C., to Thomas Lenoir, Lenoir Family Papers.

25. Thomas Felix Hickerson, *Echoes of Happy Valley: Letters and Diaries; Family Life in the South; Civil War History* (Chapel Hill, N.C.: Bull's Head, 1962), 32–33; letter dated Jan. 29, 1840, from Thomas Isaac Lenoir at Fort Defiance, N.C., to Walter W. Lenoir at Chapel Hill N.C., Lenoir Family Papers.

26. Letter dated May 30, 1839, from Thomas I. Lenoir at Chapel Hill, N.C., to Thomas Lenoir at Fort Defiance, Wilkes County, N.C., Lenoir Family Papers.

27. North Carolina's new county of Caldwell was established in 1841 from territory formerly included within Wilkes County's borders. Fort Defiance was located in Caldwell County, and the small village of Tucker's Barn, renamed Lenoir, became the county seat.

28. Letter dated Aug. 8, 1842, from Thomas I. Lenoir to Mr. J. Dunlap at Asheville, N.C., Lenoir Family Papers.

29. Information on Tom and Walter Lenoir's trip to the Northern states was taken from a letter dated Aug. 10, 1843, from Thomas I. Lenoir in Washington City to Col. Thomas Lenoir at Fort Defiance, Caldwell County, N.C., Lenoir Family Papers. Additional information was gleaned from Terrell and Terrell, "Thomas Isaac Lenoir, " in Coltman, *Legends, Tales, & History of Cold Mountain*, Book 3, 2007, p. 21.

30. Letter dated Mar. 5, 1845, from Thomas I. Lenoir at New York City to Thomas Lenoir at Fort Defiance in Caldwell County, N.C., Lenoir Family Papers.

31. Various entries in Thomas Lenoir's Haywood County journal indicate that a man by the name of Curtis was managing the affairs of the East Fork farm in the years 1837 through early 1840. Subsequently, in late 1840 A. C. Hartgrove seems to have taken over. In a journal entry dated Dec. 13, 1840, Thomas Lenoir directs "Captain Hartgrove" to settle some slave matters (Forester Collection).

32. Letter dated Mar. 6, 1844, from A. C. Hartgrove at East Fork to Thomas Lenoir at Fort Defiance in Caldwell County, N.C., Lenoir Family Papers.

33. Letter dated Oct. 24, 1845, from A. C. Hartgrove at East Fork to Thomas Lenoir at Fort Defiance in Caldwell County, N.C., Lenoir Family Papers.

34. Letter dated Jan. 3, 1846, from A. C. Hartgrove at East Fork to Thomas Lenoir at Fort Defiance in Caldwell County, N.C., Lenoir Family Papers.

Dutiful Endeavors on the East Fork

35. Thomas I. Lenoir memorandum book, folder 634, Lenoir Family Papers.

36. Letter dated Mar. 28, 1846, from Thomas Lenoir in Asheville to Thomas I. Lenoir at East Fork of Pigeon, Lenoir Family Papers.

37. Letter dated Mar. 28, 1846, from Thomas Lenoir in Asheville to Thomas I. Lenoir at East Fork of Pigeon, Lenoir Family Papers.

38. Letter dated June 14, 1846, from Thomas Lenoir at Fort Defiance in Caldwell County, N.C., to Thomas I. Lenoir at East Fork of Pigeon, Lenoir Family Papers.

39. Letter dated Nov. 29, 1852, from Louisa Lenoir at Fort Defiance in Caldwell County, N.C., to Thomas I. Lenoir at East Fork of Pigeon, Lenoir Family Papers.

40. Letter dated Apr. 7, 1846, from Rufus and Sarah Lenoir at Fort Defiance in Caldwell County, N.C., to Thomas I. Lenoir at East Fork of Pigeon, Lenoir Family Papers.

41. Letter dated June 26, 1846, from Thomas I. Lenoir at Bachelor's Hall, East Fork of Pigeon, to Sarah Lenoir at Fort Defiance in Caldwell County, N.C., Lenoir Family Papers.

42. Letter dated June 1, 1846, from Thomas Lenoir at Fort Defiance in Caldwell County, N.C., to Thomas I. Lenoir at East Fork of Pigeon, Lenoir Family Papers.

43. Letter dated May 8, 1848, from Thomas Lenoir at Fort Defiance in Caldwell County, N.C., to Thomas I. Lenoir at East Fork of Pigeon, Lenoir Family Papers.

44. Barney, *Making of a Confederate*, 30–31; letter dated Mar. 7, 1855, from Thomas I. Lenoir at Bachelor's Den, East Fork of Pigeon to Mr. Daniel Dana, Jr., in New York City, N.Y., Lenoir Family Papers; letter dated May 27, 1853, from Thomas I. Lenoir at the Den to his father at Fort Defiance in Caldwell County, Thomas Lenoir, Sr., Papers, Duke University Library (hereafter cited as Thomas Lenoir, Sr., Papers).

45. Letter dated May 27, 1853, from Thomas I. Lenoir at the Den to his father at Fort Defiance in Caldwell County, Thomas Lenoir, Sr., Papers.

46. Letter dated Sept. 9, 1854, from Thomas I. Lenoir at Bachelor's Den to his father at Fort Defiance in Caldwell County, Thomas Lenoir, Sr., Papers.

47. Letter of Sept. 23, 1851, from Thomas Isaac Lenoir at Bachelor's Den to Col. Thomas Lenoir at Fort Defiance, Terrell Collection.

48. Slave Schedule, 1860 U.S. Census, Haywood County, N.C.

49. Letter dated May 29 [about 1847] from Thomas I. Lenoir at Bachelor's Retreat, East Fork of Pigeon to Thomas Lenoir at Fort Defiance in Caldwell County, N.C., Lenoir Family Papers.

50. Letter dated Aug. 8, 1849, from Thomas I. Lenoir at Bachelor's Retreat, East Fork of Pigeon, to Sarah Lenoir at Fort Defiance in Caldwell County, N.C., Lenoir Family Papers.

51. Letter of Nov. 23, 1855, from Thomas I. Lenoir at Forks of Pigeon to Thomas Lenoir at Fort Defiance, Caldwell County, N.C., Forester collection; letter dated Dec. 14, 1855, from Thomas I. Lenoir at Forks of Pigeon to Rufus T. Lenoir at Fort Defiance in Caldwell County, N.C., Lenoir Family Papers.

52. Letter dated Sept. 18, 1856, from Thomas I. Lenoir at Asheville to brother Rufus at Fort Defiance; letter dated Sept. 23, 1856, from Thomas I. Lenoir at Waynesville to his father. In the second letter Tom recorded, "I am writing with an overcoat in a public room, & with a very bad pen" (Thomas Lenoir, Sr. Papers).

53. Letter dated Feb. 13 [c. 1847] from Thomas I. Lenoir at Forks of Pigeon to Thomas Lenoir at Fort Defiance in Caldwell County, N.C., Lenoir Family Papers.

54. Letter dated Jan. 14, 1854, from Thomas I. Lenoir at Bachelor's Den, East Fork of Pigeon to Rufus Lenoir at Fort Defiance in Caldwell County, N.C., Lenoir Family Papers.

55. Letter dated Apr. 24, 1849, from Thomas I. Lenoir at Bachelor's Retreat, Forks of Pigeon to Thomas Lenoir at Fort Defiance in Caldwell County, N.C., Lenoir Family Papers.

56. Terrell and Terrell, "Thomas Isaac Lenoir," in Coltman, *Legends, Tales, & History of Cold Mountain*, Book 3, 2007, 21.

57. Letter from Thomas I. Lenoir in New York City to James Gwyn, Esq. in Wilkesboro, N.C., in Thomas Felix Hickerson, *Happy Valley: History and Genealogy* (Chapel Hill, N.C., privately printed, 1940), 128–29.

58. Letter dated Dec. 12, 1850, from Thomas Lenoir at Fort Defiance in Caldwell County, N.C., to Thomas I. Lenoir at Bachelor's Retreat, East Fork of Pigeon, Lenoir Family Papers.

59. Letter dated Mar. 31, 1855 from Thomas I. Lenoir at Bachelor's Den to his father at Fort Defiance in Caldwell County, Thomas Lenoir, Sr. Papers.

60. Letter dated Sept. 27, 1848, from Thomas I. Lenoir at Forks of Pigeon to Rufus Lenoir at Fort Defiance in Caldwell County, N.C., Lenoir Family Papers.

61. Letter dated Aug. 5, 1854, from Thomas I. Lenoir at Bachelor's Den at East Fork of Pigeon to Rufus Lenoir at Fort Defiance in Caldwell County, N.C., Lenoir Family Papers.

62. Letters dated Oct. 7, 1854, and Nov. 18, 1854, from Thomas I. Lenoir at the Den to his father at Fort Defiance in Caldwell County, Thomas Lenoir, Sr. Papers.

63. Letter dated Aug. 7, 1848, from Thomas Lenoir at Fort Defiance in Caldwell County, N.C. to Thomas I. Lenoir at East Fork of Pigeon, Lenoir Family Papers.

64. Letter dated Nov. 3, 1854, from Thomas I. Lenoir at the Den, East Fork of Pigeon, to Rufus T. Lenoir at Fort Defiance in Caldwell County, N.C., Lenoir Family Papers; letter dated Nov. 18, 1853, from Thomas I. Lenoir at the Den to his father at Fort Defiance, Thomas Lenoir, Sr. Papers.

65. Letter dated Sept. 27, 1848, from Thomas I. Lenoir at Forks of Pigeon to Rufus T. Lenoir at Fort Defiance in Caldwell County, N.C., Lenoir Family Papers.

66. Letter dated Mar. 25, 1854, from Thomas I. Lenoir at the Den to his father at Fort Defiance in Caldwell County, Thomas Lenoir, Sr. Papers.

67. Letter dated Mar. 30, 1857, from Thomas I. Lenoir at the Den to his father at Fort Defiance in Caldwell County, Thomas Lenoir, Sr. Papers.

68. Letter dated Sept. 14, 1857, from Thomas I. Lenoir at the Den to his father at Fort Defiance in Caldwell County, Thomas Lenoir, Sr. Papers.

69. Letter dated Mar. 25, 1854, from Thomas I. Lenoir at the Den to his father at Fort Defiance in Caldwell County, Thomas Lenoir, Sr. Papers.

70. Letter dated Sept. 14, 1857, from Thomas I. Lenoir at the Den to his father at Fort Defiance in Caldwell County, Thomas Lenoir, Sr. Papers.

71. Letter dated Feb. 13 [c. 1847] from Thomas I. Lenoir at Bachelor's Retreat, Forks of Pigeon to Thomas Lenoir at Fort Defiance in Caldwell County, N.C., Lenoir Family Papers.

72. Letter dated Feb. 5, 1850, from Thomas I. Lenoir at Bachelor's Den, East Fork of Pigeon to Rufus T. Lenoir at Fort Defiance in Caldwell County, N.C., Lenoir Family Papers.

73. Letter dated Aug. 7, 1854, from Thomas I. Lenoir at Bachelor's Den to his father at Fort Defiance in Caldwell County, N.C., Thomas Lenoir, Sr. Papers.

74. Letter dated Sept. 8, 1848, from Thomas I. Lenoir at Bachelor's Retreat, East Fork of Pigeon, to Rufus T. Lenoir at Fort Defiance in Caldwell County, N.C., Lenoir Family Papers.

75. Letter dated Sept. 8, 1849, from Thomas I. Lenoir at Bachelor's Retreat, East Fork of Pigeon, to Sarah Lenoir at Fort Defiance in Caldwell County, N.C., Lenoir Family Papers.

76. Letter dated Sept. 20, 1849, from Thomas I. Lenoir at Bachelor's Retreat, East Fork of Pigeon to R. T. Lenoir, Esq. at Fort Defiance in Caldwell County, N.C., Lenoir Family Papers.

77. Letter dated July 23, 1953, from Thomas I. Lenoir at the Den to "Jonas" (his brother Walter), Thomas Lenoir, Sr. Papers.

78. Terrell and Terrell, "Thomas Isaac Lenoir," in Coltman, *Legends, Tales, & History of Cold Mountain*, Book 3, 2007, 21; Allen, *The Annals of Haywood County*, 139.

79. Letter dated June 14, 1853, from Thomas I. Lenoir at the Den to his father at Fort Defiance in Caldwell County, N.C., Thomas Lenoir, Sr. Papers.

80. Letter dated Oct. 19, 1860, from Thomas I. Lenoir at the Den, Forks of Pigeon, to Thomas Lenoir at Fort Defiance in Caldwell County, N.C., Lenoir Family Papers.

81. Barney, *Making of a Confederate*, 53.

82. The abbreviated note scribed in W. A. Lenoir's memorandum book and portending of his suicide was dated May 1, 1861. As an afterthought William wrote, "I have done harm only to myself" (Forester collection).

83. Terrell and Terrell, "Thomas Isaac Lenoir," in Coltman, *Legends, Tales, & History of Cold Mountain*, Book 3, 2007, 22.

84. Letters dated July 4, 1859, July 5, 1859, and July 18, 1850, from Joe Norwood at Lenoir, N.C., to Thomas I. Lenoir at Forks of Pigeon, Lenoir Family Papers.

85. Letter dated Dec. 14, 1860, from Thomas I. Lenoir at Forks of Pigeon to Rufus T. Lenoir at Fort Defiance in Caldwell County, N.C., Lenoir Family Papers.

86. Letter dated June 10, 1861, from Thomas I. Lenoir at Forks of Pigeon to Rufus T. Lenoir at Fort Defiance in Caldwell County, N.C., Lenoir Family Papers.

A Volunteer Company from Forks of Pigeon

87. Letter dated Nov. 23, 1860, from Thomas I. Lenoir at Forks of Pigeon to Rufus T. Lenoir at Fort Defiance, Caldwell County, Forester collection.

88. Letter dated Dec. 26, 1860, from Thomas I. Lenoir at Forks of Pigeon to Rufus T. Lenoir at Fort Defiance, Caldwell County, Thomas Lenoir, Sr., Papers.

89. Letter dated Feb. 22, 1861, from Joseph Cathey to the Rev. L. F. Siler, Cathey Collection, Special Collections, Civil War Letters and Photographs, Hunter Library, Western Carolina University (hereafter cited as Cathey Collection).

90. John C. Inscoe, *Mountain Masters: Slavery and the Sectional Crisis in Western North Carolina* (Knoxville: Univ. of Tennessee Press, 1989), 229–30.

91. Inscoe, *Mountain Masters*, 230.

92. Shelby Foote, *The Civil War, A Narrative*, vol. 1, *Fort Sumter to Perryville* (New York: Random House), 1958, 52.

93. James M. McPherson, *Battle Cry of Freedom*, 277.

94. Letter dated June 10, 1861, from Thomas I. Lenoir at Forks of Pigeon to Rufus T. Lenoir at Fort Defiance in Caldwell County, N.C., Terrell Collection.

95. Letter dated May 23, 1861, from Laura Lenoir Norwood at Lenoir, N.C., to Thomas I. Lenoir at Forks of Pigeon, Terrell Collection.

96. Letter dated June 18, 1861, from Thomas I. Lenoir at The Den, Forks of Pigeon, to Rufus T. Lenoir at Fort Defiance in Caldwell County, N.C., Terrell Collection.

97. Letter dated July 2, 1861, from Thomas I. Lenoir at The Den, Forks of Pigeon, to Walter W. Lenoir Esq., Terrell Collection.

98. Letter dated July 2, 1861, from Thomas I. Lenoir at The Den, Forks of Pigeon, to Walter W. Lenoir Esq., Terrell Collection.

99. Letter dated July 2, 1861, from Thomas I. Lenoir at The Den, Forks of Pigeon, to Walter W. Lenoir Esq., Terrell Collection.

100. Letter dated July 2, 1861, from Thomas I. Lenoir at The Den, Forks of Pigeon, to Walter W. Lenoir Esq., Terrell Collection. Uriah's age is calculated to have been twenty-six years in 1861, since in a letter from Walter Lenoir to Joe Norwood dated May 3, 1863, Uriah's age is listed as twenty-eight (Lenoir Family Papers).

101. Confederate Camp Patton was located immediately east of Charlotte Street with Chestnut Street passing east-west through it (Foster A. Sondley, *A History of Buncombe County, North Carolina* [Asheville, North Carolina: Advocate Printing Co., 1930], vol. 2, p. 690.

102. Garland S. Ferguson, "Twenty-Fifth Regiment," in vol. 2 of *Histories of the Several Regiments and Battalions from North Carolina, In the Great Civil War*, ed. Walter Clark (Goldsboro, N.C.: Nash Brothers, 1901), 291.

103. Letter dated Sept. 15, 1861, from Thomas I. Lenoir at Camp Clingman in Asheville, N.C., to Walter W. Lenoir Esq., Terrell Collection.

104. Letter dated Sept. 15, 1861, from Thomas I. Lenoir at Camp Clingman in Asheville, N.C., to Walter W. Lenoir Esq., Terrell Collection.

105. Special Order No. 335 from Headquarters N.C. Troops, Adjutant General's Office, Raleigh, dated Sept. 12, 1861, and signed by J. G. Martin, Adjutant General State Troops, www.footnote.com, accessed Jan. 22, 2009.

106. Cornelia Henry, wife of William Henry, who owned the Sulphur Springs Hotel and grounds located a few miles west of Asheville, recorded the following entry in her journal for the date of Sept. 18, 1861: "Mr. Henry & I went to Asheville today as the 25th Regiment of volunteers left there. Was a good many people in Asheville" (Karen L. Clinard and Richard Russell, eds., *Fear in North Carolina: The Civil War Journal and Letters of the Henry Family* [Asheville, N.C.: Reminiscing Books, 2008], 36).

107. Special Order No. [388?] from the Adjutant General's Office, Raleigh, dated Sept. 27, 1861, and signed by J. G. Martin, Adjutant General, www.footnote.com, accessed Jan. 22, 2009.

108. Ferguson wrote that the regiment "stopped a day or two in Raleigh and drew uniforms" ("Twenty-Fifth Regiment," in Clark, ed., *Histories of the Several Regiments*, vol. 2, 291).

109. Letter from R. P. Crawford to Wm. Eastis, Sept. 29, 1861, Civil War Letters and Photographs, Estes Collection, Special Collections, Hunter Library, Western Carolina University (hereafter cited as Estes Collection).

110. Letter from R. P. Crawford to Wm. Eastis, Sept. 29, 1861, Civil War Letters and Photographs, Estes Collection.

Captain Lenoir's Diary

111. Ferguson, "Twenty-Fifth Regiment," in Clark, ed., *Histories of the Several Regiments*, vol. 2, 291.

112. "Map of North Carolina, 1861–1865," drawn by James R. Vogt, endpaper to vol. 7, "Infantry," of Weymouth T. Jordan and Louis H. Manarin, *North Carolina Troops, 1861–1865, A Roster* (Department of National Archives, Confederate records, 2004).

113. Letter from R. P. Crawford to Wm. Eastis, Sept. 29, 1861, Civil War Letters and Photographs, Estes Collection. Crawford was attached to Company B and wrote from Mitchell's Sound (presumably Camp Davis), where the 25th Regiment N.C. was first stationed: "We Drawd our guns to Day and tha ar the Missisppi Rifels." He also duly reported to his correspondent that their uniforms were gray sack coats with a row of the finest brass buttons up the breast, and the pants nearly identical but featuring a black stripe up the legs.

114. Letter from R. P. Crawford to Wm. Eastis, Sept. 29, 1861, Civil War Letters and Photographs, Estes Collection.

115. Ferguson, "Twenty-Fifth Regiment," in Clark, ed., *Histories of the Several Regiments*, vol. 2, 291.

116. John G. Barrett, *The Civil War in North Carolina* (Chapel Hill: Univ. of North Carolina Press, 1963; repr. 1995), 32–45.

117. Barrett, *Civil War in North Carolina*, 62; O.R. 1:4, chap. 13, p. 639.

118. Department of National Archives, Confederate records, www.footnote.com, accessed December 2008.

119. Time-Life Books, *The Blockade, Runners and Raiders* (Alexandria, Va.: Time-Life Books, 1984), 31.

120. O.R. 1:6, chap. 15, p. 4.

121. O.R. 1:6, chap. 15, p. 16.

122. O.R. 1:6, chap. 15, pp. 323, 326, and Douglas Southall Freeman, *R. E. Lee: A Biography* (New York: Scribner, 1934), vol. 1, 609.

123. "Mecklenburg Declaration of Independence," www.wikipedia.org, accessed Dec. 26, 2008.

124. O.R. 1:6, chap. 15, pp. 323, 324.

125. Walter W. Lenoir's Civil War diary, p. 5, Lenoir Family Papers.

126. Freeman, *R. E. Lee*, vol. 1, p. 610.

127. O.R. 1:6, chap. 15, p. 324.

128. O.R. 1:6, chap. 15, p. 323.

129. "Civil War, Pensacola," in Floripedia, http://fcit.usf.edu/florida/docs/c/civatpen.htm, accessed Dec. 28, 2008; "Bombardment of Pensacola," *Harper's Weekly*, Dec. 7, 1861.

130. Department of National Archives, Confederate records, www.footnote.com, accessed Jan. 10, 2009. Tom signed the voucher on Nov. 23, 1861, indicating that he had received his pay from Assistant Quartermaster Captain Hutson Lee, C.S.A.

131. Douglas Southall Freeman, *Lee's Lieutenants: A Study in Command*. 3 vols. (New York: Scribner, 1942–44), vol. 3, p. 621.

132. O.R. 1:6, chap. 15, pp. 32, 33.

133. O.R. 1:6, chap. 15, p. 329.

134. "Civil War, Pensacola," in Floripedia, http://fcit.usf.edu/florida/docs/c/civatpen.htm, accessed Dec. 28, 2008; "Bombardment of Pensacola," *Harper's Weekly*, Dec. 7, 1861.

135. Walter W. Lenoir's Civil War diary, p. 7, Lenoir Family Papers.

136. McPherson, *Battle Cry of Freedom*, 389–91.

137. Walter W. Lenoir's Civil War diary, pp. 4, 5, Lenoir Family Papers.

138. "Dress Parade," http://home.att.net/~Cap1MD/DressParade.htm, accessed Dec. 29, 2008.

139. "Spanish Moss," http://hernando.fnpschapters.org/plants/spanishmoss.htm, accessed Dec. 29, 2008.

140. Grace Fox Perry, *Moving Finger of Jasper*, 2001, http://sciway3.net/clark/jasper/churches.htm, accessed Dec. 30, 2008.

141. Freeman, *R. E. Lee*, 1936, vol. 1, p. 615.

142. Barney, *Making of a Confederate*, 53 and 8–40.

143. The Marshall House, Savannah, Georgia, "History of the Marshall House," www.marshallhouse.com/history.shtml, accessed Dec. 31, 2008.

144. John Muir, *A Thousand-Mile Walk to the Gulf*, ed. William Frederic Badé (Boston and New York: Houghton Mifflin, 1916; repr. with introduction by Peter Jenkins, Houghton Mifflin Harcourt, 1998), chap. 4, http://www.sierraclub.org/john_muir_exhibit/, accessed Dec. 31, 2008.

145. Department of National Archives, Confederate records; Jordan and Manarin, *North Carolina Troops*, vol. 7, Infantry, p. 355.

146. E. B. Long, *The Civil War Day by Day, An Almanac: 1861–1865* (Garden City, N.Y.: Doubleday, 1971; repr., New York: Da Capo Press, 1985), 148.

147. "The Burning of Charleston," *Harper's Weekly*, Dec. 28, 1861.

148. Long, *Civil War Day by Day*, 148.

149. Maj. Henry Middleton Rutledge's father and sister, Frederick and Eliza Pinkney Rutledge (the major's mother had died when he was a young boy), lived in the house on Charleston's Tradd Street that was destroyed in the fire. A correspondent who lived in Charleston offered the following explanation of the origin of the fire in a letter to Mary Chesnut: "The fire began in a negro house next to the blind factory—carelessness—and the wind rose with the flames until it got beyond control." Further on in the letter the author writes, "The Tradd St. Rutledges' house could have been saved if they could have got water enough, but the firemen were exhausted" (Mary Chestnut, *Mary Chesnut's Civil War*, ed. C. Vann Woodward [New Haven, Conn.: Yale University Press, 1981], 266, 267).

150. Maj. A. Gordon, "Adjutant-General's Department," in Walter Clark, ed., *Histories of the Several Regiments and Battalions from North Carolina, in the Great War 1861–'65*, vol. 1 (Goldsboro, N.C.: Nash Brothers Book and Job Printers, 1901), 24, 25.

151. Department of National Archives, Confederate records, www.footnote.com, accessed Jan. 3, 2009.

152. O.R. 1:6, chap. 15, p. 40.

153. O.R. 1:6, chap. 15, p. 42.

154. Allen, *Annals of Haywood County*, 137, 289; Hickerson, *Echoes of Happy Valley*, 189–91.

155. William L. Barney's research reveals that Tom treaded lightly with the Reece clan after his father had given him fair warning. Sometime after Tom took over the Lenoir plantation on the East Fork he was able to release David Reece from his tenancy by overpaying him for improvements made to the property; presumably Reece was then able to purchase his own piece of land. The 1850 Haywood County census, which lists the David Reece family, enumerates his wife and five children, including nine-year old Amos. Reece is listed as "farmer" with real estate valued at $130. Interestingly, a decade later the 1860 census lists the forty-seven-year-old Reece's occupation as "miller" (Barney, *Making of a Confederate*, 31, 32).

156. Allen, *Annals of Haywood County*, 346.

157. O.R. 1:6, chap.15, pp. 66, 69, 70 , 71, 75.

158. Hickerson, *Echoes of Happy Valley*, 78–79.

159. O.R. 1:6, chap.15, p. 367.

160. Blackmun, *Western North Carolina*, 275; "Caldwell County, North Carolina," www.carolana.com/NC/Counties/caldwell_county_nc.html, accessed Jan. 8, 2009.

161. "Rubella," www.drgreene.com/21_1176.html, accessed Jan. 9, 2009.

162. Allen, *Annals of Haywood County*, 466–68.

163. 1st Lt. William Pink Welch was detailed to Co. H, 2nd Regiment Engineer Troops in May 1864. The captain of the engineering company Welch was serving with wrote a glowing

recommendation in support of the lieutenant's official transfer to the 2nd Engineers, concluding that Welch was "an officer of great energy and judgment." Pink wrote a letter of his own to Confederate adjutant and inspector general, Sandy Cooper, requesting transfer to the engineers; the transfer was signed by Wesley N. Freeman, captain commanding Co. C, 25th N.C. Troops, and Matthew N. Love, captain commanding the 25th Regiment N.C. Troops. Welch's official transfer was dated Oct. 14, 1864. Welch's service career ended with Gen. Robert E. Lee's surrender at Appomattox on Apr. 9, 1865; he was paroled with the remaining survivors of the Army of Northern Virginia (Department of National Archives, Confederate records, www.footnote.com, accessed Mar. 26, 2009).

164. Cathey family genealogy compiled by Albert C. Jones of Canton, N.C., in author's collection.

165. Department of National Archives, Confederate records, www.footnote.com, accessed Jan. 10, 2009.

166. Walter W. Lenoir's Civil War diary, p. 7, Lenoir Family Papers.

167. Allen, *Annals of Haywood County*, 375; Haywood County census data for 1850, S-K Publications, p. 194Bsecond.

168. Tom Lenoir's handwritten drafts of discharges for both Alfred Burnett and Perry Franklin are found in the Lenoir Family Papers.

169. Barrett, *Civil War in North Carolina*, 66–72.

170. Letter from Walter W. Lenoir to Rufus Lenoir dated Jan. 18, 1862, Lenoir Family Papers.

171. Walter W. Lenoir's Civil War diary, p. 7, Lenoir Family Papers.

172. The service records of the 25th Regiment N.C. Troops fail to reveal that another man in the regiment died at this time at Grahamville, S.C. Perhaps Tom was mistaken and the soldier was actually affiliated with another unit (Department of National Archives, Confederate records; Jordan and Manarin, *North Carolina Troops*, vol. 7, *Infantry*).

173. O.R. 1:6, chap. 15, p. 374.

174. O.R. 1:6, chap. 15, p. 375.

175. Letter dated Feb. 9, 1862, from Walter W. Lenoir at Camp Lee, S.C. to Rufus Lenoir at Fort Defiance, Caldwell County, N.C., Lenoir Family Papers.

176. Barrett, *Civil War in North Carolina*, 73–87.

177. Allen, *Annals of Haywood County*, 118, 119.

178. Letter dated Feb. 20, 1862, from Walter W. Lenoir at Camp Lee, S.C., to Rufus Lenoir at Fort Defiance, Caldwell County, N.C., Lenoir Family Papers.

179. A copy of the inventory of Christopher's effects is found in the Lenoir Family Papers. The document that Captain Lenoir painstakingly wrote out and signed presents a good example of the various personal items that a typical soldier in the Haywood Highlanders and the 25th Regiment N.C. Troops might have possessed. Included in Christopher's effects were the following: "one coat,

1 overcoat, 1 blanket, 1 pr. pants, 3 pr. shoes, 1 Bowie knife, 1 pocket knife, 1 padlock, 1 hat, 1 cap, 2 shirts, 2 pr. drawers, 2 cakes soap, 2 spoons, 1 comb, 12 sheets letter paper, 9 envelops, 1 inkstand, 1 Testament, 1 Spelling book, 1 Pocket Memorandum book, 1 paper needles, a small quantity of sewing thread, & 15 cents in money." Christopher was obviously a literate man and appeared to be well stocked with personal items of necessity and comfort. The fact that his effects included only fifteen cents in cash is a good indication that the volunteers had not been recently paid. In fact the company's troops received their pay just a few days after Christopher died.

180. Journalist Cornelia Henry recorded in her Civil War–era journal on Feb. 8, 1862: "Mr. Henry (her husband, William Henry) came back late in the evening & is to start to Grahamville in the morning with 3000 lbs of bacon for the army. He sold it today in Henderson to be taken to Grahamville." The next day she made the following entry: "I feel sad & lonely this morning for Mr. Henry has gone & will be away some three or four weeks (he actually returned four weeks later). I shall miss him so much.... They loaded the wagon this morning with 3,000 lbs. bacon & a barell of krout. They had some trouble in getting up the hill the other side of the mill, along the old road. The oxen had to pull up for them" (Clinard and Russell, *Fear in North Carolina*, 62, 63).

181. Freeman, *R.E. Lee*, vol. 2, p. 26.

182. James M. McPherson estimates that one-half of the Confederate army was made up of twelve-month volunteers and the balance of three-year volunteers. He also writes that Robert E. Lee pronounced the new bounty and furlough law "highly disastrous" (*Battle Cry of Freedom*, 428–31).

183. Letter written from "Camp of the 25th Regt." Feb. 15 [1862] by G. S. Ferguson to his father, Evelyn McIntosh Hyatt Papers, archive PC 1343.1, North Carolina State Archives, Raleigh, N.C. The contents of this letter also included the following news: "Well I must tell you that we have some pies baked of the fruit sent us by Freeman. They will eat well though not so nice nor as good as I have frequently eat at Mama's house." And the young soldier concluded his letter with the following sentiments: "You can only imagine how pleased I would be if peace was made and I could be at home to help the boys make corn but I now [know] they will work lively and make a good field of corn."

184. Walter wrote in his diary, "On the morning of the 15th, we marched to the rail road station, & put our large accumulation of baggage and ourselves upon the cars, during a rain" (Walter W. Lenoir's Civil War diary, p. 8, Lenoir Family Papers).

185. Walter wrote in his diary that they were traveling in freight cars, as through the whole journey, and the man was riding on top of one of the cars in disobedience to orders (Walter W. Lenoir's Civil War diary, p. 8, Lenoir Family Papers).

186. Jordan and Manarin, *North Carolina Troops*, Vol. 7, *Infantry*, 397.

187. Mary Norcott Bryan, *A Grandmother's Recollection of Dixie*, p. 397, in Documenting the American South, Wilson Library, University of North Carolina; "Confederate War Department—Ordinance of Secession of North Carolina," www.csawardept.com/documents/secession/NC/index.html, accessed Feb. 19, 2009; letter from John C. Washington to Confederate government after the war pleading for amnesty, www.footnote.com, accessed Feb. 19, 2009.

188. A Confederate States bill of sale to Jesse H. Rouse dated June 30, 1862, was for 1,400 lbs of fodder. Delivery was made to Camp Johnston and Rouse received $17.50. Another bill of sale to Rouse, dated Nov. 4, 1863, was for corn and fodder. The goods were received at Moseley Hall, located between Kinston and Goldsboro, N.C., and Rouse received payment of $215.70 (www.footnote.com, accessed Feb. 20, 2009).

189. Captain Lenoir wrote that Col. Joseph Cathey arrived at the camp near Kinston, N.C., with his two daughters, Miss Sallie and Mrs. Freeman. The daughter referred to as "Miss Sallie" is Sarah Lucinda Cathey, who was born on Dec. 20, 1839, and married William Pink Welch in 1871. Welch was attached to Company C of the 25th Regiment N.C. Troops and was stationed at the time in Kinston. The captain's diary reference to Mrs. Freeman is puzzling; there are no known marriages of Colonel Cathey's daughters to a "Freeman," and perhaps in this instance Captain Lenoir simply erred.

190. Letter dated Jan. 18, 1862, from Walter W. Lenoir at Camp Lee in Kinston, N.C., to Rufus T. Lenoir at Fort Defiance in Caldwell County, N.C., Lenoir Family Papers.

191. Letter dated Mar. 16, 1862, from A. C. Hartgrove in Forks of Pigeon to Thomas I. Lenoir at Kinston, N.C., Lenoir Family Papers.

192. McPherson, *Battle Cry of Freedom*, 430–31.

193. Letter dated Mar. 10, 1862, from Walter W. Lenoir at Camp Lee, S.C., to Joseph Norwood in Lenoir, N.C., Lenoir Family Papers.

194. Tom wrote that "Maj. Rutledge was elected Lt. Col. – About a dozen votes were cast for W^m. McDowel. The others for the Maj." (Letter dated Apr. 30, 1862, from Thomas I. Lenoir at Camp Ransom near Kinston, N.C., to Walter W. Lenoir at Fort Defiance in Caldwell County, Lenoir Family Papers).

195. Jordan and Manarin, *North Carolina Troops, 1861–1865, A Roster*, vol. 7, *Infantry*, p. 355; however, a note in the regimental muster roll return for May, 1862 in the Confederate records states that Dearing "declined reelection and [was] honorably relieved from duty by order of Brig[adier] Gen[eral] Ransom April 30, 1862" (www.footnote.com, accessed Feb. 22, 2009).

196. Confederate muster roll for May 1862, www.footnote.com, accessed Feb. 22, 2009.

197. Letter dated Apr. 30, 1862, from Thomas I. Lenoir at Camp Ransom to Walter W. Lenoir at Fort Defiance, Caldwell County, N.C., Lenoir Family Papers.

198. Barney, *Making of a Confederate*, 68–75.

199. Letter of resignation dated Dec. 5, 1862, from Walter to Col. William N. Barbour, www.footnote.com, accessed Feb. 24. 2009. Walter writes, "My right leg was amputated below the knee on 3rd Sept. last in consequence of wounds from musket balls which I received two days before in the affair of Germantown, or Ox-hill."

Barney, *Making of a Confederate,* pp. 90–93.

200. Freeman, *Lee's Lieutenants,* vol. 1, p. 273.

201. Letter dated Mar. 2, 1862, from A. C. Hartgrove at Forks of Pigeon to Thomas I. Lenoir at Camp Lee near Grahamville, S.C., Lenoir Family Papers.

202. Letters dated Apr. 18, 1862, and Apr. 28, 1862, from A. C. Hartgrove in Forks of Pigeon to Thomas I. Lenoir at Kinston, N.C., Lenoir Family Papers.

203. Letter dated Apr. 30, 1862, from Thomas I. Lenoir at Camp Ransom in Kinston, N.C., to Walter W. Lenoir at Fort Defiance in Caldwell County, N.C., Lenoir Family Papers.

204. Letter from James D. Radcliffe dated Nov. 21, 1860, requesting enrollment in the South Carolina (Palmetto) forces in case the "little triangular state secedes." In the letter Radcliffe states that he is a native of South Carolina and a graduate of the Military Academy (www.footnote.com, accessed Feb. 24, 2009).

205. True copy of Joseph Cathey's bill dated July 18, 1861, for supplies sold to the Haywood Highlanders, Lenoir Family Papers.

206. Gordon, "Adjutant-General's Department," in Clark, ed., *Histories of the Several Regiments,* vol. 1, p. 24.

207. "On the Swannanoa, Mr. George Alexander's is a pleasant stopping-place. It is twelve miles from Asheville, situated very prettily, and with a very good view on all sides" (Henry E. Colton, *Mountain Scenery: The Scenery of Western North Carolina and Northwestern South Carolina* [Raleigh, N.C.: W. L . Pomeroy, 1859], p. 85, in Documenting the American South, http://docsouth.unc.edu/nc/colton/colton.html, accessed Feb. 2009.

In War's Aftermath on the East Fork

208. Barney, *Making of a Confederate,* 101.

209. Letter dated Sept. 26, 1862 from Thomas I. Lenoir at Middleburg, Va., to Lizzie Lenoir, in Hickerson, *Echoes of Happy Valley,* 64–65.

210. Barney, *Making of a Confederate,* 131–32.

211. Barney, *Making of a Confederate,* 104–5.

212. Letter dated Jan. 18, 1862 from J. W. Benninzer at Waynesville, N.C., to Thomas Lenoir at Camp Lee in Grahamville, S.C., Lenoir Family Papers.

213. Letter dated Aug. 14, 1865, from Thomas I. Lenoir at Forks of Pigeon to Rufus Lenoir at Fort Defiance, Caldwell County, in Hickerson, *Echoes of Happy Valley,* 103–4.

214. The 1860 Haywood County, North Carolina, Slave Schedule lists the black population at approximately 313 blacks, with 2 of these having been manumitted, or freed. The entire population of the county (presumably including blacks) was 5,801 (www.werelate.org/wiki/Place:Haywood%2C_North_Carolina%2C_United_States#Population_History, accessed June 14, 2009).

215. Letter dated Aug. 14, 1865, from Thomas I. Lenoir at Forks of Pigeon to Rufus Lenoir at Fort Defiance, Caldwell County, in Hickerson, *Echoes of Happy Valley*, 103–4; and Barney, *Making of a Confederate*, 142.

216. Letter dated Aug. 14, 1865, from Thomas I. Lenoir at Forks of Pigeon to Rufus Lenoir at Fort Defiance, Caldwell County, in Hickerson, *Echoes of Happy Valley*, 103–4.

217. Letter dated June 29, 1866, from Walter Lenoir at Crab Orchard to his sister Sarah at Fort Defiance, Caldwell County, Forester collection.

218. Letter dated Mar. 27, 1866, from Thomas I. Lenoir at The Den to Rufus T. Lenoir at Fort Defiance in Caldwell County, Lenoir Family Papers.

219. Letter dated Jan. 2, 1866, from Walter Lenoir at Crab Orchard to his sister Sarah at Fort Defiance, Caldwell County, Forester Collection.

220. Thomas I. Lenoir's memorandum book dated 1866, Lenoir Family Papers.

221. Letter dated Oct. 12, 1866, from Lizzie Lenoir at Forks of Pigeon to Thomas I. Lenoir, Lenoir Family Papers.

222. Letter dated Nov. 22, 1878, from Thomas I. Lenoir at The Den to Walter B. Gywn Esq. at Asheville, N.C., Lenoir Family Papers.

223. Terrell and Terrell, "Thomas Isaac Lenoir," in Coltman, *Legends, Tales, & History of Cold Mountain*, Book 3, p 23.

224. Letter dated Sept. 8, 1870, from Walter Lenoir at Forks of Pigeon to Rufus Lenoir at Fort Defiance in Caldwell County, N.C., Lenoir Family Papers.

225. Letter dated May 29, 1874, from Walter Lenoir at Shulls Mills, Watauga County, to Capt. Thomas I. Lenoir at Forks of Pigeon, Terrell Collection.

226. Letter dated May 29, 1874, from Walter Lenoir at Shulls Mills, Watauga County, to Capt. Thomas I. Lenoir at Forks of Pigeon, Terrell Collection.

227. Letter dated June 10, 1874, from Thomas I. Lenoir at The Den to Walter W. Lenoir at Hickory Tavern, N.C., Lenoir Family Papers.

228. Letter dated Feb. 9, 1876, from Rufus T. Lenoir at Fort Defiance in Caldwell County to Thomas I. Lenoir at Forks of Pigeon, Lenoir Family Papers.

229. Note dated June 20, 1879, from Mr. R. V. Welch to Capt. T. I. Lenoir, Lenoir Family Papers.

230. Letter dated Feb. 11, 1879, from Walter W. Lenoir at Shulls Mills in Watauga County to Thomas I. Lenoir at Forks of Pigeon, Lenoir Family Papers.

231. Letter dated Dec. 23, 1879, from Mr. John H. Goodale at Nashua, N.H. to Capt. Thomas I. Lenoir, Terrell Collection.

232. Letter dated Jan 12, 1880, from Mamie Lenoir in Forks of Pigeon to Aunt Sade at Fort Defiance in Caldwell County, N.C., Lenoir Family Papers.

233. Terrell and Terrell, "Thomas Isaac Lenoir," in Coltman, *Legends, Tales, & History of Cold Mountain*, Book 3, pp. 23–24.

234. Paraphrased from letter dated Nov. 27, 1880, from Walter W. Lenoir at Shull's Mills in Watauga County to Thomas I. Lenoir c/o Springdale, N.C., Lenoir Family Papers.

Part II: History and Roster of the Haywood Highlanders
The Last Three Years

235. Letter dated Dec. 19, 1881, from Walter W. Lenoir at Forks of Pigeon to Rufus T. Lenoir at Patterson, N.C., Lenoir Family Papers.

236. 1st Lieutenant Matthew Norris Love from Henderson County, North Carolina was subsequently elected captain of his company on Apr. 30, 1862, as a result of the Confederate army's reorganization. He later was promoted to lieutenant colonel of the 25th Regiment N.C. and was paroled at Appomattox Court House in April 1865 (John C. Inscoe and Gordon B. McKinney, *The Heart of Confederate Appalachia: Western North Carolina in the Civil War* [Chapel Hill and London: Univ. of North Carolina Press, 2005], 113).

237. Letter from L. B. Northrop to the Hon. L. P. Walker, Confederate Secretary of War, dated May 17, 1861, National Archives, document image found at www.footnote.com, accessed 2008.

238. Letter from Henry M. Rutledge to the Hon. L. P. Walker, Confederate Secretary of War, undated, with note indicating receipt on Apr. 21, 1861, National Archives, document image found at www.footnote.com, accessed 2008.

239. Major Wiley Parris to Jane Parris, Apr. 13, 1862, Paris Collection, Special Collections, Hunter Library, Western Carolina University.

240. Walter W. Lenoir's Civil War diary, p. 9, Lenoir Family Papers.

241. The phrase "true music of war" was used by Garland S. Ferguson in his history of the regiment ("Twenty-Fifth Regiment," in Clark, ed., *Histories of the Several Regiments*, 291).

242. There were 93 officers and private soldiers listed on the April 1862 muster roll. From that accounting one soldier transferred out to Company I (Pvt. Napoleon Glenn) and five men transferred into Company F (Pvt. Rufus L. Deaver, Pvt. William N. Deaver, Corp. Thomas F. Henson, and Musician John A. Smith from Company C and Pvt. John C. Wilson from Company B.)

243. Company F muster roll record of events for May and June, 1862, document image found at www.footnote.com, accessed Oct. 12, 2008.

244. Ferguson, "Twenty-Fifth Regiment," in Clark, ed., *Histories of the Several Regiments*, vol. 2, p. 291.

245. General Robert Ransom, official report of brigade's actions at King's School House or Oak Grove and Battle of Malvern Hill, O.R. 1:11, part 2, chap. 23, p. 792.

246. Dispatch dated July 21, 1862, from Gen. Benjamin Huger to Gen. Robert E. Lee requesting that Lee authorize the 25th Regiment N.C. to inscribe "King's School House" on its banner, O.R., 1:11, part 2, chap. 23, p. 787.

247. Company F muster roll record of events for May and June, 1862, document image found at www.footnote.com, accessed Oct. 12, 2008.

248. Ferguson, "Twenty-Fifth Regiment," in Clark, ed., *Histories of the Several Regiments*, vol. 2, p. 291.

249. Company F muster roll record of events for July and August, 1862, document image found at www.footnote.com, accessed Oct. 12, 2008.

250. Letter dated July 22, 1862, from Thomas I. Lenoir at The Den to Walter W. Lenoir, Lenoir Family Papers.

251. Ferguson, "Twenty-Fifth Regiment," in Clark, ed., *Histories of the Several Regiments*, vol. 2, p. 291.

252. Ferguson, "Twenty-Fifth Regiment," in Clark, ed., *Histories of the Several Regiments*, vol. 2, p. 291.

253. Company F muster roll record of events for September and October, 1862, document image found at www.footnote.com, accessed Oct. 12, 2008.

254. Gen. John Walker, official report of division's actions at Harpers Ferry on Sept. 17, 1862, O.R. 1:19, part 1, chap. 31, p. 913.

255. John G. Walker, "Sharpsburg," in *Battles and Leaders of the Civil War: The Struggle Intensifies*, p. 675.

256. Ferguson, "Twenty-Fifth Regiment," in Clark, ed., *Histories of the Several Regiments*, vol. 2, p. 291.

257. Walter Clark, "Sharpsburg (or Antietam)," in *Histories of the Several Regiments*, vol. 5, p. 71.

258. Gen. Robert Ransom, official report of brigade's actions at Sharpsburg of Sept. 17, 1862, O.R. 1:19, part 1, chap. 31, p. 920.

259. Ferguson, "Twenty-Fifth Regiment," in Clark, ed., *Histories of the Several Regiments*, vol. 2, p. 291.

260. Ferguson, "Twenty-Fifth Regiment," in Clark, ed., *Histories of the Several Regiments*, vol. 2, p. 291.

261. Freeman, *R. E. Lee*, vol. 2, p. 462.

262. Gen. Robert Ransom's official report on Battle of Fredericksburg, Dec. 20, 1862, O.R. 1:21, chap. 33, p. 625.

263. Robert Ransom, "Ransom's Division at Fredericksburg," *Battles and Leaders of the Civil War: The Tide Shifts*, vol. 3, p. 94.

264. Ferguson, "Twenty-Fifth Regiment," in Clark, ed., *Histories of the Several Regiments*, vol. 2, p. 291.

265. Dispatch from J. A. Seddon, Secretary of War, to Gen. R. E. Lee dated Jan. 1, 1863, O.R. 1:18, chap. 30, p. 810.

266. William H. S. Burgwyn, "Thirty-Fifth Regiment," in *Histories of the Several Regiments and Battalions from North Carolina, In the Great Civil War*, vol. 2, p. 591.

267. Dispatch from J. A. Seddon, Secretary of War, to His Excellency Zebulon B. Vance, dated Jan. 8, 1863, O.R. 1:18, chap. 30, p. 831.

268. Message issued by Maj. Gen. D. H. Hill from "Headquarters, Goldsborough, N.C." to his North Carolina troops, O.R. 1:18, chap. 30, p. 894.

269. Message issued by Maj. Gen. D. H. Hill from "Headquarters, Goldsborough, N.C." to his North Carolina troops, O.R. 1:18, chap. 30, p. 894.

270. Message from Maj. Gen. D. H. Hill, Goldsborough, N.C., to Gen. P. T. Beauregard, Charleston, S.C., dated Apr. 20, 1863, O.R. 1:18, chap. 30, p. 1007.

271. Dispatch from Maj. Gen. J. G. Foster to Maj. H. W. Halleck, June 2, 1863, O.R. 1:18, chap. 30, p. 363.

272. Dispatch from Col. George H. Pierson to Lt. Col. Southard Hoffman, Assistant Adjutant General, May 27, 1863, O.R. 1:18, chap. 30, p. 365.

273. Dispatch from Gen. R. E. Lee to Gen. D. H. Hill, May 28, 1863, O.R. 1:18, chap. 30, p. 1075.

274. Carroll C. Jones, *The 25th North Carolina Troops in the Civil War: History and Roster of a Mountain-Bred Regiment* (Jefferson, N.C.: McFarland, 2009), 96–97; the summary of the affair at Gum Swamp is taken from this source.

275. Handwritten letter dated June 4, 1863, to Hon. James Seddon and signed by H .M. Rutledge—Col. Commanding 25 Regt. N.C.T., Lt. Col. Bryson—absent, W. S. Grady—Maj. 25th Regt. N.C.T., Lee M. McAfee—Col 49th N.C.T., J. G. Jones—Lt. Col 35th Regt N.C.T., and four other officers of these regiments, National Archives, document image found at www.footnote.com, accessed Apr. 18, 2009.

276. Ferguson, "Twenty-Fifth Regiment," in Clark, ed., *Histories of the Several Regiments*, vol. 2, p. 291.

277. Inscoe and McKinney, *Heart of Confederate Appalachia*, 122.

278. Clinard and Russell, eds., *Fear in North Carolina*, 169–70.

279. A search of the roster also found that four men from the 25th Regiment N.C. Troops were captured Oct. 16, 1863, in an unrelated incident (see Jones, *The 25th North Carolina Troops in the Civil War*, 213).

280. O.R. 1:29, part 2, chap. 41, p. 836.

281. Special Orders No. 226, O.R. 1:29, part 2, chap. 41, p. 746.

282. Barrett, *The Civil War in North Carolina*, 202–12.

283. Company F muster roll record of events for January and February, 1864, document image found at www.footnote.com, accessed Apr. 9, 2009.

284. O.R. 1:33, chap. 45, p. 98.

285. Barrett, *The Civil War in North Carolina*, 202–12; Pickett's failed attempt to capture New Bern in early 1864 is documented in this source as well as in the Official Records.

286. Clayton Charles Marlow, *Matt W. Ransom: Confederate General from North Carolina* (Jefferson, N.C., and London: McFarland, 1996), 86.

287. Ferguson, "Twenty-Fifth Regiment," in Clark, ed., *Histories of the Several Regiments*, vol. 2, p. 291.

288. Capt. Robert D. Graham, "Map of Plymouth And Defenses, April 17–20, 1864" and "Fifty-Sixth Regiment," in *Histories of the Several Regiments and Battalions from North Carolina*, vol. 5, p. 184–85.

289. Robert D. Graham, "Fifty-Sixth Regiment," in Clark, ed., *Histories of the Several Regiments and Battalions from North Carolina*, vol. 3, p. 313.

290. Graham, "Fifty-Sixth Regiment," vol. 3, p. 313.

291. Graham, "Fifty-Sixth Regiment," vol. 3, p. 313.

292. Shelby Foote, *The Civil War: A Narrative*, vol. 3, *Red River to Appomattox* (New York: Random House, 1974), 115.

293. Peter M. Chaitin, *The Civil War: The Coastal War: Chesapeake Bay to the Rio Grande*, (Alexandria, Va.: Time-Life Books, 1984), p. 96; Jones, *The 25th North Carolina Troops in the Civil War*, 109–13.

294. Graham, "Fifty-Sixth Regiment," in Clark, ed., *Histories of the Several Regiments*, vol. 3, p. 313.

295. Ferguson, *"Twenty-Fifth Regiment,"* in Clark, ed., *Histories of the Several Regiments*, vol. 2, p. 291.

296. O.R. 1:36, part 2, chap 48, p. 999.

297. William H. S. Burgwyn, "Thirty-Fifth Regiment," in Clark, ed., *Histories of the Several Regiments and Battalions from North Carolina*, vol. 2, p. 591.

298. O.R. 1:36, part 2, chap 48, p. 1002.

299. O.R. 1:40, part 2, chap 52, p. 658.

300. Freeman, *Lee's Lieutenants*, vol. 3, p. 529.

301. Burgwyn, "Thirty-Fifth Regiment," in Clark, ed., *Histories of the Several Regiments*, vol. 2, p. 591.

302. Ferguson, "Twenty-Fifth Regiment," in Clark, ed., *Histories of the Several Regiments*, vol. 2, p. 291.

303. Freeman, *Lee's Lieutenants*, vol. 3, p. 529.

304. Ransom's Brigade was actually attached to Maj. Gen. Bushrod R. Johnson's division on May 17, 1864, and soon was posted at the Howlett Line in front of General Benjamin Butler's forces to keep that Union general bottled up between the Appomattox and James rivers (O.R. 1:36, part 2, chap. 48, p. 999).

305. Letter written by Garland Ferguson on July 28 [1864] to "John," Evelyn McIntosh Hyatt papers, archive PC 1343.1, North Carolina State Archives.

306. *North Carolina Standard*, May 24, 1864, in Inscoe and McKinney, *Heart of Confederate Appalachia*, 161.

307. North Carolina State Archives, "Evelyn McIntosh Hyatt papers" contained in archive PC 1343.1; letter written by Garland Ferguson on July 28th [1864] to "John."

308. O.R. 1:40, part 1, chap 52, p. 783.

309. McPherson, *Battle Cry of Freedom*, 759.

310. Freeman, *Lee's Lieutenants*, vol. 3, p. 542.

311. Report from Lt. Gen. U. S. Grant, Aug. 1, 1864, O.R. 1:40, part 1, chap 52, p. 17.

312. Ferguson, "Twenty-Fifth Regiment," in Clark, ed., *Histories of the Several Regiments*, vol. 2, p. 291.

313. B. F. Dixon, "Additional Sketch—Forty-Ninth Regiment," in Clark, ed., *Histories of the Several Regiments and Battalions from North Carolina*, vol. 3, p. 151.

314. North Carolina State Archives, Evelyn McIntosh Hyatt papers, contained in archive PC 1343.1; letter written by Garland Ferguson on July 28 [1864] to "John." Although dated July 28, 1864, Ferguson's letter was obviously concluded after the Battle of the Crater which occurred two days later, on July 30. As a postscript he penned, "We certainly have gained a great victory [surely speaking of the battle which followed the blowup of Grant's mine under the Confederate trenches], and I hope and pray that the day may soon come when peace will rest on our banners." Sergeant Ferguson's note included a tally of the 25th N.C. Troops casualties on that day.

315. Obituary for Capt. James M. Cathey, dated Waynesville, N.C., Oct. 4, 1864, Civil War Letters and Photographs, Cathey Collection.

316. Burgwyn, "Thirty-Fifth Regiment," in Clark, ed., *Histories of the Several Regiments*, vol. 2, p. 591.

317. Letter written by Garland Ferguson on Aug. 23, 1864, from Petersburg, Va., to "Mr. Nath. J. Ferguson," Evelyn McIntosh Hyatt papers, archive PC 1343.1, North Carolina State Archives.

318. Ferguson, "Twenty-Fifth Regiment," in Clark, ed., *Histories of the Several Regiments*, vol. 2, p. 291.

319. Terrell Garren, Western North Carolina Civil War historian and author, has substantiated from family oral and documented history that his ancestor, Ensign John W. Hutchison (sometimes spelled "Hutcheson" in the Confederate records), was carrying the 25th N.C. Regiment's colors when he fell with a gunshot wound to the right arm during the action at Globe Tavern. Subsequently, Hutcheson's arm was amputated above the elbow, and he died in 1866 from continuing complications and infection arising from the wound.

320. Letter written by Garland Ferguson on Aug. 23, 1864, from Petersburg, Va., to "Mr. Nath. J. Ferguson," Evelyn McIntosh Hyatt papers, archive PC 1343.1, North Carolina State Archives.

321. Letter from Lt. Garland S. Ferguson to Mariah Henderson, widow of James Martin Henderson, dated Aug. 26, 1864, Haywood County NCGENWEB Genealogy Database, www.rootsweb.ancestry.com/~nchaywoo/database.htm.

322. Letter from Gen. R. E. Lee to Secretary of War John C. Breckenridge, Feb. 24, 1865, O.R. 1:46, part 2, chap. 57, p. 1254.

323. Inscoe and McKinney, *Heart of Confederate Appalachia*, 114; James I. Robertson, *The Civil War: Tenting Tonight* (Alexandria, Va.: Time-Life Books, 1984), 153: "One of every seven Confederates would eventually desert. In the North, one of ten would do so."

324. This paragraph is taken in its entirety from my previous history, *The 25th North Carolina Troops in the Civil War*, 153–54.

325. Archibald Rutledge, *My Colonel and His Lady* (1937), p. 94.

326. Ferguson, "Twenty-Fifth Regiment," in Clark, ed., *Histories of the Several Regiments*, vol. 2, p. 291.

327. Freeman, *Lee's Lieutenants*, vol. 3, pp. 662–74.

328. Ferguson, "Twenty-Fifth Regiment," in Clark, ed., *Histories of the Several Regiments*, vol. 2, p. 291.

329. Freeman, *Lee's Lieutenants*, vol. 3, p. 671.

330. U.S. Census, Haywood County, N.C., 1850, listing for Jessia [?] Anderson family.

Lifting the Shroud of Time

331. Although Tom wrote that "Joseph [Josiah] Anderson was shot in the shoulder while carrying his brother from the field," it is believed that Anderson was wounded in the left leg (letter dated July 22, 1862, from Thomas I. Lenoir at The Den to Walter W. Lenoir, Lenoir Family Papers).

332. U.S. Census, Haywood County, N.C., 1850, lists the names of the Henry Bug[g] family.

333. Letter dated Dec. 17, 1861, from Capt. Thomas Lenoir at Camp Lee, S.C., to his wife, Lizzie, residing at the time at Fort Defiance in Caldwell County, Thomas Lenoir, Sr. Papers.

334. Allen, *Annals of Haywood County*, 556.

335. U.S. Census, Haywood County, N.C., 1850, lists the names of the Eli Deaver family members.

336. U.S. Census, Haywood County, N.C., 1850, lists the names of the William Ferguson family; Allen, *Annals of Haywood County*, 285.

337. In a letter dated Aug. 31, 1864, to his family at home Garland Ferguson (stationed in the trenches near Petersburg) expressed deep remorse after receiving "the saddest news that was ever my lot to receive." Just days earlier Ferguson had been informed by his sister, through yet another letter, of the death of his brother, Nathan (Hattie Caldwell Davis, *Civil War Letters and Memories from the Great Smoky Mountains* [n.p., H. C. Davis, 1999]).

338. Ferguson was admitted to the hospital on Aug. 20, 1862, and returned to duty on Nov. 14, 1862 (Register of General Hospital, Petersburg, Va., www.footnote.com, accessed Sept. 26, 2009).

339. W. C. Allen wrote in his biographical sketch of William H. Hargrove that the young lieutenant rescued Lt. G. S. Ferguson at the Battle of Five Forks (*Annals of Haywood County, North Carolina*, 148). Since Ferguson was severely wounded and incapacitated less than one week before, during the Battle of Fort Stedman, I believe that Allen misstated the circumstances of Ferguson's rescue. The rescue was surely a matter of fact; however, it likely occurred during the Battle of Fort Stedman.

340. U.S. Census, Haywood County, N.C., 1850, lists the names of the A[a]ron Henson family.

341. U.S. Census, Haywood County, N.C., 1850, lists the names of the Daniel Henson family.

342. U.S. Census, Haywood County, N.C., 1850, lists the names of the Nathaniel Henson family.

343. U.S. Census, Haywood County, N.C., 1850, lists the names of the Joshua [Joseph] Inman family; Coltman, *Legends, Tales, & History of Cold Mountain*, Book 1, p. 20, and Book 3, p. 12.

344. The Confederate records and various other sources give William's middle name as "Pingree." However, his correct name was "Pinkney" per Inman family historian Cheryl Inman Haney.

345. Facts about Inman's death appear in "William Pingree 'Pinkney' Inman: The Real Story," in Coltman, *Legends, Tales, & History of Cold Mountain*, Book 2, pp. 7–9.

346. U.S. Census, Haywood County, N.C., 1850, lists the names of the Peter Meace [Meece] family.

347. U.S. Census, Haywood County, N.C., 1850, lists the names of the Thomas Pressley family. The spelling of Jemima's name appears in James E. & Vivian Wooley, *Early Marriage Bonds of Haywood County, N.C., 1808–1870* (Raleigh: North Carolina Department of Archives and History, 1963).

348. U.S. Census, Haywood County, N.C., 1850, lists the names of the Samuel Reace [Reece] family.

349. Allen, *Annals of Haywood County*, 94.

350. U.S. Census, Haywood County, N.C., 1850, lists the names of the Alexander Thompson family.

351. W. A. Newman Dorland, ed., *The American Medical Pocket Dictionary*, 16th ed. (Philadelphia and London: W. B. Saunders Company, 1938), 399.

352. Approximately 28,000 Confederate army and naval forces surrendered with Gen. Robert E. Lee at Appomattox Court House.

The Last Highlanders Standing

353. Freeman, *Lee's Lieutenants*, vol. 3, p. 718.

Afterword

354. Hartgrove's journey home from the prisoner-of-war camp and his stopover in Petersburg, Va., to "look in" on friends there in the hospitals was included in his personal diary, published as *Diary and Reminiscences of W. H. Hargrove* (Sweetwater, Tex.: Hattie Rue and Dale Campbell, 1938), copy in collection of Carroll C. Jones. I treat Hartgrove's travels in greater detail in *Rooted Deep in the Pigeon Valley: A Harvest of Western Carolina Memories* (Wilmington, N.C.: Winoca Press, 2008).

355. For more about "Captain Hack" and his contributions to Haywood County, see Jones, *Rooted Deep in the Pigeon Valley*.

356. Allen, *Annals of Haywood County*, 285–89.

Haywood Highlanders: Roster and Service Records

357. The following excerpt is taken from a letter attributed to Garland Ferguson and dated Aug. 23, 1864: "Captain J. H. [M.] Cathey—wounded, Capt. [Corp.] J. B. Mann—severely in wrist, Private H. T. Bugg—severely in leg, Ben F. Edmonston mortally in head, W. P. Inman—stunned slightly with a shell" (Hattie Caldwell Davis, *Civil War Letters and Memories*, 1999, 41, 42). It is believed that this report actually belongs to a letter that Ferguson penned on July 28, 1864, and was somehow misplaced over the years and/or transcribed incorrectly. It would likely have been included as a postscript giving the killed and wounded from the July 30, 1864, Battle of the Crater. Of importance here is the revelation that Pvt. Benjamin Edmonston received a *mortal* head wound, a fact that cannot be gleaned from the compiled Confederate records or Jordan and Manarin, *North Carolina Troops*, vol. 7, *Infantry*.

Bibliography

Books, Periodicals, and Online Publications

Allen, W. C. *The Annals of Haywood County North Carolina, Historical, Sociological, Biographical, and Genealogical.* Raleigh: North Carolina State Library, 1935; repr. Spartanburg, S.C.: Reprint Company, 1977.

Arthur, John Preston. *Western North Carolina: A History (from 1730 to 1913).* Asheville, N.C.: Edward Buncombe Chapter of the Daughters of the American Revolution of Asheville, North Carolina, 1914; repr. Johnson City, Tenn.: Overmountain Press, 1996.

Barney, William L. *The Making of a Confederate: Walter Lenoir's Civil War.* Oxford and New York: Oxford University Press, 2008.

Barrett, John G. *The Civil War in North Carolina.* Chapel Hill: Univ. of North Carolina Press, 1963; repr. 1995.

Blackmun, Ora. *Western North Carolina: Its Mountains and Its People to 1880.* Boone, N.C.: Appalachian Consortium Press, 1977.

"Bombardment of Pensacola." *Harper's Weekly*, Dec. 7, 1861.

"The Burning of Charleston." *Harper's Weekly*, Dec. 28, 1861.

Bryan, Mary Norcott. *A Grandmother's Recollections of Dixie.* New Bern, N.C.: Owen G. Dunn Printer, c. 1912. Accessed electronically via Documenting the American South, http://docsouth.unc.edu/fpn/bryan/menu.html

Canton (N.C.) Vindicator. Miscellaneous 1908 and 1909 newspaper publications on microfilm, North Carolina State Archives and Records, Raleigh, N.C.

Chaitin, Peter M. *The Civil War: The Coastal War: Chesapeake Bay to Rio Grande.* Alexandra, Va.: Time-Life Books, 1984.

Chesnut, Mary Boykin. *A Diary from Dixie.* New York: D. Appleton and Company, 1905.

Clinard, Karen L., and Richard Russell, eds., *Fear in North Carolina: The Civil War Journal and Letters of the Henry Family.* Asheville, N.C.: Reminiscing Books, 2008.

Coltman, Evelyn M. *Legends, Tales, and History of Cold Mountain: A Pigeon Valley Heritage Collection*. Books 1–3. Waynesville, N.C.: Richard L. Coltman, 2008.

Colton, Henry E. *Mountain Scenery: The Scenery of Western North Carolina and Northwestern South Carolina*, Raleigh, N.C.: W. L. Pomeroy, 1859. Accessed via Documenting the American South, http://docsouth.unc.edu/nc/colton/colton.html

Davis, Hattie Caldwell. *Civil War Letters and Memories from the Great Smoky Mountains*. N.p.: H. C. Davis, 1999.

Dorland, W. A. Newman, ed. *American Medical Pocket Dictionary*. 16th ed. Philadelphia, Pa.: W. B. Saunders, 1938.

Dowd, Clement. *Life of Zebulon Vance*. Charlotte, N.C.: Observer Publishing and Printing House, 1897.

Dowdey, Clifford, *Lee*, 1965, New York: Bonanza Books, New York 1965; repr. Gettysburg, Pa.: Stan Clark Military Books, 1996.

Esposito, Vincent J. *The West Point Atlas of War: The Civil War* (1959). New York, N.Y.: Tess Press, 1995.

Ferguson, Garland S. "Twenty-Fifth Regiment." In vol. 2 of *Histories of the Several Regiments and Battalions from North Carolina, in the Great War 1861–'65*, ed. Walter Clark. Goldsboro, N.C.: Nash Brothers, 1901.

Foote, Shelby. *The Civil War, A Narrative*. Vol. 1, *Fort Sumter to Perryville*. New York: Random House, 1958.

———. *The Civil War, A Narrative*. Vol. 2, *Fredericksburg to Meridian*. New York: Random House, 1963.

———. *The Civil War, A Narrative*. Vol. 3, *Red River to Appomattox*. New York: Random House, 1974.

Freeman, Douglas Southall. *Lee's Lieutenants: A Study in Command*. 3 vols. New York: Scribner, 1942–44.

———. *R. E. Lee: A Biography*. 4 vols. New York: Scribner, 1934.

Gordon, Maj. A. "Adjutant-General's Department," in Walter Clark, ed., *Histories of the Several Regiments and Battalions from North Carolina, in the Great War 1861–'65*, vol. 1. Goldsboro, N.C.: Nash Brothers, 1901.

Grant, Ulysses S. *Personal Memoirs: Ulysses S. Grant*. New York: Modern Library, 1999. First published New York: Charles Webster & Co., 1885, as *Personal Memoirs of U. S. Grant*, 2 vols.

Hargrove, W. H. *Diary and Reminiscences of W. H. Hargrove*. Sweetwater, Tex.: privately printed by Hattie Rue and Dale Campbell, 1938.

Hickerson, Thomas Felix. *Happy Valley: History and Genealogy*. Chapel Hill, N.C.: privately printed, 1940.

———. *Echoes of Happy Valley: Letters and Diaries; Family Life in the South; Civil War History*. Chapel Hill, N.C.: Bull's Head, 1962.

Hill, D. H., Jr. *North Carolina*. Vol. 4 of Confederate Military History: A Library of Confederate States Military History. ed. Clement Anselm Evans Atlanta, Ga.: Confederate Publishing Co., 1899; repr. Secaucus, N.J.: Blue & Grey Press, 1960.

"History of the Marshall House." www.marshallhouse.com/history.shtml, accessed Dec. 31, 2008.

Inscoe, John C. *Mountain Masters: Slavery and the Sectional Crisis in Western North Carolina*. Knoxville: Univ. of Tennessee Press, 1989.

———, and Gordon B. McKinney. *The Heart of Confederate Appalachia: Western North Carolina in the Civil War*. Chapel Hill and London: Univ. of North Carolina Press, 2005.

Johnson, Robert Underwood, and Clarence Clough Buel, eds., *Battles and Leaders of the Civil War*. 4 vols. New York: Century, 1887-88; reprint, Secaucus, N.J.: Castle, 1989.

Jones, Carroll C. *The 25th North Carolina Troops in the Civil War: History and Roster of a Mountain-Bred Regiment*. Jefferson, N.C.: McFarland, 2009.

Jordan, Weymouth T., Jr., and Louis H. Manarin. *North Carolina Troops, 1861–1865: A Roster*. Vol. 7, *Infantry*. Raleigh: North Carolina Office of Archives and History, 1979; repr. Wilmington, N.C.: Broadfoot, 2004.

Long, E. B. *The Civil War Day by Day: An Almanac, 1861–1865*. Garden City, N.Y.: Doubleday, 1971; repr. New York: Da Capo Press, 1985.

Medford, W. Clark. *The Early History of Haywood County*. Asheville, N.C.: Miller Printing Co., 1961.

Marlow, Clayton Charles. *Matt W. Ransom: Confederate General from North Carolina*. Jefferson, N.C., and London: McFarland, 1996.

McPherson, James M. *Battle Cry of Freedom: The Civil War Era*. New York: Oxford Univ. Press, 1988.

Muir, John. *A Thousand-Mile Walk to the Gulf*, ed. William Frederic Badé. Boston and New York: Houghton Mifflin, 1916. Repr. with introduction by Peter Jenkins, Houghton Mifflin Harcourt, 1998. www.sierraclub.org/john_muir_exhibit, accessed Dec. 31, 2008.

Perry, Grace Fox. *Moving Finger of Jasper*. Ridgeland, S.C.: n.p., 2001, http://sciway3.net/clark/jasper/churches.htm, accessed Dec. 30, 2008.

Robertson, James I. *The Civil War: Tenting Tonight*, Rev. ed. Alexandria, Va.: Time-Life Books, 1984.

Rutledge, Archibald. *My Colonel and His Lady*. Indianapolis and New York: Bobbs-Merrill, 1937.

Sondley, Foster A. *A History of Buncombe County, North Carolina*. 2 vols. Asheville, North Carolina: Advocate Printing Co., 1930.

Time-Life Books. *The Civil War. The Blockade: Runners and Raiders*. Rev. ed. Alexandria, Va.: Time-Life Books, 1983.

Trotter, William R. *Bushwhackers: The Civil War in North Carolina (The Mountains)*. Winston Salem, N.C.: John F. Blair, 1988.

Wheeler, Richard. *Witness to Appomattox*. New York: Harper & Row, 1989.

Wooley, James E. and Vivian. *Early Marriage Bonds of Haywood County, North Carolina, 1808–1870*. Microfilmed Raleigh: North Carolina Department of Archives and History, 1963, DH-9.

United States War Department. *The War of the Rebellion: A Compilation of the Official Records of the Union and Confederate Armies*. Washington, D.C., Government Printing Office, 1881.

Special Collections and Archives

Cathey, Paris, and Estes Collections. Special Collections—Civil War Letters and Photographs. Hunter Library, Western Carolina University.

Erwin, Thomas. *Thomas Erwin History*. Date unknown. Collection of author.

Genealogy records of the Cathey and Hargrove families of Haywood County, N.C. Compiled by Albert C. Jones, Canton, N.C.; collection of Carroll C. Jones, Pace, Florida.

Hargrove, W. H. "Wm H. Hartgrove's Book." Unpublished notebook/journal. Collection of Carroll C. Jones, Pace, Florida.

Evelyn McIntosh Hyatt Papers. North Carolina State Archives, Raleigh, N.C.

Collection of Lenoir letters and documents held by Ike Forester, Lenoir, N.C.

Lenoir family letters, papers, and historical information; unpublished diary of Thomas Isaac Lenoir. Collection of Hugh K. Terrell and the late Emily Michal Terrell, Bethel, N.C.

Lenoir Family Papers. Southern Historical Collection, Wilson Library, University of North Carolina at Chapel Hill.

Thomas Lenoir Papers, Duke University Library.

Digital collections, Joyner Library, East Carolina University.

Public documents

Haywood County, N.C. Commissioners' Court records. Waynesville, N.C.

U.S. Census, North Carolina, 1810, 1820, 1850, and 1860.

Index

Page numbers in *italics* indicate photographs, illustrations, or maps.

1st Regiment N.C. Artillery, 175
1st Regiment N.C. Calvary, 212
2nd Brigade N.C. (Ransom's Brigade), 248, 261
8th N.C. Volunteers, 98
8th Regiment N.C., 301, 303
13th Regiment S.C., 90
14th S.C. Volunteers, 153
15th Volunteers N.C., 68–69, 77; redesignated 25th Regiment N.C. Troops, 72, 77, 79; transferred to service of Confederate army, 79; *see also* Haywood Highlanders
18th Regiment N.C. Infantry State Troops, 98, 178
19th Brigade N.C. Militia, 41
25th Regiment N.C. Troops, 1, 72, 78–79, 135, 186, 191, 207, 247, 256, 294, 305, 319, 326, 330–31, 363, 369; gambling in, 120; ordnance list of, *123;* history of, 262; under Clingman, 71, 73, 203, 245
26th Regiment N.C., 190
37th Regiment N.C., 190, 205
43rd Regiment N.C., 301
48th N.C. Infantry, 261
49th N.C. Infantry, 261, 301
56th Regiment N.C., 294

Abbott, Pvt. Green B., 127, 267, 376
Allen, Pvt. David, 256, 377
Allman, Pvt. William N., 65, 306, 377
Anderson, Brig. Gen. Joseph R., 82
Anderson, Pvt. Jasper N., 263, 267, 305, 342–43, 377
Anderson, Jesse, Jr., and family (of Forks of Pigeon, N.C.), 232
Anderson, Pvt. Josiah McDonald, 35, 51, 266, 263, 267, 342–43, 377
Andy, Welch servant, 83

Antietam Run, Battle of, 250, 273, 275–78, *279*
Appomattox Court House, Va., 253, 334–35, 369
Asheville, N.C., 68, 70, 77
Avery, C. M., 223
Avery, Selina Louisa *see* Lenoir, Selina Louisa Avery
Avery, Uncle (of Thomas Isaac Lenoir), 223
Avery, Waightstill, 9; landholdings, 10–11, 408
Avery, Willy, 190

"Bachelor's Den" or "Bachelor's Retreat," *v*, 9, 32, *44*, 46, 55
Baggett, Pvt. William M., 336, 377
Ballews, William, 219, 222
Barbour, Lt. Col. William M., 190
Barringer, Maj., 211
Barton, Gen. Seth M., 299
Beauregard, Gen. P. G. T., 310–14, *312*
Bennett, F. (of Forks of Pigeon), 235
Bermuda Hundred, Va., 311–12
Best, Pvt. Rodom C., 336, 377
Big Bottom land tract, N.C., 12
Black Walnut Bottom land tract, N.C., 12
Black Walnut Cove land tract, N.C., 12
Blackburn, Pvt. William P., 377
Blake, Capt. Frederick R., 68, 84, 137, 176
Blalock, 1st Lt. Etheldred H., 46, 65, 96, 108, 142, 151, 184, 193, 195, 199, 200, 256, 375
Blalock, Pvt. George H., 338, 377
Blalock, Capt. James Allen, 84, 208, 257, 320, *321*, 354–55, 364–65, 366, 370, 375
Bonham, Cpl. William, 202, 257, 335, 355, 366, 377
Brookshire, J. (of Forks of Pigeon), 235
Brookshire, Pvt. Humphrey P., 268, 378
Brookshire, Pvt. John E., 278, 378

Bryson, Capt. Samuel C., 68, 84, 203, 257, 284, 296
Bryson, Capt. Thaddeus D., 68, 86
Bryson, Capt. William H., 135, 177, 183
Bugg, Pvt. Henry Tilman, 84, 106, 146, 159, 177, 343–44, 366, 378, 462n357
Bugg, Pvt. Jeremiah H., 336, 337, 343–34, 366, 378
Burch, Lt., 330
Burgins, Gen. (of Pleasant Gardens, N.C.), 224
Burnett, Pvt. Alfred, 127, 162–64, 183, 256, 378
Burnett, D. (of Haywood), 176
Burnett, J. G. (of Forks of Pigeon), 235
Burnett, 2nd Lt. James A., 65, 108, 183, 256, 375
Burnett, Pvt. John G., 65, 120, 141, 166, 268, 378
Byers, Pvt. William, 378

Caldwell Co., N.C., 156
Camp Beauregard (S.C.), 96
Camp Clingman, Asheville, N.C., 77
Camp Davis, Wilmington, N.C., 73, 77–84
Camp Johnston, Kinston, N.C., 191
Camp Lee (S.C.), 101–86; fortifications, 144–45, *149, 169*
Camp Patton, Asheville, N.C., 68, 70, 77
Camp Ransom, Wyse Fork, N.C., 191–205
Carroll, Augustus, 126
Case, Maj., 198
Cathey, Charles, xxi–xxiii
Cathey, Capt. James Madison, 61, 65, 96, 105, 108, 125, 187, 191, 196, 199, 207, 208–9, 245–47, *246*, 257, 265–66, 311–12, 318, 320, 335, 344, 375, 462n357
Cathey, Col. Joseph, 27, 33, 46, 50, 59–60, *65*, 266, 344, *346*; role in forming Haywood Highlanders, 1, 60–61, 62; as Highlanders' agent to state of N.C., 67; sojourn at Camp Beauregard and Grahamville, 98–109; sojourn at Camp Ransom, 195; death, 238, 430

Cathey, 3rd Lt. Joseph Turner, 61, 65, 96, 105, 125, 143–44, 184; elected new captain of Haywood Highlanders, 200–201, 209, 265–66, 305, 344, 375
Cathey, Nancy Hyatt, 344
Cathey, Sarah Lucinda (Sallie, of Forks of Pigeon, N.C.), 157, 195, 452n189
Cathey, Sgt. William Turner, 65, 202, 257, 378
Chaffin's Bluff, Va., 312
Chambers, Pvt. George W., 263, 267, 305, 341, 378, 393
Charleston & Savannah Railroad, 90, 155
Charleston, S.C., 84–90, 187, 449n149; American Hotel, 87–89; Charleston Hotel, 87
Christopher, Pvt. George E., 83, 176, 179–80, 256, 344–45, 379, 450n179
Christopher, Pvt. Henry, 83, 256, 344–45, 379
Christopher, Pvt. McDaniel, 366, 379
Clark, Pvt. Hiram, 345, 379
Clark, Cpl. Joshua A., 193, 195, 345, 366, 369, 379
Clingman, Col. Thomas L., 69, 70, 71, 72, 73, 84, 99, 134, 147, 151, 154, 178, 184, 186, 195, 203, 245, 247
Clonts, Pvt. William R., 202, 257, 272, 278, 306, 379
Coker, 1st Sgt. James, 120
Colcock, Lt. Col. (cavalry), 103
Cold Mountain (Frazier), 350
Collins, Pvt. Eli, 268, 305, 378
Colquitt, Gen. Alfred H., 311
Company A (Edney Grays), 68, 86, 106, 119, 125, 136, 143
Company B, 68, 86, 104, 120, 136, 141, 143, 175, 204
Company C, 68, 84, 104, 106, 136, 140, 160, 162, 164, 177, 195, 203, 205, 323, 330–31
Company D, 68, 84, 104, 161, 168, 177, 189, 203
Company E, 68, 84, 104, 140, 161
Company F *see* Haywood Highlanders

Company G (Highland Guards), 68, 79, 84, 120, 126, 165, 203
Company H, 68, 84, 176
Company I, 68, 86, 176, 204
Company K, 68, 86, 141, 203
Coosawhatchie Station (S.C.), 90
Corpening, Dr. Thomas (of Morganton, N.C.), 223
Crab Orchard land tract, N.C., 12, 229, 237
Crater, Battle of the, 252, 314–20, *318*
Crawford, Pvt. Amos A., 98, 262, 267, 278, 379
Crawford, R. P., 447n112, n113
Crawford, T. M. (of Forks of Pigeon), 235
CSS *Albemarle*, 288, 301–03, *303*
Curtis, Mr., manager of Lenoir's East Fork farm, 442n31

Daniel, Jeremiah, 11
Daniel, Josiah, 11
Davenport Female College, 56
Davis, Asb. (of Forks of Pigeon), 235
Davis, B. (of Forks of Pigeon), 235
Davis, Pvt. Joseph N., 379
Dearing, Lt. Col. St. Clair, 69, 70, 79, 84, 103, 127–31, 136, 139, 151, 154, 176, 178, 203, 204, 452n195
Deaver, Eli (of Forks of Pigeon), 36, 162
Deaver, Pvt. Rufus L., 162, 204, 306, 345, 380
Deaver, Pvt. William N., 204, 306, 345, 380
Devereaux, Maj. J., 215, 218
Devereaux, Maj. John, 134
Dewey, Capt. (quartermaster), 207
Dickinson, Pratt K., 86
Dillard, Lt. Lynch, 175
Drewry's Bluff, Battle of, 251, 310–311
Duncan (deceased soldier), 143
Duncan, Wiley, 141
Dunlap, J., Asheville merchant, 24
duPont, Samuel, 91

Earp, William, 11
Edmiston brothers (of Patterson, N.C.), 220

Edmonston, Pvt. Basil, 177
Edmonston, Pvt. Benjamin F., 110, 177, 262, 267, 335, 380, 462n357
Edmonston, Ninian (of Forks of Pigeon), 176
Edney, Capt. Balis M., 68, 86, 119, 215–18
Edwards, Col. Oliver, 90
Edwards, T. L. (of Haywood), 176
Erwin, Lenoir slave, 38
Estes, Pvt. Robert J. H., 369, 380
Evans, Pvt. John C., 278, 337, 380
Evans, 1st Sgt. William J., 256, 338, 380–81

Ferguson, 3rd Lt. Ebed J., 310, 335, 346–47, 355–56, 376
Ferguson, 2nd Lt. Garland Sevier, 65, 139, 184, 262, 272, 273–74, 282, 297, 313, 319, 321–22, 323–24, 330–32, 336, 337, 346–47, *346, 361,* 366, 370–72, 376, 451n183, 459n314, 461n337, n338, n339, 462n357
Ferguson, Pvt. Nathan J., 110, 336, 381, 461n337
Fitzgerald, J. A. B. (of Haywood Co., N.C.), 208
Five Forks, Battle of, 252, 332–34, *367*
Fletcher, Dr. George, 197
Florence, S.C., 87, 188
Forester, Lt., 212
Forks of Pigeon, N.C., 6–7, *passim;* during postwar years and Reconstruction, 227–35
Fort Beauregard (S.C.), 91, *92*
Fort Defiance, Lenoir family plantation, Wilkes Co., N.C., 12, 22
Fort Stedman, Battle of, 252, 328–32, *329, 333*
Fort Sumter, S.C., *61*
Fort Walker (S.C.), 91, *92*
Foster, Gen. J. G., 294–95
Francis, Capt. John W., 68, 84, 168, 203, 257, 337
Francis, Pvt. William F., 336, 366, 381
Franklin, D. S., 209
Franklin, Pvt. David N., 338, 381
Franklin, Pvt. Henry J., 381

Franklin, Pvt. Perry B., 132, 139, 141, 162–64, 183, 256, 381
Franklin, Thomas, 162
Franklin, Va., 299, 300
Frazier, Charles, 350
Frederick, Va., 272–73
Fredericksburg, Battle of, 282–85, *287*
Fredericksburg, Va., 251
Freeman, Mrs. (of Forks of Pigeon, N.C.), 195, 452n189
Freeman, 2nd Lt. Wesley, 146, 203, 208

Gaddis, Pvt. David W., 338, 381
Garrett, Martha Jane Rogers, 56
Garrett, Mary Elizabeth (Lizzie), *see* Lenoir, Mary Elizabeth
Garrett, William Green Berry, 56, 146, 421
Garysburg, N.C., 296, 298
Glade land tract, N.C., 12
Glenn, Pvt. Napoleon L., 204, 256, 381
Globe Tavern, Battle of, 252
Godwin, Pvt. Leonard, 337, 382
Goldsboro, N.C., 190–91, 212–13, 289
Gordon, Pvt. Alson, 268, 335, 356, 382
Gordon, Gen. John B., 328–30
Gracie, Gen. Archibald, 313–14
Grady, Capt. William S., 68, 126, 203
Grahamville, S.C., 99–186, *117, 169*
Green, Pvt. Samuel B., 306, 382
Green, Pvt. Thaddeus M., 200–201, 338, 382
Green, William, UNC professor, 22–23
Gum Swamp, N.C., 294–95
Gum Swamp, Va., 251
Gwyn & Hickerson, Wilkesboro, N.C., 27, 43
Gwyn, Amanda Harper Foster, 237
Gwyn, James II, 26–27, 43, 237, 431
Gwyn, James, Jr. (237)
Gwyn, W. B., 434
Gwyn, Walter, 236

Hall, Pvt. George R., 267, 369, 382

Hall, Pvt. George, Jr., 338, 382
Harding, Mr. (brother-in-law of Lt. Col. Dearing), 127
Harp, Tobias, 11
Harper, George, 219
[Harper, Col. James C.], 196
Harper, James C., 221
Harper's Ferry, Va., 250, 272–74, *273*
Harrell, Pvt. Ezekiel T., 338, 382
Hartgrove, 1st Lt. William Harrison, 171, 201, 202, 257, 322–24, 334, 337, *346,* 347–48, *361,* 366, 369–72, 376, 462n354, n355
Hartgrove, Augustus C., Haywood Co. overseer, 27–28, 32, 33, 46, 67, 109, 111, 171, 198, 210, 410, 442n31
Hartgrove, Pvt. Rufus P., 334, 337, 347–48, 366, 383
Hawkins, Sgt. J. B., 323, 330–31
Haywood Co., N.C., 14, 454n214; during postwar years and Reconstruction, 227–35,
Haywood Highlanders (Co. F., 15th Volunteers N.C./25th N.C. Troops), *passim;* formation of, 1, 61ff, 422–26; overview, 1–5; election of officers, 6, muster roll of, 258–59; service records of, 341–61, 363–91; desertion from, 326, 365; last members of, 363–68; in aftermath of war, 369–70; casualties; 393

Summary of movements during Civil War, *244,* 249–53, 255, 395–405; departure from Haywood Co., 67–68; mustered into service, 68, 77, 395; Carolina coastal duty, 84–187, 255–57, 395–96; encamped at Wilmington, N.C., 71–73, 78, 395; army life, 71–72, 81; church services, 82, 119, 134, 158; 166; ordered to Charleston, S.C., 84, 395; in Charleston, 86–89; at Coosawhatchie Station (S.C.), 89–96; at Camp Beauregard (S.C.), 96–99, 395; ordered to Grahamville, S.C., 99–100; at Grahamville, S.C., 101–86, 395; ordered to prepare for march, 104; pay received, 106–10, 183, 185, 209–10;

departed Grahamville, 187; disease and illness, 113–14, 119, 120, 125, 126, 127, 132, 139, 147, 151, 166, 179, 266; manning pickets, 120; ordance of, 123; clothing and uniforms of, 134–35, 159, 198, 215–18, 281; gives ball for ladies of Grahamville, 156–57, 165, 175; nearby battles and skirmishes, 173–74; reacts to Bounty and Furlough Act and options for reenlisting, 184, 198–99, 204, 246–47; ordered to New Bern and Kinston, N.C., 186–90, 395; at Camp Johnston, N.C., 190, 395; at Camp Ransom and Kinston, N.C., 191–205, 396; election of new officers, 199–203, 256–57; in Seven Days' Battles, 261–68, 396–97; at Battle of Malvern Hill, 263–64, 396; marches to Petersburg, Va., 265, 396; in the Maryland Campaign, 271–79, 397; travels to Richmond, 271, 397; crosses Potomac River, 272; arrival at Frederick, Md., 272–73, 397; marches to Shepherdstown, Va., 273; participates in capture of Harper's Ferry, Va., 272–74, 397; in the Battle of Antietam Run, 275–78, 397; encamped at Martinsburg, Va., 277, 281, 397; at Fredericksburg, 281–87, 398; marches to Madison Courthouse and Fredericksburg, Va., 281–82, 398; in Battle of Marye's Heights and Battle of Fredericksburg, 282–85, 398; serves in North Carolina/Virginia coastal defense, 289–306, 398–403; departs Fredericksburg for North Carolina, 290; participates in affair at Gum Swamp, N.C., 294–95, 400; skirmishes with Tories at Warm Springs, N.C., 296–98, 402; participates in assault on New Bern, N.C., 298–300, 402; participates in capture of Suffolk, Va., 300, 403; participates in capture of Plymouth, N.C., 300–04, 403; participates in defense of Richmond and Petersburg, Va., 309–37, 403–05; participates in Battle of Drewry's Bluff, 310–11, 404; participates in defense of Petersburg, 311–14; ordered to support General Beauregard, 313; at Battle of the Crater, 314–20, 459n314; participates at Globe Tavern, 320–24; during winter of 1864–65, 325–28; participates in Battle of Ft. Stedman, participates in Battle of Five Forks, 332–34; at end of war, 334–39, 405

Henderson, Pvt. Harper, 268, 383

Henderson, Pvt. James Martin, 109, 113, 120–24, 126, 141, 166, 172, 176, 201, 323, 335, 383

Henderson, Pvt. William, 65, 268, 348, 383

Henry, Mrs. Cornelia (of Sulphur Springs, N.C.), 297–98, 446n106, 451n180

Henry, William (of Sulphur Springs, N.C.), 179

Henson, Aaron and Elizabeth, 348

Henson, Alfred (of Cold Creek, N.C.), 232)

Henson, Pvt. Burton H., 176, 348–49, 383

Henson, Charles, 12

Henson, Daniel and Mary, 348

Henson, Elijah, 12

Henson, Pvt. Elijah L., 306, 349, 383

Henson, Pvt. Fidellio W., 191, 267, 349, 383

Henson, Pvt. Henry, Jr., 356–57, 366, 383

Henson, J. M. (of Forks of Pigeon), 235

Henson, Cpl. Thomas F., 202, 204, 257, 306, 349, 383

Henson, Pvt. William, 278, 336, 337, 366, 384

Henson, Sgt. Wesley, 96, 336, 337, 348, 366, 384

Henson, Sgt. Wiley, 209, 278, 306, 348–49, 384

Herbert, 1st Lt. William, 161

Hickerson, Charley, 193

Hickory, N.C., 219, 223

Hill, Maj. Gen. Daniel Harvey, *291*, 292–94, 295

Hoke, Gen. Robert F., *291*, 300, 301, 310

Holland, Pvt. Humphrey P., 65, 357, 366, 384

Holland, Pvt. Matthias, 306, 384

Holland, Pvt. Thomas, 316, 335, 384

Holton, Virginia (of Lenoir, N.C.), 219
Holy Trinity Episcopal Church, Grahamville, S.C., 119, 121, 134, *148*
Hood, Pvt. Pleasant B., 268, 385
House, Pvt. Ambrose, 337, 366, 385
Howell, F. (of Forks of Pigeon), 235
Howell, Capt. George W., 68, 86, 176
Huger, Gen. Benjamin, 262–63
Hutchinson (Hutcheson), Ensign John W., 460n319
Hyatt, Pvt. Robert H., 65, 171, 202, 257, 357–58, 366, 385
Hyatt, 1st Lt. Thaddeus C. S., 84, 200, 257, 298, 305, 358, 376

Inman, Joshua and Mary Polly Smith, 349
Inman, Pvt. Joshua E., 162, 349–50, 385
Inman, Pvt. Lewis Hezekiah, 338, 349–50, 385
Inman, Pvt. William Pinkney, 263, 267, 336, 338, 349–50, 385, 462n357
Isaac, Lenoir slave, 39
Island land tract, N.C., 12
Ivester, H. C. (of Forks of Pigeon), 235
Ivester, I. (of Forks of Pigeon), 235
Jackson, John, servant, 83
Johnson, Gen. Bushrod R., *312,* 314, 320
Johnstone, Capt. Francis W., 68, 84
Jones, Byrum, 11
Jones, Carroll C.: *The 25th North Carolina Troops in the Civil War*, xxiv, 3
Jones, Edmund W. (cousin of Thomas Isaac Lenoir), 207, 214
Jones, Pvt. George W., 267, 385
Jones, Pvt. Isaac W., 337, 366, 385
Jones, Col. James, 153
Jones, Musician John R., 159, 202, 335, 386
Jones, Capt. John T., 207
Jones, Robert, 12

Kemper's Brigade, 301, 303
Kenansville, N.C., 290

Kent, Lawrence Massilon, 97
King's School House, Battle of, 250
Kinston, N.C., 186, 190, 261, 289, 300
Knight, N. (of Forks of Pigeon), 235

Lane, Mr. (of North Carolina), 89
Larkin, Lenoir slave, 38
Latham, Capt. Alexander C., 175–76
Laughter, Pvt. Arthur, 338, 369, 386
Lee, Gen. Robert E., 95, 121, *122,* 155, 290, 299, 325–26, 329, 334–35
Lemmonds, John, 12
Lenoir family, xv, , 440n16
Lenoir, Col. Thomas (father of Thomas Isaac Lenoir), 9, *11, 34,* 439n5, as surveyor, 10–11; settlement in Haywood Co., N.C., 14–18; appointed to N.C. state militia, 15–16; family, 16; return to Wilkes Co., 18–19; management and division of Haywood Co. landholdings, 27–29, 31–35, 55, 420; letters to and from family, 408, 409, 411, 412
Lenoir, Capt. Thomas Isaac: portrayed, *frontispiece, 24;* youth and education, 21–23; early career, 23–28, 43–45, 409; move to "Bachelor's Den" in Haywood Co., 9, 31ff; farm management, 46–52, 410, 411, 420; as surveyor, 48; encounter with a bear, 51–52, 412; recreation at The Den, 52; trips from the Den, 54; hospitality, 52–53; marriage to Lizzie Garrett, 56–57, 64, 423, 424; civic involvement, 45–46; and slaves, 32–33, 37–41, 419 425; and religion, 36–37; appointed to N.C. state militia as cavalry captain, 41, 42; political sentiments, 59–60, 112, 138, 428; diary of, *xx, xxii,* 75–76, 77–225; elected captain of Haywood Highlanders, 1–2, 62–65, 66, 68, 372–73, 375, 423, 426; with Haywood Highlanders Nov. 1861–May 1862, *see entries under* Haywood Highlanders; letters to and from wife, 75, 108, 155, 181, 191; letters to and

from family, 407–36 *passim;* administrative responsibilities for Co. F, 80, 101, 103, 146, 152, 163, 183, 204, 208–10, 215–18; health problems, 34, 83, 96, 119, 127, 151, 167, 178, 191–93, 197, 223, 224, 237–38, 239, 414–17, 430; attitudes toward alcoholic beverages, 83, 151; brews yaupon tea, 95, 112; visits sick soldiers, 111, 127, 176; observations on nature and culture, 115–16, 129–30, 131, 132, 145; on furlough to Savannah, Ga., 127–31; plays billiards, 127, 130; designs fortifications for Camp Lee, 144–45; appointed to regiment's court-martial, 161; builds log cabin in camp with brother Walter, 166; surveys camp road with Walter, 167; reprimands men for drinking, 171–72, 175; declines to run again for captaincy, 199–200, 245, 256; participates in election committee, 201; honorably relieved of duty, 204; collects final pay, 207; departs Haywood Highlanders, 211–14; visits government offices in Raleigh, 214–219; travels to Lenoir, N.C., and reunites with Lizzie and family, 219–21; returns to Forks of Pigeon with Lizzie, 223–25; resumes farming on East Fork, 227–41, 429, 432; writes to Walter about Haywood Highlanders' actions, 265–66; serves in home guard, 228–29; travels to Virginia in search of brother Walter, 229; suffers loss in federal raid, 230–31; on freeing former slaves, 231–35; starts a family, 235, 239, 240–41; manages tenants, 234–36; founds church in Waynesville, N.C., 236–37; builds mill, 238–39, 433; final illness, death, and burial, 241–42, 437, 438

Lenoir, Henry Uriah, 67, 127, 132–33, 212, 214, 42

Lenoir, infant daughter of Walter Waightstill Lenoir and Nealy Lenoir, 124

Lenoir, infant child (b. & d. 1880) of Thomas Isaac and Mary Elizabeth, 240–41, 436

Lenoir, Laura (b. 1872), 235, 241–42, 422

Lenoir, Mary (Mamie, b. 1865), 235, 240, 241–42, 435

Lenoir, Mary Elizabeth (Lizzie) Garrett, 44, 56–57, 219, 231, 236, 421, 423, 424; death and burial, 240–42

Lenoir, N.C., 156, 436

Lenoir, Nealy (wife of Walter Waightstill Lenoir), 124

Lenoir, Rufus (brother of Thomas Isaac Lenoir), 38, 55, 220, *228,* 241, 413, 414–17, 418, 419, 421, 423, 424, 428, 429, 437, 438

Lenoir, Sarah ("Aunt Sade," sister of Thomas Isaac Lenoir), 34, 220, 241, 435

Lenoir, Sarah (Sallie, b. 1875), 235, 240, 241–42

Lenoir, Selina Louisa Avery, 9, 34, 220, 221–22, 408; death, 229

Lenoir, Walter Waightstill (brother of Thomas Isaac Lenoir), 25–26, 55, 65–66, 114, 124, 139–40, 153–54, 160, 166, 167, 187, 191, 192, 196, 205, 207, 220, 221, 223, *228;* 232, 234; 236–37, 238, 241, 249, 426, 430, 431, 432, 436, 437, 438, 445n82

Lenoir, Gen. William, 9, 13, 22, 23, 156, 167, 408

Lenoir, William Avery (brother of Thomas Isaac Lenoir), 23, 55, 440n16

Lenoir, William Ballard (uncle of Thomas Isaac Lenoir), 25–26, 43–45

Lewis, R. T., 196

Long, Pvt. Joseph F., 336, 386

Love, 1st Lt. Mathew Norris, 455n236

Love, Tom, 14–15

Luther, Pvt. Dillard T., 338, 386

Mahaffey, Pvt. Francis M., 285, 334, 337, 358–59, 366, 386

Mahaffey, Pvt. John W., 256, 306, 386

Mahaffey, Pvt. Joseph H., 366, 386

Mahone, William, 320

Malvern Hill, Battle of, 250, 263–64

Mann, Cpl. Joseph B., Sr., 336, 387, 462n357
Mann, Pvt. William B., 387
Marion, N.C., 223–24
Marshall, Pvt. John H., 136
Martin, Adj. Gen. James G., 134
Martinsburg, Va., 177
Marye's Heights, Battle of, 251, 282–86
McDowell, William, 203
McMinn, Jesse (of Henderson Co., N.C.), 143–44
McMinn, Pvt. James N., 143–44
Meares, Lt. Col. Oliver, 178
Meece, Pvt. James Bradford, 202, 257, 306, 350–51, 387
Meece, Pvt. John Medford, 177, 262, 265, 267, 268, 350–51, 387
Meece, Pvt. Morgan, 336, 350–51, 387
Meece, Pvt. William R., 305, 387
Miller, Pvt. Francis M., 193, 195, 305, 387
Miller, G. W. (of Forks of Pigeon), 235
Miller, L. F. (of Forks of Pigeon), 235
Mitchell (Confederate paymaster), 106
Mood, Rev. John and family (of Lenoir, N.C.), 219
Moore, Capt. Alex D., 138
Moore, Capt., 97
Moore, Cpl. Elisha, 177
Moore, Pvt. John C., 337, 366, 387
Morgan's Bottom land tract, N.C., 12
Morrison, John, 11
Murray, 1st Sgt. Luther W., 171, 278, 334, 337, 359, 366, 369–370, 387–88

New Bern, N.C., 186, 207, 298–300
Nichols, Pvt. James, 160
Norton, Pvt. James E., 202, 388
Norwood, James H. (of Waynesville, N.C.), 140
Norwood, Joseph, 56, 67, 219, 222, 223
Norwood, Pvt. John Wall, 140
Norwood, Laura Lenoir, 56, 63–64, 67, 219, 222
Norwood, Thomas (of Lenoir, N.C.), 222

O'Hagan, Dr. Charles, 212
Osborn, Ephraim, 50
Osborne, Pvt. Roland Calloway, 110, 171, 267, 388

Paris, Va., 281
Patsy, Lenoir slave, 40–41
Patterson, Mr. (minister), 158
Patterson, N.C., 220
Patterson, Rufus, 214
Patton, J. W. (of Asheville, N.C.), 39, 233
Pemberton, Brig. Gen. John C., 158
Peninsula Campaign, *see* Seven Days' Battles
Petersburg, Va., 261, 290, 299, 311–39, *324, 327, 339*, siege of, 252
Phinizy, Lt. John, 165
Pickett, Maj. Gen. George E., 298–99
Pierce, Capt. W. W., 215, 218
Pigeon River land tract, N.C., 12
Pinkney, Dr., 176
Pleasants, Lt. Col. Henry, 317
Pless, Isaac (of Forks of Pigeon), 235
Pless, L. (of Forks of Pigeon), 235
Pless, W. P. (of Forks of Pigeon), 235
Plott family, of Forks of Pigeon, 51
Plymouth, Battle of, 251, 309–10
Plymouth, N.C., 300–04, 309–10
Poplar Bottom land tract, N.C., 12
Port Royal, Battle of, 91–94, *92*
Port Royal, S.C., 88, 153
Port Royal Sound, S.C., 88–95
Poston, Pvt. Robert, 184, 268, 388
Poston, R. (of Forks of Pigeon), 235
Pressley, Pvt. Daniel N., 306, 351, 388
Pressley, Pvt. Joshua A., 267, 351, 388
Pressley, Pvt. Nelson A., 267, 351, 388
Pressley, Thomas and Jemima, 351

Queen, Pvt. Robert H., 209, 306, 388

Radcliffe, Col. James, 178, 213, 453n204
Raleigh, N.C., 78, 214–19; Plantation Hotel, 214

Rankin, Capt. William R., 190
Ransom, Gen. Matt W., *291,* 296, 302, 314, 330–31
Ransom, Brig. Gen. Robert, 72, 204, 207, *249,* 257, 261, 264, 282–84, 295–96, 311
Ransom's Brigade (2nd Brigade N.C.), 248, 261
Reece, Mr., Haywood stock keeper, 28
Reece, Pvt. Amos M., 141–43, 146, 210, 256, 388
Reece, David, 142, 210, 449n155
Reece, Musician John V., 256, 388–89
Reece, Pvt. Jonathan K., 351–52, 366, 389
Reece, Pvt. Isaac N., 263, 267, 351–52, 388
Reece, Samuel and Lucinda, 351–52
Reece, Pvt. William L., 389, 383
Rhodes, Pvt. William B., 166–67, 172–73, 256, 389
Rice, Pvt. Henry, 120
Richmond, Va., 261
Riley, Lenoir slave, 37–38
Ripley, Brig. Gen. R. S., 95
Robbins, John, 11
Roberson, Pvt. Isaac W., 65, 359–60, 366, 389
Roberts, Capt. Charles M., 68, 86, 203
Robinson, 2nd Lt. John, 161
Rogers, Pvt. John C., 202, 257, 389
Rogers, Pvt. Matthew McA., 339, 389
Rouse, Jesse H. (of Kinston, N.C.), 192–93
Rutledge, Maj. Henry Middleton, 69, 79, 84, 132, 137, 151, 176, 203, 211, *248,* 257, 284, 330, 332, 449n149

St. Clair, Capt. (Confederate navy), 95–96
Salisbury, Pvt. Walter, 113, 119
Sanders, J. A., 84
Satchwell, Dr. Solomon S., 89, 157, 192, 197
Savannah, Ga., 127–31; Bonaventure Cemetery, 128–30; Marshall House, 127–28
Scott, Pvt. James P., 338, 366, 389
Seven Days' Battles, 250, 261–68; *269*
Sharp, Pvt. Richard H., 189

Sharpsburg, Md., 250, 272, 273–78
Singleton, Cpl. James Anderson, 272, 278, 352, *353,* 366, 370, 390
Singleton, Pvt. James M., 193, 195, 305, 390
Singleton, Pvt. John C., 200, 352, *353,* 366, 370, 390
Singleton, Pvt. Samuel P., 306, 390
Singleton, Pvt. William A. S. C., 171, 268, 352, *353,* 369, 390
Sloan, Capt. James, 213–14
Smith, E., 96
Smith, I., 11–12
Smith, Musician John A., 202, 204, 262, 265, 267, 306, 390
Smith, Rowland, 11–12
Sorrells, Cpl. Henry Jackson, 171, 202, 257, 267, 390
South Mills, N.C., 300
Spivey, William, 12
Spivey, Cpl. William M., 162–64
"Springdale" (Lenoir farm), 237, 241, 431
Stamey, Pvt. John, 267, 390
Stevenson, Pvt. James H., 164
Stiegel, William, 12
Suffolk, Va., 300
Swain, David, UNC president, 22

Terrell, Emily Michal, xxi, xxv–xxvi
Terrell, Hugh K., v
Thomas, Pvt. John G., 306, 390
Thompson, Alexander and Isabella (of Forks of Pigeon, N.C.), 352
Thompson, Pvt. Joseph M., 262, 267, 352–53, 391
Thompson, Pvt. William, 267, 352–53, 391
Tindle, Pvt. J. R., 337, 366, 391
Trevezant, Captain (cavalry), 102
Trull, B. H. (of Forks of Pigeon), 235
Trull, D. T. (of Forks of Pigeon), 235
Trull, Pvt. John W., 89, 285, 360, 391
Trull, Polly, 37

Tucker, Pvt. Samuel, 140
Tucker's Barn (Lenoir), N.C., 156, 219

Uriah, Lenoir slave, see Lenoir, Henry Uriah
USS *Southfield*, 302

Vance, Pvt. William P., 268, 315, 391
Vance, Gov. Zebulon B., 59–60, *62*, 190, 289
Vause, R. B., (of Kinston, N.C.), 197–98, 211–12
Vines, Ben, 11
Vines, Thomas, 11

Walker, Capt. John W., 196, 207
Ware Bottom Church, Va., 311
Warm Springs, N.C., 251, 296–98
Washington, John (of Kinston, N.C.), 190
Washington, N.C., 293–94
Waynesville, N.C., 236–37
Welch, R. V., 433
Welch, William, 157
Welch, 1st Lt. William Pink, 157, 298, 449n163

Weldon, N.C., 296, 298m 300
Wessells, Gen. Henry W., 304–05
Western N.C., *33*, settlement, 12–13; Native Americans in, 15; Unionist sentiment in Civil War, 60–61; involvement in Civil War, 62–63
Wigfall, Rev. Arthur, 119, 121
Williams, Pvt. William H., 306, 391
Wilmington and Weldon Railroad, 321–23
Wilmington, N.C., 73, 77, 86, 188–89
Wilson, A. J., 143
Wilson, Andrew J., 141
Wilson, Pvt. John C., 204, 285, 338, 391
Winchester, Pvt. James, 125–26
Wright, Aaron, 172–73
Wright, 2nd Lt. William M., 172, 212, 306, 376

Young, Capt. Ephraim, 109
Young, Pvt. George H., 188–89

This book was set in the Adobe Caslon Pro, Cezanne, and Trajan faces in Adobe InDesign CS4 for the Macintosh computer.

www.ingramcontent.com/pod-product-compliance
Lightning Source LLC
Chambersburg PA
CBHW051357070526
44584CB00023B/3200